Advances in Data Science and Analytics

Scrivener Publishing
100 Cummings Center, Suite 541J
Beverly, MA 01915-6106

Advances in Data Engineering and Machine Learning

Series Editors: Niranjanamurthy M, PhD, Juanying XIE, PhD, and Ramiz Aliguliyev, PhD

Scope: Data engineering is the aspect of data science that focuses on practical applications of data collection analysis. For all the work that data scientists do to answer questions using large sets of information, there have to be mechanisms for collecting and validating that information. Data engineers are responsible for finding trends in data sets and developing algorithms to help make raw data more useful to the enterprise.

It is important to have business goals in line when working with data, especially for companies that handle large and complex datasets and databases. Data Engineering Contains DevOps, Data Science, and Machine Learning Engineering. DevOps (development and operations) is an enterprise software development phrase used to mean a type of agile relationship between development and IT operations. The goal of DevOps is to change and improve the relationship by advocating better communication and collaboration between these two business units. Data science is the study of data. It involves developing methods of recording, storing, and analyzing data to effectively extract useful information. The goal of data science is to gain insights and knowledge from any type of data - both structured and unstructured.

Machine learning engineers are sophisticated programmers who develop machines and systems that can learn and apply knowledge without specific direction. Machine learning engineering is the process of using software engineering principles, and analytical and data science knowledge, and combining both of those in order to take an ML model that's created and making it available for use by the product or the consumers. "Advances in Data Engineering and Machine Learning Engineering" will reach a wide audience including data scientists, engineers, industry, researchers and students working in the field of Data Engineering and Machine Learning Engineering.

Publishers at Scrivener
Martin Scrivener (martin@scrivenerpublishing.com)
Phillip Carmical (pcarmical@scrivenerpublishing.com)

Advances in Data Science and Analytics

Concepts and Paradigms

Edited by
M. Niranjanamurthy
Hemant Kumar Gianey
and
Amir H. Gandomi

Scrivener Publishing

WILEY

This edition first published 2023 by John Wiley & Sons, Inc., 111 River Street, Hoboken, NJ 07030, USA and Scrivener Publishing LLC, 100 Cummings Center, Suite 541J, Beverly, MA 01915, USA

For more information about Scrivener publications please visit www.scrivenerpublishing.com.

Wiley Global Headquarters
111 River Street, Hoboken, NJ 07030, USA

For details of our global editorial offices, customer services, and more information about Wiley products visit us at www.wiley.com.

Library of Congress Cataloging-in-Publication Data

ISBN 978-1-119-79188-1

Front cover images supplied by Pixabay.com
Cover design by Russell Richardson

Set in size of 11pt and Minion Pro by Manila Typesetting Company, Makati, Philippines

Contents

Preface

Data science is an inter-disciplinary field that uses scientific methods, processes, and algorithms systems to extract knowledge and insights from many structured and unstructured data. Data science is related to data mining, deep learning, and Big Data. Data analytics software is a more focused version of this and can even be considered part of the larger process. Data Analysis is a process of inspecting, cleansing, transforming, and modelling data with the goal of discovering useful information, suggesting conclusions, and supporting decision-making. Analytics is devoted to realizing actionable insights that can be applied immediately based on existing queries. This book provides the information related to components of data science, including Machine Learning, Big Data, and Business Intelligence and four types of Analytics, including Descriptive Analytics, Diagnostic Analytics, Predictive Analytics, and Prescriptive Analytics. The main goal of this book is to explore the concept and solutions for analysis and develop multidisciplinary applications using advances in Data Science and Analytics techniques. This book features innovative research on advances in Data Science and Analytics techniques and applications which put a great impact on human lives. Highlighting the possible data science applications in multiple domains to ease the day to day challenges, this book is a critical reference source for academicians, professionals, engineers, technology designers, analysts, and students. Topics discussed in this book are implementation tools for generating statistical consequence using data visualization techniques, decision making and Predictive Analysis for real-time data, optimizing water quality with Data Analytics and machine learning, lip reading framework using deep learning and machine learning, a new perspective to economic growth and debt nexus analysis through evidence from the Indian economy, data-driven Delay Analysis with applications to railway networks, a proposed framework to analyze breast cancer in mammogram images using global thresholding, Gray Level Co-Occurrence Matrices And Convolutional Neural Networks (CNN), IoT technologies for smart healthcare, enhancement of scalability of SVM classifiers for Big

Data, electrical network-related incidents prediction based on weather factors, Green IoT, an environment-friendly approach to IoT, Big Data Analytics as a new paradigm shift in the micro-finance industry, Big Data storage and analysis, and a framework for analyzing social media and digital data by applying machine learning techniques for pandemic management.

1

Implementation Tools for Generating Statistical Consequence Using Data Visualization Techniques

Dr. Ajay B. Gadicha[1]*, Dr. Vijay B. Gadicha[2], Prof. Sneha Bohra[2] and Dr. Niranjanamurthy M.[4]

[1]*Department of Computer Science and Engineering, P.R. Pote College of Engineering and Management Amravati (Maharashtra), India*
[2]*Department of Computer Science and Engineering, G H Raisoni University Amaravati, Maharashtra, India*
[3]*Department of Computer Application, M.S. Ramaiah Institute of Technology, Bangalore, Karnataka, India*

Abstract

The measure of computerized information that exists is developing at a quick rate, multiplying at regular intervals, and changing the manner in which we live. It is assessed that by 2020, about 1.7MB of new information will be made each second for each person on the planet. This implies we have to have the specialized devices, calculations, and models to clean, measure, and comprehend the accessible information in its various structures for dynamic purposes. Information science is the field that contains everything identified with cleaning, planning, and breaking down unstructured, semi-organized, and organized information. This field of science utilizes a mix of measurements, arithmetic, programming, critical thinking, and information catch to extricate bits of knowledge and data from data. Figure 1.1 shows various stages in the field of information science. Information researchers use programming devices, for example, Python, R, SAS, Java, Perl, and C/C++, to remove information from arranged information. To remove this data, they utilize different fit-to-reason models dependent on machine inclining calculations, insights, and numerical strategies. This chapter predominantly centers around the information representation strategies and their relationship with the information relationship component to secure, decipher, and contrast information all together

**Corresponding author*: ajjugadicha@gmail.com

M. Niranjanamurthy, Hemant Kumar Gianey and Amir H. Gandomi (eds.) Advances in Data Science and Analytics: Concepts and Paradigms, (1–20) © 2023 Scrivener Publishing LLC

to unmistakably impart complex thoughts, along these lines encouraging the distinguishing proof and examination of important examples.

Keywords: Data Science, Data Visualization, Python, R, SAS, Java, Perl, and C/C++

1.1 Introduction

Data can be defined as a collection of facts and statistics gathered together in order to perform some analysis. In order to deliver quality service, organizations may utilize various forms of data, analyze it, and manage the data. Data can be in various form like numbers, words, measurements, observations, or just descriptions of things. Analysis of large amounts of data is difficult to project without any visual aid. Visualization can be one of the exceptional ways of analyzing and sharing information [4].

Big data is a concept that describes the vast amount of data that inundates a company on a regular basis — both structured and unstructured. It is regarded as one of the major challenges of the 21st century because of the volumes of information, the speed at which the data is being generated,

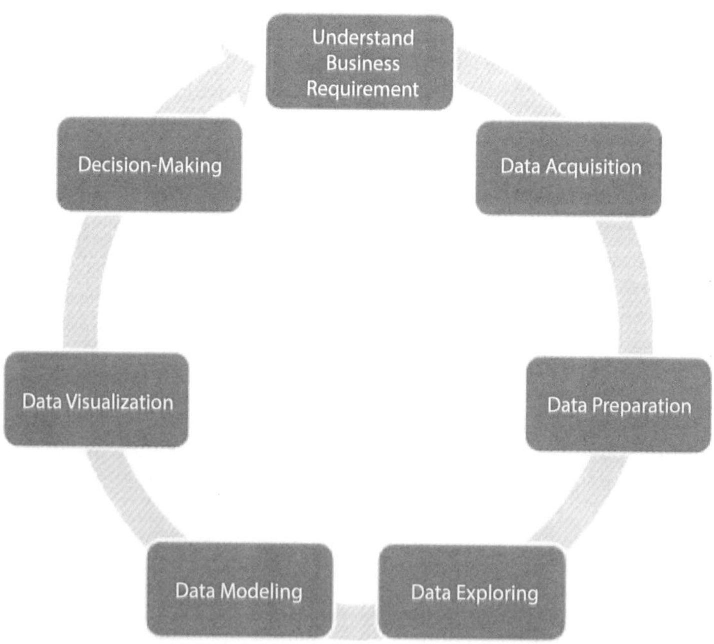

Figure 1.1 Stages of Data Science.

and even the complexity of the data [7]. The factors that contribute to the invariant proliferation of this big data mainly include growth and complexity of big data, including the data generated by internet of things (IOT) enabled devices, user clicks over the internet, and social media, hence it has become an important part of the digital industry, social media, scientific analysis, and a variety of other fields [12].

Subsequent growth in generation of big data necessitates efficient methods for analyzing these large datasets. Data Visualization techniques are considered to be a key method for data analysis since they attract visual and cognitive capabilities of humans to analyze and perceive data faster.

Data visualization involves the use of graphics to display vast volumes of data according to certain criteria or classifications, such as data represented using charts, maps, graphs, scatter plots, Venn diagrams, ordinogram, or any other visualization types [2, 9].

Depending upon the relation among the data, Data Visualization can be grouped into five categories: Temporal, Hierarchical, Network, Multidimensional, and Geospatial [15].

Visuals describing linear data fall under the category of Temporal Data Visualization. These techniques generally characterize graphs or charts which either focus on a single line or overlapping lines. For example, Timelines, Line graphs, Scatter plots, Polar area diagrams, or time series sequences [15].

Use of Hierarchical Data Visualization techniques is suggested when data or information is available in the form of clusters which originate from a single source. Tree diagrams, Ring charts, and sunburst diagrams are examples of Hierarchical Data Visualization techniques.

Network Data Visualizations can be used when the user needs to demonstrate relations between datasets. Some widely used charts in this kind of visualization are Matrix charts, Node-link diagrams, Word clouds, and Alluvial diagrams [15].

Multidimensional Visualization techniques are ideal for data with multiple dimensions. The striking feature of this technique is the use of many concurrent layers to display the information. Visuals of this category include pie charts, histograms, Venn diagrams, etc. [15].

Geospatial Data Visualization techniques are used to represent geographically related data in order to correlate various attributes of geographical locations with each other. Examples of this technique include heat maps, density maps, flow maps, and cartograms [15].

In order to implement these data visualization techniques, the user must be acquainted with various tools available. The literature review gives insight about the tools.

1.2 Literature Review

Big Data has become a vital to business since it empowers organizations to achieve various objectives by applying analytics to data available and transform it to make real time decisions and solve real time problems of the organizations. These visualizations of data also aid the organization to have insight and develop optimized decisions [1].

Big Data is said to have attributes like Volume, Speed, Variety, Veracity, and Value. The real challenge is not only to process this enormous amount of data, but also to process it with a significant diversity [6]. Efficient data visualization techniques can be used to condense, analyze and demonstrate important facts from the data gathered. These techniques can also aid the user to make efficient decisions, thereby leading to better planning [8].

There are several factors that directly or indirectly affect the choice of method or tool for data visualization. In [5], the author discusses factors including Audience, Content, Context, Dynamics, and Purpose of Data visualization. The role of the target audience is vital in order to understand what sort of data is expected by them. For example, share holders of any company will be interested in Annual Profit instead of Annual Investment. The type of visual being chosen is equally important to demonstrate the information precisely [5].

Data visualization tools should address challenges like scalability, flexibility, and response time. Data reduction techniques like filtering, sampling, and aggregation can be used to get reduced data. This reduced data can then be used for visualizations [14].

Large volume and diversity in the data makes it difficult to visualize the trends in data [13]. In [10], the authors suggest some requirements for data visualization tools in order to interpret proper insights. This requirement list included reduction in dimension, rate of retrieval, level of assistance to user, and interactiveness among data and scalability.

Some of the areas where Big Data visualization and analysis play vital roles include the fields of Travel and Hospitality, Healthcare, the government sector, and retail [11].

1.3 Tools in Data Visualization

Data visualization tools offer an simpler way for data visualization designers to construct visual representations of vast sets of data. Automating the process of making a visualization, at least in part makes the task of a designer considerably simpler when working with data sets that contain hundreds of thousands or millions of data points.

These data visualizations can then be used for a number of purposes including dashboards, annual reports, sales and marketing materials, slide decks for investors, and information that needs to be quickly interpreted almost everywhere else.

There are a few things in common amongst the best data visualization instruments on the market. Their ease of use is first. For visualizing data, there are some extremely complex apps available. Some are built in ways that sound natural to the user and have excellent documentation and tutorials. In such regions, others are missing, excluding them from any list of "best" instruments, irrespective of their other capabilities.

Large sets of data can also be managed by the right methods. In fact, single visualization can even manage multiple sets of data. An array of different types of charts, graphs, and maps can also be created with the best resources. Both images and interactive graphs can be created by most of the tools below. There are exceptions to the range of conditions for production, however. Some methods for visualizing data concentrate on a single form of chart or map and do it very well.

Another component to be considered is cost considerations. While a higher price tag does not inherently disqualify a tool, in terms of better service, better features, and better overall value, the higher price tag must be justified.

To generate visualizations of large data sets, there are dozens, if not hundreds, of applications, software, and scripts available. Several are very basic and have a lot of overlapping characteristics.

There are highlights that either have more ability to create or are much easier to use for the types of visualizations they can create than the other options out there. We have surveyed and listed various tools available for Data Visualization.

1. Microsoft BI

It is a cloud based visualization and analytics tool by Microsoft supported by both mobile and browsers. It allows its user to connect with a varicty of data sources, designs, and reports [15].

It is a set of tools for business analytics that can quickly simplify, prepare, and analyze data. It is the most popular tool because it can be easily integrated with Microsoft tools and can be used and downloaded absolutely free of charge.

For both mobile and desktop versions, the tool is available, so it can be a big advantage for them if a company uses Microsoft tools.

Key Features:

a) Generates visualizations of interactive data through multiple data centers
b) It provides both business data processing and self-service on a single platform
c) Even non-data scientists can easily build models for machine learning

2. Google Chart:

It is one of the most powerful, easy, and interactive free tools for data visualization used over browsers and mobile devices. It supports a variety of charts which allows users to customize the visuals per their needs.

Google Charts is a powerful free tool for visualizing data that is specifically designed to create interactive charts for online embedding. It works with dynamic data and the outputs are based purely on HTML5 and SVG, so without the use of additional plugins, they work in browsers. Google Spreadsheets, Google Fusion Tables, Salesforce, and other SQL databases are included as data sources.

A variety of types of charts are available, including maps, scatter charts, column and bar charts, histograms, region charts, pie charts, treemaps, timelines, gauges, and many others. Through simple CSS editing, these charts can be fully personalized.

Pros

a) Free to use
b) Wide range of available chart formats
c) Compatible with cross-browsers since it utilizes HTML5 / SVG
d) Operates with dynamic data

Cons

a) There is little support outside the guides and forums available.

3. Tableau

Tableau is a paid and licensed business intelligence tool that helps users visualize and understand their data. It is commonly used in the business intelligence sector to design interactive graphics and charts in the form of dashboards and worksheets for company visions.

A variety of options are available for Tableau, including a desktop app, server, and online hosted versions, and a free public alternative. From CSV files to Google Ads and Analytics data to Salesforce data, there are hundreds of data import options available.

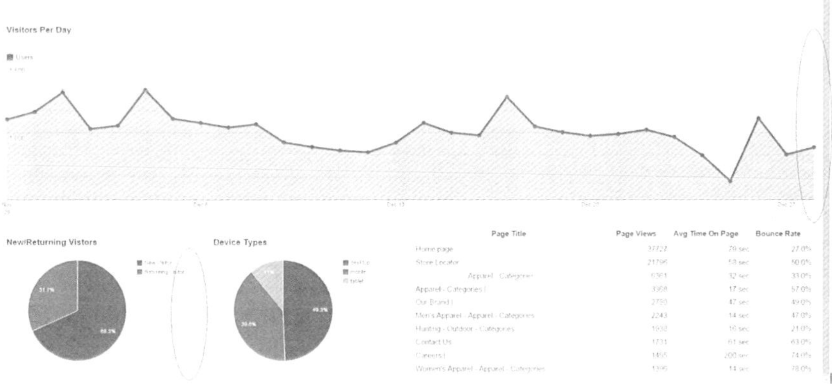

Figure 1.2 Google chart dashboard [18].

Multiple chart formats as well as mapping capabilities provide performance options. This means that designers can create color-coded maps that display geographically significant data in a format that is far easier to absorb than any table or chart shown in the above Figure 1.2.

Advantages of Tableau

a) Hundreds of choices for importing data
b) Capability for mapping
c) Accessible public free edition
d) Lots of video tutorials on how to use Tableau to direct the user

Cons

a) Although free versions are available for use, paid versions are expensive
b) Public version does not allow you to keep data analyses private

Figure 1.3 shows a dashboard of Tableau tools. It shows how different forms of charts can be used to represent data [Caldarola, S. M. Ali].

4. IBM's Watson Analytics: It offers automated data visualization that helps to recognize patterns, trends, and complex relationships in business data [15].

5. XPlenty

Xplenty is a licensed cloud based data integration framework that prepares data for your data visualization applications. It can combine data from

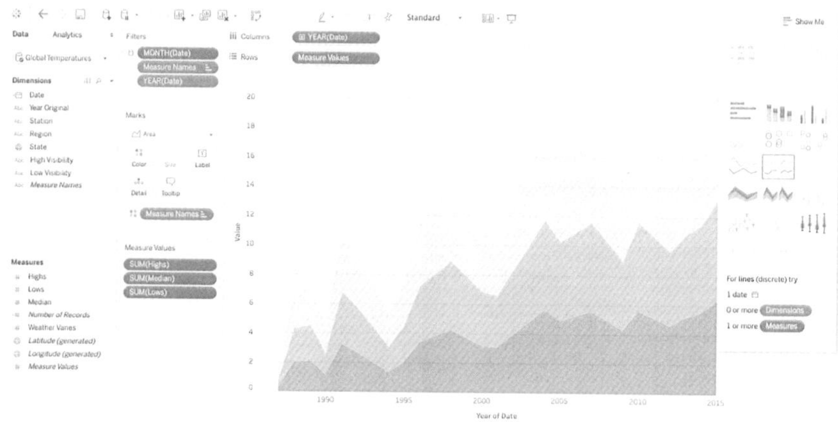

Figure 1.3 Tableau dashboard [17].

more than 100 data stores and SaaS applications. It provides flexible and versatile infrastructure and helps the user with basic replication tasks and complex transformations [15].

6. HubSpot
HubSpot is a free licensed tool which provides a sales report that will give maximum insight in the sales process. It provides the reporting features built around the dashboard. The dashboard is an adjustable series of files. It also provides provision for custom report generation [15].

7. WhataGraph
Whatagraph is a popular marketing data reporting tool for companies to use. It makes it simple to handle several clients while providing you with a variety of integrations and automation capabilities [15].

8. Sisense
Sisense is a licensed tool that facilitates immediate insights to all, anywhere in the company. It helps to create visual dashboards and reports from any piece of data, discover underlying trends and patterns, and make data-driven decisions. It is useful when the user has huge datasets. Its excellent support and easy upgrades make it very user friendly [15].

Sisense provides a total analytics solution. The visualization capabilities include an uncomplicated alternative for drag and drop that can easily accommodate complex graphics, charts, and interactive visualizations.

It enables documents to be accumulated in easily accessible libraries where they can be quickly stored on the dashboards. Dashboards can then be shared across groups to ensure that even non-technical workers can find the answers they need to fix their issues.

Key Features:

a) Provides users with different resources in a visual environment to understand collected data
b) You may link directly to several sources of knowledge at once
c) Data scientists may use this method to connect different maps and charts together

9. Adaptive Discovery
Adaptive Discovery is yet another licensed tool which allows focusing on analysis and decision making on important aspects of data. It provides complete perspective that is required to drive for financial, sales, and operational performances. It connects to almost all data sources, allowing modeling, planning, and forecasting to make better decisions [15].

10. TeamMate Analytics
This licensed tool is a package of over 150 computer-aided audit tools and productivity tools. The data visualization tools support analytics, relational display, simulation models, and filtered views. The attractive user interface makes it very user friendly. TeamMate has extremely good integration of both common APIs and tools which increases the efficiency in automating workflows.

11. JupyteR
Jupyter is an opensource and free tool for data visualization. It makes use of programming scripts to provide prototypes [15].

12. Infogram
It is a web-based tool for data visualization. It allows its users to create and share digital charts, infographics, and maps. Although the basic version of this tool is free to use, a licensed version is also available on a payment amount specified by the company [3, 13].

Infogram is a fully featured drag-and-drop visualization tool for marketing reports, infographics, social media articles, charts, dashboards, and more that enables even non-designers to create powerful data visualizations.

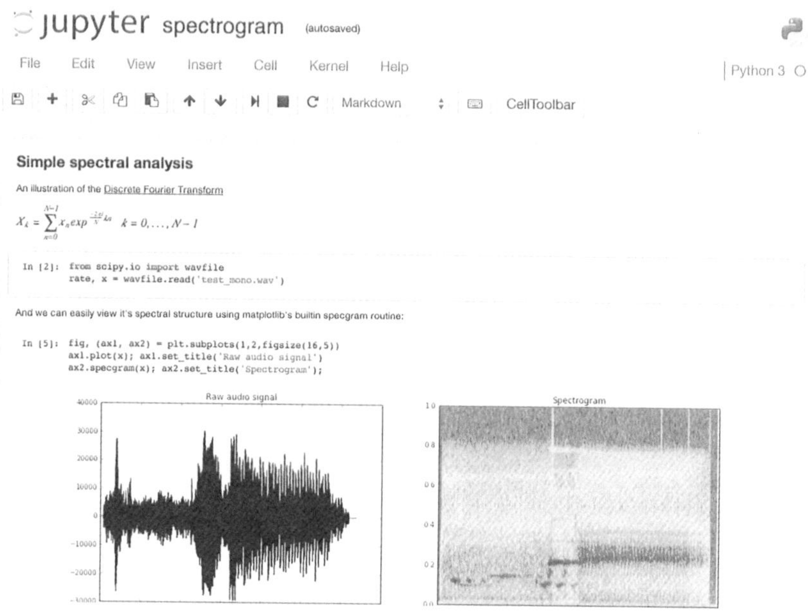

Figure 1.4 Jupyter dashboard [16].

It is possible to export completed visualizations to a variety of formats: .PNG, .JPG, .GIF, .PDF, and .HTML. Interactive visualizations are also possible and, ideal for embedding in websites or applications shown in the above Figure 1.4.

Pros

a) Tiered pricing, like a free plan with fundamental characteristics
b) Includes 35 + types of graph and 550 + types of maps
c) Editor Drag and Drop
d) API for importing extra sources of data

Cons

a) Considerably less data sources built-in than certain other applications

13. ChartBlocks

ChartBlocks claims that data can be imported using their API, even from live feeds. Although they state that "only a few clicks" can be done to import data from any source, it is bound to be more complex than other apps that have automated modules or extensions for specific data sources.

The app allows comprehensive customization of the final visualization generated and, before importing the data, the chart building wizard helps users select exactly the right data for their charts.

Designers can produce virtually any form of graph and the output is sensitive, a significant benefit for designers of data visualization who want to incorporate graphs on websites that are likely to be displayed on a number of devices.

Pros

a) Free and reasonably priced paid plans are available
b) Easy to use wizard for importing the necessary data

Cons

a) Unclear how robust their API is
b) Does not appear to have any mapping capability

14. Datawrapper

Datawrapper was created specifically for adding charts and maps to news stories. The charts and maps created are interactive and made for embedding on news websites. Their data sources are limited, though, with the primary method being copying and pasting data into the tool.

Once data is imported, charts can be created with a single click. Their visualization types include column, line, and bar charts, election donuts, area charts, scatter plots, choropleth and symbol maps, and locator maps, among others. The finished visualizations are reminiscent of those seen on sites like the New York Times or Boston Globe. In fact, their charts are used by publications like Mother Jones, Fortune, and The Times.

Pros

a) Specifically designed for newsroom data visualization
b) Free plan is a good fit for smaller sites
c) Tool includes a built-in color blindness checker

Cons

a) Limited data sources
b) Paid plans are on the expensive side

15. D3 Java Script Framework

D3.js is a JavaScript library for data-based manipulation of documents. D3.js requires at least some JS expertise, but there are apps out there that allow the library to be used by non-programming users.

These applications include NVD3, which provides D3.js reusable charts, Plotly's Chart Studio, which also allows WebGL and other charts to be created by designers, and Ember Charts, which also use the Ember.js framework.

Pros

a) Extremely powerful and customizable
b) Huge number of possible chart types
c) A concentration on web standards
d) Tools available for the creation of visualizations by non-programmers
e) The Free and Open Source

Cons

a) Requires programming knowledge to use
b) Less available support than with paid tools

16. Grafana

Grafana is software for open-source visualization that allows users to create dynamic dashboards and other visualizations. It supports mixed data sources, annotations, and customizable alert functions, and hundreds of available plugins can be used to extend it. That makes it one of the most powerful tools available for visualization. Export features let designers share dashboard snapshots as well as invite other users to collaborate. Over 50 data sources are supported by Grafana via plugins. If there is a paid cloud-hosted version available, a free version is available for download. There are also support plans available for the downloadable version, something a lot of other open-source tools do not offer.

Pros

a) Open source, with accessible free and paid options
b) Large selection of available sources of data
c) Variety of available chart types
d) Making it easy to create dynamic dashboards
e) Can work with mixed data feeds

Cons

a) Overkill to create simple visualizations
b) Does not offer as many options for visual customization as some other resources
c) Not the best option for generating images for visualization
d) Not capable of embedding dashboards in websites for individual panels

17. Plotly

Plotly is capable of handling complex visualizations. This provides a way for it to be combined with Python, Matlab, and R analytics-oriented programming languages.

It is built on top of JavaScript 's free d3.Js visualization libraries, but this commercial kit (with a possible non-industrial license available) provides user-friendliness and support layers in addition to built-in support for Salesforce-inclusive APIs.

Key Characteristics:

a) It provides built-in permissions and SAML Integrations
b) Super-fast and simple deployment of the tool for data visualization
c) Provides links to users for rapid prototyping and exploration

18. Qlikview:

QlikView is a Tableau-like software, but before using it for commercial purposes, you need to pay. It is a forum for business intelligence that transforms knowledge into valuable information.

This software helps enhance the process of visualizing data. Well-established data scientists prefer this instrument to analyze large-scale data. Qlikview is used and has a very large culture spanning 100 countries.

Key Characteristics:

a) The software combines with a wide variety of sources of data such as EC2, Impala, HP Vertica, etc.
b) When it comes to data analysis, it is extremely fast
c) This method for data visualization can be quickly deployed and configured

19. E-Charts

We have E-Charts, which is an enterprise-level chart data visualization application from the Baidu expert team, in the list of best data visualization software. It is possible to refer to E-Charts as a pure Javascript chart library that runs smoothly on different platforms and is compatible with most browsers as well.

Key Characteristics:

a) Has multidimensional processing of data
b) For all sized devices, charts are available
c) It offers a platform for the rapid creation of visualizations based on the Internet
d) These are completely free of charge to use

20. FusionCharts

FusionCharts is based on a JavaScript charting process. As one of the best in the market, this visualization tool has established itself. It can build 90 types of one-of-a-kind graphs and integrates with a wide range of systems and frameworks, offering a large amount of versatility. Any type of visualization can be generated by FusionCharts from scratch and this is one of its unique features. Customers also have the option to choose from a range of models for "live" examples.

Key Characteristics:

a) It offers insightful tooltips to support users
b) The tool ensures that users can understand the various functions
c) The values of different data points can be compared with each other

21. HighCharts

This also includes a license for business use, like FusionCharts, although it can be used openly as a trial, for non-business or non-public use.

Its website claims that it is used by 72 of the world's 100 largest agencies and is always chosen when it is necessary to introduce a fast and scalable solution, with a minimal requirement for specialist statistical visualization training before it can be put to use.

Key Characteristics:

a) The data visualization application offers good usability with its users
b) One of the most commonly used data analyzing methods is HighCharts
c) Adding interactive charts to advanced applications is a helpful tool

1.4 Methodology

Big Data analysis requires the implementation of innovative and specialized tools and methods. These tools ensure that customer-centric applications have some additional features, such as real-time access to information, flexible application domains, etc. These techniques are more reliable and efficient for generating accurate results after the analysis of large data.

Nowadays, data visualization is core to data analysis and data relationships play a vital role. In this chapter, data relationship strategies explain using python programming.

1.4.1 Plotting the Data

The item oriented interfaces to the python library matplotlib that allows you to visualize measured records in greater bendy and extendable workflow. The widespread plotting paintings waft looks like this:

In this plotting a data point, we have discussion relation between "time" versus "distance". The x-axis shows use time in hours and the y-axis considers distance in miles and the relationship between the two entities shown below:

```
import matplotlib.pyplot as plt
r, p = plt.subplots()
x= [0.0,1.0,2.0, 3.0, 4.0,5.0,6.0]
y= [0.00,44.05, 107.16, 148.44, 196.40,254.44, 300.00]
p.plot (x, y, color="red", linestyle="--", marker="s")
plt.show()

# Create figure and axis objects using subplots()
fig, axis = plt.subplots()
# Plot line using the axis.plot() method
line = axis.plot(x , y , linestyle=" ", marker="o", color="red")
plt.xlabel ('X Data, Time in Hours') plt.ylabel ('Y Data, Distance
   in Miles') # Set a title.
# Use the plt.show() method to display the figure
plt.show()
```

1.4.2 Plotting the Model on Data

Figure 1.5 and 1.6 explore the data relationship both with line and without line. Here, we can combine both data points to give an idea about the data

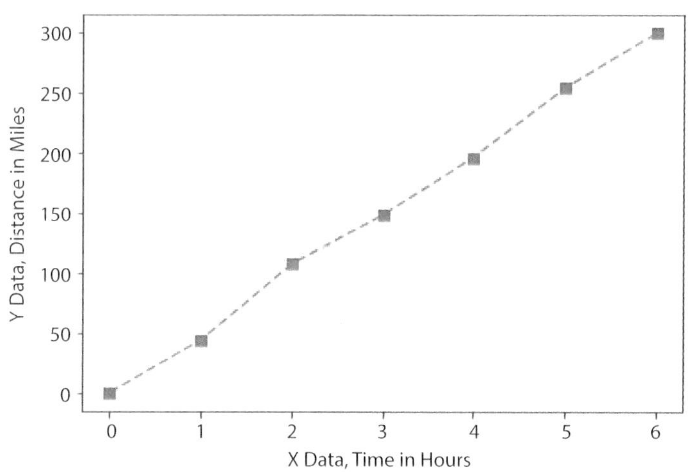

Figure 1.5 Relationship between Time (in hours) & Distance (in miles).

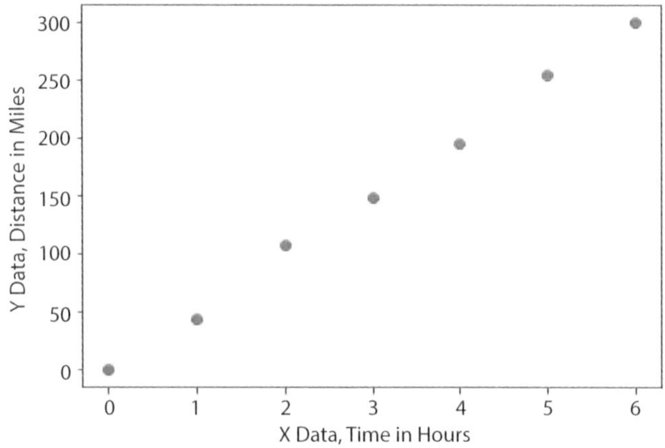

Figure 1.6 Relationship between Time (in hours) & Distance (in miles) (only markers no lines).

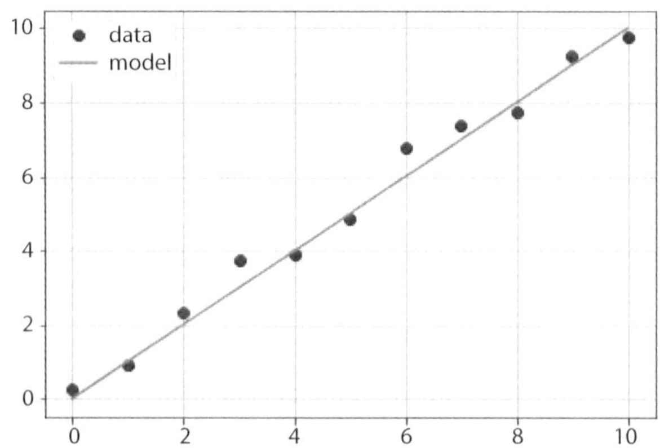

Figure 1.7 Model Data.

relationship between time and distance. The above Figure 1.7 represents the data model of X data, time in hours and Y data, distance in miles.

1.4.3 Quantifying Linear Relationships

Now, the major task is to quantify the data using Mean, Deviation, and Standard deviation. The mean describes the center of the data. The standard deviation describes the spread of the data, but to compare two variables it is convenient to normalize both. The below Figure 1.8 represents the quantifying data of normalized deviations of X and Y.

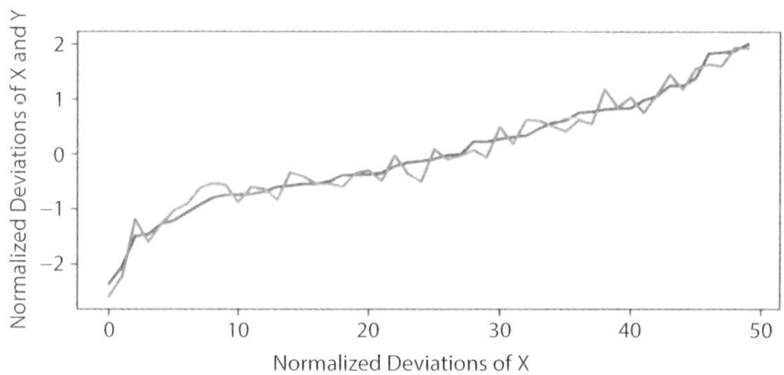

Figure 1.8 Quantifying data.

1.4.4 Covariance vs. Correlation

Covariance is a degree of whether or not two variables alternate ("range") together. It is calculated by means of computing the products, factor by means of point, the deviations seen in the previous workout, dx[n]*dy[n], after which finding the average of all the products. Correlation is in essence the normalized covariance. In this work, you are provided with arrays of records, which can be especially correlated and you will visualize and compute both the covariance and correlation. The below Figure 1.9 represents the relationship between covariance vs. correlation.

```
# Compute the covariance from the deviations.
import matplotlib.pyplot as plt
x=[0.0,1.0,2.0, 3.0, 4.0,5.0,6.0]
y=[0.00,44.05, 107.16,148.44,196.40,254.44,300.00]
dx = x - np.mean(x)
dy = y - np.mean(y)
covariance = np.mean(dx * dy)
print("Covariance: ", covariance)
# Compute the correlation from the normalized deviations.
zx = dx / np.std(x)
zy = dy / np.std(y)
correlation = np.mean(zx * zy)
print("Correlation: ", correlation)

# Plot the normalized deviations for visual inspection.
fig = plt.plot(zx, zy)
plt.show()
```

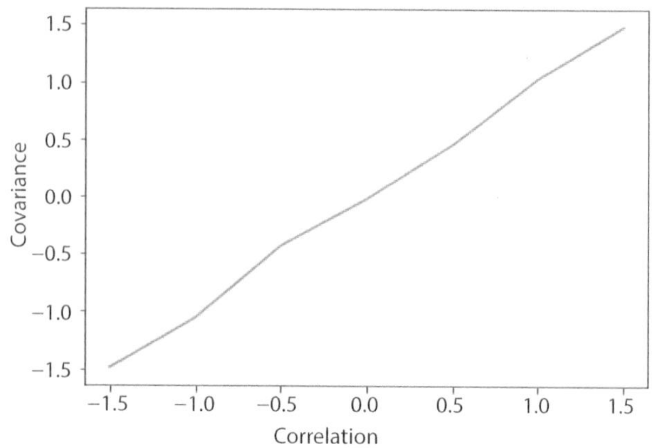

Figure 1.9 Relationship between covariance vs. correlation.

1.5 Conclusion

Information or Data Visualization confers associations of data with pictures. This is noteworthy considering the way that it licenses examples and guides to be even more successfully watched. With the rising of gigantic data upon us, we ought to have the choice to translate logically greater groups of data. Man-made intelligence makes it less difficult to coordinate assessments, for instance, insightful examination, which would then have the option to fill in as obliging discernments present. Nonetheless, data portrayal is not only noteworthy for data scientists and data specialists, it is critical to appreciate data recognition in any livelihood. Whether or not you work in finance, exhibiting, tech, plan, or whatever else, you need to imagine data. That reality includes the hugeness of data recognition.

Information representation is entering another time. Rising wellsprings of knowledge, hypothetical turns of events, and advances in multidimensional imaging are reshaping the potential worth that examination and experiences can give, with perception assuming a key job. The standards of compelling information representation will not change. Nonetheless, next generation advances and developing intellectual structures are opening new skylines, moving information perception from workmanship to science.

References

1. A. S. Syed Fiaz, N. Asha, D. Sumathi, A.S. Syed Navaz Data Visualization: Enhancing Big Data More Adaptable and Valuable ,International Journal of

Applied Engineering Research ISSN 0973-4562 Volume 11, Number 4 (2016) pp 2801–2804.

2. Bibhudutta Jena :A Review on data visualization tools Used for Big Data International Research Journal of Engineering and Technology (IRJET), Volume: 04 Issue: 01 , Jan -2017
3. Caldarola, Enrico G. & Rinaldi, Antonio. (2017). Big Data Visualization Tools: A Survey - The New Paradigms, Methodologies and Tools for Large Data Sets Visualization. 10.5220/0006484102960305.
4. D. Beaver, S. Kumar, H. C. Li, J. Sobel and P. Vajgel, "Finding a needle in Haystack: facebook's photo storage", Proceedings of the 9th USENIX conference on Operating systems design and implementation, Vancouver, BC, Canada, (2010) October 4–6, pp. 1–8.
5. Dr. D. Sridevi, Dr A. Kumaravel, Dr S. Gunasekaran, A Review on Big Data Visualization Tools, IRE Journals , Volume 3 Issue 7,JAN 2020 , ISSN: 2456–8880
6. Jin X, Wah BW, Cheng X, and Wang Y, "Significance and challenges of big data research," Big Data Research, 2015 Jun 30;2(2):59–64
7. Katal, A., Wazid, M., Goudar, R.H.: Big data: issues, challenges, tools and Good practices. In:2013 6th International Conference on Contemporary Computing, IC3 2013, pp. 404–409 (2013). https://doi.org/10.1109/IC3.2013.6612229
8. Kochhar D., Meenakshi S.P., Dubey S. (2020) Applications of Visualization Techniques. In: Anouncia S., Gohel H., Vairamuthu S. (eds) Data Visualization. Springer, Singapore. https://doi.org/10.1007/978-981-15-2282-6_6
9. L. Meloncon and E. Warner, "Data visualizations: A literature review and opportunities for technical and professional communication," 2017 IEEE International Professional Communication Conference (ProComm), Madison, WI, 2017, pp. 1–9, doi: 10.1109/IPCC.2017.8013960.
10. Lowe J., Matthee M. (2020) Requirements of Data Visualisation Tools to Analyse Big Data: A Structured Literature Review. In: Hattingh M., Matthee M., Smuts H., Pappas I., Dwivedi Y., Mäntymäki M. (eds) Responsible Design, Implementation and Use of Information and Communication Technology. I3E 2020. Lecture Notes in Computer Science, vol 12066. Springer, Cham. https://doi.org/10.1007/978-3-030-44999-5_39
11. Ms. Suman Choudhary Dr. Mahaveer Sain, Critical Analysis of Big Data Analytics Tools, Subodh Journal of Recent Trends in Information Technology, Volume 10, Issue-02, June 2019
12. Olshannikova, E., Ometov, A., Koucheryavy, Y., Olsson, T.: Visualizing big data with augmented and virtual reality: challenges and research agenda. J. Big Data 1–27 (2015). https://doi.org/10.1186/s40537-015-0031-2
13. S. M. Ali, N. Gupta, G. K. Nayak and R. K. Lenka, "Big data visualization: Tools and challenges," 2016 2nd International Conference on Contemporary Computing and Informatics (IC3I), Noida, 2016, pp. 656-660, doi: 10.1109/IC3I.2016.7918044

14. Tri Wahyuningsih, Problems, Challenges and Opportunities Visualization on Big Data, Journal of Applied Data Science, Vol. 1, No. 1, September 2020, pp. 20–28.
15. https://www.klipfolio.com/resources/articles/what-is-data-visualization (March 2021)
16. https://www.dataquest.io/blog/jupyter-notebook-tips-tricks-shortcuts (March 2021)
17. https://www.tableau.com/new-features/10.0 (March 2021)
18. https://stackoverflow.com/questions/27786822/google-charts-overflow-with-bootstrapMarch (March 2021)

2

Decision Making and Predictive Analysis for Real Time Data

Umesh Pratap Singh

Shri Ramswaroop Memorial Group of Professional Colleges, Lucknow

Abstract

Data Analysis is required for any business either starting a new venture, planning marketing decisions, or going for a shuttle down the business. The statistical probabilities calculated using data analysis help to make the critical decisions over human bias. Before selecting a data analytical tool, it is necessary to take into account the scope of work, economic feasibility, infrastructure constraints, and the final report is prepared. Analytics models aim to understand business planning and operations for future improvements in business models by using systematic data-driven processes which link historical data about the business. Sometimes a with dramatic change in an uncertain world, we need a predictive analytic model to improve business areas. The need for predictive analytics applications comes with better risk management, fraud, system failure, or interaction of customers in any business. Predictive analytics makes artificial business decisions and usage of IT helps to identify the operational tradeoffs that impact the business decisions being simulated. It can reduce technical debt and financial costs included with the decision and understanding the customers. IT's role is complex for the selection of an architecture that fulfills future demands around manifold analytical data preparation tasks, reducing model building duration and deploying operational model systems. Technology is required with the needs of business analysts, marketing data scientists, and domain experts. Analytical data preparation is different in every business problem-solving model with the help of statisticians or business analysts using a lot of interactive and collaborative effort. The creative ability to look at data from various perspectives and quickly manipulate for finding missing data or variables, eliminating unnecessary data, and bringing unique new data to improve results from the modeling exercise.

Email: usgemini@gmail.com

M. Niranjanamurthy, Hemant Kumar Gianey and Amir H. Gandomi (eds.) Advances in Data Science and Analytics: Concepts and Paradigms, (21–38) © 2023 Scrivener Publishing LLC

Predictive analytics benefits all small companies as well as large companies for making better decisions in uncertain worlds. Predictive analytics are a key strategy for growing successful businesses in the long run. This is the critical concept of analysts to develop model performance monitoring systems for business.

Keywords: Model, business decision, data analytics, performance, innovation, process

2.1 Introduction

Data analytics are required for more worthy utilization of predictive analytics to eliminate hidden patterns and their relationships to visualize and explore the information. Predictive analytics has given another technique for auto-driven computerization and choice administration that has a choice for cutting operational edge. It is the part of information mining with the prediction of future probabilities and patterns and furthermore anticipates risk, division, and associations. With predictive analytics, associations can accomplish growth development and revenues by key measurements. Various models are used in predictive analytics to monitor various boundaries at various stages of the business system.

The aim of business analytics is to help managers understand their organization's components, market trends, and challenges existing. While estimating stock requirements and recruiting talent, companies are grasping systematic statistical analysis methods for improving effectiveness and earnings.

Predictive analytics is an advanced approach for analyzing the current and previous data for predicting the future by hiring techniques using statistics, artificial intelligence, and machine learning. Organizations can use big data for finding their profit by applying predictive analytics. It helps organizations with a proactive approach that is forward-looking and decision-based on the data [1, 2]. The importance of key market dynamics is emerging as a wide variety of tools and applications for data analytics are available.

The value of data knowledge is growing as a rising organization selects buyer-oriented marketing decisions to help key business shortcoming analytics.

Suppose an e-commerce company employs their retailing company globally via the internet and sells numerous products. Millions of customers browse the company website to search for their needed products. They examine the features, price, and offers related to that product displayed on the website. A lot of products are in demand on a seasonal basis [3, 4].

For example, air-conditioner's demand increases in summers and geysers' demand increases in winter. Customers browse for the item requirement in the season. The organization collects the customer searching data on a season-wise product interest with its price [5, 6]. How do offers attract customers to products? What additional products are bought by customers with selected products? The organization will apply analytics after collecting data to identify the customer requirements and then approach the customers through various mediums such as emails and messages. If the customer browses the website again to buy the same product, then the organization will suggest the new products in combination. If a customer starts frequently buying, then the company increases the price and removes the offer for that individual customer. This is an example of one of the many applications of predictive analytics .

2.2 Data Analytics

The classification of data analytics are as follows.

2.2.1 Descriptive Analytics

Descriptive Analytics are used for data illustration. An example of a product is an administration (SaaS) organization that sold 500 licenses in the current year and 200 licenses last year. Descriptive analysis responds to the number of licenses sold in current versus last year.

2.2.2 Diagnostic Analytics

Diagnostic Analytics is the reason for descriptive analytics. Utilizing the past model, the symptomatic analysis takes information a stride further. An information expert can bore down into quarterly programming permit deals and decide deals and promote endeavors inside every district to reference them against deals development [7, 8]. They could likewise check whether a business increment was an aftereffect of high-performing sales reps or rising enthusiasm inside a specific industry.

2.2.3 Predictive Analytics

Predictive Analytics uses techniques, for example, data mining and machine learning to anticipate what may occur straight away. Data analysis can develop predictive models after gathering large amounts of information to achieve an expected outcome. Predictive analytics is different from data mining on the grounds that it spotlights the revelation of the shrouded connections between factors. A SaaS organization can demonstrate authentic deal data against showcasing uses over every area to make a predicted model for future income dependent on marketing expenses.

2.2.4 Prescriptive Analytics

Prescriptive Analytics makes the last stride and provides a suggestion determined by an anticipated result. When a prescient model is set up, it can suggest activities dependent on recorded information, outer information sources, and machine learning calculations [9, 10].

2.3 Predictive Modeling

Predictive modeling is most firmly identified with the predictive analytics classification. It is a cycle that utilizes information to predict results with data models. This technique can be utilized to predict anything from a rating of television and cricket results. This model is also called:

- Predictive Analysis
- Predictive Analytics
- Machine Learning

Predictive Analytics are frequently used by businesses for predictive modeling. Machine learning is additionally particular from predictive modeling that scientists demonstrate and is characterized by the utilization of statistical methods to permit a system for developing predictive models.

2.4 Categories of Predictive Models

Parametric and non-parametric predictive models are the various forms of predictive models. The main distinction is that parametric models make more precise assumptions about the properties used in the model's construction. Such examples of the different types of predictive models involve:

- Logistic Regression for predicting the outcome
- Splines for Multivariate Adaptive Regression (MARS)
- Ordinary Least Squares

- Decision-Tree
- Neural Networks

2.5 Process of Predictive Modeling

Predictive analytics consists of different steps. A data analyst may predict the future primarily depending on modern-day and historical facts. The predictive analytics process model is designed in given Figure 2.1.

Figure 2.1 Process of Predictive Analytics.

2.5.1 Requirement Gathering

During prediction, which type of information will be picked up ought to be characterized. For instance, a pharmaceutical company needs to predict the medicine's sale in a specific territory. The data analysts ask the customers for the prerequisites to build up the predictive model. How will the customer benefit from these predictions? It distinguishes what information the customer will require in building up the model.

2.5.2 Data Gathering

According to the requirements of the customer, the analyst will collect data from multiple sources which will be used to construct the predictive model. These datasets may be in a well-organized or unorganized state. On their own websites, the analysts verify the information obtained from customers [11].

2.5.3 Data Analysis and Massaging

Data analysts break down the gathered data and it as required in the model to convert the unstructured data into a structured form in this progression. The quality is tested when total data is accessible in the structure form. There are potential outcomes that unusable data is available in the main dataset against the characteristics that must be addressed. The adequacy of the model absolutely relies upon the information behavior.

2.5.4 Machine Learning Statistics

The most widely used methods in analytics are regression analysis and probability theory. Artificial intelligence approaches are used in different predictive analytics jobs. With the development of any predictive model, machine learning techniques are in higher demand than traditional statistical methods.

2.5.5 Predictive Modeling

It is based totally on statistical and machine learning strategies for the dataset. It is tested on a dataset after the development of the model. It is a suitable model if successful validity testing of the main gathered dataset is performed. Once suited, this model makes correct predictions on the other dataset applied as an input to the system.

2.5.6 Prediction and Decision Making

The model is installed at the customer's site for regular predictions and complex decision-making processes after passing effective tests in predictions. The model is consistently observed to ensure that it is producing the desired results and making correct predictions. We have shown that predictive analytics is not a one-step process for making future predictions, but rather a step-by-step procedure that involves a variety of options.

2.6 Predictive Analytics Opportunities

Despite the fact that predictive analytics has a strong tradition and has been used widely in a range of domains for a long time, the modern age of predictive analytics has advanced technology and reliance on data. Many businesses are turning to predictive analytics to boost their profits and bottom lines.

The need to use predictive analytics to explore experiences from large amounts of data is being driven by the growth in volume. Computers that are faster, less costly, and easier to use are available for processing. A variety of software is available and more innovations are being made in software that would be easy to use for clients. The competitive landscape of building a company for profit, as well as the company's financial situation, forces them to use predictive analytics. Predictive analytics is no longer limited to analysts and mathematicians, enabling the development of extremely simple and advanced applications and their accessibility. It is being used in an entire decision-making phase by market analysts and managers. The ones that are probably the most well-known in the field of predictive analytics are as follows.

2.6.1 Detecting Fraud

By applying different research methods, it is possible to enhance the detection and avoidance of suspicious ethical standards. The development of network security is becoming a source of concern. Social inspection could be used to constantly track the activities of the company. It could also be able to detect unusual exercises that might lead to cheating. This concept can be used to identify dangers.

2.6.2 Reduction of Risk

The default probability by a purchaser/shopper of assistance might be evaluated ahead of time by applying predictive analytics using the credit score.

This score is produced by a predictive model utilizing all the information identified by an individual's reliability. It is used with Visa backers and insurance agencies to recognize false clients.

2.6.3 Marketing Campaign Optimization

The reply of clients to the acquisition of data could be determined by using predictive analytics. It allows companies to attract and keep the most valuable customers.

2.6.4 Operation Improvement

The framework of predictive models can be used to forecast stock and deal with property. Predictive analytics is being used by aircrafts to set ticket prices. Hotels may use predictive models to predict the number of customers on a given weekend in order to increase occupancy and revenue. By using predictive analytics, a management team needs to function much more effectively.

2.6.5 Clinical Decision Support System

Expert systems based on statistical models could be used for patient analysis. They could also be used in the development of medications to help any disease.

2.7 Classification of Predictive Analytics Models

Predictive Modeling requires scoring data and then deciding the output. The data processing approach is introduced into the discipline that is used to make strategic decisions. The following are examples of how to sort these orders.

2.7.1 Predictive Models

Predictive models demonstrate that there is still a connection between a unit's performance and its qualities. This model provides an assurance that the relative unit in a different example has indicated the same performance. This model is widely used in ads, where acceptable client execution responses are anticipated. It stimulates individual interactions in order to provide answers to a query. It calculates during a client's exchange to identify the risk depending on the transaction.

2.7.2 Descriptive Models

The model basically makes a link between the data and various clients. Predictive models only take one client or output into account. Descriptive models take into account a variety of relationships with customers. A number of selected agents can be simulated together to make a prediction in a descriptive simulation.

2.7.3 Decision Models

The relationship between the data as well as the decision is illustrated by decision models. This relationship represents the decision model, which can be used to forecast the outcome of an intra decision. These models are used to boost and simplify certain performance. It is used to create strategic rules that determine the right plan of action for each customer in any given situation. A predictive analytics system is defined as a model that predicts at a detailed level. It assigns each person a credit score. This will assist in making an educated decision. The accuracy of the model's performance is defined as the degree of data analysis.

2.8 Predictive Analytics Techniques

Various types of predictive analytics models involve classification and regression. Classification trends demand values that belong to particular classes at the same time that regression models predict a number. We can make a list of the most used methods for developing and enhancing predictive models.

2.8.1 Predictive Analytics Software

Predictive analytics is used to review current and historical data. It is used to distinguish possible threats from possible improvements. Predictive Analytics phases will be complex products that will require the use of current abilities and skills. If you have access to expert data analysts and researchers, predictive analytics can be a very useful tool. It can predict what product an online buyer would most likely buy right now based on a client's actions for financial prediction forecasts for the next quarter.

2.8.2 The Importance of Good Data

Relevant information is the reason for good predictive outcomes. For example, reliable data about what clients have previously purchased and characteristics of purchased goods are required to make predictions about purchases in the future.

It is developed using techniques such as regression tests, decision trees, or other methods. It always quantifies the degree of relationship between variables to help predict future decisions if there is better information.

2.8.3 Predictive Analytics vs. Business Intelligence

Business knowledge and Predictive Analytics tools are strongly intertwined. They are occasionally recognized as part of the world of Business Intelligence. Predictive Analytics is concerned with trying to uncover hidden patterns in data and predicting future outcomes using complex mathematical simulations. Big Data stages like Hadoop, as well as rapid in-memory analytics products, have created a gap between Big Data and Predictive Analytics.

2.8.4 Pricing Information

A few well-known incumbent brands control a significant part of the market, so these resources would be significantly more expensive than younger upstart products with a much smaller market share.

The R programming language, which is free and open-source has over 3,000 network-developed software tools, but this can be difficult to use. It is code-based and lacks a simplified visual workspace.

2.9 Data Analysis Tools

Various analytics tools have their own set of features. The methods are chosen depending on the different data analyzed. There are multiple tools outlined below.

2.9.1 Excel

With additional plugins enabled, it has a different collection of supporting features. It controls a large amount of information. As an outcome, Excel is an effective tool for analyzing Big Data.

2.9.2 Tableau

The Pivot-Table is the core of Tableau. This is user-friendly data representation via a Pivot Chart. It also performs a data mining feature along with an analytical function.

2.9.3 Power BI

It began as an Excel plugin and developed into one of the most supportive data analytic tools. It is available in 3 different versions: free, pro, and premium. Both Power Pivot and DAX languages can be used to fine-tune progress analytics similar to the way Excel formulas can.

2.9.4 Fine Report

Fine Report is really a simple drag-and-drop operation. It is used in the preparation of various report types and the development of a data decision analysis system. It can be associated with a variety of databases and has a similar Excel feature.

2.9.5 R & Python

It is a wonderful and adaptable programming language. For normal distribution and regression analysis, R specializes in statistical analysis. It executes individual predictive analysis such as client actions, spends, and products preferred by him.

2.10 Advantages & Disadvantages of Predictive Modeling

2.10.1 Advantages

Predictive modeling fundamentally decreases the budget needed for organizations to estimate business outcomes, competitive intelligence, and economic situations. The utilization of competitive intelligence can offer some forecast value:

- Forecasting demand
- Churn measurement and workforce planning
- External factor forecasting

- Competitor evaluation
- Maintenance of a fleet or machinery
- Credit or financial risk modeling

2.10.2 Disadvantages

Besides various benefits, predictive modeling absolutely has some disadvantages. Predictive modeling may not give accurate potential output if certain conditions are met. In reality, if these requirements are not met, predictive models may not provide any advantage over heritage strategies or traditional thinking.

2.10.2.1 Data Labeling

A computer is developing the predictive model using machine learning and data should be labeled and properly classified. This process can be uncertain and full of errors. Nonetheless, if appropriate characterization and labeling cannot be finished, then any predictive model will produce poor outcomes and difficulties related to inappropriate order.

2.10.2.2 Obtaining Massive Training Datasets

In order for statistical methods to be consistently accurate at predicting outcomes, one key concept should be followed: appropriate sample size. If a predictive modeling expert does not have enough data to build a model, the model generated will be strongly affected by noise in the data used. Currently, the number of records needed to achieve adequate model output differs from thousands to millions. The data used must be representative of the primary audience. If the sample size is particularly high, for model refinement, the data should include a wide range of records, including unique or unusual examples.

2.10.2.3 The Explainability Problem

When more unpredictable and complex models and methodologies become available, disentangling models to determine why a particular decision is made can often be an extraordinary test. Factors that may explain predictions become crappy as models and consume more data records, posing a significant restriction in some areas. The need to record recorded processes and decisions may disrupt the use of dynamic models in companies that involve reasoning in important legal or administrative outcomes. These limitations are in the new methodologies that can deal with large data volumes and complexities while preserving data integrity.

2.10.2.4 *Generalizability of Learning*

Generalization is the model's ability to be described beginning with one use case and moving on to the next. In general, when a model is created for a specific case, it should not be used for another case. Despite the development of strategies such as exchange learning, a technique that aims to solve this issue, predictive modeling's generalization remains a significant limitation.

2.10.2.5 *Bias in Algorithms and Data*

Despite the fact that it is more of a moral or ethical problem than a technological one, some believe that researchers and experts building predictive models should be careful about which data to use and ignore. Since past perceptions can be established even with the smallest amount of data, extreme caution should be exercised when attempting to correct them. Otherwise, their implications can be propagated into the future by predictive models.

2.11 Predictive Analytics Biggest Impact

The uprising of Big Data has arrived. Companies are scrambling to hire a new generation of analysts known as "data scientists" and universities have responded by incorporating data science courses into degrees from software engineering to business. Companies seem to still be investing in Big Data frameworks because they believe it will result in quantitative development.

Based on surveys and consultancy studies, it is unclear what specific use cases would push this positive initial capital expenditure return from big data. A real-world example of how Big Data has benefited companies is those that have collaborated with Microsoft's analytics teams. These examples reveal the circumstances in which Big Data Predictive Analytics will create unique and high-esteem solutions.

2.11.1 Predicting Demand

Predicting demand for buyer goods in the "long tail" of use is one of the most common use cases. Since stock is expensive to maintain on the market and stock-outs, then for both short-term revenue and long-term customer engagement, companies place a premium on precise demand forecasting. Using time-series macroeconomics with historical deal data is the standard method of solving a problem. This technique works well for conventional goods in large districts, but it keeps failing when data becomes limited. On the current time-series data, a big data solution for this problem is to use encrypted and collected web search or sentiment data related to each store's location. This method is being used by Microsoft data scientists to work with assistance forecasting firms for estimating car sales. As compared to conventional time series models, building models with web search information as one of the data sources reduces total forecast error. A typical proportion of forecast accuracy is for the month-to-month public sales expectations on the request by 40% from the trend for cars, making small proportions of the manufacturing market.

2.11.2 Transformation Using Technology and Process

In this case, the massive data arrangement makes use of previously undiscovered data that people do to ensure comprehensive social research and online research before buying a car. As a result of higher expectation predictives, it is now possible to achieve operational productivity by getting the right stock in the right areas. Anonymized web search data has proven to be useful for a variety of channels. In order to make a successful prediction, you should first handle search information and combine it with conventional sources: simple search query volume is insufficient in filtering out the signs that lead to genuine product demand according to our findings. When deciding which signals to derive from big data, best practices can be case-specific. For example, a single question from a client could be less important than a series of questions from clients.

2.11.3 Improved Pricing

Since the portion of the demand curve which could be profitably fulfilled is driven out of business using a single price is financially inefficient, businesses consistently deliver based on limitations, innovations, and segment-based pricing to connect to a wide range of customers. E-commerce websites have a distinct advantage in adopting such a technique. They monitor comprehensive information on customer browsing, not only the products they purchase, and effectively adjust prices over time. These price changes are a form of exploration when combined with big data that allows companies to research their customers' value response.

By tracking customers through mobile phone availability and logging which customers enter the store to look at and buy the product in offline mode, machine learning applied to this data will computationally generate client portions based on value responsiveness and preferences. Our role in evaluating advertising on the Bing web search has also shown that using Big Data to better-fit sponsors to customers will result in substantial gains. The success of algorithmic focusing has been highly published and it is a major source of revenue in the online advertising industry.

2.11.4 Predictive Maintenance

Predictive maintenance solutions can be used in a wide range of industries, for example, using continuous flight data to predict the useful life of an airplane motor. Utilizing sensor data to predict the failure of an ATM money withdrawal exchange and using flight data to predict the failure of electric sub-siphons used to refuel aircraft, machine learning can strengthen supply chains and minimize the impacts of disruptions for some items and services [12, 13].

2.12 Application of Predictive Analytics

Predictive analytics has many applications in different domains, from stock market prediction to clinical decision analysis to prediction to where an infection can be anticipated dependent on indications and profit for a stock. We will list out some important applications below.

2.12.1 Financial and Banking Services

Predictive analytics is widely used in the banking and financial sectors. Data and money play an important role in both businesses for extracting data. Predictive analytics assists in the identification of false customers and suspicious transactions. It reduces the credit risks that industries face when lending money to their customers. It assists in strategically cross-selling and up-selling strategies and attracting and profiting from large customers. Predictive analytics returns the value for assets and helps in decision-making in budgetary businesses where capital is invested in stocks or other tools.

2.12.2 Retail

Predictive analytics assists the retail industry in identifying and recognizing its customers. They will predict the client's response to a product using this technique. Following the identification of client purchasing behavior, businesses can regulate prices and make special deals on goods. It also helps the retail industry in forecasting how profitable a particular product is during a specific season. Retailers may also benefit from predictive analytics to improve their supply chains. They can identify and predict interest in a product in a specific region that can help them increase demand for products.

2.12.3 Health and Insurance

Predictive analytics is used in pharmaceutical companies for drug preparation and supply chain improvement. These companies can use this approach to predict that the shortage of supply due to prescriptions will expire in a specific region. Predictive analytics models are used in the insurance industry to identify and forecast client-reported misrepresentation claims. This procedure is being used by the health insurance industry to identify clients who are most at risk of true infection.

2.12.4 Oil and Gas Utilities

Predictive analytics techniques are being used by the oil and gas industry to predict the failure of industrial machinery in order to minimize risk. They use these models to predict future asset requirements. Energy-based companies should anticipate the need for assistance in order to avoid a fatal mishap in the future.

2.12.5 Public Sector

To predict possible crimes in a geographic area, government bodies are employing Big Data-based predictive analytics strategies. They use web-based media information to identify and forecast their future behavior. Predictive analytics are being used by governments to forecast population patterns at the national and state levels. Predictive analytics procedures are used for improving cyber security.

2.13 Future Scope of Predictive Modeling

Artificial intelligence is closely tied to the development of predictive modeling. Computers come to generating models as computing capacity grows, data collection keeps growing, and new technologies and methods evolve. The future of predictive modeling is connected to artificial intelligence as computing power grows, data collection expands rapidly, and new advancements and techniques emerge.

2.13.1 Technological Advancements

Advances in calculation capacity and data volume for predictive modeling have increased the impact of ordinary relevant developments. In several areas, including computer vision, natural language processing, and complex games, predictive algorithms may become more advanced.

2.13.2 Changes in Work

In other professions, intelligent computers developed by predictive modeling experts will adjust to adapt to recently available predictive technology. Individuals who work in predictive modeling will also not become redundant, but their careers will evolve and include new predictive technical features and capabilities.

2.13.3 Risk Mitigation

Advances in predictive innovation are extremely encouraging in terms of generating commercial and scientific benefits. The importance of securing information from programmers and reducing other privacy issues grows with massive increases in data volume.

2.14 Conclusion

Statistical models were used as predictive models and they are based on sample data from a broad data index. The advancements in the fields of artificial intelligence and machine learning have changed the world of computing in which intelligent computation strategies and algorithms are presented.

Machine learning models are being used as predictive models. The field of predictive analytics has already been taken over by artificial neural networks. The performance can be estimated based on the input parameter. Advancements in the field of machine learning and the growth of deep learning methods has caused and increase in the use of deep learning models in predictive analytics.

References

1. Elsayed Elashkar, Fares Aldeek, Alaa Shoukry, Business predictive analysis from business insurance data using business strategic planning techniques, Knowledge Management Research & Practice, PP. 1, 2020.
2. M. S. Prasada Babu; S. Hanumanth Sastry, Big_Data_and_Predictive_Analytics_in_ERP_ Systems_ for_Automating_Decision_Making_Process, IEEE 5th International Conference on Software Engineering and Service Science, 2014.
3. Poornima Selvaraj, Pushpalatha Marudappa, A survey of predictive analytics using big data with data mining, 2018.
4. Shivam Gupta, Xiaoyan Qian, Bharat Bhushan, Zongwei Luo, Role of cloud ERP and big data on firm performance: a dynamic capability view theory perspective, Management Decision, 2018.
5. Snijders, C. Matzat ,U. Reips, Big data, Big gaps of Knowledge in the Field of Internet, International Journal of Internet Science, PP. 1–5 2007.
6. Vaibhav Kumar, M. L. Garg, Predictive_Analytics_A_Review_of_Trends_and_Techniques, International Journal of Computer Applications , Volume-182, 2018.
7. David Dietrich, Barry Heller, Beibei Yang: Data Science and Big Data Analytics, PP. 25-45, EMC Education Series, 2015.
8. Michael Berthold, David J. Hand: Intelligent Data Analysis, PP. 442–443, Springer,, 2003.
9. Paul Zikopoulos, Chris Eaton, Paul Zikopoulos: Understanding Big Data: Analytics for Enterprise Class Hadoop and Streaming Data, McGraw Hill, 2017.
10. A. Shi-Nash, David R. Hardoon, Data analytics and predictive analytics in the era of big data, in: Internet of Things and Data Analytics Handbook, PP. 329–345, 2017.
11. Transforming Data With IntelligenceTM, https://tdwi.org/adv-all-ebook-leading-trends-in-data -analytics.aspx , 2019.
12. B. Pavithra, M. Niranjanmurthy, J. K. Shaker and F. M. S. Mani, "The study of big data analytics in E-commerce", International Journal of Advanced Research in Computer and Communication Engineering , vol. 5, no. 2, pp. 126–131, Oct. 2016.
13. K. R. Swetha, N. M, A. M. P and M. Y. M, "Prediction of Pneumonia Using Big Data, Deep Learning and Machine Learning Techniques," 2021 6th International Conference on Communication and Electronics Systems (ICCES), 2021, pp. 1697-1700, doi: 10.1109/ICCES51350.2021.9489188.

3

Optimizing Water Quality with Data Analytics and Machine Learning

Bin Liang*, Zhidong Li, Hongda Tian, Shuming Liang, Yang Wang and Fang Chen

Data Science Institute, University of Technology Sydney, Australia

Abstract

It is critical to continuously maintain the high quality of drinking water in water distribution network management. However, it remains challenging to predict water demand and optimize dosage to ensure safe drinking water. This paper details solutions that utilize data analytics and machine learning to provide water demand forecasting and chemical dosing optimization. Key environmental factors are used to build a Bayesian linear model to predict the water demand for each supply zone. To ensure safe drinking water, chlorine residual is one of the most important indicators. However, as the water age becomes high, the chlorine residual decays very fast. Thus, we provide a data-driven solution to determine the chlorine set points and optimize the ammonia dosage for reservoirs. The optimization results can determine the set point of the dosage devices to be installed at reservoirs. Evaluation results demonstrate that the solutions achieve reasonably consistent results.

Keywords: Water quality modelling, water demand forecasting, hydraulic modelling, chemical dosing optimization, bayesian model

3.1 Introduction

Clean and safe drinking water is essential to public health. It is critical for water utilities to ensure the continued supply of high-quality drinking water to residents. Water quality can be measured in terms of taste, odor, appearance, and chlorine concentration along with other parameters. It

**Corresponding author*: Bin.Liang@uts.edu.au

M. Niranjanamurthy, Hemant Kumar Gianey and Amir H. Gandomi (eds.) Advances in Data Science and Analytics: Concepts and Paradigms, (39–66) © 2023 Scrivener Publishing LLC

can be impacted by the components of the water distribution network (such as pipe materials, tanks, and valves) and other risks related to water distribution [1]. Therefore, maintaining water quality through the water distribution network until the point of consumption is one of the most challenging tasks faced by the water utility industries [2]. The treatment process involves the removal of contaminants from raw water and chemical dosing, aiming to produce water that is pure enough for human consumption without any risk of adverse health effect. Chlorination is the most widely used method for disinfecting water supplies [3]. The disinfected water may be polluted again when the water is being transported for long time. A disinfectant residual should be maintained throughout the distribution system at all times.

Since the water quality is changing with time, it is difficult to identify the connections based on upstream observations. To address this issue, we utilize the hydraulic modelling to have the connection between the components in the delivery system. The distribution of water travel time is then estimated from reservoirs to customer connections using the proposed demand forecasting method. Then the estimated distribution can be used to link total chlorine in reservoir and customer connections. Furthermore, climate change and the increase in water demand has put pressure on the water distribution network. This highlights the importance of using the prediction of water demands as an effective approach for optimizing the operation and management of the network or planning for future expansion or reduction under the variability of climate and socio-economic factors [4, 5]. In this work, Bayes linear models are constructed for water demand forecasting because the models are simple and able to describe uncertainty.

The maintenance of residual chlorine concentrations within a particular range is necessary to suppress microbial growth during water supply and to prevent the occurrence of diseases that could be attributed to cross-contamination between the water supply and sewer, due to leaky pipes, a lack of water pressure, and operational failures [12–14]. It was found that low doses of chlorine disinfectant could adequately achieve quality standards when compared to traditional injection methods for the water source. In order to minimize the residual chlorine concentrations at the previously determined re-chlorination injection points, re-chlorination optimization is required to determine the set point of the auto dosage device that is planned to be installed at the reservoir.

This work includes three steps to optimize water quality in the delivery system. 1) The hydraulic system is utilized to connect the components in the delivery system. 2) Water demand is forecasted by Bayesian models. 3) Re-chlorination optimization is conducted to determine the optimized set point.

3.2 Related Work

Different methods and models have been applied in previous studies to predict water demand, including traditional, machine learning, and hybrid models [6–8]. Traditional methods, such as time-series analysis and regression [9, 10], were firstly employed in water demand prediction. However, they lack accuracy when predicting water demand, which may cause significant issues in the operation and management of the water distribution network. Furthermore, the impact of climate change and urbanization can cause high uncertainty, making the prediction and forecasting more complex. This has motivated researchers to further improve their approaches [11], including the use of machine learning and data analytics techniques. Zubaidi *et al.* investigated the impact of climate change on water consumption and developed an ANN model to forecast monthly water demand [20]. A singular spectrum analysis technique was used to decompose and reconstruct water consumption in relation to weather variables. Monthly water demand was estimated in relation to previous water consumption using ANN which is optimized with a Backtracking Search Algorithm [21]. A comparative study between ANNs and SVMs was conducted in the forecasting of water demand [22]. The work observed that ANNs perform significantly better than SVMs. Chen *et al.* adopted discrete wavelet transformation to decompose raw time series into low- and high-frequency parts and then applied RF to the prediction of daily urban water consumption [23]. Furthermore, data pre-processing, model architecture, and optimization algorithms have big effects in the performance of the prediction model. Therefore, hybrid models have been used in these models where machine learning approaches act as the primary model while others work as pre-processing or post-processing algorithms [6–8].

Water travel time plays an important role in the prediction of water quality since chlorine residuals decrease depending on the travel time in the network. The calculation of travel time from a source to any demand node in the network is a problem that has been studied over the past few decades. Various methods have been developed, which can be broadly categorized into steady-state and dynamic models. Steady-state models [24] [26] determine the travel times by assuming that all flows throughout the distribution network are steady. However, it is limited to most real-world applications where the flow varies slowly as demand and other factors change. Dynamic models [27, 28] aim to overcome this weakness. Islam *et al.* proposed a dynamic hydraulic solution that takes the spatial and temporal variations of flows, pressures, and constituent concentrations into account [25].

Studies related to the maintenance of residual chlorine concentrations within a particular range started by minimizing the mass of the disinfectant at the previously planned chlorine injection facilities. Munavalli and Kumar [15] studied the optimal chlorine concentration injection using a genetic algorithm (GA). Tryby *et al.* [16] and Lansey *et al.* [17] developed a mixed integer linear programming model to determine the minimal disinfectant injection points. With respect to studies on the operation and maintenance of re-chlorination, Propato and Uber [18] proposed an operation method that allows for the sums of the squared deviations of the residual concentrations to be minimized, in which the linear least-squares (LLS) optimization model was used. Ostfeld and Salomons [19] attempted to simultaneously optimize the pump operation and the re-chlorination injection facilities by combining a water quality simulation model with a GA, in which the operation and construction costs were used as the objective functions.

3.3 Data Sources and Collection

This research work includes various data sources from an Australian water utility, including network topology data, monitoring and control data, water quality data, and customer consumption data. Each of the data sources presents various issues and challenges. This section briefly describes each of them.

The network topology data has been extracted from the water utility's GIS system. This provides a comprehensive snapshot of the network topology. The topology data contains the connections between pipes and includes pipe characteristics. We mainly use diameter and pipe length for the estimation of water travel time. The data also includes the locations of the flow meters to collect the water flow data and the on/off status of pumps and valves that are used to determine the path of water. They do not change very often in the reality. The network is separated by reservoirs into several reservoir zones. Customer connections are usually connected to only one reservoir and the connections using the same reservoir compose a reservoir zone.

At reservoirs, the data includes flow meter readings, total chlorine measurements, water levels, and water temperature. At customer connections, total chlorine is measured by field and lab operators in charge of sampling sites. Samples are collected from a set of sparsely located customer taps. The compliance data includes the measurements of total chlorine, monochloramine, dichloramine, pH, and turbidity.

In order to estimate the water travel time, we need to investigate the water usage of each customer connection. Each customer connection involved in the delivery system is equipped with a water meter (different from flow meter for monitoring a part of the network). This device accurately tracks water usage and ensures customers can be billed only for the water that has passed through the meter. The acquired data includes the location of each water meter and which reservoir zone it belongs to. However, only the historical monthly consumption is recorded as the meters are mainly designed for billing purposes.

3.4 Water Demand Forecasting

Predicting the future demand for water is critical to ensuring a sufficient supply of water into the supply planning process. The supply planning process takes the predicted water demand over the next 28 hours and generates a series of pumping control laws that enable this demand to be met in a cost-effective manner. This section examines the available data that allows water demand to be measured and subsequently builds a probabilistic model that allows the key environmental data to be used to predict the water demand for each reservoir supply zone. This is performed on an individual zone level. The fine-grained model will also be important for subsequent re-chlorination optimization.

3.4.1 Network Flow and Zone Demand Estimation

Based on information extracted from InfoWorks, Hydra, and IICATS, a topological network has been constructed. This comprises of two types of nodes: Storage Zones and Flow Zones. A Flow Zone represents a collection of connected pipes that do not have any internal storage and may supply water to customers. Flow Zones typically represent reduced pressure zones, demand management areas, or remainder zones and are typically separated by flowmeters. A Storage Zone has one or more hydraulically connected internal storage reservoirs and does not have any connected customers. Zones are interconnected with links to form a graph that represents the macroscopic topology of the network.

It is of interest to use the available flowmeter and reservoir level sensors to estimate the water demand for each zone. By combining these

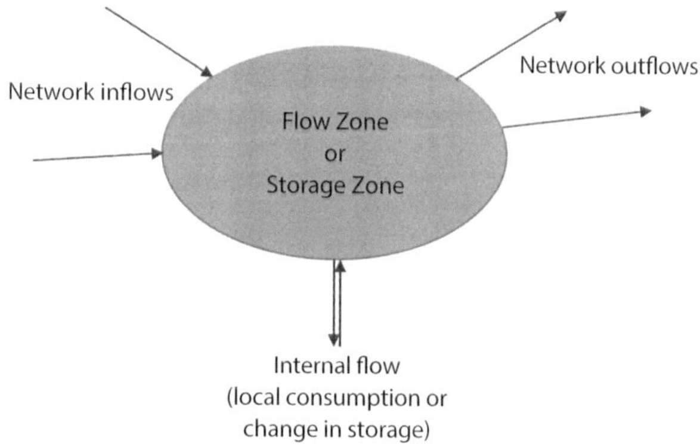

Figure 3.1 For any time, if all but one of the flows are known, the remainder can be estimated using conservation of mass.

measurements with the law of mass conservation, most unmeasured link flows and zone demands can be estimated. For a flow zone with internal customer connections, the demand requires all the in and out flows to be measured. Similarly, for a storage zone, an in or out flow can be estimated if the internal storage is measured and all other in/out flows are also measured (see Figure 3.1). This flow estimation is performed at a temporal resolution of 15 minutes, corresponding to the availability of SCADA flow and level measurements for all zones.

3.4.2 Demand Forecasting

To aid operational planning, it is of interest to forecast the amount of future water that will be used over the next 24 to 48 hours. Typically, the amount of water used varies with the time of year and the day of the week. For instance, residential areas use more water during the weekend. In addition, water used for garden and lawn irrigation is heavily dependent on the weather. The observed daily variations in the water consumed by customers directly supplied by a reservoir are depicted in Figure 3.2. The vertical axis is the flow in ML per day.

In building a forecast model that can predicts future water usage, several features have been explored:

- Calendar information including the year, the month of the year, and whether the day of interest is a weekday or part of the weekend.

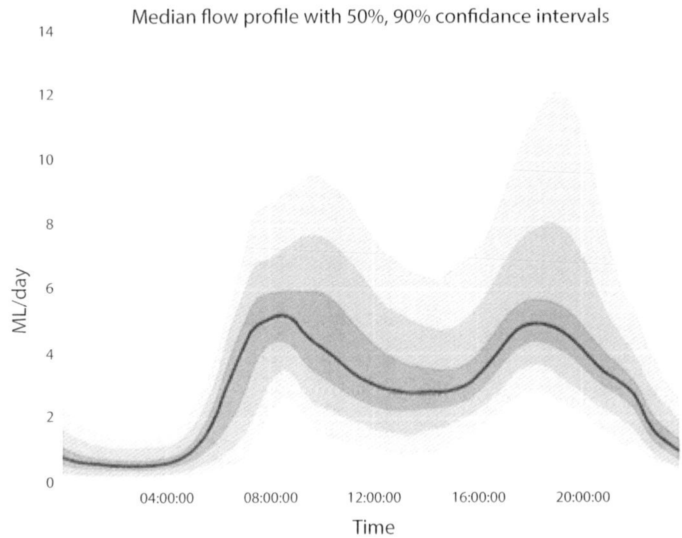

Figure 3.2 Variations in water consumed during a day.

- Past consumption is the cumulative amount of water consumed over the previous *N* days (where *N* ranges from 1 to 14).
- Past weather including total rainfall, maximum temperature, and total pan evaporation measured over the previous *N* days (where *N* ranges from 1 to 14).
- Forecasted weather including the forecast maximum temperature and rainfall for the day being forecasted.[1]

3.4.2.1 Feature Importance

Of the possible features considered above, it is expected that only a few are important for predicting future demand. To explore these, a Bayesian linear model is constructed and trained on the daily cumulative flow data. Feature importance is measured using an incremental stepwise procedure by which at each step the feature is added that achieves the greatest performance improvement. Here, performance improvement is measured through cross validation to avoid overfitting.

[1] Historical forecasts have not been obtained and the actual measured maximum temperature and rainfall is used for all training and characterisation purposes.

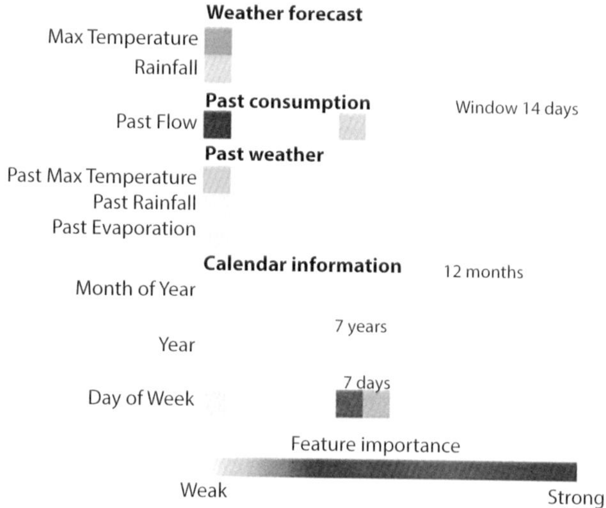

Figure 3.3 Importance of different features in forecasting future water demand.

The results are shown below in Figure 3.3. It is noted that the previous day's flow is the most important feature. Information about whether the day of interest is a weekday or not is the next most useful feature, followed by the forecasted weather conditions and the past day's weather. Another key outcome of lower importance of the year and the month of the year. Although consumption does vary with the year and month, the variation can be better explained through the weather and past flow based on the analysis.

3.4.2.2 *Forecast Horizon*

Based on the results obtained above for the cumulative daily flow data, a series of Bayesian linear models is constructed to predict the demand for each hour within a forecast horizon of 24 hours. As the horizon may span more than one day, additional weather forecast information is incorporated. For instance, a forecast generated at 12pm, with a 24-hour horizon will be based on the weather information for that day and the next day. An example is given in Figure 3.4.

3.4.3 Performance Characterization

To assess the performance of the forecast approach, two evaluations have been conducted. The first considers the error between the forecasted

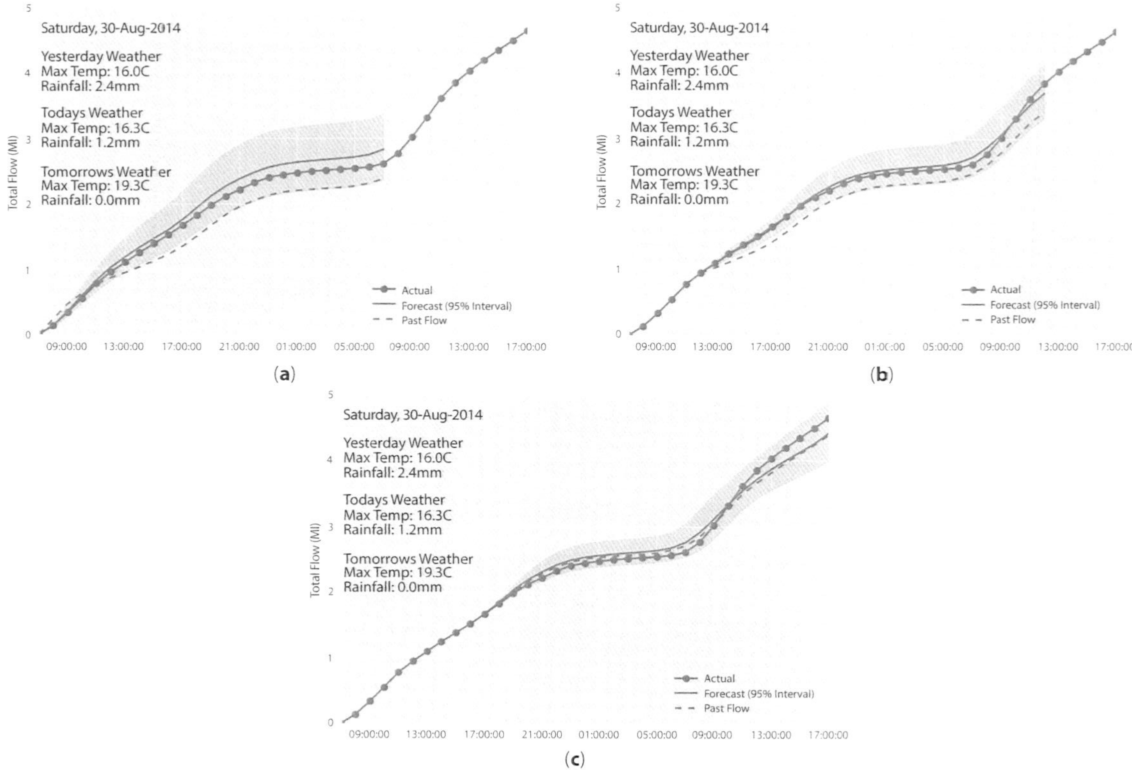

Figure 3.4 Forecasted cumulative demand over 24-hour horizon for one supply zone. Forecast is generated at 7am in (a), 12pm in (b), and 5pm in (c). Each figure shows the actual demand, the demand recorded over the past 24 hour horizon and the forecasted demand, including a 95% confidence interval.

demand and the actual demand. The second considers the uncertainty interval around this single estimate. Each of these measures is created by using mean values within the forecast horizon. Cross validation is also employed that splits the data into 3 sets, with two used to train a model and the predictive performance measured on the third. This is performed 3 times and the results averaged again.

The forecast performance is shown in Figures 3.5 and 3.6 and covers the root mean square error (RMSE) and percentage of measurements that lie within the forecasted confidence interval. These figures show the performance separately for each of the supply zones, as well as the total demand across the entire distribution network. Figure 3.5 also shows the RMSE when the past flow is used to forecast the future demand. Figure 3.6 highlights the consistency between the confidence interval and the inherent variability in the forecast. All the supply zones have approximately 95% of the data within the confidence interval, with the outliers generally spread equally above and below.

The performance has demonstrated the ability to build probabilistic forecast models that can accurately capture the variability in the demand for water. The models allow operational demand to be estimated over a horizon that matches the supply planning requirements of approximately 24–48 hours.

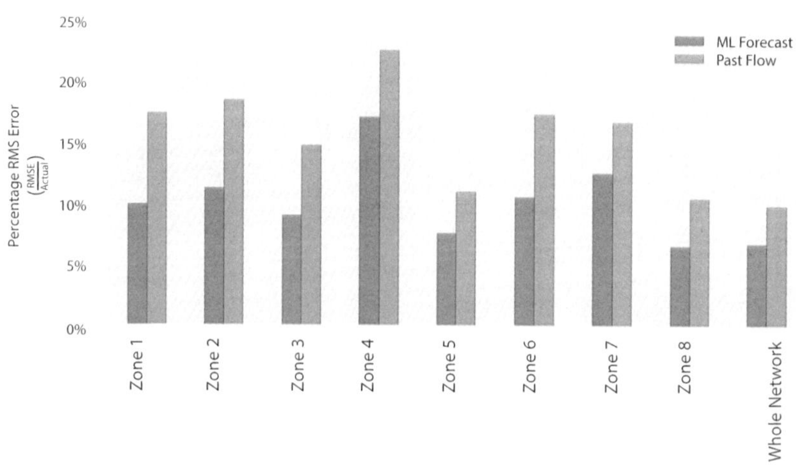

Figure 3.5 Average forecast error measured as average ratio of root mean square error to actual demand.

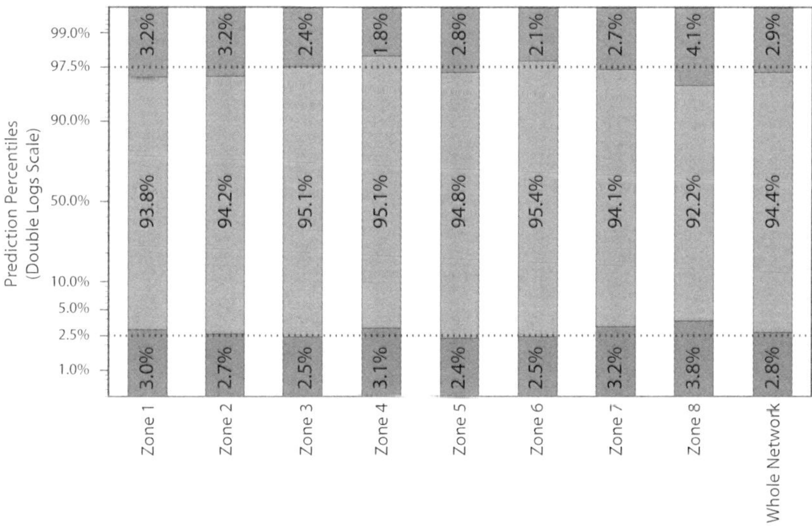

Figure 3.6 Average number of points that fall above/inside/below the forecasted 95% confidence interval.

3.5 Re-Chlorination Optimization

This section describes the objectives that the re-chlorination strategy tries to balance, how these are codified within an optimization model, and how they are solved. The objective of the intelligent decision for dosage optimization is to determine the set point of the auto dosage device that is planned to be installed at a reservoir.

To ensure safe drinking water, appropriate chlorine residual levels must be maintained through the network. However, the level can decay very fast with water age (time from last treatment). To reduce the decay rate and the formation of chlorinated disinfection by-products, chloramine (NH_2Cl) is often used. The water is treated by coagulation/flocculation/direct filtration, followed by chlorination and ammonization. As is shown in Figure 3.7, the total chlorine can be best kept when the ration between Cl and N is 4:1. The dosing needs to consider this and keep the chlorine as Monochloramine to prevent it from decay as free chlorine. When the ratio is greater than this, more free chlorine will not only decay faster, but also create taste concerns. On the other hand, high levels of ammonia are also not suitable for a healthy water supply. Therefore, the water in high standard is to optimize the dosing to keep the total chlorine in a range.

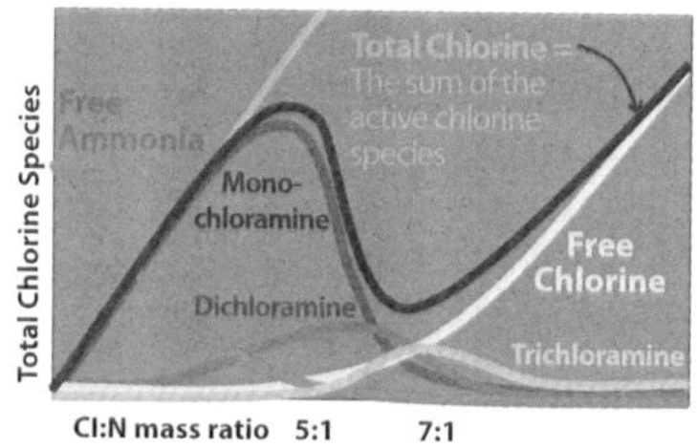

Figu re 3.7 The Cl:N ratio and total chlorine decay rate [29].

In the actual dosing, two kinds of chemicals are used, one is chlorine dosing and the other is ammonia dosing. In the water plant, which is usually the source of water supply, both chlorine and ammonia are dosed. It is easy to control the Cl:N ratio to be 4:1 and keep the chlorine level. However, the situation is much more complex for the intermediate reservoirs. The traditional dosing for chlorine in reservoirs is performed by the water utility manually, e.g., twice per week. However, the modern dosing strategy uses an auto dosing device that can continuously add chlorine into a reservoir. It enables the function to keep the chlorine level to a set point.

We provide a data-driven intelligent framework to determine the chlorine set points for all the reservoirs as a network and optimize the ammonia dosage for the water source (in the water plant). As the result of optimization, we hope to let the water users get high standard water from their taps. However, the tap data is sparse and we take advantage of water demand forecasting in the previous section for performance evaluation. We tested our method in the water utility where the chlorine set point we optimized can reduce the probability of not using water in high standard by 50%. The ammonia set point is also optimized. The results are stable, so the main contributor of optimizing is the set point of chlorine devices.

In this work, three challenges evolved.

- First, a high frequency set point update, e.g., per 15 minutes, requires high frequency ammonia observation. However, there is no device to monitor ammonia in such a high frequency. Usually the samples are taken weekly, so it is challenging to fill in these missing intervals of optimization
- Secondly, we need to maintain sufficient chlorine to ensure the 4:1 Cl:N ratio in downstream reservoirs in the network. Except the decay itself, the ammonia volume can change

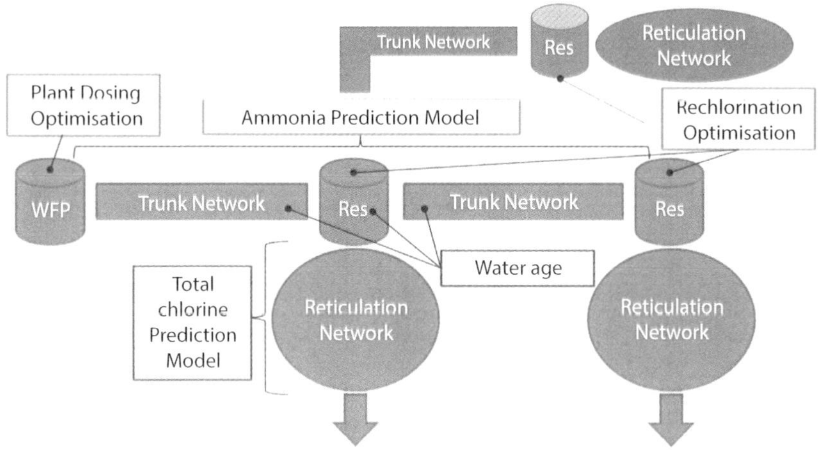

Figure 3.8 Re-chlorination framework (rectangles are components needed for optimization).

given the water will be staying in the reservoir for a certain time (residential time) before it travels to the next reservoir. In that case, the ammonia could become less and less passing more reservoirs since it can only be dosed in the water plant. Thus, we need to find out how much impact this has to change optimization.

- Thirdly, we need to consider the joint optimization problem for all reservoirs and water plant with chlorine and ammonia.

The framework is illustrated in Figure 3.8. We consider the network from upstream reservoirs (or water plant) to downstream reservoirs. It can be seen that we need to predict the ammonia level in reservoirs, water age (including travel time and residential time), and predicted chlorine in the reticulation network (taps).

3.5.1 Data

We will use the data in the water plant as the main source in optimization, including "Ammonia in NH3" and "Total Chlorine" as shown in Figure 3.9. The water plant applied different dosing strategies within the observation time and we represented this as different colors in the figure. It is important to consider this given that the observation period is long and strategies could change from time to time. The analytics can confirm the smooth

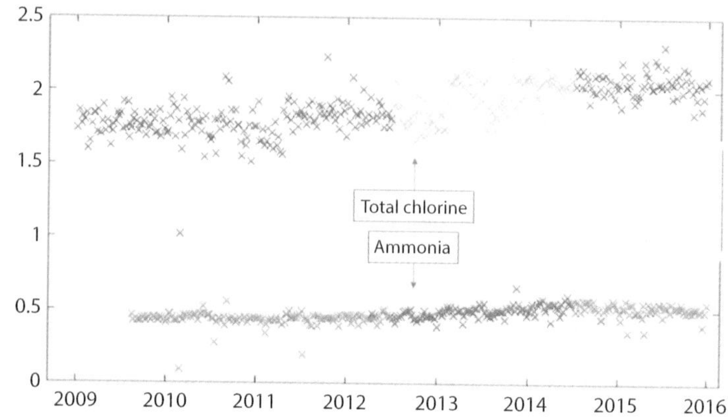

Figure 3.9 Water plant data in time series. All observations are included.

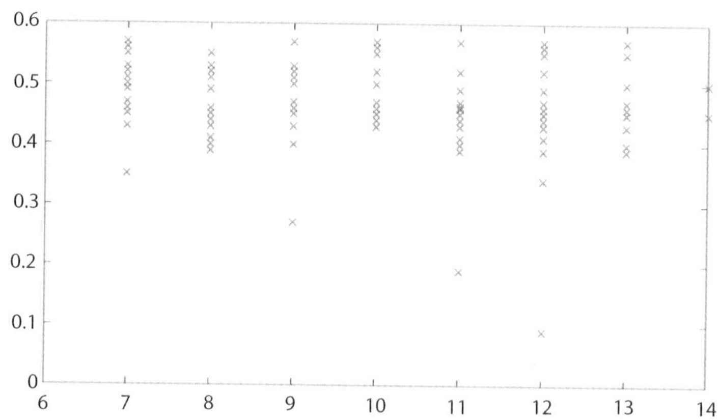

Figure 3.10 Ammonia data in different times of day (each point is an observation).

connection between different strategies so we can use them together in one batch. In addition, it can be seen that the ammonia level is stable across years. The stability can also be observed in different times in one day (7:00–14:00), as shown in Figure 3.10. The samples are extracted from different days and the ammonia level is around 0.4–0.6 mg/L.

3.5.2 Water Age Estimation

The water age is an important factor that influences the delay for both chlorine and ammonia. The water age must include the time delay in two parts: travel time and default residential time.

3.5.2.1 *Travel Time Estimation*

In order to achieve the proper connections between the components in the delivery system, a hydraulic system is built based on the collected data. Travel time is a key component in the hydraulic system. It can be used to predict water quality and is a critical part of water age. It is noted that the travel time cannot be measured directly and must be estimated indirectly.

Based on the constructed hydraulic system, we propose to estimate the travel time of water from reservoirs to customer connections. After demand forecasting, travel time can be estimated based on the forecasted corresponding volume. To do so, each zone is considered separately and the available flow data combined. The total incoming and outgoing flows of each zone can be estimated by considering the data from the flowmeters and reservoir level sensors. These are available at a high frequency of one measurement per 15 minute period. In addition to this, the meter data of individual customers provides detailed spatial data on the outflows on the network, but at a very low temporal resolution of once per month (interpolated from quarterly meter readings). To estimate the time it takes water to travel from, e.g., the upstream reservoir to a location in the network, an assumption must be made on the temporal variation in the demand at the customer locations. Here, it is assumed that all the customers consume a fixed proportion of the total water that is consumed within the zone, as illustrated in Figure 3.11.

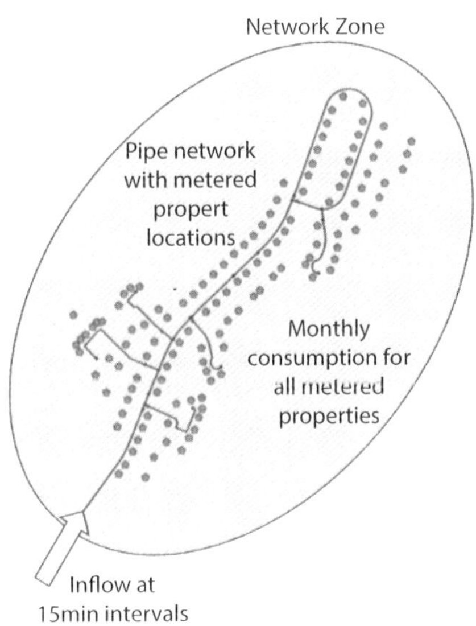

Figure 3.11 Travel time estimation for each zone.

For example, if during a peak demand time the total consumption within the zone is twice the average, it is assumed that all customers will be consuming twice their average demand. This assumption provides a way to use the high frequency flowmeter data to interpolate temporally the individual customer demand. It is noted that this does not differentiate between residential, commercial, or industrial customers that may consume water at different times during the day. Such an extension could be considered in the future. It is acknowledged that this assumption on how water is used by customers is an explicit simplification and any network flows that are estimated with this assumption will be wrong. Nevertheless, it provides a good starting point for estimating the travel time between two points in the network. The travel time estimation can be performed using standard hydraulic flow simulators by first computing the flow rates on each pipe segment, followed by a path tracing algorithm to compute the total travel time.

3.5.2.2 Residential Time Estimation

Default residential time can be estimated from the water volume in the reservoir and inlet flow. Specifically, default residential time calculation can be performed according to the following steps:

1. The local maxima and minima of volume for each reservoir are first extracted from the whole historical period.
2. The durations in hours (*total_period*) between two consecutive timestamps of local maxima and minima are then calculated.
3. The volume at the current timestamp and next timestamp with maximum volume are denoted as *v_start* and *v_max*, respectively, so the difference between these two volumes can be calculated as *delta_v = v_max – v_start*.
4. The residential time during one period is calculated via *(0.5 + vstart / delta_v) * total_period*.
5. Finally, the default residential time is represented as the average value of the calculated residential time for each reservoir during the whole historical period.

3.5.3 Ammonia Prediction

The ammonia can only easily be added at the water plant, which means it will consistently decay through the network with water age. As it is shown in Figure 3.12, it is quite important to determine the dosage volume for

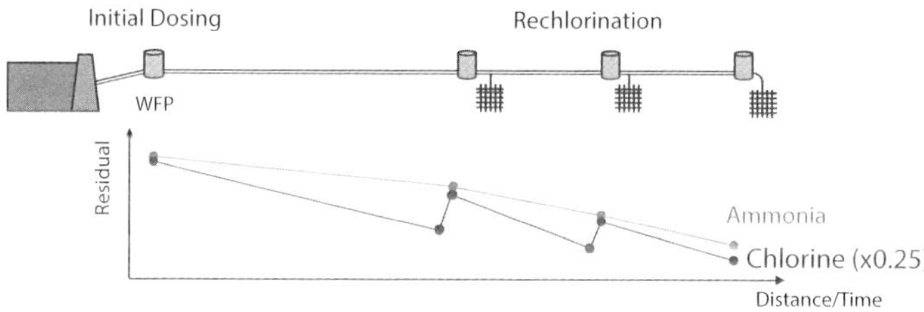

Figure 3.12 Decay and re-chlorination.

re-chlorination to keep the ratio of 4:1. However, the ammonia can vary in different sites because of decay and other reasons.

There are many challenges to predict ammonia. For example, the ammonia decay is not proportional to the distance between reservoirs. It can also be affected by many factors such as pump running, reservoir level, demand, water temperature, water age, weather, etc. Due to its complexity and importance, we use data-driven methods to estimate the ammonia volume in each reservoir.

For prediction, first we will investigate the importance of factors that could cause the variation of ammonia. After reviewing all the factors, we mainly consider 5 factors, including ammonia in WFP, water age, temperature, and Chlorine in upstream, as the features of prediction. Using one reservoir as an example, in Figure 3.13 we put the abovementioned features as the inputs to a machine learning model. We use a 10-fold cross-validation method to select 90% data to train the model and the remaining 10% data to test the model performance. The average performance is used. For each training-testing iteration, we add 1 feature from the feature set, ordered by ammonia in WFP, water age, temperature, and Chlorine in the upstream. The corresponding performances are shown as the bar chart in Figure 3.13. All the performances are combined with random prediction which predict the testing data as the average of training data.

The performance is measured by Mean Absolute Error (MAE) where the absolute value between predicted ammonia and observed ammonia in that reservoir are used. In the comparison, we can see that the Ammonia in WFP is the largest increment (decrement of error). The significant increments can also be observed for adding water age and temperature. However, adding the chlorine volume from the upstream does not give significant increment. As a result, using only Ammonia in WFP, water age, and temperature is enough to make the prediction good.

The similar results are also observed when we extend the prediction to all the other considered reservoirs. In the Figure 3.14, we can see that

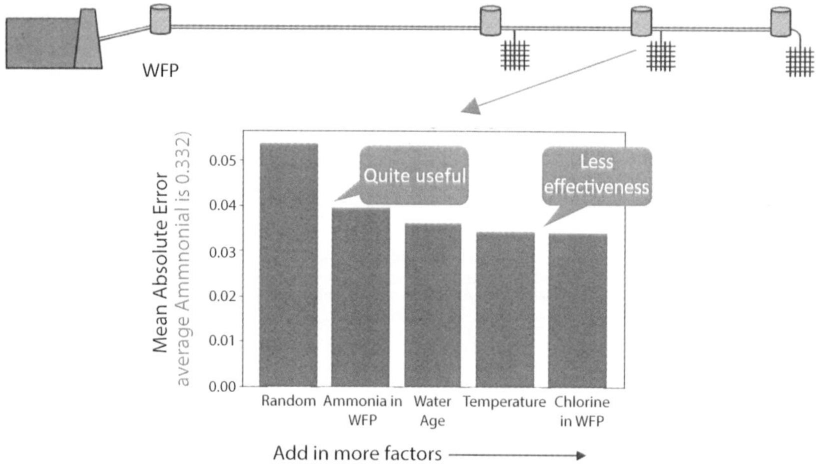

Figure 3.13 Feature importance.

adding the Ammonia in WFP can drastically increase the prediction accuracy, while adding other features is less effective. To evaluate the effectiveness quantitatively, we compare the increment by adding chlorine from upstream reservoirs. It is represented by:

$$E_{effectivness} = \frac{MAE_{before\ adding\ factors} - MAE_{after\ add\ factors}}{Actual\ Ammonia}.$$

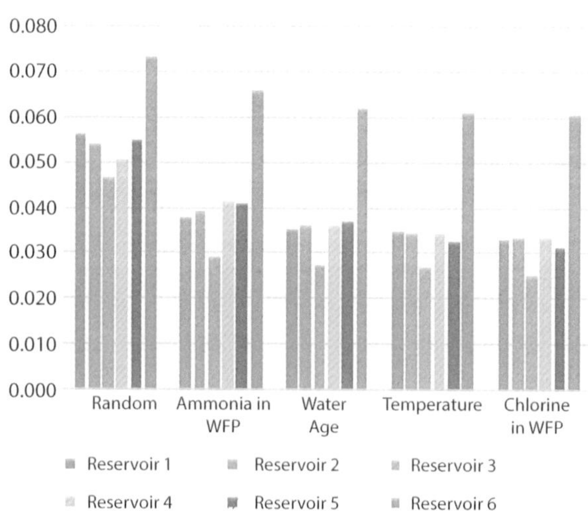

Figure 3.14 Prediction error for more reservoirs.

Table 3.1 Average ammonia in observations for each reservoir.

Reservoir 1	Reservoir 2	Reservoir 3	Reservoir 4	Reservoir 5	Reservoir 6
0.385	0.332	0.446	0.333	0.357	0.376

As a result, from Figure 3.13 and Figure 3.14, we can see that the effectiveness of adding upstream chlorine is minor, given the average of observed ammonia in Table 3.1. The observation can benefit to our optimization from two respects, first, when considering the ammonia prediction, we do not need to use the chlorine from upstream since the chlorine will be dynamic so the uncertainty of aligning the time between the upstream chlorine and downstream ammonia is large. Secondly, in the set point optimization we do not need to consider its influence on ammonia in the downstream reservoirs since the impact is small.

Given the predictions, we can set our direct objectives for optimizing the set point in each reservoir (based on the outlet of reservoirs):

- Minimum level of total chlorine (set to 0.6 in the experiments)
- Maximum level of total chlorine (set to 1.8 in the experiments)
- Chlorine to ammonia ratio (set to 4:1 in the experiments)

3.5.4 Optimization Model Definition

To introduce the optimization objective, we define the following notations first:

C_R: the set point of chlorine in reservoir R, where $R \in \{6\ reservoirs\}$;
A_R: the predicted ammonia in reservoir R;
C_t: the predicted chlorine for tap site t;
lower: the lower threshold for chlorine level in the tap site. The chlorine level cannot be too low to keep the water clean, 0.6mg/L is used in the experiments.
upper: the upper threshold for chlorine level in the tap site. The high chlorine level could cause odor in the water, 1.8mg/L is used in the experiments.

The optimization loss function for reservoir R on time i can be formally written as:

$$L(R,i) = \left|\frac{C_R}{A_R} - 4\right| + \sum_{t=1}^{T}(\delta(C_t < lower) + \beta\delta(C_t > upper)).$$

where

$$A_R = f(A_{WFP}, WA, Temperature)$$

and C_t is the predicted tap chlorine from the previous section from C_R. $\delta(\mathbf{X})$ is a function with:

$$\delta(\mathbf{X}) = \begin{cases} 1, & f \text{ logic statement } \mathbf{X} \text{ is true} \\ 0, & \text{otherwise} \end{cases}$$

Then, the optimization is to find C_R given any time i that can minimise $L(R, i)$.

More details of the objective function can be found in Figure 3.15. The map in the middle indicates the examples for reservoir investigated and possible locations for taps. We will use two taps in the optimization, one is close to the reservoir while the other is far away from it. These two taps are representative for the reticulation network. Our algorithm is easily generalized to more tap locations. As it is shown, when C_R is changing, the loss part for ammonia ratio will change as the top-left curve. At the same time, the loss for tap chlorine prediction is shown as the curve in the top right corner.

The importance of the upper limit and lower limit can be manually adjusted by changing β. For example, when the upper limit is less important than the lower limit, β can be set to values less than 1. It can be seen from Figure 3.16 that by setting β to higher values, the > 1.8 part is considered more, so less probability that the tap chlorine is > 1.8. For a smaller β, the less tap chlorine is < 0.6.

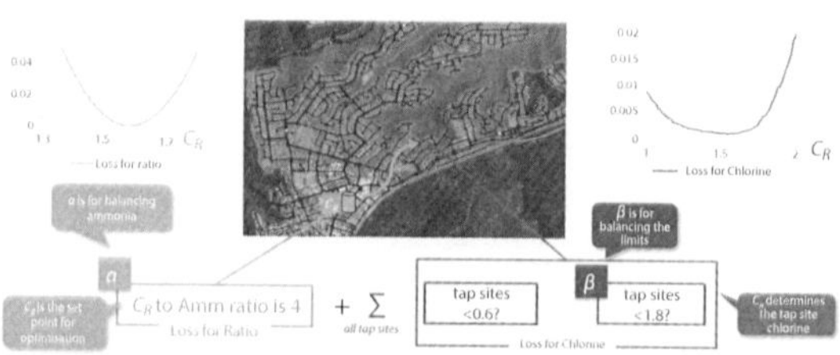

Figure 3.15 Explanation of objective function.

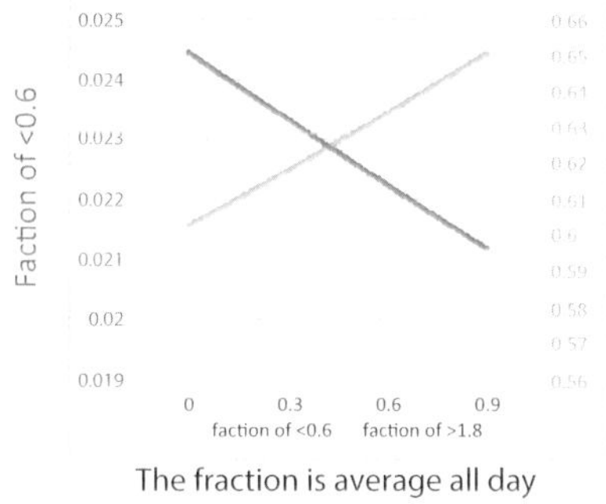

Figure 3.16 Balance between upper limit and lower limit when setting different β. The x axis is value of β.

3.5.5 Improvements in Customer Water Quality

The probability that chlorine is out of lower-upper range is used to evaluate the results in individual reservoirs. We compare the optimized chlorine and actual chlorine in the reservoirs. All the results are evaluated on actual data. Using one reservoir as an example, the left figure in Figure 3.17 shows the distribution of predicted chlorine residual at tap sites. The mean and media values of the predicted tap chlorine based on the optimized set point is larger than the predicted tap chlorine based on the actual reservoir chlorine on that day. The right figure shows the probability of the distribution in the left figure for the case that the tap chlorine is less than 0.6mg/L, which is the *lower* limit in our optimsation. It can be seen that the probablity based on the optimsed set point is 60% less than the current observed chlorine.

More details about the suggested set points are shown in Figure 3.18. The whole testing duration is from 0:00am on the first day till 0:00am on the second day. The set points are optimized every 15 minutes. In the

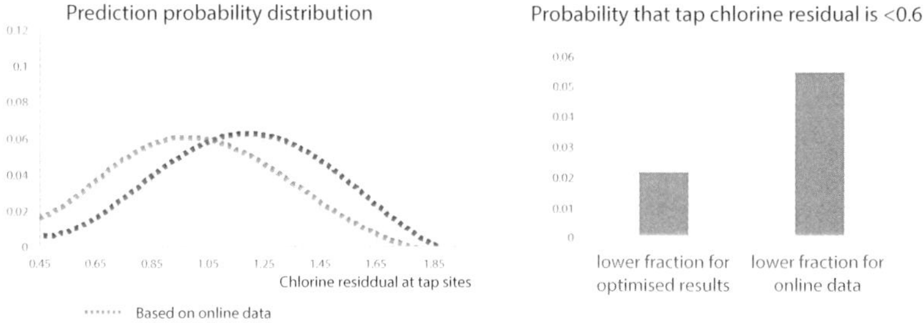

Figure 3.17 Evaluation on one reservoir.

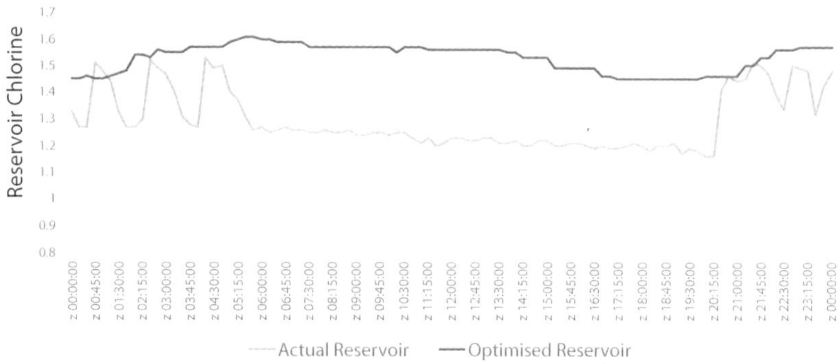

Figure 3.18 Suggested chlorine level (mg/L) on 1, Feb 2014.

practical use, the set points can be suggested under any time scale. It can also be planned ahead of time. For such usage, the prediction of ammonia must be done for the needed time ahead. In the experiment, the chlorine is unstable which is because of the water inlet from upstream with different levels of chlorine. There is no manual dosing in the experiment. Dosing is also needed in the middle of the day, especially in the morning time (5:00am – 6:00am) even water with higher chlorine levels in the morning time. This is a reasonable case because of the residential time of water.

We also examine the performance every 5 minutes on the same day. The performance is evaluated by the probability that the tap chlorine residual is lower than the *lower* bound (0.6mg/L, in Figure 3.19). It can be seen that in the morning peak time, the optimized set point can drastically keep the chlorine residual, therefore the method can provide larger probability (at most 8% more) to tap users to consistently use water with chlorine residual which is higher than 0.6mg/L.

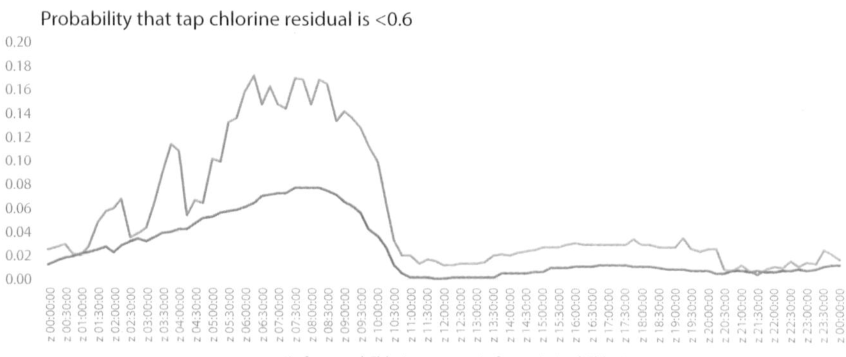

Figure 3.19 Performance examination for every 5 minutes.

Figure 3.20 shows the actual distribution of the chlorine residual in a tap site. The curve in the middle is the median value for the distribution, while the shaded areas present 95% confidence interval area, which means with 95% probability that the tap chlorine is in the shaded area. The distribution using the actual chlorine is lower than the optimized one.

Similar testing is performed on all 6 investigated reservoirs (see Figure 3.21). Here, Reservoir 2 and Reservoir 5 are closer to the water plant and the chlorine and ammonia level is still high in these reservoirs. As a result, we found that they have much less chance to provide water with chlorine residual less than 0.6. The improvement for reservoirs that are further from the water plant is more significant, such as Reservoir 3 where the probability for chlorine level under 0.6 is high but lowered by more than a half. The improvements of Reservoir 1 and Reservoir 5 are also more than a half.

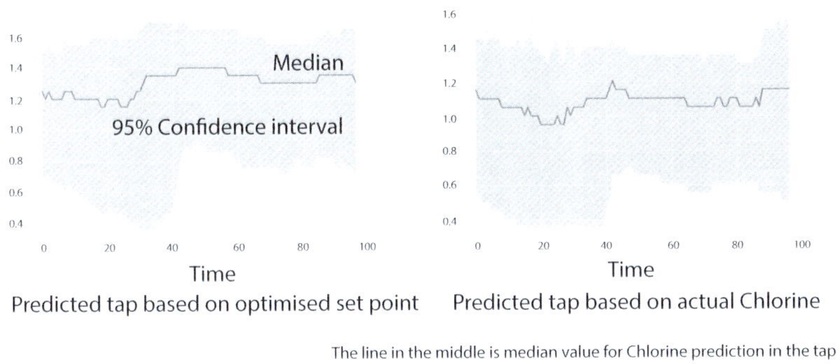

Figure 3.20 Confidence interval for tap users.

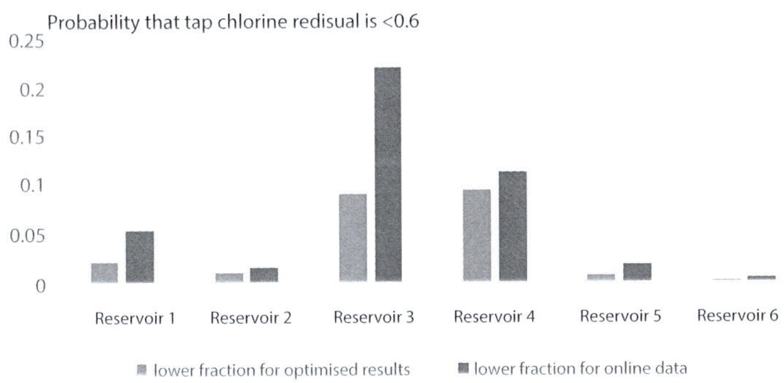

Figure 3.21 Performance on other reservoir zones.

3.5.6 Plant Dosing Optimization

In this section, we investigate the effectiveness by optimizing the ammonia dosing volume in the water plant as well. The above optimization model will be re-defined to include the plant ammonia and chlorine dosing to be controllable. The updated objective is to minimize the total loss by considering all the reservoirs. The formal objective to optimize is:

$$L_{total}(i) = \sum_{R=1}^{6} \alpha \left| \frac{C_R}{A_R} - 4 \right| + \sum_{t=1}^{T} (\delta(C_t < lower) + \beta\delta(C_t > upper)).$$

In this optimization, the target becomes to find $\{C_R, A_W\}$. More details of the objective function can be found in Figure 3.22.

A similar evaluation is then presented in Figure 3.23. In the evaluation, if Ammonia in the water plant is optimized, the predicted tap chlorine can be a bit better. In this case, the optimized Ammonia is still around 0.5mg/L.

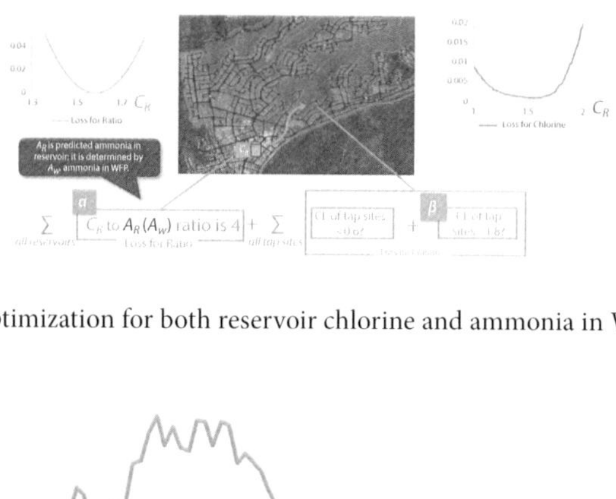

Figure 3.22 Optimization for both reservoir chlorine and ammonia in WFP.

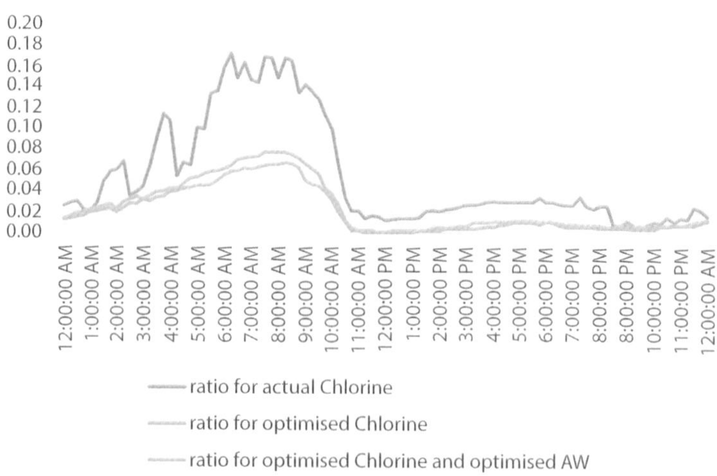

Figure 3.23 Evaluation for optimized reservoir chlorine and ammonia in WFP.

3.6 Conclusion

The present work uses data analytics and machine learning to develop models for optimizing water quality within the delivery system. The proposed models enable us to effectively forecast water demand and accurately capture the variability. The outcomes allow operational demand to be estimated over a horizon that matches the supply planning requirements. A data-driven intelligent framework has been provided to determine the chlorine set points for all the reservoirs and optimize the ammonia dosage for reservoirs. A hydraulic model is built in order to estimate the water age including travel time and residential time. Furthermore, the proposed approach identifies the important factors in forecasting water demand and optimizing re-chlorination.

Acknowledgements

We would like to thank Ronnie Taib, Shiyang Lu, and George Mathews from CSIRO's Data61 for their contributions to this work.

References

1. Cordoba, G. C., Tuhovčák, L., Tauš, M., Using artificial neural network models to assess water quality in water distribution networks. *Procedia Engineering*, 70, 399–408, 2014.
2.. Clement, J., Powell, J., Brandt, M., Predictive models for water quality in distribution systems. *American Water Works Association*, 2005.
3. World Health Organization, Guidelines for drinking-water quality. *World Health Organization*, 1993.
4. Banihabib, M. E., Mousavi-Mirkalaei, P., Extended linear and non-linear auto-regressive models for forecasting the urban water consumption of a fast-growing city in an arid region. *Sustainable Cities and Society*, 48, 101585, 2019.
5. Msiza, I. S., Nelwamondo, F. V., Marwala, T., Water demand forecasting using multi-layer perceptron and radial basis functions. *2007 International Joint Conference on Neural Networks*, 2007
6. House-Peters, L. A., Chang, H., Urban water demand modeling: Review of concepts, methods, and organizing principles. *Water Resources Research*, 47(5), 2011.
7. Ghalehkhondabi, I., Ardjmand, E., Young, W. A., Weckman, G. R., Water demand forecasting: review of soft computing methods. *Environmental monitoring and assessment*, 189(7), 1–13, 2017.

8. de Souza Groppo, G., Costa, M. A., Libânio, M., Predicting water demand: a review of the methods employed and future possibilities. *Water Supply*, 19(8), 2179–2198, 2019.
9. Gato, S., Jayasuriya, N., Roberts, P., Forecasting residential water demand: Case study. *Journal of Water Resources Planning and Management*, 133(4), 309–319, 2007.
10. Gato, S., Jayasuriya, N., Roberts, P., Temperature and rainfall thresholds for base use urban water demand modelling. *Journal of hydrology*, 337(3–4), 364–376, 2007.
11. Zubaidi, S. L., Dooley, J., Alkhaddar, R. M., Abdellatif, M., Al-Bugharbee, H., Ortega-Martorell, S., A Novel approach for predicting monthly water demand by combining singular spectrum analysis with neural networks. *Journal of hydrology*, 561, 136–145, 2018.
12. Payment, P., Robertson, W., The microbiology of piped distribution systems and public health. *Safe, Piped Water: Managing Microbial Quality in Piped Distribution Systems*, 2004.
13. Gonelas, K., Chondronasios, A., Kanakoudis, V., Patelis, M., Korkana, P., Forming DMAs in a water distribution network considering the operating pressure and the chlorine residual concentration as the design parameters. *Journal of Hydroinformatics*, 19(6), 900–910, 2017.
14. Kanakoudis, V., Tsitsifli, S., Potable water security assessment–a review on monitoring, modelling and optimization techniques applied to water distribution networks. *Desalin. Water Treat*, 99, 18–26, 2017.
15. Munavalli, G. R., Kumar, M. M., Optimal scheduling of multiple chlorine sources in water distribution systems. *Journal of water resources planning and management*, 129(6), 493–504, 2003.
16. Tryby, M. E., Boccelli, D. L., Uber, J. G., Rossman, L. A., Facility location model for booster disinfection of water supply networks. *Journal of Water Resources Planning and Management*, 128(5), 322–333, 2002.
17. Lansey, K., Pasha, F., Pool, S., Elshorbagy, W., Uber, J., Locating satellite booster disinfectant stations. *Journal of Water Resources Planning and Management*, 133(4), 372–376, 2007.
18. Propato, M., Uber, J. G., Linear least-squares formulation for operation of booster disinfection systems. *Journal of water resources planning and management*, 130(1), 53–62, 2004.
19. Ostfeld, A., Salomons, E., Conjunctive optimal scheduling of pumping and booster chlorine injections in water distribution systems. *Engineering optimization*, 38(03), 337–352, 2006.
20. Zubaidi, S. L., Dooley, J., Alkhaddar, R. M., Abdellatif, M., Al-Bugharbee, H., Ortega-Martorell, S., A Novel approach for predicting monthly water demand by combining singular spectrum analysis with neural networks. *Journal of hydrology*, 561, 136–145, 2018.
21. Zubaidi, S. L., Ortega-Martorell, S., Al-Bugharbee, H., Olier, I., Hashim, K. S., Gharghan, S. K., Al-Khaddar, R., Urban water demand prediction for a

city that suffers from climate change and population growth: gauteng province case study. *Water*, 12(7), 1885, 2020.

22. Msiza, I. S., Nelwamondo, F. V., Marwala, T., Water demand prediction using artificial neural networks and support vector regression. 2008
23. Chen, G., Long, T., Xiong, J., Bai, Y., Multiple random forests modelling for urban water consumption forecasting. *Water Resources Management*, 31(15), 4715–4729, 2017.
24. Boulus, P. F., Altman, T., Sadhal, K. S., Computer modeling of water quality in large multiple-source networks. *Applied mathematical modelling*, 16(8), 439–445, 1992.
25. Islam, M. R., Chaudhry, M. H., Clark, R. M., Inverse modeling of chlorine concentration in pipe networks under dynamic condition. *Journal of environmental engineering*, 123(10), 1033–1040, 1997.
26. Males, R. M., Clark, R. M., Wehrman, P. J., Gates, W. E., Algorithm for mixing problems in water systems. *Journal of Hydraulic Engineering*, 111(2), 206–219, 1985.
27. Rossman, L. A., Boulos, P. F., Altman, T., Discrete volume-element method for network water-quality models. *Journal of Water Resources Planning and Management*, 119(5), 505–517, 1993.
28. Farmani, R., Walters, G., Savic, D., Evolutionary multi-objective optimization of the design and operation of water distribution network: total cost vs. reliability vs. water quality. *Journal of Hydroinformatics*, 8(3), 165–179, 2006.
29. Kirmeyer, G. J., Optimizing chloramine treatment. *American Water Works Association*, 2004.

4

Lip Reading Framework using Deep Learning and Machine Learning

Hemant Kumar Gianey*, Parth Khandelwal, Prakhar Goel, Rishav Maheshwari, Bhannu Galhotra and Divyanshu Pratap Singh

Department of Computer Science & Engineering, Thapar Institute of Engineering and Technology, Patiala, Punjab, India

Abstract

Lip reading from the lip movements of an individual is a task to interpret the speech being spoken without actually listening to the speech. This ability of lip-reading helps speech-impaired individuals to engage in various social activities. Previous research has primarily been based in offline modes. In this research, we explore a real-time Visual Speech Recognition System specifically designed for speech-impaired individuals. The proposed model uses a Spatio-temporal encoder to deliver lip-tracking sequences followed by a decent-based decoder to produce high-quality speech. The corresponding text transcriptions are generated with the help of a speech recognition API that aids hearing-impaired individuals. We are building a large dataset, for training and testing of Lip-to-Speech activities in natural settings. This perspective shows that real-time speech recognition systems are achievable.

After studying this chapter, you should be able to understand the concept of the Lip-Reading System, its emergence and definition, and dimensions and components in detail. The work is solely focused on generating speech from the lip movement of single speaker in a frame at a time. In the last section, various issues and challenges associated with the Lip Reading System and different models are also discussed in detail. With the assistance of the deep learning, we will be looking at the cutting-edge innovations that we have encountered. The goal here is to produce a sound that is audible and interpretable. Hence, more effort is put into the correctness of the speech instead of naturalness, so we need to study the concept of the Lip-reading system in light of various issues, their challenges, and different applications of a Visual Speech Recognition System.

**Corresponding author*: hgianey@gmail.com

M. Niranjanamurthy, Hemant Kumar Gianey and Amir H. Gandomi (eds.) Advances in Data Science and Analytics: Concepts and Paradigms, (67–88) © 2023 Scrivener Publishing LLC

***Keywords*:** Lip-reading system, motivation, background of domain, audio-visual, implementation aspects, identified problems, preprocessing

4.1 Introduction

4.1.1 Overview

Lip reading is the function of decoding text from lip movements of individuals. It is accustomed to interpret or understand speech without hearing it. Recent advances in computer vision and signal processing have led to the desire to make the lip-reading processes more effective, which is often known as Visual Speech Recognition (VSR). VSR mainly deals with the visual domain of speech. The purpose of the VSR system is to provide machines with the ability to understand languages in noisy environments. The objective of this study is to develop an AI model for generating speech based on the lip movements of individuals. The model takes real-time or pre-captured video feed as input to generate the corresponding speech. A dataset consisting of preprocessed video and audio files is provided as input. The training takes place on the silent lip videos frame-by-frame using a spatio-temporal encoder to extract sequences of lip movements, which is followed by an attention-based decoder for high-quality speech generation. The audio files are used to calculate the error between generated speech and ground truth. The main advantages of this system include generating speech for individuals who cannot produce voiced sounds (aphonia). Other areas in which the VSR plays a major role include video conferencing in quiet environments, background speech retrieval, surveillance, and speech retrieval from corrupted videos.

4.1.2 Motivation

Being able to communicate is one of the most important life skills. Lack of good interpersonal skills means an absence of existence itself. People who shortfall the most are the ones who suffer from difficulty in speech or those hard of hearing. People suffering from speaking disorders often fallback in many situations especially in a fast-paced working environment. In today's world, being able to present your views in front of others is a challenging task which every person should learn to accomplish. Technology has always assisted individuals with disabilities to break barriers and be independent without any restrictions. Thus, there was a need to develop a system which would be able to generate speech just by watching the lip movements of

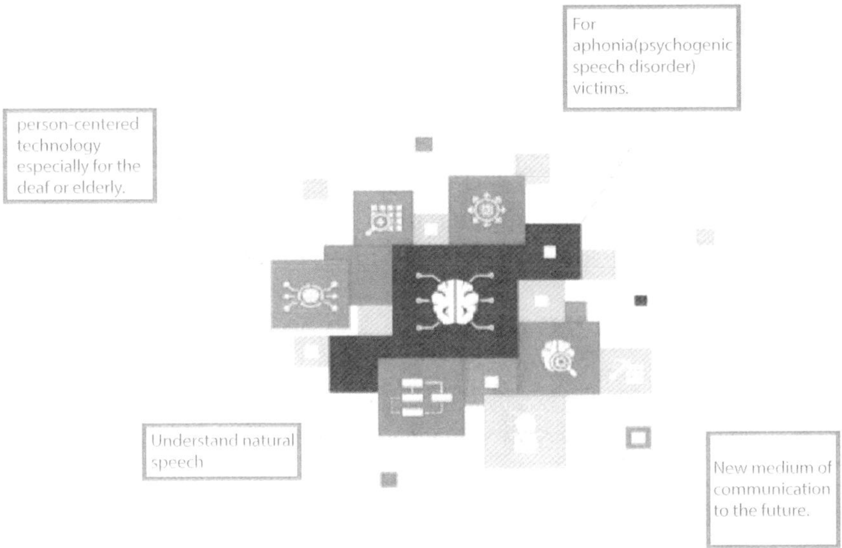

Figure 4.1 Lip-reading system.

an individual. Hence, with the implementation of this project, we hope to develop a system which would be capable of producing voice for individuals dealing with the problem of communication due to aphonia which is one of the most common psychogenic speech disorders also known as "no voice". This project will help reinforce our knowledge and expertise in the field of speech recognition as well as broaden our understanding in various deep learning constructs. This will probably lead to some major contributions in the future shown in Figure 4.1.

4.1.3 Lip Reading System Outcomes and Deliverables

The following are the outcomes of the Lip-Reading System which are designed based on the requirements and specifications of the client:

1. Documentation for providing implementation details
2. We will be able to provide a software that will generate natural speech from the lip movement of speech-impaired individuals.
3. The purpose of our program is to understand natural speech, mostly composed of sentences, which requires access to information that contains telephone words, phrases, and limited sentences and models that can work well in these.

4. Depending on how we design our Lip-Reading System, this program is a person-centered technology especially for the deaf and the elderly.

4.2 The Emergence and Definition of the Lip-Reading System

In this section, the lip-reading framework, apparatuses, various capacities, prerequisites, and different variables are discussed to give a thorough portrayal of the lip-reading framework.

4.2.1 Background of Domain

People are always paying close attention to the movement of their lips in order to 'visually hear' [1] speech in a very noisy environment, but the same principle applies to deaf people who often learn to read lips. Typical lip-reading methods include flexible newly installed models and hidden Markov models with different stages of the feature extraction process [3]. With a rapid growth in the artificial neural networks field, in the past few years many new techniques have emerged to tackle the problem of lip reading. Recently, the various proposed end-to-end speech recognition systems include a neural network which is trained to predict character sequences which can be further converted to words or word sequences. For an end-to-end system, the most appropriate architecture is a causal model, such as a unidirectional RNN, trained with a CTC objective function [4]. In 2016, a new model named LipNet [6] was proposed which claimed to be the first of its kind to perform sentence-level lip reading. Later, several different sentence-level models came into the picture, such as the WLAS (Watch, Listen, Attend, Spell) network which uses a curriculum learning strategy to accelerate training and reduce overfitting [8]; TM-seq2seq [19] which used teacher forcing decay to train an encoder-decoder architecture; and LipSound [12] which uses a front-end and back-end kind of architecture to predict the text transcriptions out of the generated Mel spectrograms. The pseudo-convolutional policy gradient (PCPG)-based approach addresses two issues of outstanding bias due to the "teacher-forcing" strategy, as well as the inconsistency between the intent to discriminate (usually cross-entropy loss) and the final testing metric (usually character/word error rate) [9]. Recently, Google introduced a TTS system which revolutionized the development of speech generation by taking a character sequence as input and producing the corresponding spectrogram. Tacotron and Wavenet were the two algorithms used in this system which generated natural sounding speech. After the success of Tacotron

Table 4.1 Literature survey.

Ref. no.	Input type	Techniques/ methods	Performance metrics	Word level/ sentence level	Dataset	Speaker dependency	Output
1.	Audio-Visual	Attention based seq2seq technique + Teacher forcing decay	1. Short-Time Objective Intelligibility (STOI) 2. Extended Short-Time Objective Intelligibility (ESTOI) 3. Perceptual Evaluation of Speech Quality (PESQ)	Sentence Level	Unconstrained (Lip2Wav dataset)	Speaker Dependent	Speech
2.	Audio-Visual	Cross-modal distillation + Teacher-Student approach	1.Word Error Rate (WER)	Sentence Level	Unconstrained (Voxceleb)	Speaker Independent	Text
3.	Silent Video	-	1. Accuracy (in percentage) 2.Training time (in hrs.)	Sentence Level	Constrained (Ouluvs2)	Speaker Independent	Text

(Continued)

Table 4.1 Literature survey. (*Continued*)

Ref. no.	Input type	Techniques/ methods	Performance metrics	Word level/ sentence level	Dataset	Speaker dependency	Output
4.	Audio	Teacher-Student learning + Curriculum learning + Label smoothing	1.Word Error Rate (WER)	Sentence Level	Unconstrained (Microsoft U.S Cortana)	Speaker Independent	Speech
5.	Silent Video	SE attention mechanism	1. Accuracy 2. Dilation rate 3. Growth rate	Word Level	Constrained (LRW, LRW-1000)	Speaker Independent	Text
6.	Silent Video	-	1. Character Error Rate (CER) 2. Word Error Rate (WER)	Sentence Level	Constrained (GRID)	Speaker Independent	Text
7.	Silent Video	Attention based seq2seq technique	1. Character Error Rate (CER) 2. Word Error Rate (WER) 3. Training Time	Sentence Level	Unconstrained (LRS2)	Speaker Independent	Text

(*Continued*)

Table 4.1 Literature survey. (*Continued*)

Ref. no.	Input type	Techniques/ methods	Performance metrics	Word level/ sentence level	Dataset	Speaker dependency	Output
8.	Audio-Visual	Attention based seq2seq technique + Curriculum learning	1. Character Error Rate (CER) 2. Word Error Rate (WER) 3. BLEU	Sentence Level	Unconstrained (LRS2)	Speaker Independent	Text
9.	Silent Video	Pseudo-Convolution Policy Gradient seq2seq method	1. Character Error Rate (CER) 2. Word Error Rate (WER)	Sentence Level	Constrained (GRID, LRW, LRW-1000)	Speaker Independent	Text
10.	Audio-Visual	Attention Technique	1. Active Shape Mode (ASM) 2. PCA	Word Level	Unconstrained	Speaker Independent	Text
11.	Silent Video	Griffin-Lim Reconstruction	1. Quality and intelligibility of the reconstructed speech 2. Short Time Objective Intelligibility (STOI) 3. Extended Short Time Objective Intelligibility (ESTOI)	Sentence Level	Constrained (GRID, TCD-TIMIT)	Speaker Dependent	Speech

(*Continued*)

Table 4.1 Literature survey. (*Continued*)

Ref. no.	Input type	Techniques/ methods	Performance metrics	Word level/ sentence level	Dataset	Speaker dependency	Output
12.	Audio	Attention mechanism	1. Word Error Rate (WER) 2. Character Error Rate (CER)	Sentence Level	Constrained (GRID)	Speaker Dependent	Text
13.	Silent Video	1. Attention based method 2. Motion based method	1. Recognition Accuracy	Sentence Level	Constrained	Speaker Dependent	Speech
14.	Silent Video	Deformation Flow Network	1. Model Accuracy (In Percentage)	Word Level	Unconstrained (LRW)	Speaker Dependent	Speech
15.	Audio-Visual	Clustering Technique	-	Word Level	Constrained	Speaker Independent	Speech
16.	Audio-Visual	-	1. Model Accuracy (In Percentage)	Word Level	Unconstrained (MIRACL-V1)	Speaker Independent	Speech

(*Continued*)

Table 4.1 Literature survey. (*Continued*)

Ref. no.	Input type	Techniques/ methods	Performance metrics	Word level/ sentence level	Dataset	Speaker dependency	Output
17.	Audio-Visual Continuous Speech	Weighted Finite State Transducer (WFST) using hybrid DNN-HMM + t-Distributed Stochastic Neighbor Embedding (t-SNE)	-	Word Level	Constrained (TCD-TIMIT)	Speaker Independent	Speech
18.	Video Frames	Attention based seq2seq technique + Hidden Markov Models (HMM)	1. Character Error Rate (CER) 2. Word Error Rate (WER) 3. BLEU	Word Level	Constrained (Grid, Lipnet, LRSW, LRW)	Speaker Independent	Text
19.	Silent Video + Audio-Visual Video	Spatio-Temporal Visual Front-End + Attention based seq2seq technique	1. Word Error Rate (WER)	Sentence Level	Unconstrained (LRS2-BBC) L RS, MV-LRS, LRS-TE, LRS3-TED	Speaker Independent	Text

(*Continued*)

Table 4.1 Literature survey. (*Continued*)

Ref. no.	Input type	Techniques/ methods	Performance metrics	Word level/ sentence level	Dataset	Speaker dependency	Output
20.	Audio-Visual	Coupled Generative Adversarial Networks (CoGAN) framework + Attention based seq2seq technique + Cross Model Alignment Structure	1. Character Error Rate (CER)	Word Level	TCD-TIMIT	Speaker Independent	Text
21.	Audio-Visual	Spatio-Temporal Fusion Module (STFM) + Temporal Focal Blocks	1. Word Error Rate (WER)	Word Level	GRID, LRW, LRS2-BBC, LRS3-TED	Speaker Independent	Text
22.	Audio-Visual	Domain Adversarial Training	1. Word Accuracy 2. p-value	Sentence Level	GRID	Speaker Independent	Speech

(*Continued*)

Table 4.1 Literature survey. (*Continued*)

Ref. no.	Input type	Techniques/ methods	Performance metrics	Word level/ sentence level	Dataset	Speaker dependency	Output
23.	-	Apache Mahout Skytree Server	-	-	HDFS	Speaker Independent	-
24.	-	Stochastic techniques, logic-based techniques	1. Accuracy 2. Precision 3. Recall 4. ROC	-	German Credit Data	Speaker Independent	-
25.	Huge volume of data	Density based method Grid based method	1. Silhouette Coefficient 2. Adjusted RAND Index	-	-	Speaker Independent	Prediction

and Wavenet algorithms, multiple attempts were made to reconstruct the audio by mapping the image sequence of the mouth region directly to Mel spectrograms. Griffin-Lim, which is one of the spectrogram syntheses approaches [11], appeared to be a promising algorithm which was used in many research works for speech reconstruction of the predicted spectrograms. Several datasets were released to train the models for speech recognition. These datasets were mainly divided under two categories: constrained and unconstrained. The constrained datasets included GRID, LRW, Ouluvs2, and TCD-TIMIT and the unconstrained datasets included Lip2Wav, Voxceleb, LRS, and LRS2. Traditionally, only constrained datasets were present, but lately unconstrained datasets have gained a lot of popularity. The literature survey shown in Table 4.1.

4.2.2 Identified Problems

A lot of research and paperwork has been carried out in the visual speech recognition field in the past few years, but none of it was powerful enough to be converted into a full-fledged application. We believe that taking on this challenge of developing a visual speech generation system for speech-impaired individuals will help reduce the communication gap for these people and will also be a stepping stone in the visual speech recognition field.

4.2.3 Tools and Technologies Used

1. Language: Python
2. IDE/Development Tools: IDE, VSCode DevOps Tools, GitHub
3. Software Libraries: Deep learning libraries, TensorFlow, Keras, NumPy Face detection library, OpenCV
4. External Components
   1) Web Camera
   2) Speaker
5. Internal Components
   1) Operating System: Windows 10 or above
   2) Main Memory: 16GB RAM or more
   3) GPUs: A single GPU with 16GB VRAM or more

4.2.4 Implementation Aspects

The entire project can be divided in three phases:

A) Dataset Generation: Creation of a file consisting of images and audio of the videos of a specific speaker recorded at varying parameters like face angle, lighting, gestures, etc.

B) Preprocessing: Working on the images and audio to make them ready for the model. Processes include naming the different audio and video files, putting them into separate folders for testing and training, and implementing certain image processing and audio processing techniques to remove elements that may obstruct correct functioning of the Deep Learning Model [27, 28].

C) Model Creation: This module consists of the study of different available models to learn their merits and demerits and to use the knowledge to build our own encoder-decoder based model to generate speech. The aim is to build a model to deliver clear and understandable speech.

4.2.4.1 *Data Preparation*

A) Image Processing

This is the first and foremost step in data preparation. A set of videos each of a length of 3 seconds is downloaded from the GRID dataset for a specific speaker. There are a total of 1000 videos per speaker in the GRID dataset. To make the data, the model ready following steps are carried out:

1. Each video is read and its corresponding frames are generated. This is done with the help of OpenCV. The videos run at a rate of 25 frames per sec and an entire video is of 3 secs. A total of 75 frames are generated per video.
2. Face detection is performed on each of the frames using a haar cascade classifier to extract the desired region of interest for speech generation shown in Figure 4.2.

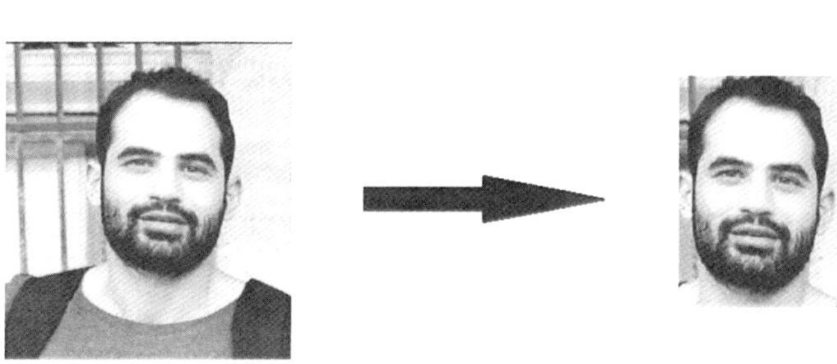

Figure 4.2 Face detection.

3. The cropped images consisting of only faces are resized to 96x96 and converted to grayscale to reduce computational power and to keep a consistent size across all images.
4. A NumPy array consisting of pixel values of these images is formed to store the data. An npy file is created to store all the NumPy arrays corresponding to the images formed out of the 1000 videos. An npy file helps in fast loading of data during processing and reduces the overall training time shown in Figure 4.3.

→

[[0, 0, 0, ...],
[120, 150, 132, 140, ..],
:
:
.........., 165, 163, 177]]

Figure 4.3 RGB matrix representation of detected face.

B) Audio Processing

The audio for each of the videos is extracted and processed separately to form a set of target values for training the model. Some of crucial terms for understanding audio processing are:

1. Spectrogram: A spectrogram is a visual representation of the signal strength or "loud noise" of a signal over a period of time in various wavelengths.
2. Mel Scale: Scale used to measure unit height so that equal pitch distances sound equal to the listener.
3. Mel Spectrogram: A spectrogram in which the frequencies are converted to Mel scale.

Steps followed for audio processing:

1. The audio is extracted from the video with the help of an ffmpeg tool and a .wav file is generated out of it. This step is done for all the videos.
2. The generated .wav file is used to form Mel spectrograms. For 3 sec audio, 6 different Mel spectrograms are

formed with an overlap of 0.6 secs. The calculations are as follows:

25 frames ---------> 1s

Therefore,

1 frame ---------> 1/25
15 frames ---------> 0.6 s

Table 4.2 Frames in seconds.

Time (in sec)	Frames
[0.0–1.0]	[0–25]
[0.4–1.4]	[10–35]
[0.8–1.8]	[20–45]
[1.2–2.2]	[30–55]
[1.6–2.6]	[40–65]
[2.0–3.0]	[50–75]

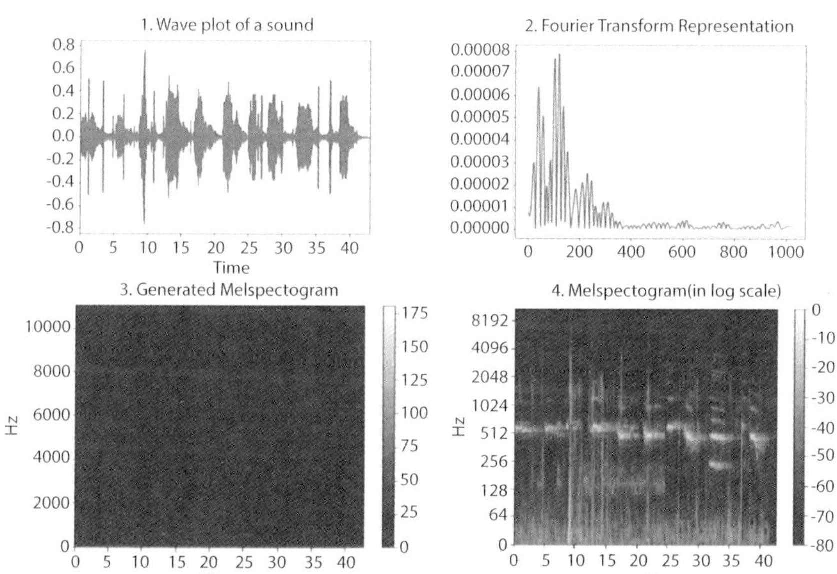

Figure 4.4 Mel spectrogram.

The model is designed to process 25 frames at a time with an overlap of 15 frames. The overlap value is decided by a series of trials and errors to find the best fit. Overlapping plays an important role in model training as it allows the model to learn the "context" of speech. For a 3 sec video, a total of 75 frames are formed which are selected in a group of 25 frames at a time with an overlap of 15 frames. This allows 6 different sets of images and 6 different Mel spectrograms. Table 4.2 shows the frames in seconds.

3. An npy file is formed to store the Mel spectrograms in a NumPy array from. This allows fast loading of data and less processing time shown in Figure 4.4.

4.3 Design and Components of Lip-Reading System

The first process is we take raw data from the GRID Corpus (GRID has the original videos of a specific speaker from the grid dataset, which has a total of 34 speakers), which consist of a series of videos of different speakers. Now the data read from it is converted into sets of video frames.

This data is given as an input to the Image Processing part. It performs face detection and stores detected images to form a data set out of it. The dataset is further passed to the VSR Model which is used for training purposes. It uses different kinds of methods to improve the accuracy and calculates the suitable set of weights. The VSR Model gives an output as a spectrogram feature vector, which is processed to reconstruct speech.

4.4 Lip Reading System Architecture

The System Architecture Diagram (Figure 4.5) starts with Unlabeled data. The Unlabeled data consists of data which is taken from nature or created by humans to explore the scientific patterns behind it. In the system, the unlabeled data means videos which do not have a text transcript. The unlabeled data is further processed and divided into audio and silent videos. The silent videos are given as an input to the VSR Model. The VSR Model consists of a 3D Convolutional Encoder which is used to extract Spatio-temporal features out of the frames of our silent videos shown in Figure 4.6.

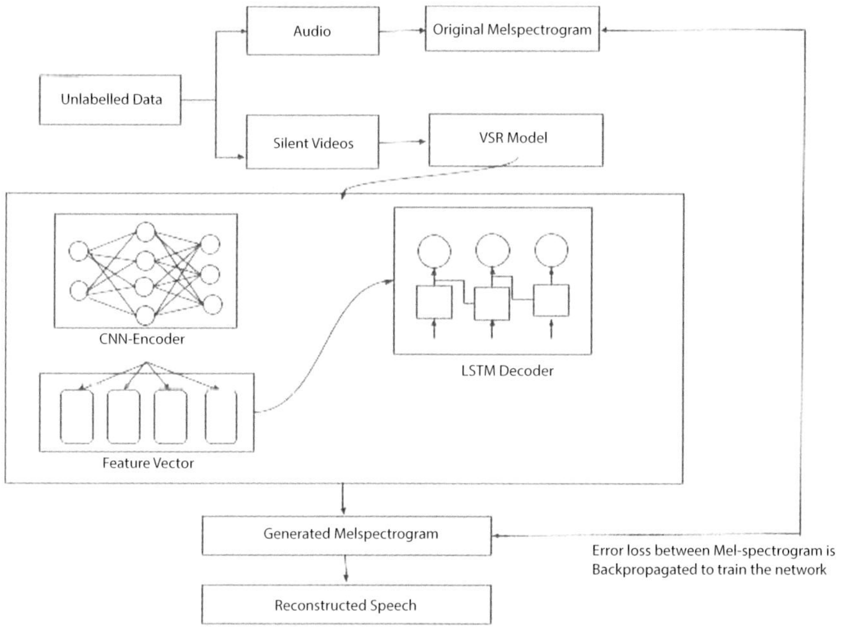

Figure 4.5 System architecture.

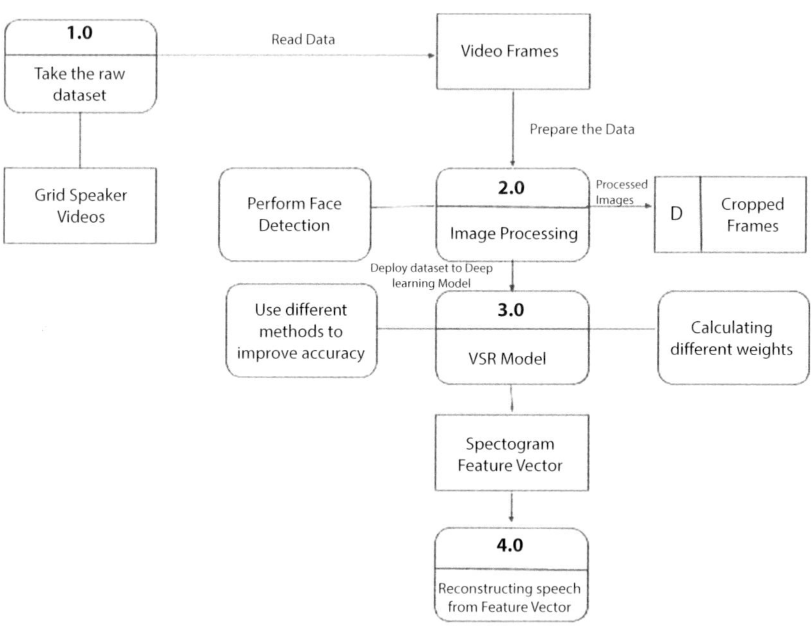

Figure 4.6 System flowchart of a lip-reading system.

The extracted Spatio-temporal features are compressed to form a feature vector and this feature vector is passed to our LSTM Decoder. The LSTM Decoder takes the feature vector and decodes it to learn the sequence-to-sequence linkage between the values. Output which is produced by LSTM Decoder is used to generate the Mel spectrogram. Now, the Mel spectrogram generated is compared with the original Mel-spectrogram which we have obtained from the Original Audio. The difference between the generated and original Mel-spectrogram gives the loss function which helps us to train the model and the generated Mel-spectrogram is used to reconstruct the speech.

4.5 Testing

1. Testing in different light intensity, motion, and expression
2. Testing for different face angles of the speaker
3. Testing for real-time application
4. Testing the time delay taken for the generation of speech
5. Testing the behavior of the model with respect to homophones
6. Testing for correctness and audibility of speech
7. Testing the intelligibility of generated speech within the context
8. Testing for end-to-end working of the machine learning model [26]

4.6 Problems Encountered During Implementation

1. The initial setup in the local environment can take a lot of time and will require high-computation processing power so we can use any cloud environment.
2. The preprocessing stage can take time, as we are initially considering processing each frame separately. We can overcome this by storing the compressed data in npz files, reducing storage and data retrieval time.
3. Real time video capture was not possible in the cloud environment as the hardware of the local machine could not be connected to the cloud servers easily, as well as the cost required to rent an extra VM on top of an existing cloud environment is much higher, so we can perform the real-time deployment of the model in the local environment.

4. Also, it can take much time to decide the data preparation parameters as it could onlybe determined after multiple trial and crror attempts.

4.6.1 Assumptions and Constraints

The following are the assumptions made for the Lip-Reading System:

- Lip movement must be clear
- Video should be focused on lips of the speaker
- Speaker must speak English language

Constraints:

- Works for only English language
- Speaker must be sitting in position that his/her face is in the center of the frame
- Video quality must be above 360px

4.7 Conclusion

In this work, we investigated the problem of composing speech based on lip movements. We studied various deep learning models like CNN, RNN, and LSTMs and also did thorough research on the various approaches used to tackle the same problem. This helped us gain a clear understanding of spatio-temporal modeling and the sequence-to-sequence paradigm which is used extensively in this domain.

In this phase of our study, we were able to perform the required installations and successfully completed the environment setup for implementation purposes. We are able to complete the data preprocessing stage using the GRID Dataset which involved face detection, image resizing, and audio processing. We also decided upon the model architecture which will be implemented in the next phase.

4.8 Future Work

Our next step will be to build the model as per the design and to train it to achieve the desired results. The model will be tested on an unseen test set and the generated speech will be cross verified by an objective human evaluation. A pre-trained version of the model will be used to generate real-time speech. Analysis will be performed on varying hyperparameters to achieve the best results.

References

1. Prajwal, K. R., *et al.* "Learning Individual Speaking Styles for Accurate Lip to Speech Synthesis." *Proceedings of the IEEE/CVF Conference on Computer Vision and Pattern Recognition*. 2020.
2. Afouras, Triantafyllos, Joon Son Chung, and Andrew Zisserman. "ASR is all you need: Cross-modal distillation for lip reading." *ICASSP 2020-2020 IEEE International Conference on Acoustics, Speech and Signal Processing (ICASSP)*. IEEE, 2020.
3. Fung, Ivan, and Brian Mak. "End-to-end low-resource lip-reading with maxout CNN and LSTM." *2018 IEEE International Conference on Acoustics, Speech and Signal Processing (ICASSP)*. IEEE, 2018.
4. Kim, Suyoun, *et al.* "Improved training for online end-to-end speech recognition systems." *arXiv preprint arXiv:1711.02212* (2017).
5. Ma, Pingchuan, *et al.* "Lip-reading with Densely Connected Temporal Convolutional Networks." *arXiv preprint arXiv:2009.14233* (2020).
6. Assael, Yannis M., *et al.* "Lipnet: Sentence-level lipreading." *arXiv preprint arXiv:1611.01599* 2.8 (2016).
7. Afouras, Triantafyllos, Joon Son Chung, and Andrew Zisserman. "Deep lip reading: a comparison of models and an online application." *arXiv preprint arXiv:1806.06053* (2018).
8. Chung, Joon Son *et al.* "Lip Reading Sentences in the Wild." *2017 IEEE Conference on Computer Vision and Pattern Recognition (CVPR)* (2017): 3444–3453.
9. Luo, Mingshuang, *et al.* "Pseudo-Convolutional Policy Gradient for Sequence-to-Sequence Lip-Reading." *arXiv preprint arXiv:2003.03983* (2020).
10. Lu, Yuanyao, and Hongbo Li. "Automatic Lip-Reading System Based on Deep Convolutional Neural Network and Attention-Based Long Short-Term Memory." *Applied Sciences*9.8 (2019): 1599.
11. A. Ephrat, T. Halperin and S. Peleg, "Improved Speech Reconstruction from Silent Video," 2017 IEEE International Conference on Computer Vision Workshops (ICCVW), Venice, 2017, pp. 455–462, doi: 10.1109/ICCVW.2017.61.
12. Qu, Leyuan *et al.* "LipSound: Neural Mel-Spectrogram Reconstruction for Lip Reading." *INTERSPEECH* (2019).
13. Shirakata, Tasuya, and Takeshi Saitoh. "Lip Reading using Facial Expression Features."

14. Xiao, Jingyun, *et al.* "Deformation Flow Based Two-Stream Network for Lip Reading." *arXiv preprint arXiv:2003.05709* (2020).
15. Fernandez-Lopez, Adriana, and Federico M. Sukno. "Automatic viseme vocabulary construction to enhance continuous lip-reading." *arXiv preprint arXiv:1704.08035* (2017).
16. Gutierrez, Abiel, and Z. Robert. "Lip Reading Word Classification." (2017).
17. Thangthai, Kwanchiva, and Richard W. Harvey. "Building Large-vocabulary Speaker-independent Lipreading Systems." *INTERSPEECH*. 2018.
18. Xu, Kai, *et al.* "LCANet: End-to-end lipreading with cascaded attention-CTC." *2018 13th IEEE International Conference on Automatic Face & Gesture Recognition (FG 2018)*. IEEE, 2018.
19. T. Afouras, J. S. Chung, A. Senior, O. Vinyals and A. Zisserman, "Deep Audio-visual Speech Recognition," in IEEE Transactions on Pattern Analysis and Machine Intelligence, doi:10.1109/TPAMI.2018.2889052.
20. Fernandez-Lopez, Adriana, *et al.* "Cogans for Unsupervised Visual Speech Adaptation To New Speakers." *ICASSP 2020-2020 IEEE International Conference on Acoustics, Speech and Signal Processing (ICASSP)*. IEEE, 2020.
21. Zhang, Xingxuan, Feng Cheng, and Shilin Wang. "Spatio-temporal fusion based convolutional sequence learning for lip reading." *Proceedings of the IEEE International Conference on Computer Vision*. 2019.
22. Wand, Michael, and Jürgen Schmidhuber. "Improving speaker-independent lipreading with domain-adversarial training." *arXiv preprint arXiv:1708.01565* (2017).
23. Meenu Dave, Hemant Kumar Gianey, "Analysis of big data for data-intensive applications." *2016 International Conference on Recent Advances and Innovations in Engineering (ICRAIE)*, IEEE, 2017.
24. Rishabh Choudhary, Hemant Kumar Gianey, "Comprehensive Review on Supervised Machine Learning Algorithms." *2017 International Conference on Machine Learning and Data Science (MLDS)* IEEE, 2018.
25. Meenu Dave, Hemant Kumar Gianey, "Different clustering algorithms for Big Data analytics: A review." *2016 International Conference System Modeling & Advancement in Research Trends (SMART)* IEEE, 2016.
26. E. Naresh, B. P. Vijaya Kumar. Kumar, M. Niranjanamurthy and B. Nigam, "Challenges and issues in test process management", Journal of Computational and Theoretical Nanoscience, vol. 16, no. 9, pp. 3744–3747, 2019.
27. B. Pavithra, M. Niranjanmurthy, J. K. Shaker and F. M. S. Mani, "The study of big data analytics in E-commerce", International Journal of Advanced Research in Computer and Communication Engineering , vol. 5, no. 2, pp. 126–131, Oct. 2016.
28. K. R. Swetha, N. M, A. M. P and M. Y. M, "Prediction of Pneumonia Using Big Data, Deep Learning and Machine Learning Techniques," 2021 6th International Conference on Communication and Electronics Systems (ICCES), 2021, pp. 1697–1700, doi: 10.1109/ICCES51350.2021.9489188.

5

New Perspective to Management, Economic Growth and Debt Nexus Analysis: Evidence from Indian Economy

Edmund Ntom Udemba[1], Festus Victor Bekun[1*], Dervis Kirikkaleli[2] and Esra Sipahi Döngül[3]

[1]*Faculty of Economics Administrative and Social Science, Istanbul Gelisim University, Istanbul, Turkey*
[2]*European University of Lefke, Faculty of Economic and Administrative Science, Department of Banking and Finance, Lefke, Northern Cyprus Mersin, Turkey*
[3]*Aksaray University, Faculty of Health Science, Department of Social Work, Aksaray, Turkey*

Abstract

Recently, Indian economic performance has been on a continuous upward trajectory in terms of GDP growth amidst external debt. This study considers in the context of management the measure of maintaining the positive trend of Indian economic growth, taking into account the potentially damaging impact of debt in the near future. To this end, the annual time series frequency data from 1975-2016 is employed for econometrics analysis. The study utilizes the co-integration technique in conjunction with Granger causality tests for causality direction among the variables under consideration in this study. The empirical findings of our study are as follows: debt ratio to GDP has a significant positive relationship with GDP growth and trade openness is significant but exerts a negative relationship with the economic growth of India. Furthermore, FDI has a positive and significant link with the economic growth of India, investment has a positive and significant link with economic growth of India, capital has a positive and significant link with the economic growth of India, and population has a negative and significant link to the economic growth of India. Based on our study findings, we conclude that in the long-run, debt ratio to GDP, FDI, investment, capital, and inflation are all positively related to the economic growth of India, while the likes of trade openness and population have a dampening effect on the economic growth of India.

**Corresponding author*: fbekun@gelisim.edu.tr

M. Niranjanamurthy, Hemant Kumar Gianey and Amir H. Gandomi (eds.) Advances in Data Science and Analytics: Concepts and Paradigms, (89–114) © 2023 Scrivener Publishing LLC

***Keywords*:** GDP growth, economic sustainability, external debt, FDI, openness, India, management

5.1 Introduction

The recent and steady upward trend in Indian economic growth is widely applauded. This revelation is made known by recent world development bank statistics (Hodge, 2018). This was affirmed by Robert *et al.* (2017) when they maintained that India passes China in becoming the fastest-growing economy. However, as the economy is positively growing, it is pertinent to ask and address some salient questions such as: Is the growth induced by or debt-oriented (external debt)? Is the economy growing in a multi-facial trend or single trend? Is the growth affecting and correcting the poverty rate in the economy? Is the growth accommodating the explosive population growth rate of the country? Is the growth enhancing the openness of the economy as a response to an increase in imports? Also, it is very important to sort out ways of sustaining the upward growth trend.

However, it is worth noting that the economy is not trending upward without capital backing. Among the capital backings of the Indian economy are both the internal and external debts included and others such as FDI and investments. External debt has proved to be an important factor and source of financing and sustaining economic growth for both developed and developing countries even though it is still being debated. The developing economies finance their economic growth through capital accumulations, infrastructural development, and human resources development. Furthermore, Ayadi and Ayadi (2008) alluded to the fact that demand from LDC (less domestic blocs) in terms of investment cannot offset by domestic savings, and export earnings which are insufficient to finance import demand. To bridge the saving-investment gap, developing countries tend to borrow from external sources. The steady increase in government spending widens the gap of the budget deficit and this forces the government to depend on public debt from both internal and external sources (Rath and Bal, 2014). The Indian government tried hard to limit the budget deficit by promoting and encouraging foreign direct investment and reducing government spending and this makes it a bit challenging for the economy to sustain lower deficit because of high subsidies on food and agricultural input. The economic consequences of the fiscal policy of budget deficit are heavily dependent on external debt, which draws the attention of many researchers to shift dimension and focus towards analyzing the implication. No doubt, this results in diverse views emanating from different findings from different authors. Currently, there is a concern that the current debt burdens in several economies around the globe are not sustainable, pointing towards a risk to long-term growth and stability. An example is Japan's debt-to-GDP of about 233%, which is recorded as the highest debt-to-GDP among the world's developed countries. The USA debt-to-GDP ratio is at 102% and after the government's debt ceiling was lifted, several cases of economic rescues meted out for some depressed economies in Europe. An example of such a European country is Greece with a 165.3% debt-to-GDP ratio. The case of India is unique as its economy accounts for a growth rate of 6.7% and −3.5% of (GDP) government deficit in 2017 alongside a debt to GDP ratio of 67.67%.[1] The projections of debt-to-GDP ratios seem even worse, especially when expected future age-related spending is taken into account (Cecchetti *et al.*, 2011). As sensitive and important as growth-debt related policy is, many researchers have picked interest on this topic with many coming out with positive findings on the grounds of backing debt while so many others have equally countered this with their negative findings. This rich case of Indian economic dynamics trajectory, including the debt to GDP ratio and the economic growth rate, is a plausible explanation as to why the economy is enlisted in the BRICS blocs reputed as among the fastest-growing economies by Goldman Sachs. This has far-reaching implications which inform our interest in researching this topic.

This study examines the implication of external debt to the trend of economic growth in India and the measures to sustain and prevent the full harm of external debt in the long run. We based this research on addressing some macroeconomics variables and augmenting the growth model with economic development indicators that will aid in balancing and making multiple economic growths. The current work differs from existing literature in the following ways: first, unlike other studies like (Rangarajan and Srivastava, 2005; Liu *et al.*, 1999; Gautam, 2015 and Balassone *et al.*, 2011), this study added some key macroeconomic indicators such as trade openness and foreign direct investment (FDI) to the growth equation and examines the relationship between debt and economic growth in an extended growth accounting framework for India. This is an attempt by this study to leverage the positive inducement of the added indicators in establishing a remedial effect in the long-run, where the debt burden becomes heavier than projected. Secondly, this study applied a clear statistical methodology

[1] For brevity, more insights regarding Indian economic fact are available at CIA fact book see https://www.indexmundi.com/india/#Economy

to explore and explain both the short-run and long-run effects of external debt on economic growth using a vector error correction model (VECM) with Granger causality as a boost on showing the direction of the relationship between the chosen indicators. Thirdly, most of the previous studies are almost a decade old and focus more on the serious economic problems facing the Indian economy before now which formed their opinion about the Indian economy. The present study expanded the series from 1975-2016 to accommodate recent activities in the economy and focuses on the upward trending of the economic growth of the Indian economy and ways of sustaining the trend.

The remaining part of this work is grouped as follows: Section 5.2 reviews the literature, Section 5.3 involves the analytical framework and data sources, Section 5.4 presents methodology used in the study and the results, and Section 5.5 includes the discussion and conclusions and implications for policymakers, accordingly.

5.2 Literature Review

The review will be based in a comparative manner, that is reviewing the existing literature that deals with each variable on economic growth. The sections will be external debt and economic growth, trade openness and economic growth, FDI, and economic growth.

5.2.1 External Debt and Economic Growth

On the growth effect of external debt, the conventional view suggests that external debt positively affects economic growth in the short run by stimulating the aggregate demand (Elmendorf and Mankiw, 1999). However, theoretical literature mostly points to a negative debt-growth link in the long run through different channels. External debt is capable of crowding out private investments and hampering economic growth through higher long term interest rates (Sugin, 2004; Woo and Kumar, 2015), higher inflation (Barro, 1979 and Cochrane, 2011), and higher future distortion through higher taxation policy (Barro, 1979; Woo and Kumar, 2015). The effect of external debt on economic growth is categorized into the short-run and long-run impacts by Mohanty (2012), who found the existence of a negative but very minimal impact in the short run, but positive impact in the long run through the multiplier effect. Singh (1999) found the Ricardian equivalence hypothesis which implies the neutrality of domestic debt to economic growth for the case of India.

Bal *et al.* (2014) in their study for the case of India found a long-run equilibrium relationship between public debt and economic growth and in the short run, found central government debt, total factor productivity (TFP) growth, and debt-services affecting the economic growth in the short-run. Saxena and Shanker (2018), for the case of India, found a negative relationship between GDP and both external debt and the debt servicing ratio. Chipalkatti and Rishi (2001) utilized a simultaneous equation model to test the link between capital flight and external debt in the Indian economy and their study confirms the existence of a financial revolving door link between the two endogenous variables.

The impact of external debt is at a moderate level and it enhances economic growth and improves welfare (Cecchetti *et al.*, 2011). The findings of their study revealed a threshold (at 85%) that poses as a ceiling at which government debts are not supposed to exceed and anything above this ceiling is a danger to the economic performance of the country. Mohanty (2012) empirically examined Pakistan's economic growth and external debt. The study found an inverse relationship between debt and economic growth. Their findings established that external debt slows down economic growth when compared with domestic debt. A panel study of euro area countries for 40 years revealed a non-linear impact of debt on economic growth which is a negative growth impact to 70-80 percent of GDP (Baum *et al.*, 2013). They found the relationship between external debt and economic growth to be monotone. The finding suggests that a growth debt might necessarily shrink economic growth but a surplus budget to curb debt might reduce growth. Christie and Rioja (2012) made a finding on the long run impact of external debt. The finding suggests that it is not the initial debt that reduces growth, but additional debt obtained by the government to finance government expenditure. It impacts negatively on economic growth through debt servicing costs. The study of Nigerian and South African economies by Ayadi and Ayadi (2008) revealed both positive and negative impacts on economic growth. It first starts with a positive impact and when it gets to a certain level, will reverse to negative thereby supporting the notion of a threshold. Furthermore, Onogbosele and Ben (2016) studied the Nigerian economy utilizing the same methods the author applied in this present work, using a combination of both Vector Error Correction techniques and Granger Causality tests to decide both the long run and short-run impact and causality relationship and direction between external debt and economic growth. The findings revealed an insignificant long-run relationship but a bi-directional relationship between the external debt and economic growth in Nigeria in the short run.

5.2.2 Trade Openness, FDI, and Economic Growth

Trade-growth led economic growth can positively or negatively affect the enhancement of the economic activities of a country. The following justify the author's claim: Dollar (1992) and Frankel and Romer (1999) are of opinion that trade openness promotes good economic performance and this leads to economic growth and sustenance. Motiur *et al.*, 2006; Almfraji and Almsafir 2014; Alesina and Wacziarg, 1998 found trade openness to be positively related to economic growth. On the other hand, Greenaway and Sapsford, 1994 and Giles and Williams, 2000 all found no support for the trade-growth relationship. The comparative advantage theory maintains that an economy specializes in the production of goods and services in which it has comparatively better factor endowments than its trading partner (Dollar and Kraay, 2004) and this will lead to the increase in economic growth because of the production and exportation of that product or service. Brueckner and Lederman (2015) contributed to this theory by arguing that productivity and economic growth are impacted by trade openness by specialization and economies of scale. Buiter and Kletzer (1991), alongside the study of Zilibotti (1995), supported the view by endogenous growth theory that there exists a strong positive trade-growth link as a result of advancement in technology and dissemination of technological knowledge. Also, developing countries are disadvantaged in trade openness if they only depend on exporting unprocessed products to developed countries (Lall, 1994). Kim and Lin (2009) studied trade–growth relationships in 61 selected developing countries and found an income threshold level of 41.5 percent above which greater trade enhances economic growth and by an average of 12.4 percent. Below the threshold level, however, trade openness has detrimental effects on economic growth by about 14.2 percent.

5.2.3 FDI and Economic Growth

Some literature has justified the bases of linkage between FDI and economic growth. Udemba (2019), for the case of China, found a positive link between FDI and economic growth. Udemba *et al.* (2019) for Indonesia found a positive link between FDI and economic growth. Almfraji and Almsafir (2014) have worked on the impact of FDI and economic growth and found a positive relationship between economic growth and FDI. Sahoo and Sethi (2017) empirically researched the FDI and economic growth of India and found a positive relationship in the long run. For this, they advised that the Indian government should give more attention to the FDI in their economic policy. Chanda *et al.* (2006) tested the relationship between FDI and economic growth and found that FDI has a negative relationship with the primary sector but a positive role in the manufacturing sector. Additionally, Murari (2017) explored the relationship between financial development and economic growth, using panel data of south Asian countries that belong to middle-class incomes for the years 1980-2013. He, however, established that FDI, as well as domestic investment, contribute significantly to the economic growth of countries.

The Granger causality between FDI and growth is explored by Anyanwu (2012) on East and South African regions and Almfraji and Almsafir, 2014; Irandoust 2001 found causality between economic growth and the FDI, while Almfraji and Almsafir (2014) for Malaysia found no causality between the FDI and economic growth.

5.3 Data

The authors used annual data for India that covers the span of 1975-2016 (i.e., a total of 42 observations on an annual frequency basis) to explore the dimension of historical specificity and capture the underlying relationship between the variables under research. We sourced our data from the World Bank's world development indicator (WDI). As mentioned earlier, the authors use per capita GDP at 2010 market prices, urban population, investment, secondary school and enrollment as a measure of human capital, openness to trade and the consumer price index (CPI) as a measure to inflation, and foreign direct investment measures as inflow. The definition and summary of the variables are presented in Table 5.1.

Table 5.1 Variables and their measurements.

Full description of the variable	Codes	Measurement/calculation
Real GDP per capita	GDP	Constant 2010 US dollars (ΔlogGDP)
Trade Openness	OPEN	Export+Import/GDP
External Debt	DEBT	Debt/GDP
Inflation	INF	ΔlogCPI
Human Capital	Capital	Secondary School Enrolment %
Urban Population	POP	ΔlogPop
Foreign Direct Invest Inflow	FDI	FDI%GDD
Investment	INV	GCF/GDP%

Source: Authors Compilation.

5.3.1 Analytical Framework and Data Description

The analytical framework used in this study involves the Augmented Dickey-Fuller (ADF) unit root test, Johansen cointegration test, Vector Error Correction Model, and Granger Causality test.

5.3.2 Theoretical Background and Specifications

Cochrane (2011) opines that economic models are inevitably incomplete characterizations of the sophisticated and complicated reality of economic life and suggests that like rays of light they illuminate a part of a whole and leave the rest in shadow. Also, Sousa (2010) comes up with a view that formulating a sufficiently general initial model to capture all the substantively relevant influences is a fundamental challenge encountered in all empirical modeling procedures.

The critical decision in all empirical studies revolves around the set of variables for which the survey should be gathered, analyzed, and then interpreted, which will be a small subset of all the variables in the economy. Following both the relevant economic theory and the previous empirical results, our strategy incorporates the growth model specification and estimation of the equation based on the growth literature by Woo and Kumar (2015) and we expanded and augment the growth equation with external debt to assess if the latter has an impact on economic growth over and above other indicators.

The initial empirical specification is derived from the neoclassical growth model of Solow, where the rate of real per capita GDP (Y_t) for a given country is:

$$y_t = a + \gamma y_{t-1} + \sum_{i=1}^{n} (\delta_i z_{it} + \beta d_t + x_{\mu t}) \tag{5.1}$$

where y_{t-1} is the lagged value of the initial real per capita GDP (to capture the conditional convergence of the economy to its steady-state) and y_t is the initial GDP, z_{it}(i=1,...,n) is a set of independent or explanatory variables, and d_t is the net external debt-to-GDP ratio.

Regarding z_{it}, we considered a set of explanatory variables that proved to be consistent with the construction of growth analyses in the literature: openness to trade measured by the absolute sum of export and import over GDP (OPEN), foreign direct investment inflow (FDI), investment measured by the gross capital formation as a ratio to GDP (INV), human capital measured by secondary school enrollment (CAPITAL), population measured by the urban population (POP), and inflation measured by CPI, constant=2010(INF).

The justification of the selected variables is based on economic growth literature, the labor growth rate is used in the production process, and the accumulation of physical capital as suggests investment are the key determinants of growth (Felipe and Fisher, 2010). Empirical evidence has shown the relationship between population and economic growth in a mixed manner and differs between countries. Levine and Renelt (1992), in their survey of 41 growth studies, are of the opinion that there exist negative relationships and insignificance. Mankiw and Romer (1992), in their study of developing and developed countries, are of the opinion supporting the negative and significant relationship between population and growth, while Sachs and Warner (1997) support a positive relationship between population and economic growth for the case of Sub-Sahara African countries. The population has been found to exhibit either a positive or a negative relationship with economic growth. Also, according to many literature reports, a positive and statistically significant impact of investment on economic growth is expected. Many studies have found human capital is essential in growth studies because of its attractiveness to investors, the capability of absorbing ideas from the rest of the world, and enhancement of innovative contributions. Grossman and Helpman (1991) confirmed from the evidence, a positive relationship with economic growth (Cecchetti *et al.*, 2011) and Barroand McCleary (2003) found a negative relationship. Consequently, the effect of human capital could either be positive or negative. On the other hand, trade openness is suggested to boost productivity via the transfer of knowledge and efficiency gains (Levine and Renelt, 1992). Many studies found that openness impacts economic growth positively (Fetahi-Vehapi *et al.*, 2015; Keho, 2017; Edwards, 1998). With regards to the inflation rate, it has been argued that inflation is a good macroeconomic indicator of whether the economy is managed (Felipe and Fisher, 2003; Cecchetti *et al.*, 2011). Low inflation brings about economic growth because, through the price mechanism, economies can allocate scarce resources to their best economic application (Balassone *et al.*, 2011). However, inflation could either be positive or negative, as informed by the divided opinion on this. De Gregorio (1993), Liu *et al.* (1999), and Easterly and Bruno (1998) are of the opinion that inflation has a negative relationship with economic growth. He backs his claim with the cost of capital and reduction of capital accumulation and lowering its productivity, which will eventually bring about long-run growth. Tobin (1965) argued that inflation can increase capital per head as households shift their assets away from real money balance. Dotsey and Sarte (2000) are among the defenders of inflation with the opinion that it increases precautionary savings and, in response to higher expected inflation, the investment pool enhances economic growth.

5.3.2.1 *Model Specification*

The model is specified as:

$$y_t = a + \gamma y_{t-1} + \sum_{i=1}^{n} (\delta_i z_{it} + \beta d_t + x_{\mu t}) \tag{5.2}$$

where y_t is the initial real per capita GDP and y_{t-1} is the lagged value of the initial real per capita GDP (to capture the conditional convergence of the economy to its steady-state), z_{it}(i=1,..., n) is a set of independent or explanatory (OPEN, FDI, INV, CAPITAL, POP and INF) variables, and d_t is the net external debt-to-GDP ratio.

Since we are estimating our model with VECM approach, we first of all specified the VAR(p) model as:

$$Y_t = C + \Pi 1\ Y_{t-1} + \Pi 2\ Y_{t-} 2 + \dots\dots\dots + \Pi\ p\ Y_t - p + \epsilon t \tag{5.3}$$

where Y_t is a vector of the endogenous variables: *GDP*; *OPEN*; *FDI*; *INV*; *CAPITAL*; *POP*; *INF*.

C is a Vector of intercept term, Π i is an (n × n) coefficient matrix, and ϵt is a vector of error term.

The long-run cointegrating equation is specified as:

$$\begin{aligned} U_t = GDP - \alpha_0 - \beta_1 DEBT - \beta_2 OPEN - \beta_3 FDI - \beta_4 INV - \\ \beta_5 CAPITAL - \beta_6 POP - \beta_7 INF \end{aligned} \tag{5.4}$$

The VECM is specified as

$$y_t = c + \sum_{i=1}^{K} \Gamma\ y_{t-1} + \gamma(U_{t-1}) + E_t \tag{5.5}$$

where C = vector of constant terms, y_t = vector of endogenous variables, Γ = Short-run coefficient matrices, γ = Error correction term/speed of adjustment, Δ = Short-run operator, u_{t-1} = One lag of long-run cointegrating equation, and E_t = Vector of the error term.

5.4 Methodology and Findings

Recently, Indian economic performance has been on a continuous upward trend in terms of GDP growth amidst external debt. It is on this premise that the current study seeks to investigate this phenomenon. Table 5.2 shows the distribution statistics which clearly shows the distribution of the variables, namely inflation, FDI, and GDP, are not normally distributed. In the same statistical tabulation, the increasing nature of the Indian population, coupled with the rate of inflation and other sensitive variables, is the obvious reason for the gap between the maximum and minimum values.

5.4.1 Unit Root Testing

For the proper model specification and to reduce the likelihood of arriving at misleading or spurious results, it is essential to survey the time-series features of the data by testing the stationarity. This also includes tests for the order of integration of the variables. The outcomes of the ADF unit root test show that all of the variables are non-stationary and integrate to the order of one 1(1) and are seen in Table 5.3.

5.4.2 Cointegration

With a non-stationary variable that integrated in order I(1), testing whether a long-run relationship (cointegration) exists among the series is equally essential. Failure to account for cointegration would amount to misspecification if the variables are cointegrated and this might undermine the validity of the parameter estimates (Engle and Granger, 1987). Among many techniques that can test and estimate cointegration relationships in the literature, we consider (Mohanty, 2012; Tiwari, 2011) the maximum likelihood test procedure the most efficient because it recognizes the number of cointegrating vectors between the non-stationary level variables in the framework of VECM. Because of this, the study applied the Johansen cointegration test and the result is presented in Table 5.4.

Table 5.4 presents the cointegration test results. With Johansen's cointegration methodology, there are basically two tests that are employed: the Trace test and Maximum Eigen Value test. Under each of the tests, the null hypothesis is rejected if the t-statistics are greater than the critical value at a 5 percent level of significance. Based on the results presented, it is clear that in both tests the null hypothesis of the existence of, at most, one cointegration equation was rejected. Hence, from the result, the author concludes

Table 5.2 Descriptive statistics.

	GDPPCG	DEBT	T__OPEN	FDI	INV	CAPITAL	U_POP	CPI
Mean	791.2373	1.41E+08	15.15662	0.770822	2.54E+08	45.83140	2.69E+08	50.96027
Median	639.5004	1.40E+08	12.83144	0.541033	2.24E+08	45.22224	2.59E+08	39.31064
Maximum	1861.491	2.78E+08	31.84807	3.656951	4.42E+08	75.17671	4.39E+08	154.9534
Minimum	372.6426	36966736	5.243633	−0.030083	1.07E+08	25.67899	1.33E+08	7.658689
Std. Dev.	428.1370	68596182	7.962024	0.905782	1.08E+08	14.37872	91015413	42.38577
Skewness	1.031553	0.354175	0.594239	1.219341	0.491202	0.521891	0.257029	1.008017
Kurtosis	2.904809	2.471086	2.054144	3.885650	1.788588	2.320860	1.883749	3.011976
Jarque-Bera	7.464574	1.367642	4.037465	11.78020	4.257112	2.713749	2.642972	7.112942
Probability	0.023938	0.504685	0.132824	0.002767	0.119009	0.257464	0.266739	0.028539
Sum	33231.97	5.92E+09	636.5781	32.37451	1.07E+10	1924.919	1.13E+10	2140.331
Sum Sq. Dev.	7515352.	1.93E+17	2599.147	33.63808	4.78E+17	8476.654	3.40E+17	73658.71
Observations	42	42	42	42	42	42	42	42

Source: Authors Computation.

Table 5.3 Augmented Dickey-Fuller (ADF) test result.

Variables	Level		1st Difference		Status
	ADF	Critical Value@5%	ADF @	Critical Value@5%	
GDP	3.268512	−3.523623	−4.695710	−3.526609**	I (1)
DEBT	−0.166433	−1.949319	−2.708329	−1.949319**	I (1)
OPEN	−3.105682	−3.523623	−9.778032	−3.526609**	I (1)
FDI	−3.017490	−3.523623	−7.172584	−3.562882**	I (1)
INV	−1.418685	−3.523623	−4.991988	−3.526609**	I (1)
CAPITAL	−1.071965	−3.523623	−6.534481	−3.526609**	I (1)
POP	0.826428	−1.949609	2.382134	−1.949609**	I (1)
INF	1.579797	−3.557759	−4.456708	−3.540328	I (1)

Source: Author's Computation.
*, **, and *** signifies statistical significance at 10%, 5%, and 1%, respectively.

Table 5.4 Johansen cointegration test results.

Hypothesized								
Null(H_0)	**Alt(H_1)**	**Maxi-Eigen Statistic**	**0.05 C.Value**	**Prob**	**Trace Statistic**	**0.05 C.Value**	**Prob**	**Decision**
r=0	r=1	76.245	52.362	0.000	242.984	159.529	0.000	Reject Ho
r=0	r=1	55.098	46.231	0.004	166.738	125.615	0.000	Reject Ho
r=0	r=1	42.490	40.077	0.026	111.640	95.753	0.002	Reject Ho
r=0	r=1	25.615	33.876	0.344	69.149	69.818	0.056	Reject Ho
r=0	r=1	22.519	27.584	0.194	43.533	47.856	0.120	Accept Ho
r=0	r=1	13.953	21.131	0.368	21.014	29.797	0.356	Accept Ho
r=0	r=1	7.049	14.264	0.483	7.060	15.494	0.570	Accept Ho
r=0	r=1	0.011669	3.841466	0.913	0.011669	3.841466	0.913	Accept Ho

Note: Trace and Max-eigenvalue test indicates 4 cointegrating vectors each at the *** and ** denotes statistical rejection level at 0.01% and 0.05%, respectively.

that in both tests there is presence of three (3) cointegrating equations. The finding of the test is a direction to the fact that there is a long run association among the variables. The maximum lag length of three is selected according to AIC information criteria.

5.4.3 Vector Error Correction Model

The VECM is designed for a multivariate equation. It is considered advantageous over just a bivariate or single equation which is limited by the weakly exogenous for the parameters of interests. The VECM is considered better than any other single equation because of its ability to contain numerous co integration relationships, all the variables are treated as endogenous variables, and tests relating to the long run parameters are possible. The VECM was estimated to retrieve the short-run dynamics of the model, as well as the error correction term (ECT). Table 5.5 presents the output of the estimate of ECT. The presence of a stable long-run relationship is further affirmed by the significant ECT. The coefficient of the ECT shows the speed of adjustment of the economy towards long run equilibrium following a shock in the economy. The result shows that, following a shock in the economy, about 14.4 percent convergence towards long-run equilibrium is completed in one year.

In the short-run estimate, the author observed the following: first (−1) and second (−2) lag of trade openness were found to have a negative relationship with the GDP in the short-run, but only the second lag was found to be significant. Debt ratio to GDP was found to have a negative relationship with the GDP, but insignificant in the second lag (−2) within the short run period. Also, the population was found to have a negative relationship with the GDP and is significant in the first lag (−1) but maintains a positive relationship with the GDP and significant in lag (−2). The inflation was found to have a negative relationship with the GDP but was insignificant only in lag (−1) in the short run. The explanatory power of the independent variables was determined by the value of R-Squared, which is 88 percent. This means that 88 percent variations in GDP are explained by the independent variables. Also, the Adjusted R-squared shows the power of the independent variables on the dependent variable by imposing restrictions on the inclusion of additional variables. Its coefficient is a 78 percent variation in GDP, which is explained by the independent variables. The overall significance of the model is determined by the F-statistics and probability and the values are 5292.82 and 0.050, respectively. With this, we can conclude that the model is well fit and significant overall.

Table 5.5 Error correction test results.

Variables	Coefficient	T-statistic	P-value
ECT	−0.143984	1.16084	0.0546*
Δ (DEBT(−1))	1.31E-06	0.233814	0.8154
Δ (DEBT(−2))	−7.24E-07	−0.111298	0.9115
Δ (OPEN(−1))	−49.13912	−1.466768	0.1443
Δ (OPEN(−2))	−56.53389	−2.154381	0.0326**
Δ (FDI(−1))	137.4498	0.638690	0.5239
Δ (FDI(−2))	39.02332	0.194167	0.8463
Δ (INV(−1))	−5.96E-08	−0.010523	0.9916
Δ (INV(− (−2))	8.70E-06	1.414712	0.1590
Δ (CAPITAL(−1))	−30.09943	−0.768759	0.4431
Δ (CAPITAL(−2))	11.11094	0.278107	0.7813
Δ (POP(−1))	−0.001287	−3.962697	0.0001***
Δ (POP(−2))	0.001658	4.650496	0.0000 ***
Δ (INF(−1))	−12.53022	−0.133467	0.8940
Δ (INF(−2))	51.61517	0.644662	0.5200
C	−2227.692	−1.327989	0.1860
R-squared	0.880830		
Adj. R-squared	0.784359		
F-statistic	5292.821		
Prob.	0.050		

Source: Author's Computation.

Note: Here, Superscript *,**, and*** signify statistical significance at 10%, 5%, and 1%, respectively. The estimated models are free from both the problem of serial correlation and heteroscedasticity problems.

5.4.4 Long-Run Relationship Estimation

The test of the possibility of long-run association among the variables with Balassone *et al.* (2011) came with the unrestricted normalized long run relationship among the variables. The next step is to present, examine, and analyze the long-run relationship between the variables. Hence, the normalized long-run relationship among the variables is presented in Table 5.6.

Table 5.6 and Equation (5.5) present the long-run relationship estimates. Since some of the variables are in log form and the other remaining variables are expressed in percentage form, the relationship between the variables is expressed in its elasticity form. While real GDP per capita, Inflation, and Urban Population variables are in log form, Trade Openness, External Debt, Human Capital, Foreign Direct Invest Inflow, and Investment variables are expressed in percentage form. The Debt ratio to GDP was found to have a significant positive relationship with GDP and this supposes that a one percentage point increase in Debt ratio to GDP leads to having a 1.1 percent increase in GDP. This finding aligns with the finding of Balassone *et al.* (2011) in their work on public debt and the Indian economy. Trade openness was found to be significant but with a negative relationship with the economic growth of India. This is not surprising looking at India's half openness to trade policy and, even with the recent attempt to open up the economy to trade, the economy is still more

Table 5.6 Normalized cointegrating coefficients.

Dep. variable	Ind. variables	Coefficient	STD error	T-statistics
GDP	DEBT	−1.09E-06	(−1.7E-07)	6.412***
	OPEN	0.370938	(−2.07095)	−0.179*
	FDI	−34.27362	(−8.68913)	3.944**
	INV	−3.64E-06	(−3.6E-07)	10.11***
	CAPITAL	−7.642968	(−1.83255)	4.171**
	POP	5.02E-06	(−3.6E-07)	−13.94***
	INF	−10.31142	(−0.37305)	27.64**

Source: Author's Computation.

*,**, and *** signifies statistical significance at 10%, 5%, and 1%, respectively.

import oriented. This is not a good trend for a developing economy like that of India, especially at the early stages of openness (short-run period). The domestic industries will face external forces competing with them locally, though it is generally agreed that, in the long run, the competition will enhance the production efficiency of local industries through innovations and restructuring. Hence, a one percent point increase in trade openness will lead to a 0.37 percent decrease in GDP. This finding is in consonance with the findings by Hye and Lau (2015), where the FDI was found to be positive and significant to the economic growth of India. Therefore, a one percent point increase in FDI will lead to 34.3 percent in GDP. This is not far from the reality in India's economic development, hence, as put by an Indian Economic Strategy 2035 (2018), ''*India is keen to attract foreign investment. It has made substantial progress in liberalizing foreign investment policy settings. The stock of inward and outward direct and portfolio investment has grown from a little over 1 percent of GDP in 1990 to more than 30 percent in 2017. India's reforms to foreign portfolio investment (FPI) are impressive and ongoing*". The investment was found to be positive and significant to the economic growth of India. Also, Irandoust (2001) found a u-shape pattern in his work on investment with economic growth which incorporates both positive and negative relationships. Hence, a one percent point increase in investment will lead to a 3.6 percent increase in GDP. Capital was found to be positive and significant to the economic growth of India, which is following the past literature. Also, one percent point increase in capital will lead to a 7.6 increase in GDP. The population was found to be negative and significant to the economic growth of India. This is understandable with the explosive population growth ratio to the GDP of the country. One percent increase in population will lead to 5.0 percent decrease in GDP and inflation was found to be positive and significant to the economic growth of the country. Most times, inflation is seen as an enemy to economic growth, but according to Philips, curve inflation can be a cure to the high rate of unemployment. According to Williams Philips, if the rate of inflation is high, the unemployment rate is low and the growth of a nation depends, to a large extent, on employment. This could be the reason foreign direct investment and investment seem to be positive and significant to the economic growth of India because of the availability of Human Capital. However, the authors conclude that in the long run, Debt ratio to GDP, FDI, investment, capital, and inflation all have a positive impact on the economic growth of India, while the likes of trade openness and population harm the economic growth of India. On average, the coefficients are statistically significant at the one (1%) percent level.

5.4.5 Causality Test

Although the cointegration which the author has estimated confirmed the presence of causality, it is limited in determining the direction of the causality or transmission. This gives the author a sense of further testing the model with the granger causality test to ascertain the transmission direction of the selected variables, which will aid in forming the policy for the sustainability of the economic growth of India. The causality is referred to as the ability of one variable to predict and cause variables. From the causality finding as reported in Table 5.7, there is no Granger causality among the two variables. This is just for the DEBT and GDP.

Table 5.7 Granger causality tests analysis.

Null hypothesis	F-stat	P-value	Causality	Direction
$\Delta^{DEBT}\rightarrow\Delta^{GDP}$ $\Delta^{GDP}\rightarrow\Delta^{DEBT}$	0.44128 1.94857	0.7251 0.1416	NO	Neutrality
$\Delta^{OPEN}\rightarrow\Delta^{GDP}$ $\Delta^{GDP}\rightarrow\Delta^{OPEN}$	0.99245 3.90203	0.4088 0.0175**	 YES	UNI-DIRECTION
$\Delta^{FDI}\rightarrow\Delta^{GDP}$ $\Delta^{GDP}\rightarrow\Delta^{FDI}$	1.63493 8.09484	0.2007 0.0004***	YES	UNI-DIRECTION
$\Delta^{INV}\rightarrow\Delta^{GDP}$ $\Delta^{GDP}\rightarrow\Delta^{INV}$	1.02439 3.22560	0.3948 0.0354**	YES	UNI-DIRECTION
$\Delta^{OPEN}\rightarrow\Delta^{DEBT}$ DEBT→OPEN	1.61969 0.30185	0.2042 0.8238	NO	Neutrality
$\Delta^{FDI}\rightarrow\Delta^{OPEN}$ $\Delta^{OPEN}\rightarrow\Delta^{FDI}$	1.47055 4.72797	0.2411 0.0077***	YES	UNI-DIRECTION
$\Delta^{FDI}\rightarrow\Delta^{DEBT}$ $\Delta^{DEBT}\rightarrow\Delta^{FDI}$	1.73391 0.46462	0.1798 0.7090	NO	Neutrality
$\Delta^{INV}\rightarrow\Delta^{DEBT}$ $\Delta^{DEBT}\rightarrow\Delta^{INV}$	3.34181 3.14011	0.0313** 0.0387**	YES	BI-DIRECTION
$\Delta^{INV}\rightarrow\Delta^{FDI}$ $\Delta^{FDI}\rightarrow\Delta^{INV}$	6.14316 0.61343	0.0020*** 0.6113	YES	UNI-DIRECTION
$\Delta^{INV}\rightarrow\Delta^{OPEN}$ $\Delta^{OPEN}\rightarrow\Delta^{INV}$	11.3427 0.94227	0.0005*** 0.4317	YES	UNI-DRETON

Source: Author's computation.

*,**, and *** signify statistical significance level at 10%, 5%, and 1%, respectively.

In other words, there is no Granger causality passing between GDP and DEBT (i.e., they are independent of each other). Interestingly, there are causalities passing between GDP and trade openness (i.e., uni-direction), between GDP and FDI (i.e., uni-direction), INV and GDP (i.e., uni-direction), trade openness and FDI (i.e., uni-direction), FDI and DEBT (i.e., uni-direction), INV and DEBT (i.e., bi-direction), INV and FDI (i.e., uni-direction), and INV and trade openness (i.e., uni-direction). In summary, all the Granger causality results agree with error correction on the causality between trade openness and GDP, hence, the authors conclude that there is a strong causality between trade openness and GDP in India over the sampled period under review.

5.5 Conclusion and Policy Implications

This study aims to explain measures to maintain current upward economic growth in India's debt-in-debt economic performance in the context of management. The study equally seeks to address the highlighted questions in the first paragraph of the introduction, including: Is the growth induced by or debt-oriented (external debt)? Is the economy growing in a multi-facial trend or single trend? Is the growth affecting and correcting the poverty rate in the economy? Is the growth accommodating the explosive population growth rate of the country? Is the growth enhancing the openness of the economy as a response to increasing imports? Also, is the upward growth sustainable? The study is performed with a combination of VECM and Granger causality (long run and short run) estimation approaches. Long-run equilibrium is established and some key variables displayed a positive and significant relationship with economic growth.

The relationship that exists between the economic growth and explanatory variables is well spelled out from the output of the long-run relationship displayed in Table 5.3. Considering the result of the long run estimation, it is observed that the following variables are significantly and positively related to the economic growth of India: Debt ratio to GDP, FDI, human capital, and inflation. Investment has a positive relationship with economic growth but is not significant. The findings of this study have paved the way for the adherence of the authors to the group that thinks positivity about debt and GDP growth relative to the Indian economy. This supposes that as long as there is a good policy to moderate the activities in the Indian economy, the growth is sustainable and will go as far as addressing the highlighted questions from the first paragraph in the introduction. Hence, the question "Is growth induced by external debt?" is answered with the finding that supports a positive relationship between economic growth and external debt. Again, for the question bordering on whether the growth is a multi-facial trend or single trend and whether it is affecting or correcting the poverty rate in the economy, Indian economic growth is multi-trending and equally curbing the poverty rate in India. Hence, the majority of the variables are pointing toward a positive relationship with economic growth. For the case of explosive population and trade openness, they are considered to be hurting the economic growth of India. However, with the insight from the findings in this study, Indian economic growth can be sustained if the policymaking process is tailored towards improving and sustaining the variables inducing the economic growth of India. This could be done with moderation in the handling of the external debt so as not to be a burden through debt servicing. This has not closed the door of researching on this same topic and it is still open for study.

With these results confirming the significant positive relationship of some vital variables such as debt ratio to GDP, FDI, and human capital, it will amount to good policy formulation in pursuit of sustaining the current positive growth of India in creating a conducive environment to encourage the variables that are viable to the growth and sustenance of Indian economic activities. Anyanwu (2012) deduced in his paper why FDI goes where it goes, that human capital, natural resources, and endowments such as oil attracts FDI, and among the findings here, according to our results, the Granger causality is amongst FDI, OPEN, and INV. Considering the advantage India has in terms of population, which constitutes part of the human capital, justifies the claim that there is a positive relationship between FDI and growth. Hence, FDI is attracted by the availability of human resource and the FDI will turn around, influencing the rate of trade via trade openness and this will create an avenue for a virtuous economic growth and a sustainability circle if policy implication is managed well. Also, human capital should be considered among the indicators to give rapt attention because of its impact on the economic performance of the Indian economy. This will form a ground for the policy implication of this research work.

Declarations

Availability of Data and Materials

The data for this present study are sourced from the World Development Indicators (https://data.worldbank.org/). The current specific data can be made available upon request but all are available and downloadable at the earlier mentioned database and weblink.

Competing Interests

I wish to disclose here that there are no potential conflicts of interest at any level of this study.

Funding

I hereby declare that there is no form of funding received for this study.

Authors' Contributions

All authors have contributed to the manuscript significantly and have approved final submission.

Acknowledgments

Author gratitude is extended to the prospective editor(s) and reviewers that will/have spared time to guide toward a successful publication.

References

Alesina, A. and Wacziarg, R., 1998. Openness, country size and government. Journal of public Economics, 69(3), pp. 305–321.

Alfaro, L., Chanda, A., Kalemli-Ozcan, S. and Sayek, S., 2006. How does foreign direct investment promote economic growth? Exploring the effects of financial markets on linkages (No. w12522). National Bureau of Economic Research.

Almfraji, M.A. and Almsafir, M.K., 2014. Foreign direct investment and economic growth literature review from 1994 to 2012. Procedia-Social and Behavioral Sciences, 129, pp. 206–213.

Almfraji, M.A. and Almsafir, M.K., 2014. Foreign direct investment and economic growth literature review from 1994 to 2012. Procedia-Social and Behavioral Sciences, 129, pp. 206–213.

Anyanwu, J.C., 2012. Why Does Foreign Direct Investment Go Where It Goes?: New Evidence From African Countries. Annals of Economics & Finance, 13(2).

Ayadi, F.S. and Ayadi, F.O., 2008. The impact of external debt on economic growth: A comparative study of Nigeria and South Africa. Journal of Sustainable Development in Africa, 10(3), pp. 234–264.

Balassone, F., Francese, M. and Pace, A., 2011. Public debt and economic growth in Italy. Bank of Italy Economic History Working Paper, (11).

Bal, D. P., & Rath, B. N. (2014). Public debt and economic growth in India: A reassessment. *Economic Analysis and Policy*, *44*(3), 292–300.

Barro, R.J. and McCleary, R., 2003. Religion and economic growth (No. w9682). National Bureau of Economic Research.

Barro, R.J., 1979. On the determination of the public debt. Journal of political Economy, 87(5, Part 1), pp. 940–971.

Baum, A., Checherita-Westphal, C. and Rother, P., 2013. Debt and growth: New evidence for the euro area. Journal of International Money and Finance, 32, pp. 809–821.

Brueckner, M. and Lederman, D., 2015. Trade openness and economic growth: Panel data evidence from Sub-Saharan Africa. Economica, 82, pp. 1302–1323.

Buiter, W.H. and Kletzer, K.M., 1991. Persistent differences in national productivity growth rates with a common technology and free capital mobility: The roles of private thrift, public debt, capital taxation, and policy toward human capital formation. Journal of the Japanese and International Economies, 5(4), pp. 325–353.

Cecchetti, S.G., Mohanty, M.S. and Zampolli, F., 2011. The real effects of debt. Rev. Finance Stud. 22, pp. 25–27.

Chipalkatti, N., & Rishi, M. (2001). External debt and capital flight in the Indian economy. Oxford Development Studies, 29(1), 31–44.

Christie, T.A. and Rioja, F.K., 2012. Debt and Taxes: Financing Productive Government Expenditures. Job Market Paper.

Cochrane, J.H., 2011. Presidential address: Discount rates. The Journal of finance, 66(4), pp. 1047–1108.

De Gregorio, J., 1993. Inflation, taxation, and long-run growth. Journal of monetary economics, 31(3), pp. 271–298.

Dollar, D. and Kraay, A., 2004. Trade, growth, and poverty. The Economic Journal, 114(493), pp. F22–F49.

Dollar, D., 1992. Outward-oriented developing economies really do grow more rapidly: evidence from 95 LDCs, 1976-1985. Economic development and cultural change, 40(3), pp. 523–544.

Dotsey, M. and Sarte, P.D., 2000. Inflation uncertainty and growth in a cash-in-advance economy. Journal of Monetary Economics, 45(3), pp. 631–655.

Easterly, W. and Bruno, M., 1999. Inflation crises and long-run growth. The World Bank.

Edwards, S., 1998. Openness, productivity and growth: what do we really know?. The economic journal, 108(447), pp. 383–398.

Elmendorf, D.W. and Mankiw, N.G., 1999. Government debt. Handbook of macroeconomics, 1, pp. 1615–1669.

Engle, R.F. and Granger, C.W., 1987. Co-integration and error correction: representation, estimation, and testing. Econometrica: journal of the Econometric Society, pp. 251–276.

Felipe, J. and Fisher, F.M., 2003. Aggregation in production functions: what applied economists should know. Metroeconomica, 54(2–3), pp. 208–262.

Fetahi-Vehapi, M., Sadiku, L., & Petkovski, M. (2015). Empirical analysis of the effects of trade openness on economic growth: an evidence for South East European countries. Procedia Economics and Finance, 19, 17–26.

Frankel, J.A. and Romer, D.H., 1999. Does trade cause growth?. American economic review, 89(3), pp. 379–399.

Gautam, K., 2015. Semi-Presidentialism under the Indian Constitution.

Giles, J. and Williams, C.L., 2000. Export-led growth: a survey of the empirical literature and some non-causality results. Part 1. The Journal of International Trade & Economic Development, 9(3), pp. 261–337.

Greenaway, D. and Sapsford, D., 1994. What does liberalisation do for exports and growth?. Weltwirtschaftliches Archive, 130(1), pp. 152–174.

Gregory, A.W. and Hansen, B.E., 1996. Practitioners corner: tests for cointegration in models with regime and trend shifts. Oxford bulletin of Economics and Statistics, 58(3), pp. 555–560.

Grossman, G.M. and Helpman, E., 1991. Trade, knowledge spillovers, and growth. European economic review, 35(2-3), pp. 517–526.

Hodge, G., 2018. Privatization: An international review of performance. Routledge.

Hye, Q. M. A., & Lau, W. Y. (2015). Trade openness and economic growth: empirical evidence from India. *Journal of Business Economics and Management*, *16*(1), 188–205.

Irandoust, J.E.M., 2001. On the causality between foreign direct investment and output: a comparative study. The International Trade Journal, 15(1), pp. 1–26.

Keho, Y. (2017). The impact of trade openness on economic growth: The case of Cote d'Ivoire. Cogent Economics & Finance, 5(1), 1332820.

Kim, D.H. and Lin, S.C., 2009. Trade and growth at different stages of economic development. Journal of Development Studies, 45(8), pp. 1211–1224.

Lall, S., 1994. The East Asian miracle: Does the bell toll for industrial strategy?. World development, 22(4), pp. 645–654.

Levine, R. and Renelt, D., 1992. A sensitivity analysis of cross-country growth regressions. The American economic review, pp. 942–963.

Liu, R.Y., Parelius, J.M. and Singh, K., 1999. Multivariate analysis by data depth: descriptive statistics, graphics and inference,(with discussion and a rejoinder by Liu and Singh). The annals of statistics, 27(3), pp. 783–858.

Mankiw, N.G., Romer, D. and Weil, D.N., 1992. A contribution to the empirics of economic growth. The quarterly journal of economics, 107(2), pp. 407–437.
Mohanty, R.K., 2012. Fiscal deficit-economic growth nexus in India: A cointegration analysis. New Delhi: Centre for Economic Studies & Planning, School of Social Sciences Jawaharlal Nehru University.
Motiur, R.M., Furukawa, Y., Kawata, I., Rahman, M.M. and Alam, M., 2006. Role of homestead forests in household economy and factors affecting forest production: a case study in southwest Bangladesh. Journal of Forest Research, 11(2), pp. 89–97.
Murari, K., 2017. Financial development–economic growth nexus: Evidence from South Asian middle-income countries. Global Business Review, 18(4), pp. 924–935.
Onogbosele, D.O. and Ben, M.D., 2016. The Impact of Domestic Debt on Economic Growth of Nigeria. Asian Research Journal of Arts & Social Sciences, 1(3), pp. 1–13.
Rangarajan, C. and Srivastava, D.K., 2005. Fiscal deficits and government debt: implications for growth and stabilisation. Economic and Political Weekly, pp. 2919–2934.
Rath, B.N. and Bal, D.P., 2014. Do fdi and public investment crowd in or crowd out private domestic investment in India. The Journal of Developing Areas, pp. 269–284.
Robert, M., Thomas, A., Sekhar, M., Badiger, S., Ruiz, L., Raynal, H. and Bergez, J.E., 2017. Adaptive and dynamic decision-making processes: A conceptual model of production systems on Indian farms. Agricultural systems, 157, pp. 279–291.
Sachs, J.D. and Warner, A.M., 1997. Sources of slow growth in African economies. Journal of African economies, 6(3), pp. 335–376.
Sahoo, K. and Sethi, N., 2017. Impact of foreign capital on economic development in India: An econometric investigation. Global Business Review, 18(3), pp. 766–780.
Saxena, S. P., & Shanker, I. (2018). External debt and economic growth in India. *Social Science Asia*, *4*(1), 15–25.
Singh, C. (1999). Domestic debt and economic growth in India. *Economic and political Weekly*, 1445–1453.
Sousa, R.M., 2010. Housing wealth, financial wealth, money demand and policy rule: evidence from the euro area. The North American Journal of Economics and Finance, 21(1), pp. 88–105.
Sugin, L., 2003. Sustaining Progressivity in the Budget Process: A Commentary on Gale & (and) Orszag's An Economic Assessment of Tax Policy in the Bush Administration, 2001-2004. BCL Rev., 45, p. 1259.
Tiwari, A.K., 2011. A structural VAR analysis of renewable energy consumption, real GDP and CO2 emissions: evidence from India. Economics Bulletin, 31(2), pp. 1793–1806.

Tobin, J., 1965. Money and economic growth. Econometrica: Journal of the Econometric Society, pp. 671–684.

Woo, J. and Kumar, M.S., 2015. Public debt and growth. Economica, 82(328), pp. 705–739.

Zilibotti, F., 1995. A Rostovian model of endogenous growth and underdevelopment traps. European Economic Review, 39(8), pp. 1569–1602.

6

Data-Driven Delay Analysis with Applications to Railway Networks

Boyu Li, Ting Guo*, Yang Wang and Fang Chen

Data Science Institute, University of Technology Sydney, Sydney, Australia

Abstract

Reliability is one of the key evaluation criteria in railway service. Many factors contribute to the measure, such as delays spanning over spatiotemporal dimensions. A common method used to improve reliability is to design a better timetable to reduce the mutual influence between trains. Recently, machine learning shows great potential in improving the effectiveness and efficiency of decision-making to increase operational performance. For railway system management, this seems like an opportunity worth further exploration. In this chapter, we focus on analyzing railway disruptions and their impact on the traffic in the whole network. Specifically, we build three different data-driven models: (1) a conditional Bayes Net Model with the introduction of Markov property for delay propagation prediction, (2) a primary delay tracking back model, and (3) a dwell improvement evaluation model which can estimate the potential network benefits of the dwell improvement on single or multiple platforms. All the delay analysis models have been validated and deployed to the railway network in the Great Sydney area and the outcome of this application of the intelligent delay analysis technology significantly reduces delay-caused losses, increases the operation efficiency, and enables the train operating system to meet performance metrics and recover from incidents.

***Keywords*:** Data-driven, transport, delay analysis, railway network, bayesian modelling

**Corresponding author*: ting.guo@uts.edu.au

M. Niranjanamurthy, Hemant Kumar Gianey and Amir H. Gandomi (eds.) Advances in Data Science and Analytics: Concepts and Paradigms, (115–144) © 2023 Scrivener Publishing LLC

6.1 Introduction

The urban railway network is a significant part of the modern transportation system and its performance is always related to the daily life of residents [1]. However, when a trip is delayed, the following trips are affected and suffer from a secondary delay, which will significantly affect the entire railway system's performance, creating a domino effect. In this way, the performance and service of the railway system have been greatly affected. Therefore, the railway system managers and controllers are very concerned about the train delay and delay propagation [2]. Although some solutions have been applied to solve train delay problems, including applying buffer time for the entire train system or considering systematic delays for railway schedules design, there is still a multitude of stochastic factors that cause train delays: (1) Train factors such as mechanical or equipment failure and error operation of the train driver; (2) Passenger factors including sudden growth of train demand and the behavior of the passengers; and (3) External factors including delays caused by extreme weather, such as high temperature or heavy rain. Due to these factors, current solutions are insufficient to solve the delay problem in complex railway networks. In the railway network, delays can spread from one trip to other trips very easily and quickly. As an example, trains run continuously along the track line, so the delay of a single train will not only affect itself but also cause a secondary delay for the following trips. Hence, the railway network suffers from passenger satisfaction reduction and economic problems caused by the delays. Accordingly, it is crucial and valuable to analyze the factors that can cause train delays and to implement delay prediction and control strategies based on historical operating data to ensure the train system's stability.

With the development of modern technology, the modern railway system is highly digitalized. However, in actual train operation, the delay prediction and response still highly relies on the train driver or controllers' accumulated experience and intuition, not the results of comprehensive data analysis from the historical data [3–5]. Considering a complex railway network in which different lines are interleaved with each other and dependencies between different stations, it is difficult for local train managers to consider the impact of the entire network on local train delays. In most cases, they can only estimate train delay time and propagation by observing local line situations. However, in the real world, the secondary delays can be caused by route conflicts from the problem of cross-lines, merged lines, and train connections. Simultaneously, as the scale of the city grows, the railway network needs to expand and become more complex to meet the increasing urban traffic demand. Therefore, in order to improve the management and planning of the subway network more accurately, a data-driven application for railway delay analysis can provide effective help to railway managers. By the advanced application, they can quickly identify the cause of the delay problem, estimate the accurate delay severity, and respond to the accident in quick time.

In this chapter, we propose a conditional Bayesian model to predict the delay propagation from the real-world operating data of the Sydney Trains railway network. The major challenges in this work can be divided into two aspects: (1) The Sydney Trains railway network is a very complex and large system and the stations generate vast amounts of data every day. It is very difficult to process this data and obtain the delay patterns on the station level. (2) Currently, there is no suitable model that can simultaneously consider the delay dependence between multiple trips among complex railway network structures and predict delay propagation. Based on these challenges, we design a conditional Bayesian model. A Bayesian-based methodology is a representational tool that can be used to process complex structures and combine specific knowledge and situations into a coherent whole [6]. In addition, Bayesian-based methods applied here can merge a large amount of historical data to identify contingencies between multiple events and use real-time data to renew the different variables' status.

At the same time, based on the consideration of the railway system, we can assume the delay propagation is a continuous Markovian process because in the railway network, the future delay of a trip is only affected by the current status. Although the complete operation history might be recorded, the past situation has no influence on the future. By introducing Markov properties, we can obtain the dependence of different delays more clearly and reduce the complexity of the model. Regarding the different types of delay propagation caused by the very complex structure of the railway network, we study the different scenarios of the delayed trips. We divide the delay propagation into four classifications: (1) Self-delay when the current train is running and there is a problem from itself causing the primary delay; (2) Backward propagation where in the same service line, the following trips are affected by previously delayed trips; (3) Cross-line propagation where current trips at intersection stations interact with the trips from cross-service lines; and (4) Train-connection propagation when trips have train connections[1] with the current trips. By studying real-world

[1] *Train connection*: It means the train needs to start a new trip after finishing its current trip because these trips used the same train, so the current trip delay may cause a delay for the next trip and it can be called secondary delay.

scenarios, we have determined all the dependencies of different trips in the railway network, reducing the complexity of delay propagation. Therefore, our model benefits from scalable computing time and simplified complexity over the Markov property. Compared with traditional probabilistic models, our conditional Bayesian model shows good feasibility and accuracy on the Sydney train system operating data.

After implementing the conditional Bayesian model for delay propagation, we also design a delay trace-down model to find the root causes of delays (primary delays). It can help us understand clearly when the first train delay happens so as to understand the overall process of delay propagation better. Lastly, based on the delay propagation model and trace-down model we developed, we build a model for dwell improvement evaluation. This model can help estimate the benefits for a railway network from improving dwell time as a buffer for some platforms. It will provide sufficient support for the design and optimization of the timetable of the train system.

The following structure of the chapter is as follows. We introduce some current related work on train delays in Section 6.2. The background knowledge about train delay and preliminaries are in Section 6.3. In Sections 6.4 to 6.6, we introduce details of our three models about delay propagation, primary delay trace back, and dwell time improvement. Section 6.7 provides the experimental results based on our models to show performance in real-world applications. Finally, we summarize our work in Section 6.8.

6.2 Related Works

With modern technique development, more and more researchers have started using machine learning methods for analyzing delay patterns and propagation effects. Some studies considered the unstable characteristics of the actual train departure time to enhance the empirical estimation method [7]. Carey and Kwiecinski calculated delays by simulating trains randomly and studied the effects of planned distance between trips and delay propagation [8]. However, these studies on delay propagation, including some methods that have been applied, have not achieved success in complex network structures. Florio and Mussone proposed a solution that can be used in moderately complex railway networks [9]. In [8], the authors calculate how the delay of a single train propagates by introducing a theory about how to delay transfer in consecutive trains at a station. In [10], this paper discusses the distribution of buffers between trains in a periodic schedule. Nevertheless, in reality, this method did not consider run-time delay and dwell delay.

Some studies tried to solve this problem by using regression analysis to predict the departure delay from the affection of the arrival delay, involving the variance of run-time and dwell time. This method is easy to apply to real-world data, but it cannot be applied to complex geographic situations [2]. In [11], the authors proposed a random model based on the Monte Carlo method to predict the distribution of departure delay from the distribution of late arrival delays and dwell delays. However, this method does not analyze the dependence of the delays. In [12], Briggs used a super-statistical model to analyse the train delay on the railway network and found the train delay can be represented by a q-exponential function.

In [13], the authors proposed a model that can be applied to the entire network structure by using the initial delay within a timetable period to analyze delay propagation. The authors also designed a graph algorithm that can store the propagated delay in the bucket to calculate the train delays. However, the disadvantage of this model is that it does not consider the distribution of run-time and dwell delay because it is built from a linear system. In [14], Cerreto uses clustering methods to find delay patterns by identifying large data sets of train systems, but this is a hard assignment method (K-means). Probabilistic interpretation cannot be used and it cannot be used to analyze the influence of different conditions on delay. With the development of deep learning methods, many studies start to use neural networks for delay propagation prediction [15–17]. In [18], Wu *et al.* used deep learning methods such as LSTM to predict some common major train delays. However, this method is still in development and has not been tested in large real data sets. In the latest work, authors have designed an algorithm to predict the delay of the train at the following trips after the initial delays occur. However, the authors simplified the analysis by ignoring the influence of the train delay on train drivers' behavior and complex train delay scenarios [19].

6.3 Background Knowledge

To design a high-performance railway system schedule and optimize utilization of train carriages efficiently, it needs the help of accurate prediction of the stability and reliability of train operation. These predictions mainly depend on train delays and their propagation. Through analysis, train delays occur more frequently during train departure or arrival at the station. This is because a large number of lines and platforms in the railway network are cross-used and merged. In this section, we introduce different delay scenarios and background knowledge.

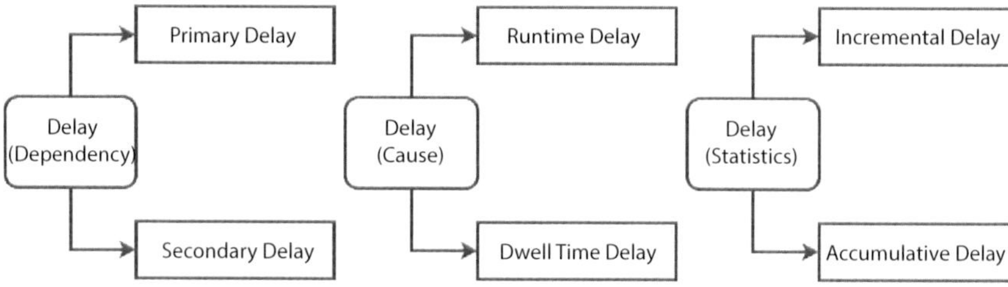

Figure 6.1 Delay types under different standards.

6.3.1 Background and Problem Formulation

6.3.1.1 *Train Delay*

The definition of delay is the variation between the originally planned time and the actual time. In the railway network, we divide delays into different types according to different delay dependencies, as shown in Figure 6.1[2]. In this chapter, both the primary and secondary delay are considered. We will distinguish delays based on different causes and estimate the incremental delay distribution of stations by using historical data and finally calculate the accumulative delays and their impacts on the entire railway network.

The variation from the planned run-time and dwell time of a train is defined as run-time delay and dwell delay. Therefore, the incremental run-time from Station i to Station j is defined as:

$$R_{ij} = t_j^a - t_i^d \tag{6.1}$$

where t_j^a is the time that the train arrives at Station j and t_i^d is the time that it departs at Station i. Therefore, the incremental run-time delay from Station i to Station j can be calculated by $A(t_j^a) - S(t_i^d)$, where $A(\cdot)$ is used to calculate the actual time and $S(\cdot)$ is used to calculate the scheduled time. Similarly, the incremental dwell time at Station j is:

$$D_j = t_j^d - t_j^a \tag{6.2}$$

---

[2] The type of train delays could be classified into many types: 1) Primary and Secondary Delay (by dependency): The primary delay is a self-caused delay and the delays caused by it are called secondary delays, 2) Run-time delay and Dwell time delay (by causes): It means the variation between the actual run-time/dwell time and the planned time, 3) Incremental delay and accumulative delay depend on whether the delay of a single train is stacked.

Therefore, the incremental dwell delay can be calculated by

$$\mathcal{A}(t_j^d - t_j^a) - \mathcal{S}(t_j^d - t_j^a).$$

6.3.1.2 *Delay Propagation*

Delays of a trip affect not only itself but also others, just like the domino effect we discussed in the Introduction section. When a single trip has a delay (primary delay), it may affect the following trips and crossing-line trips, causing them to become delayed as well (secondary delays). This phenomenon is called delayed propagation, as shown in Figure 6.2. More specifically, we have defined four standard scenarios to cover all delay propagation situations, as shown in Figure 6.3.

- Self-Propagation: When train T_1 is delayed at Station 3, this delay propagation will cause delays in the following subsequent stations of T_1.
- Cross-line Propagation: When train T_1 is delayed at Station 3, the delay will cause the delay of all cross-line trains arriving at Station 3 during the time that T_1 stops at this platform.
- Backward Propagation: When train T_1 is delayed at Station 3, the delay will cause the delay of all following trains arriving at this platform during the time period that T_1 stopped at Station 3, which is not as the plan.

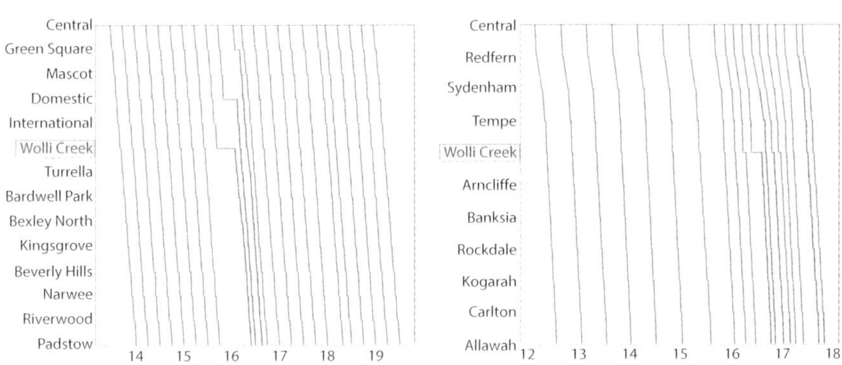

Figure 6.2 Delay propagation and impacts.

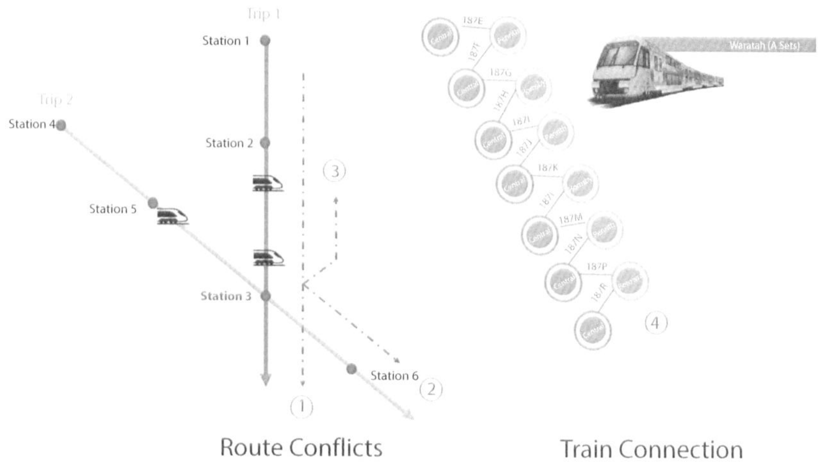

Figure 6.3 Four scenarios of delay propagation: ① Self-propagation; ② Cross-line Propagation; ③ Backward propagation.

- Train Connection Propagation: For the reason that trains need to run multiple times or connected trips every day, there is a train connection effect[3]. If the time that the train arrives at the destination is late, the next trip of the train will be delayed.

Please note, for the delays of trips which influence Cross-line and Backward trips, they can be collectively called route conflict effects.

6.3.2 Preliminaries

The daily operation of the railway system will be greatly affected by delay propagation. To solve this problem, we establish a reliable train delay propagation prediction model to provide reliable support for the planners and controllers of the railway system. In this way, we developed a conditional Bayesian model with Markov properties to predict delayed propagation. This model can be applied to a variety of complex scenarios in the real world, including the consideration of both run-time delay and dwell delay. To comprehend the model clearly, we introduce background knowledge here.

[3] In addition to the train connection effect, due to the delay of a current trip, the crew of the next trip could not be able to switch from the current trip on time. As a result, the next trip needs to wait for the crew, so it cannot depart on time and causes the delay.

6.3.2.1 *Bayesian Inference*

Our model uses a Bayesian inference framework. The function $P(A \mid B) = \frac{P(B \mid A)P(A)}{P(B)}$ of Bayes' Theorem has been deeply studied in many empirical machine learning materials, which can be used to model various random variables. In Bayes' theorem, the denominator is generally called an evidence or normalization constant, so the formula is usually written as $P(A|B) \propto P(B|A)P(A)$, where $P(A|B)$ is the posterior distribution and is proportional to the likelihood $P(B|A)$ times prior $P(A)$. Under normal circumstances, we need to form the prior at first, then use Bayes' theorem to calculate the posterior distribution to construct the Bayesian inference framework. Unfortunately, if the conjugate prior is not applicable, it is impossible to calculate the postponement distribution analytically because we need to calculate the intractable integrals.

6.3.2.2 *Markov Property*

The Markov property refers to the independence between the past and present. When we define a single-parameter process X as a Markov process relative to filtration $\{\mathcal{F}\}_t$, X_t is adapted to the filtration, and for any $s > t$, X_s is independent of $\mathcal{F}_t$ in X_t, which can be written as $X_s \perp \perp \mathcal{F}_t|X_t$. In the railway system, any delay which is self-propagation caused is only influenced by the delay status of the immediate preceding station. To illustrate, when a train has a delay (primary delay) at Station , this propagates the delay at Station 2, and after the train runs to Station 3 with a delay, the delay of the train on Station 3 will be only influenced and related to the delay on Station 2. Formally, it can be written as $P(\tau_{i+1}^{delay} \mid \tau_i^{delay}, \tau_{i-1}^{delay}, \cdots, \tau_1^{delay}) = P(\tau_{i+1}^{delay} \mid \tau_i^{delay})$.

6.4 Delay Propagation Model

In this section, we will give details about our conditional Bayesian model to predict the delay propagation in the railway network. Our model cannot only predict the effect of a single train's delayed propagation but also apply to all scenarios, as we defined in Section 3.

6.4.1 Conditional Bayesian Delay Propagation

In this part, we will introduce our conditional Bayesian models for different delay propagation situations based on Section 6.3.1.2.

6.4.1.1 *Delay Self-Propagation*

As shown in Scenario 1 of Figure 6.3, it is a case of self-delay propagation. It shows the delay of a single trip at a station can propagate to the following stations. As we introduced, this delay propagation situation follows Markov property and the accumulative delay (secondary delay) is only affected by the previous delays. To better explain, we use a trip that has continuous delays at two consecutive stations as an example. It can explain how a delay propagates from one station to other stations from the interpretation of Bayes' theorem and how it continues to propagate to subsequent trips.

If we define $R_{i(i+1)}$ as the normal incremental run-time[4] from Station i to the next Station $i + 1$ (consecutive stations), and D_{i+1} as the normal incremental dwell time at Station $i + 1$, in this way, both $R_{i(i+1)}$ and D_{i+1} follow normal distributions[5] as we assumed. Then, we can learn the distributions by historical data, expressed as $R_{i(i+1)} \sim N(\mu^{R}_{i(i+1)}, \sigma^{R}_{i(i+1)})$ and $D_{i+1} \sim N(\mu^{D}_{i+1}, \sigma^{D}_{i+1})$.

When there is a primary/secondary delay at Station i (departure delay of Station i: Δt^d_i), the behaviors of train drivers can be influenced (e.g. accelerate the train speed to reduce the delay that has already occurred) and the passenger flow will be different from the no-delay situation (e.g. more passengers will accumulate at the platform) with arrival delay (Δt^a_{i+1}) of Station i+1. Therefore, the run-time between Station i and $i + 1$ and the dwell time at Station $i + 1$ following the Markov property will be:

$$R'_{i(i+1)} = R_{i(i+1)} + (\Delta R_{i(i+1)} \mid \Delta t^d_i) \tag{6.3}$$

$$D'_{i+1} = D_{i+1} + (\Delta D_{i+1} \mid \Delta t^a_{i+1}) \tag{6.4}$$

where the incremental delays $\Delta t^a_{i+1} = \Delta t^d_i + (\Delta R_{i(i+1)} \mid \Delta t^d_i)$, $(\Delta R_{i(i+1)} \mid \Delta t^d_i)$, and $(\Delta D_{i+1} \mid \Delta t^a_{i+1})$ are caused by Δt^d_i for the run-time and dwell time, respectively.

---

[4] Normal incremental run-time: there is no run-time delay at the train stops station.

[5] After analyzing the data, we found the run-time delay and dwell time delay follow a gamma distribution and there is a long tail on the right side of the distribution. However, for the aim to develop the delay propagation model, we adopt normal distribution for delay patterns. Although normal distribution is symmetric, we only use the right side of the X-axis and after experiments, it shows accuracy loss of normal distribution is not much. In this chapter, the historical data of different stations are fitted by a different normal distribution.

6.4.1.2 Incremental Run-Time Delay

When a trip is delayed at Station i (Δt_i^d), the train driver will speed up to make up for the delay in the following trips, so that the actual train run-time will be different from the planned schedule. For different values of Δt_i^d, there are different incremental run-time delays. If Δt_i^d is small, it means the driver can speed up a little bit and there may be no delay at the next station, but when Δt_i^d is very large, no matter how fast the train speeds up, it cannot arrive at the next Station $i+1$ on time. So in our model, we divide Δt_i^d into the following intervals: (1) $\Delta T_i^1: 0 < \Delta t_i^d \le 3\ mins$; (2) $\Delta T_i^2: 3\ mins < \Delta t_i^d \le 5\ mins$; (3) $\Delta T_i^3: 5\ mins < \Delta t_i^d \le 10\ mins$; and (4) $\Delta T_i^4: \Delta t_i^d > 10\ mins$. For different intervals, our model learns different normal distributions to fit them respectively, *i.e.*, $(\Delta R_{i(i+1)} \mid \Delta t_i^d, \Delta t_i^d \in \Delta T_i^k) = (\Delta R_{i(i+1)} \mid \Delta T_i^k) \sim N(\mu_{i(i+1)}^{\Delta T_i^k}, \sigma_{i(i+1)}^{\Delta T_i^k})$.

Therefore, the incremental run-time delay by giving $\Delta t_i^d \in \Delta T_i^k$ can be re-written as:

$$\begin{aligned} R_{i(i+1)}^{k'} &\sim N(\mu_{i(i+1)}^{R}, \sigma_{i(i+1)}^{R}) + N(\mu_{i(i+1)}^{\Delta T_i^k}, \sigma_{i(i+1)}^{\Delta T_i^k}) \\ &\sim N\left(\mu_{i(i+1)}^{R} + \mu_{i(i+1)}^{\Delta T_i^k}, \sqrt{(\sigma_{i(i+1)}^{R})^2 + (\sigma_{i(i+1)}^{\Delta T_i^k})^2}\right) \end{aligned} \tag{6.5}$$

6.4.1.3 Incremental Dwell Time Delay

When a train arrives at Station i with a delay (the arrival delay at Station i is: Δt_i^a), which will cause the accumulative increase in the number of passengers at Station i, this situation will lead the train to stay longer to get passengers on board at Station i, which increases dwell time. By analyzing the historical data of the Sydney Trains system, a significant linear relationship between the dwell time and the increasing passengers has been found. From Figure 6.4, we can see that when the dwell time is between 30 seconds and 60 seconds and it shows a strong linear pattern (because

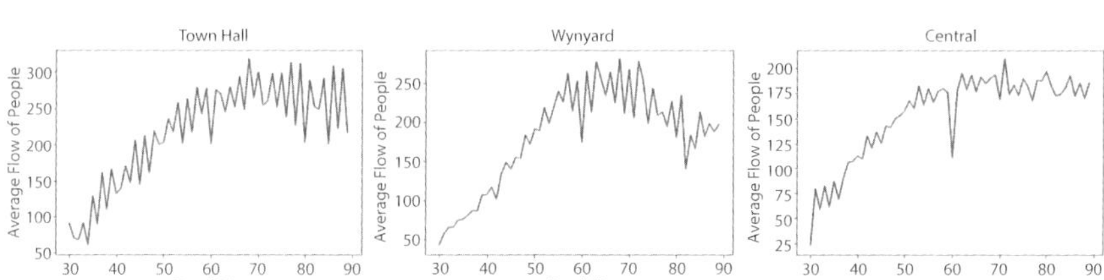

Figure 6.4 Relationship between dwell time and average passenger flow on three stations.

the Sydney Trains system sets a 30 second planned dwell time for most stations). The discovery leads us to design and learn a piecewise function to represent this relationship.

Based on our experiments, similar patterns can be found on most of the other stations.

$$\Delta D_i \mid \Delta t_i^a = \begin{cases} \alpha_i(\Delta t_i^a) + \beta_i, \Delta t_i^a < 60s \\ c_2, \qquad \Delta t_i^a \geq 60s \end{cases} \tag{6.6}$$

Therefore, the incremental dwell delay at Station $i + 1$ by giving Δt_1^d can be re-written as:

$$D'_{i+1} \sim \begin{cases} N(\mu_{i+1}^D + \alpha_{i+1}(\Delta t_{i+1}^a) + \beta_{i+1}, \sigma_{i+1}^D), \Delta t_{i+1}^a < 60s \\ N(\mu_{i+1}^D + c_2, \sigma_{i+1}^D), \qquad \Delta t_{i+1}^a \geq 60s \end{cases} \tag{6.7}$$

where $\Delta t_{i+1}^a = \Delta t_i^d + (\Delta R_{i(i+1)} \mid \Delta t_i^d)$.

6.4.1.4 *Accumulative Departure Delay*

In the case of delayed propagation in a single trip, the accumulated delay of each station will be considered, but not the incremental run-time/dwell time. On the contrary, Δt_i^d always follows the normal distribution of the delay propagation from the last station instead of a fixed value when Δt_i^d is a secondary delay, *i.e.* $\Delta t_i^d \sim N(\mu_i, \sigma_i)$. Therefore, the delay part we considered should be $(\Delta R_{i(i+1)} \mid \Delta t_i^d)$ and $(\Delta D_{i+1} \mid \Delta t_{i+1}^a)$. These can be written by Bayes' theorem as:

$$P(\Delta R_{i(i+1)} \mid \Delta t_i^d) = \sum_{k=1}^{4} R_{i(i+1)}^{k'} \mid_{t_i^d \in \Delta T_i^k} \tag{6.8}$$

where $R_{i(i+1)}^{k'}$ is calculated by using Equation 6.5 and with $a_i < \Delta T_i^k < b_i$, we have $P(t_i^d \in \Delta T_i^k) = \int_{a_i}^{b_i} \frac{1}{\sigma_i \sqrt{2\pi}} \exp(-\frac{(x-\mu_i)^2}{2\sigma_i^2}) dx$. The probability of the arrival delay and dwell delay at Station $i + 1$ can be expressed as:

$$P(\Delta t_{i+1}^a) = P(\Delta t_i^d + (\Delta R_{i(i+1)} \mid \Delta t_i^d)) \tag{6.9}$$

$$(\Delta t_{i+1}^{a} \mid \Delta t_{i}^{d}) \sim \sum_{k=1}^{4} N(\mu_i + \mu_{i(i+1)}^{\Delta T_i^k}, \sqrt{(\sigma_i)^2 + (\sigma_{i(i+1)}^{\Delta T_i^k})^2})\,\big|_{t_i^d \in \Delta T_i^k} \quad (6.10)$$

$$\begin{aligned}(\Delta D_{i+1} \mid \Delta t_{i+1}^{a}) \sim\ & N(\alpha_{i+1}(\Delta t_{i+1}^{a}) + \beta_{i+1}, \sigma_{i+1}^{D})\,\big|_{\Delta t_{i+1}^{a} < 60s} \\ & + N(c_2, \sigma_{i+1}^{D})\,\big|_{\Delta t_{i+1}^{a} \geq 60s}\end{aligned} \quad (6.11)$$

where $P(\Delta t_{i+1}^{a} < 60s) = \int_{0}^{60} f(x)dx$, $P(\Delta t_{i+1}^{a} \geq 60s) = \int_{60}^{+\infty} f(x)dx$ and we have $f(x) = \frac{1}{\sigma_{i+1}\sqrt{2\pi}} \exp\left(-\frac{(x-\mu_{i+1})^2}{2\sigma_{i+1}}\right)$, given $\Delta t_{i+1}^{a} \sim N(\mu_{i+1}, \sigma_{i+1})$.

Finally, with the given departure delay of Station *i*: $\Delta t_{i+1}^{a} \sim N(\mu_i, \sigma_i)$, the departure delay of Station $i+1$ (Δt_{i+1}^{d}) is:

$$\Delta t_{i+1}^{d} = \Delta t_{i}^{a} + (\Delta R_{i(i+1)|\Delta t_i^a}) + (\Delta D_{i+1} \mid (\Delta t_{i}^{a} + (\Delta R_{i(i+1)} \mid \Delta t_{i}^{a}))) \quad (6.12)$$

By using the equation above, we can calculate any delay propagation between two consecutive stations for a single trip.

6.4.2 Cross-Line Propagation, Backward Propagation and Train Connection Propagation

In other delay scenarios, we found a common delay propagation structure: if the preceding train does not arrive at the planned time, the delay will propagate in the network (cross-line train, preceding train, or itself with round-trips). Because these types of delay scenarios have a common delay propagation structure, the same model can be applied to them. Please note that Train *x* and Train *y* (with different starting stations but ending at the same Station *i* + 1) will be in a time conflict at station *i* + 1. From the scheduled timetable, if Train *x* plans to arrive earlier than Train *y*, to assume the delay that Train *x* propagate to Train *y*, we have:

Train *x* and Train *y* are two consecutive trains planned to stop at Station *i* + 1. If the following train *y*'s expected arrival time at Station *i* + 1 is earlier than the expected platform accessible time, then Train *y* has to wait and is delayed.

- Train *x*:
  - Scheduled arrival time at Station $i+1$: $t_{i+1}^{a,x}$
  - Scheduled departure time at Station $i+1$: $t_{i+1}^{d,x}$

- Accumulative arrival delay at Station $i + 1$ with a departure delay $\Delta t_i^{d,x}$ at Station i:

$$\Delta t_{i+1}^{a,x} = \Delta t_i^{d,x} + (\Delta R_{i(i+1)^x} \mid \Delta t_i^{d,x})$$

- Accumulative departure delay at Station $i + 1$ with a departure delay $\Delta t_i^{d,x}$ at Station i:

$$\Delta t_{i+1}^{d,x} = \Delta t_i^{d,x} + (\Delta R_{i(i+1)^x} \mid \Delta t_i^{d,x}) + (\Delta D_{i+1}^{x} \mid \Delta t_{i+1}^{a,x})$$

- Estimated arrival time at Station $i+1$: $t_{i+1}^{a,x} + \Delta t_{i+1}^{a,x}$
- Estimated departure time at Station $i+1$: $t_{i+1}^{d,x} + \Delta t_{i+1}^{d,x}$

- Train y:
  - Scheduled arrival time at Station $i+1$: $t_{i+1}^{a,y}$
  - Accumulative arrival delay from Station j to Station $i + 1$ with a departure delay $\Delta t_j^{d,y}$ at Station j:

$$\Delta t_{i+1}^{a,y} = \Delta t_j^{d,y} + (\Delta R_{j(i+1)}^{y} \mid \Delta t_j^{d,y})$$

- Estimated arrival time at Station $i+1$: $t_{i+1}^{a,y} + \Delta t_{i+1}^{a,y}$

As Figure 6.5 shows, Train x will affect Train y. When Train y arrives at Station $i + 1$, the arrival time of it will overlap with the arrival time period of Train x and platform accessibility. Here, the minimum interval time (headway) is defined as S between Train x and Train y at Station $i + 1$ and

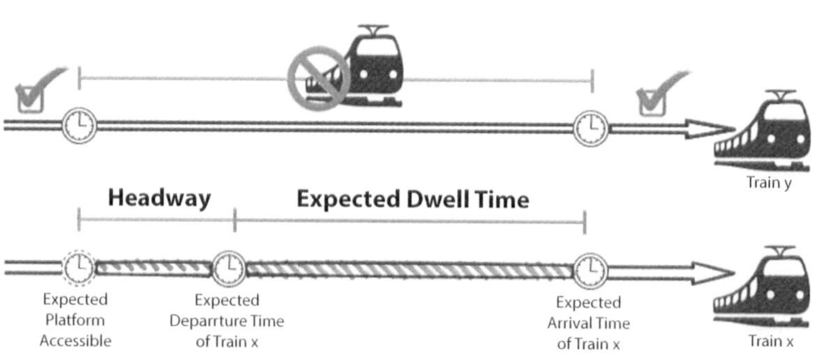

Figure 6.5 Delay propagation between trains.

this time is used to guarantee that Train x does not influence Train y, *i.e.* $Z_1 = t_{i+1}^{a,y} + \Delta t_{i+1}^{a,y} - t_{i+1}^{a,x} - \Delta t_{i+1}^{a,x} > 0$ and $Z_2 = t_{i+1}^{a,y} + \Delta t_{i+1}^{a,y} - t_{i+1}^{d,x} - \Delta t_{i+1}^{d,x} - S < 0$. Then, the probability of the delay which Train x propagates to Train y is as the following equation:

$$\begin{aligned} P(\delta t_{i+1}^{a,y} > 0 \mid \Delta t_{i+1}^{a,y}, \Delta t_i^{d,x}) &= P(Z_1 > 0, Z_2 < 0) \\ &= P(t_{i+1}^{a,y} + \Delta t_{i+1}^{a,y} - t_{i+1}^{a,x} - \Delta t_{i+1}^{a,x} > 0, \\ &\qquad t_{i+1}^{a,y} + \Delta t_{i+1}^{a,y} - t_{i+1}^{d,x} - \Delta t_{i+1}^{d,x} - S < 0) \end{aligned} \tag{6.13}$$

where $\delta t_{i+1}^{a,y}$ is the delay that Train x propagates to Train y. For Δt_{i+1}^{a} and Δt_{i+1}^{d}, both of them follow a normal distribution in our propagation model. It is hard to directly calculate the probability in Equation 6.13. In this way, we still estimate it by a normal distribution. Given the scheduled interval between two trains are $t_s^{x,y}$, $\Delta t_{i+1}^{a,y} \sim N(\mu_{a,y}, \sigma_{a,y})$, and $\Delta t_{i+1}^{d,x} \sim N(\mu_{d,x}, \sigma_{d,x})$, then the secondary delay that Train x propagated to Train y can be estimated as:

$$\Delta t_{i+1}^{x \to y} \sim N\left(\mu_{a,y} + \mu_{d,x} + S - t_s^{x,y}, \sqrt{(\sigma_{a,y})^2 + (\sigma_{d,x})^2}\right) \tag{6.14}$$

Note that we only consider the positive part of $\Delta t_{i+1}^{x \to y}$. We can incorporate the estimated delay propagation (secondary delay of Train y) from Train x to Train y into the departure delay estimation equation and get estimated accumulative departure delay at Station $i + 1$ of Train y as the equation below:

$$\Delta t_{i+1}^{d,y} = \Delta t_{i+1}^{a,y} + (\Delta D_{i+1}^{y} \mid \Delta t_{i+1}^{a,y}) + \Delta t_{i+1}^{x \to y} \tag{6.15}$$

By applying normal distribution, the scale of the fitted delay distributions is $(-\infty, +\infty)$. It means all trains that pass the same station have a certain chance of delay interaction. However, it cannot happen in real life. Therefore, only a 95% confidence interval of each delay distribution and corresponding propagation to other trains in this chapter are considered. From the result of the experiment, the computational complexity is greatly reduced and the accuracy remains.

6.5 Primary Delay Tracing Back

At the peak hour period of the urban railway system, a small delay can easily propagate to other trains (as shown in Figure 6.6). The delay that first happened is called the primary delay and secondary delay is the delay which is caused by the primary delay. Based on the relationship, we are trying to avoid primary delays to stop the delay propagation. However, in the real world, it is almost impossible to prevent all primary delays. If we could reduce some which happen frequently, it can avoid many delays which are propagated from the primary delays in the railway system. In view of the above-mentioned reasons, we developed a model to identify primary delays, which influence other following trains by analyzing operating schedules and historical operational data, which is TLS-OTR data from Sydney Trains. This data set includes detailed records about each trip.

6.5.1 Delay Candidates Selection

A train T_1 stopped at platforms $(p_1, p_2, \cdots, p_{n-1}, p_n)$, where p_1 is the platform of departure and p_n is the terminal station. Suppose the arrival delays of T_1 at each platform are denoted by $(da_1, da_2, \cdots, da_{n-1}, da_n)$, where da_i is calculated by the variation between actual arrival time at Platform p_i and the planned arrival time at p_i. If $\exists da_i \geq \varepsilon_1$, $1 \leq i \leq n-1$ and the delay at the terminal stop is $da_n \geq \varepsilon_2$, we regard this trip as delayed trip and append it to candidature set C, where ε_1 and ε_2 are the control thresholds to determine delay candidates.

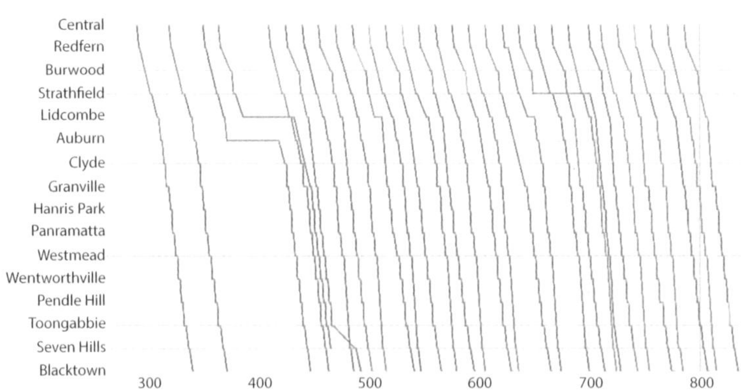

Figure 6.6 Delays gradually increase and spread out.

6.5.2 Relation Construction

After selecting the delay candidates set from historical operational data, now we aim to construct the relations between each delay trip in and its preceding trips, following trips or connecting trips. Under this circumstance, there are two scenarios that need to be considered: one is the preceding train and the following train and the other is the preceding train and the connecting train. The first scenario considers the relation between the preceding train and the following train that stopped at the same platform, while the latter scenario figures out the relation between the preceding train and the connection train because the terminal station of the preceding train is usually the departure station and if the preceding train has a delay at the terminal station, this will affect the connecting train.

6.5.2.1 *Preceding and Following Trains*

For each delayed trip T_i in candidature set C, suppose T_i is comprised of platforms of $(p_{i1}, p_{i2}, \cdots, p_{i(n-1)}, p_{in})$. For each platform p_{ij}, *where* $1 \le j \le n$, the preceding train passing through the same platform p_{ij} is denoted by TP_i. If the actual departure time of the preceding train TP_i at p_{ij} is too close to the planned arrival time of the candidate train T_i at platform p_{ij}, then it can be inferred that the preceding train might affect the following train. The time variation Δ_t can be calculated as $\Delta_t = ta(p_{ij}) - td(p_{ij})$, where *ta* means the planned arrival time and *td* is the actual departure time of the preceding train. A time threshold ε_t is set here to control the relationship between the preceding and following trips. If $\Delta_t \le \varepsilon_t$, it can be derived that TP_i affects T_i and we have the relation pair $[TP_i, T_i]$.

Similarly, let the following train at platform p_{ij} denote TP_i. If the planned arrival time of the following train TP_i is too close to the actual departure time of the candidate train T_i, we can also infer that T_i has affected the following train TF_i and we have a relation pair $[T_i, TF_i]$.

6.5.2.2 *Preceding and Connecting Trains*

The connection trips of each delay candidate in C should also be considered because the connecting train might depart late if the preceding train arrives at the terminal station late. For each T_i in C, suppose we have its connecting train, denoted by TC_i, and TC_i is comprised of platforms $(p_{i1}, p_{i2}, \cdots, p_{i(n-1)}, p_{in})$. The departure delay at the departure platform p_{i1} is denoted by dp_{i1}, which is calculated by the actual departure time of connecting train

TC_i minus the planned departure time of TC_i at platform p_{i1}. If $dp_{i1} \geq \varepsilon_c$, where ε_c is another threshold, it can be inferred that the connecting trip TC_i is affected by T_i and we have an order of $[T_i, TC_i]$ to indicate the relation between them.

After scanning all the delay candidates and constructing relations, we can find the primary delay trips that have not been affected. For each primary delay, we can also build the delay tracing down the tree by searching the relation pairs.

6.6 Evaluation on Dwell Time Improvement Strategy

Adding more dwell time as a buffer time to stations that are prone to delay is another effective way to avoid delay propagation. Therefore, it will be useful to add dwell time reasonably and evaluate the benefits it can bring. In this section, we introduce the model of dwell time improvement evaluation.

Similar to when a train has a delay time at a station, our conditional Bayesian delay propagation model can be applied to quantify the influence. Based on this idea, we can transfer the train delay time situation to train dwell time improvement. If dwell time at some platforms is improved, this improvement will make the afterward stations' accumulative delay distribution move to the left. As shown in Figure 6.7, if an improved dwell time has been witnessed at a station, then the accumulative delay distribution (i.e., orange line) will move to the left of the blue distribution and the mean value also moves from x_1 to x_2, while the variance keeps the same.

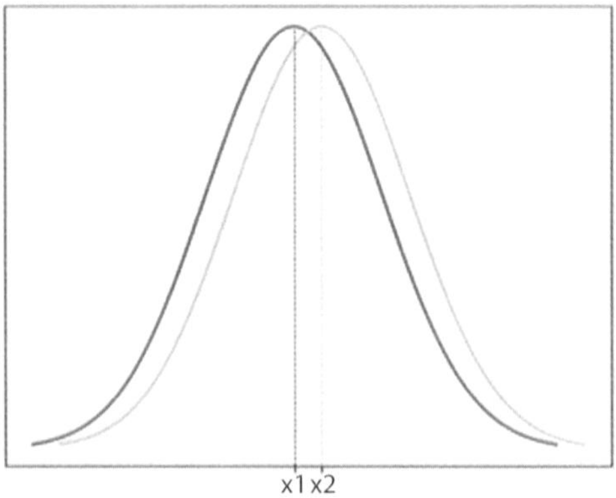

Figure 6.7 Effect of dwell improvement on delay distribution.

For a better understanding, the following equation is how we quantify the improvement:

$$\frac{\int_{x_1+x_2}^{+\infty}}{2} |f_1(x) - f_2(x)| \bullet xdx \tag{6.16}$$

In this equation, $f_1(x)$ represents the previous distribution before the dwell time improvement strategy is applied and $f_2(x)$ is the distribution function with dwell time improvement applied. x_1 and x_2 are the mean values of normal distribution, $f_1(x)$ and $f_2(x)$, respectively.

To evaluate if the different time intervals are positive or not, the time range is divided into different time intervals with a duration of 1 minute and they are [0, 1], [1, 2], [2, 3], [3, 4], [4, 5], and [5, +∞), as Figure 6.8 shows. The following equation is then used to evaluate the improved values for time intervals $[a,b]$:

$$\int_a^b f_1(x) - f_2(x)dx \tag{6.17}$$

Then, we need to take the primary trip (the trip with dwell improvement), following trips, and connected trips and other affected trips into consideration for estimating the overall influence by dwell time improvement. Take Figure 6.9 as an example, where we improve dwell time for Station (Platform) S_k. Also, Trip 1 is the primary trip that influences Trip 2. Therefore, both the affected following stops of Trip 1 and the affected

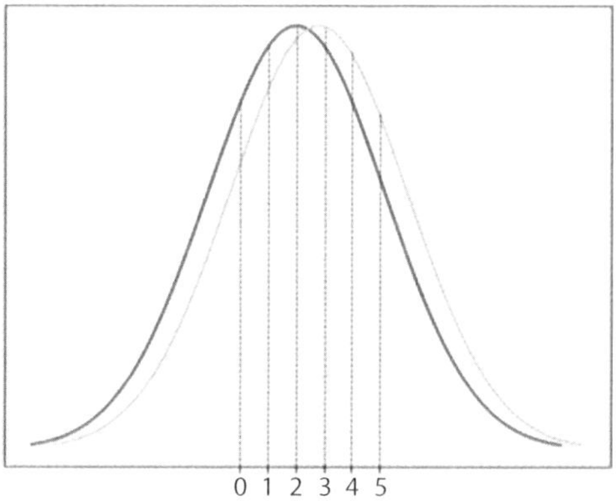

Figure 6.8 Effect of dwell improvement on different delay time bins.

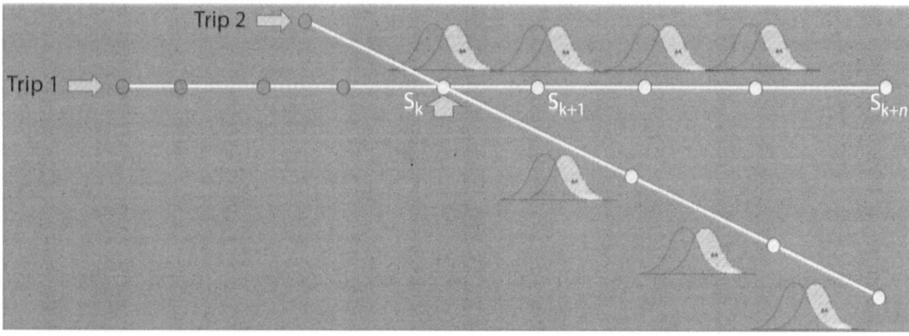

Figure 6.9 An example of dwell improvement estimation.

following stops of Trip 2 need to be considered. In this way, if ΔA represents the sum of the delay improvement of one trip, then we have:

$$\Delta A(\mathrm{Trip}^1_{\mathrm{self}}) = \Delta A(\mathrm{S}_k) + \Delta A(S_{k+1}) + \cdots + \Delta A(S_{k+n}) \tag{6.18}$$

$$\begin{aligned}\Delta A(Trip^1) \quad &= \Delta A(\mathrm{Trip}^1_{\mathrm{self}}) + \Delta A(\mathrm{Trip}^2_{\mathrm{affected}}) + \Delta A(\mathrm{Trip}^3_{\mathrm{affected}}) + \\ &\cdots + \Delta A(\mathrm{Trip}^{\mathrm{m}}_{\mathrm{affected}}) + \cdots\end{aligned} \tag{6.19}$$

Therefore, given a platform Z and a time period M (assume peak hours) with N number of trips passing this platform and the historical delay rate R is:

$$U(Z) = \frac{\left[\sum_{i=1}^{N} \Delta A(Trip_i)\right]}{M} \times R \tag{6.20}$$

where $U(Z)$ is the expected improved value per hour at Platform Z. If we take the number of customers C_i onboard each trip, we have:

$$U(Z) = \frac{\left[\sum_{i=1}^{N} \Delta A(Trip_i) \times C_i\right]}{M} \times R \tag{6.21}$$

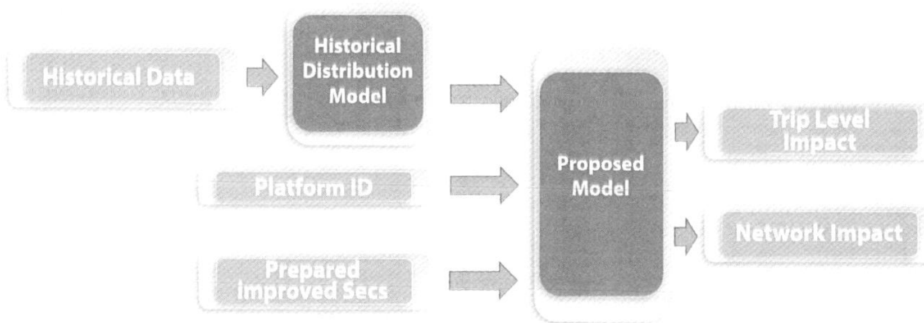

Figure 6.10 Dwell improvement expectation: inputs and outputs.

where $U(Z)$ is the expected customer impact per hour at Platform Z and the structure of dwell improvement expectation is as shown in Figure 6.10.

6.7 Experiments

The models we proposed have been applied to the Sydney Trains system and the data-driven delay analysis applications achieve great success in supporting Sydney Train System management. It helps the Sydney Trains system reduce the cost to manage the delayed trains and improve operation efficiency. Meanwhile, it helps the Sydney Train maintain higher performance and recovers from the incident more easily. For Sydney Trains, it is an NSW Government agency of Australia that runs, maintains, and operates railway services in the Greater Sydney area (as shown in Figure 6.11). For details, Sydney Trains covers 1,617km of track and 175 stations (700+ platforms) over nine main lines, with a total of 377.1 million passengers last year [20]. Its responsibilities include managing and maintaining all tracks, trains, signals, overhead wiring, stations, and facilities. In railway networks management, the operation performance depends more and more on how to obtain useful information from a large amount of historical data and make decisions. In this section, we use the proposed models to predict the train delay in the real-world data from Sydney Trains and evaluate the model performance.

6.7.1 Experiment Setting

In order to verify the performance of our model and its applicability to the complex large-scale railway network in the real world situation, we

Figure 6.11 Geographical map of Sydney trains railway network.

used data from the Sydney Train system. This data contains the operating schedule and historical operating data (TLS-OTR) of the trains in the Sydney Train Network. This data set records in detail the information on each train trip, including the unique ID of each trip every day. The data *set also* records the actual arrival/departure time and planned arrival/departure time of each trip at each station. Thus, we can know whether the train is delayed or not. In order to verify the performance of our models in more complex situations, we selected data of July 2019, which is the last month of the Australian financial year, so people need to take the train

more frequently than usual to meet more demands. As a result, the number of people using railway services increased and the railway system faced heavier tasks, which may cause a delay of trips more frequently. In this experiment, we selected 10 stations in the core areas of the Sydney Train system, such as densely populated residential areas and core business areas (as shown in Figure 6.12). The flow of people in these train stations is much larger than that of other train stations. Also, these stations are

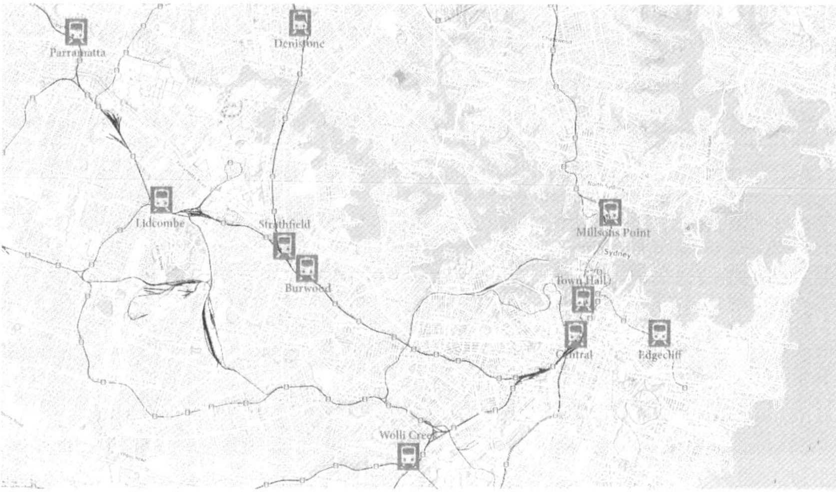

Figure 6.12 Location of 10 selected stations.

the most critical connection points in the Sydney Railway Network. As a result, they are more prone to delays and spreading delays to other lines.

6.7.2 Temporal Prediction of Delay Propagation

For temporal prediction, the captured accumulated delay time of delayed trips which passed the selected 10 stations are input into our model to predict the following 6 stops running status. In this experiment, we consider and predict all delay trip types from the different scenarios defined in Section 3.1.2. Then, we compare the predicted result with the real operational data to evaluate our model performance. The results are shown in Table 6.1 and we selected the mean absolute error (MAE) to evaluate the results. Taking the first cell of the table as an example, when the train has a delay at Central Station, we predict the delay propagation of the trips for the next 6 stops and 15.36 means the MAE between the predicted result and real operational data. For the last rows, it is the average MAE among the selected 10 stations. Most of the MAE for the predicted results in the following 6 stops is lower than 1 minute. Note that these 10 core stations are related to the operating performance of the entire Sydney Railway, so managers will manually control these stations more frequently and this artificial control pattern is very difficult to capture. In this way, our model predicts the delay propagation without considering human control.

Table 6.1 Performance of next-6-station temporal prediction by capturing delays on 10 stations.

Station \ MAE	1st	2nd	3rd	4th	5th	6th
Central	15.36	21.33	25.26	32.52	42.99	37.15
Town Hall	19.41	25.25	42.02	58.20	46.59	54.84
Burwood	24.72	34.32	37.96	38.72	49.25	44.07
Wolli Creek	40.46	44.15	49.45	51.47	54.92	61.43
Edgecliff	12.13	17.88	36.34	46.92	46.61	49.94
Lidcombe	38.61	48.79	58.40	57.63	62.13	71.21
Strathfield	38.74	47.46	51.85	54.22	56.77	60.93
Denistone	11.43	23.71	25.90	27.03	29.75	37.33
Parramatta	32.40	43.35	48.16	52.48	65.25	74.48
Milsons Point	43.33	53.73	42.80	48.85	54.95	75.33
Average	**28.27**	**37.21**	**42.80**	**48.40**	**52.94**	**57.44**

However, the performance is quite acceptable and our model is applicable for real-world complex railway network prediction tasks.

6.7.3 Spatial Prediction of Delay Propagation

For spatial prediction, the main delayed trips of the selected 10 stations have been input to our model. Then, we apply the model to predict the following trips which pass the same stations and may be influenced by the previous delay. Through the spatial prediction, we can get the other trips that are influenced by previous delayed trips and learn better about how delay propagates from a station to other stations. It could support the railway controller for decision making on how to avoid delay propagation from one line to other lines. A delayed trip is defined when the arrival time at the destination is 5 minutes longer than the scheduled time. For the evaluation method, we used the prediction success rate. The reason we use is that a train delay may be caused by many factors and we want to learn better how the delay propagates to other trips in different lines. The experiment results

Table 6.2 Performance of spatial prediction on 10 stations.

Station affected	Predicted delay	Real delay	Accuracy
Central	169	230	73.47%
Town Hall	170	231	73.59%
Burwood	56	87	64.36%
Wolli Creek	159	188	84.57%
Edgecliff	141	171	82.45%
Lidcombe	48	51	94.11%
Strathfield	388	436	88.99%
Denistone	73	80	91.25%
Parramatta	110	125	88.00%
Milsons Point	156	204	76.47%
Average	**147**	**180.3**	**81.53%**

are shown in Table 6.2. Taking the first cell as an example, after selecting the delayed trips at Central Station, our model predicted the total number of following delayed trips that pass Central Station is 169. Besides, the real delayed trips passed Central is 230. It means the accuracy of prediction is 73.47%. Moreover, the total accuracy for 10 stations is 81.53%. Note that the factors that cause the train delay may not only be because of delays from the stations we selected. Therefore, the performance of our model is fairly accurate in the complex real-world situation.

6.7.4 Case Study of Primary Delay Tracing Down

We provide a case study of identifying the primary delays and constructing primary delay tracing down tree. In this study, the thresholds aforementioned in Section 6.5.1 are set as: $\varepsilon_1 = 5min$, $\varepsilon_2 = 2.5min$, $\varepsilon_t = 0$, $\varepsilon_c = 3min$. The candidature set C is determined by using the TLS-OTR data.

C = [('Central Coast', 'N167'), ('Central Coast', 'N169'), ('Central Coast', '291G')]

```
========================================
'N167', 'Epping', 'EPG3', '2019-10-25 17:06:39'
('Central Coast', 'N167', 'Epping', EPG3')
└── ('Central Coast', 'N168')
    └── ('Central Coast', '291G')
========================================
```

Figure 6.13 Primary delay tracing down tree generated by our model.

For each delay candidature in C, construct the relations between itself and the preceding, following, or connecting trips. The constructed relations by considering the above two scenarios are listed as follows.

Relation Set = [[('Central Coast', 'N167'), ('Central Coast', 'N169')], [('Central Coast', 'N169'), ('Central Coast', '291G')]]

By scanning all the elements in the relation set, we can infer that trip 'N167' is the primary delay trip because it is not affected by any trip. Then, the primary delay tracing down tree is plotted as shown in Figure 6.13. The first line of the tree provides detailed information about the primary delay trip name, the first delay occurred station, platform, and its corresponding timestamp.

6.7.5 Evaluation of Dwell Time Improvement Strategy

For evaluating the dwell time improvement strategy, we choose the platform HVL3, which is a main platform located in Sydney's densely populated residential area. Here, we improve the dwell time for 10 seconds for this platform and there are a total of 38 trips planned stopped at HVL3 during the AM peak hours (i.e., 06:00 AM to 10:00 AM) from the planned timetable on the day of 02/09/2019. For every trip that passed HVL3, we select all trips which are impacted by this improved dwell time trip via the conditional Bayesian delay propagation model. For example, for the trips 303B pass HVL3 and it impacts the 32 following trips. For every affected trip, we evaluate the improved dwell time value by our Dwell Time Improvement model. Table 6.3 shows the improved value for the affected trip '322B and because we improved dwell time at HVL3, the improving values at the following stops after HVL3 could be viewed and are listed in the column of improved values. Meanwhile, the improved value at different time bins of [0, 1], [1, 2], [2, 3], [3, 4], [4, 5], and [5, $+\infty$) are also shown in the corresponding columns.

Table 6.3 Improved values of trip '322B' Affected by Trip '308B'.

Trip name	Affected by	Planned stop station	Planned stop node	Improved value (s)	Bin [0,1] (%)	Bin [1,2] (%)	Bin [2,3] (%)	Bin [3,4] (%)	Bin [4,5] (%)	Bin [5,+∞) (%)
322B	308B	Hurstville	HVL3	5.4	0.13	0.57	0.74	0.65	0.42	0.35
322B	308B	Wolli Creek	WCI3	5.2	0.15	0.48	0.62	0.56	0.4	0.41
322B	308B	Sydenham	SYD5	5.1	0.16	0.47	0.59	0.54	0.39	0.42
322B	308B	Redfern	RD11	5.2	0.13	0.42	0.56	0.53	0.4	0.46
322B	308B	Central	CE24	4.7	0.21	0.44	0.52	0.47	0.35	0.41
322B	308B	Town Hall	THL5	4.3	0.28	0.47	0.51	0.44	0.31	0.34
322B	308B	Martin Place	MPL2	4.5	0.25	0.44	0.5	0.44	0.32	0.38
322B	308B	Kings Cross	KGX2	4.2	0.29	0.46	0.5	0.43	0.3	0.34
322B	308B	Edgecliff	EDG2	4.2	0.29	0.46	0.5	0.42	0.3	0.34
322B	308B	Bondi Junction	BJN2	4.3	0.25	0.42	0.48	0.42	0.31	0.38

6.8 Conclusion

In this chapter, we propose three novel models for the analysis of delay propagation problems in railway systems. They are delay propagation conditional Bayesian model, primary delay traceback model, and dwell improvement evaluation model. We add Markov properties to our models based on the delay propagation feature. They can handle complex real-world scenarios and are successfully applied to Sydney Train operating data. From the experiment result, our models achieve reasonably applicable results for both spatial and temporal delay prediction and dwell time improvement evaluation. It shows great performance in sizeable complex railway networks. Consequently, our data-driven delay analysis for railway networks can improve railway system performance and support railway managers in multiple aspects and handle complicated real-world situations.

References

1. Bowman, L. A., Turnquist, M. A., Service frequency, schedule reliability and passenger wait times at transit stops. *Transp. Res. A.*, 15(6):465–471, 1981.
2. Goverde, R. M., Hansen, I. A., Delay propagation and process management at railway stations, *World Conference on Railway Research (WRCC)*, 2001.
3. Martin, L. J, Predictive reasoning and machine learning for the enhancement of reliability in railway systems, *RSSRail.*, pp. 178–188, Springer, 2016.
4. Prokhorchenko, A. V., Panchenko, A., Parkhomenko, L., Nesterenko, H. I., Muzykin, M. I., Prokhorchenko, H., Kolisnyk, A., Forecasting the estimated time of arrival for a cargo dispatch delivered by a freight train along a railway section, 2019.
5. Lessan, J., Fu, L., Wen, C., A hybrid bayesian network model for predicting delays in train operations. *CAIE.*, 127:1214–1222, 2019.
6. Darwiche, A., Modeling and reasoning with Bayesian networks. Cambridge university press, 2009.
7. Chen, B., Harker, P. T., Two moments estimation of the delay on single-track rail lines with scheduled traffic. *Transp. Sci.*, 24(4):261–275, 1990.
8. Carey, M., Kwieciński, A., Stochastic approximation to the effects of headways on knock-on delays of trains. *Transp. Res. B.*, 28(4):251–267, 1994.
9. Florio, L., Mussone, L. An analytical model for the simultaneous calculation of capacity of lines, junctions and station tracks. WIT Transactions on The Built Environment, 37, 1998.
10. Jovanović, P., Kecman, P *et al,* Optimal allocation of buffer times to increase train schedule robustness. Eur. J. Oper. Res., 256(1):44–54, 2017.

11. Yuan, J., Goverde, R. M. P., Hansen, I. A., Propagation of train delays in stations. WIT Transactions on The Built Environment, 61, 2002.
12. Briggs, K., Beck, C., Modelling train delays with q-exponential functions. *PHYSICA A.*, 378(2):498–504, 2007.
13. Goverde, R. M., A delay propagation algorithm for large-scale railway traffic networks. *Transp. Res.* C., 18(3):269–287, 2010.
14. Cerreto, F., Nielsen, B. F *et al,* Application of data clustering to railway delay pattern recognition. *J Adv Trasnsport.*, 2018.
15. Oneto, L., Fumeo, E., Clerico, G *et al,* Train delay prediction systems: a big data analytics perspective. *Big Data Res.*, 11:54–64, 2018.
16. Jiang, C., Huang, P., Lessan, J *et al,* Forecasting primary delay recovery of high-speed railway using multiple linear regression, supporting vector machine, artificial neural network, and random forest regression. *Can. J. Civ. Eng.*, 46(5):353–363, 2019.
17. Oneto, L., Fumeo, E *et al,* Dynamic delay predictions for large-scale railway networks: Deep and shallow extreme learning machines tuned via thresholdout. *IEEE Trans. Syst. Man Cybern. Syst.*, 47(10):2754–2767, 2017.
18. Wu, J., Zhou, L *et al,* Towards a general prediction system for the primary delay in urban railways, *IEEE Intelligent Transportation Systems Conference (ITSC),* pp. 3482–3487. 2019.
19. Xu, W., Tang, C., Ma, J., A delay propagation algorithm for trains on a single railway line, *Chinese Control And Decision Conference (CCDC),* pp.4152–4156, 2020.
20. Sydney Trains., Sydney trains 2017-2018 annual report. Report, 2018.

7

Proposing a Framework to Analyze Breast Cancer in Mammogram Images Using Global Thresholding, Gray Level Co-Occurrence Matrix, and Convolutional Neural Network (CNN)

Ms. Tanishka Dixit and Ms. Namrata Singh*

Department of Computer Science and Engineering, Naraina Vidhyapeeth Engineering & Management Institute, Panki, Kanpur (U.P.), India

Abstract

Based on the review and survey I will get a way out to analyze breast cancer in a more precise manner at the initial stage itself by using mammogram images. Initially, pre-processing methods will be applied to align and remove labels and noise from an image. Further, we will be proceeding with segmentation methods where we will be finding the Region of Interest (ROI) and pectoral muscle removal using Global Thresholding and will apply an Artificial Neural Network (ANN). Once this is done, then morphological operations and feature extraction using GLCM will help us in getting more into the details of mammogram images. After this, I will use one of the classification methods, i.e., Convolutional Neural Network (CNN), which will help in obtaining the output with either benign or malignant tissues that will help in taking out a preventive step to cure breast cancer within the human body.

Keywords: Segmentation, mammography, computer-aided system (CAD), region of interest (ROI), convolutional neural network (CNN)

**Corresponding author*: nam2817120@gmail.com

M. Niranjanamurthy, Hemant Kumar Gianey and Amir H. Gandomi (eds.) Advances in Data Science and Analytics: Concepts and Paradigms, (145–180) © 2023 Scrivener Publishing LLC

7.1 Introduction & Purpose of Study

Mammography is a technique where mammary tissue has been adapted, allowing inspection and internal analysis of the breast. These images are examined by radiologists so that they can detect possible abnormalities [1]. However, with the increase in number and difficulty in diagnosing, the use of CAD tools is becoming really important. Many of them have developed the techniques in this matter to analyze the mammographic images automatically. Many of these require a step to pre-process so that the ROI (Region of Interest) can be separated in an image and analyzed from what are considered as residue intruders into the image of breast, such as the pectoral muscle, image background, and labels [1, 2, 5]. Also, the boundary of the breast may have some crucial data regarding the percentage of right and left breast structure similarities, the position of the nipple, and the regularity of the breast's shape. All these details give indications regarding the possible presence of cancer [1, 2, 5, 13, 16].

Around the world, cancer in breast is considered to be the second foremost cancer in women. The American Cancer Society committee has given an estimate for deaths due to breast cancer as 40,610 every year. So, early detection of cancer using some effective ways is becoming more important so that chances for successful treatment increase. To give an exceptional way to find breast cancer beforehand, mammography is an advanced technique. Mass segmentation becomes a main task to operate the diagnosis of cancer. The features of masses (size, location, shape) should be used so that we can inspect and categorize the mass as malicious or benign and the performance depends mainly on segmentation. In quite a few years, many people have studied and suggested enhancements for the accuracy and quality of the CAD system and many of them have majorly concentrated on mass segmentation [1, 2, 5, 17–19, 27].

7.1.1 Segmentation

Image segmentation is a method where a digital image has been partitioned into multiple segments which are basically sets of pixels, majorly known as image objects. This method is good to locate boundaries (lines, curves, etc.) and objects in an image [7, 10–12, 14]. Segmentation has different types which helps in detecting medical imaging and helps in detecting label pixels which further represents a cancer in patients organs (Figure 7.1).

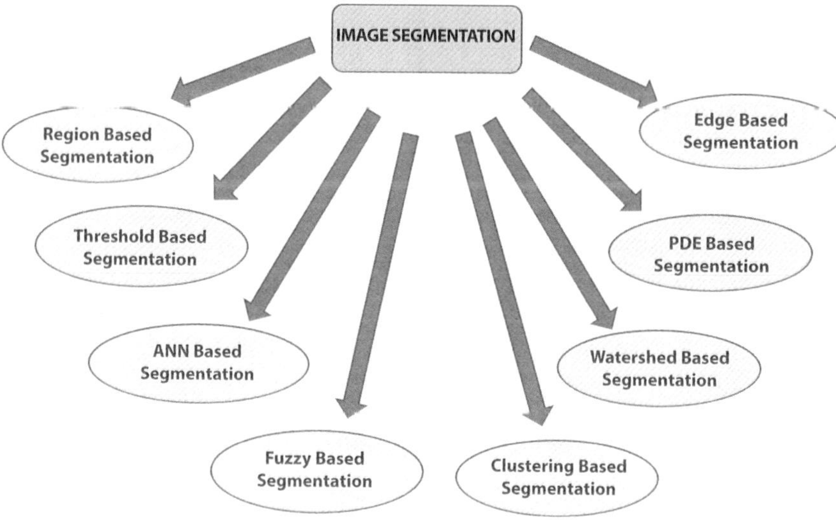

Figure 7.1 Types of image segmentation.

7.1.1.1 Types of Segmentation

i. Region-Based Segmentation: It is a process for finding the area directly and is a simple region growing segmentation process. As it involves finding of initial points of seed, it is also known as pixel-based image segmentation.
In this process, the different types of objects are divided by some other types of emotive boundaries and neighborhood features. These are used to define the classes and are homogeneous in nature. The approaches in this set are based on region growing, thresholding, region merging-splitting, and clustering in feature space [7, 10–12, 21, 32].

ii. Threshold Based Segmentation: This is another and one of the most preferred methods to segment medical images which exploit the certainty that doubtful areas of an image are signified by intensities of pixels above, within, or below a definite range of values. As detection of edge has its basis where a pixel value change is from region to region, similarly, thresholding methods also have the same. This method is extensively used in tasks that require the separation of an image into a background which is supposed to be rejected and a set of foreground objects or foreground [7, 10–12, 21, 32].

iii. ANN-Based Segmentation: An ANN, or Artificial Neural Network, is a strategy based on the method of the biological nervous system which also resembles the human mind. These methods are motivated by the way human intelligence works and are an information dispensation model. Further, there are some basic processing elements of neural networks which are known as "Artificial Neurons" or sometimes, simply as "Neurons". Generally, neurons divide some features of biological neural networks. It also swaps its arrangement basis on external or internal information that means it is an adaptive system that flows from one point to another inside the system. Many tools are used for modelling, particularly when an original data relationship is not conceded [7, 34, 36, 37].

Types of Learning in ANN

- Supervised Learning: This is a kind of learning is based on an error between input and output data. The supervisor and teacher are trained on every input pattern. Here, the process of learning is compared between expected output and obtained output. Whenever an error is generated, then it is used to adjust the network framework which results in improved results. To accomplish supervised learning, global information should be there, but this method is offline as its operation and learning period are different. Supervised learning has a few examples, such as Backpropagation Networks and Least Mean Square [7, 15, 20, 34, 36, 37].
- Unsupervised Learning: There is no involvement of teachers to teach to the network and it is very difficult and complex to implement. Also, the expected outcome is not presented to the network. The system is intelligent enough to learn by its own adapting and discovery to the structural parameters in the input sample of data. It is based on local information and a neural network is also supposed to learn online and operate at the same time. There are a few examples of this, including Competitive Learning and Hebbian Learning [7, 15, 20, 34, 36, 37.
- Reinforced Learning: This is a method where it deals with output-based learning. In this case, a teacher does

exist with the procedure, however, the teacher is not going to present the exact output. The teacher is only there to indicate whether the result is correct or incorrect. Also, for every right answer, a reward is given and for every wrong answer, a penalty is applied. Generally, it is a less used type of learning method in ANN [7, 15, 20, 34, 36, 37].

iv. Fuzzy Based Segmentation: One of the effective clustering methods that is well known is the Fuzzy C means method. This method computes a general membership value for each pixel depending on the similar basis which is calculated for it. This technique allows a pixel to own one or more areas in an image that has different values of membership function per region per pixel. This function is also found repetitively on each allotment of pixels to an area and the finishing criteria are given as a threshold value. It is an optimization algorithm which aims to execute fuzzy membership where hard boundaries are not present and unlikely in hard clustering methods like k-means [8, 9, 22, 28, 39].
v. Clustering Based Segmentation: It is the same as region growing as it choose pixels, along with labels, that are based on set criteria. However, the gap is that it does not engage fixed seed pixels to evolve the image areas. Here, it generally aims to allot every pixel to the nearby cluster and repetitively converts the cluster and label heads to initiate bigger regions based on specific conditions. In this scenario, the condition does not straight away calculate the similarity of 2 neighboring pixels. To measure and assign labels to pixels, it measures using the sum of squared distances and means of them. One of the frequent and famous techniques is k-means clustering [1, 2, 23, 28, 31].
vi. Watershed Based Segmentation: It necessitates the hypothesis of an image as a surface that has peaks and troughs, where the altitude of the surface is denoted by the gray level intensity of a pixel. The term watershed refers to the edges of the regions which have persistent intensities which are examined as flat zones. Further, the catchment basins are gradients that are sharp in the topographical form of the grayscale image signifying where the watersheds lie and surround a region. In this

segmentation, its transformations are known as a flooding technique where water drops fall on the basin and drip down to the bottommost sides of the basin/watersheds. This helps in marking the areas which are divided by the edges and also helps objects come into focus [1, 2, 6, 21, 28].

vii. PDE Based Segmentation: These are the most efficient, effective, and convenient techniques under image segmentation. Its main benefit is that the theory behind the solution and concept methods are well established in other fields. The full form of PDE is "Partial Differential Equation" which is used to segment an image. The most popular method is Curve Propagation, where there are numerous applications to object tracking, object extraction, stereo reconstruction, etc. The core idea is to generate an initial curve towards less potential of a cost function in which it defines the task to be addressed. There are a few image segmentation methods which are based on PDE, as follows: [29, 30, 32, 36, 39]
    - Level Set Methods
    - Parametric Methods
    - Fast Marching Methods

viii. Edge Based Segmentation: One of the old segmentation techniques is the Edge Detection in which an image is intricate with a specific derivative/gradient matrix, known as an operator, that generates a binary mask which shows regions of unexpected changes in values of pixel intensity, signifying objects and areas in an image. It generally works on a norm that highlights the edges/boundaries between regions and objects in an image and pixel intensity dissimilarity [29, 30, 32, 36, 39].

7.1.2 Compression

The compression of an image is basically reducing the size in bytes of a file without any effect on the standard of an image to an inadmissible extent. This allows the storage of images to be increased in a certain amount of memory space or disk and there are many ways in which image files can be compressed. It is applied generally to digital images to decrease their storage cost or transmission. Though this method might

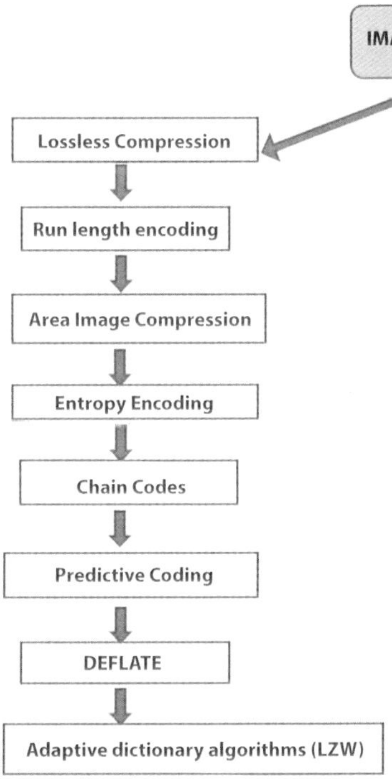

Figure 7.2 Types of image compression.

have the advantage of statistical and visual perception features of data images to give good output, whereas generic ones are used for other digital data [24–26, 40]. Here, we get to know types of compression named Lossy and lossless techniques. Moreover, efficiency and usability of these techniques are different. Lossy technique gives loss of information where size has to be compromised, however in lossless techniques it doesn't have any loss of information (Figure 7.2).

Types of Compression

i). Lossless Compression: It is proposed for record purposes and mostly for medical imaging, comics, clip art, or technical drawings. The one which causes insignificant dissimilarity may be known as Visually Lossless [24–26, 40].

Types of Lossless Compression

- Run-Length Encoding: It is used in PCX and also in TGA, BMP, and TIFF
- Area Image Compression

- Entropy Encoding: The most efficient and common entropy techniques are Huffman coding and Arithmetic coding
- Chain Codes
- Predictive Coding: Used in DPCM
- DEFLATE: Used in MNG, PNG, and TIFF
- Adaptive Dictionary Algorithms (LZW): Used in TIFF and GIF

ii). Lossy Compression: It is proposed mostly when it is used at a low bit rate and introduces the compression artifacts. The lossy technique is acceptable for images which are natural, such as photographs or images in applications where a small loss of constancy is admissible to get a considerable reduction in bit rate [24–26, 40].

Types of Lossy Compression

- Chroma Subsampling: It generally takes benefit of the truth that the eyeball of a human being recognizes spatial changes of luminosity more intensely than those of dropping and color and by averaging a few of the aspect data in the image [24–26, 40].
- Lowering the color space to the most ordinary image colors. The color palette has specified colors on the header of the image which is compressed. Here, every pixel refers to the color index in the palette and this thing can be combined with fluctuating to keep away from posterization [24–26, 40].
- Transform Coding: It is considered to be the most used technique [24–26, 40].
    a). Discrete Cosine Transform (DCT): It is one of the most used techniques in lossy compression and uses Fourier-related transforms. It was generally developed by Nasir Ahmed, K.R. Rao, and T. Natarajan. It is also known as "DCT-II", where its context is of the family with DCT (Discrete Cosine Transforms). Generally, everyone uses this method as it is one of the most logical forms of image compression.
    b). The most recently built wavelet transform is being used broadly, which follows entropy coding and quantization.
    c). Also, DCT is being used in JPEG which is the most accepted format of lossy and one of the recent HEIFs.
- Fractal Compression

7.2 Literature Review & Motivation

In [1], the author proposed a method where mass can be extracted from the ROI (Region of Interest) based on FCM (Fuzzy C-Means), having setting c=2 and texture features, where the consumer manually picks the region of interest. Further, the procedure of clustering is applied with a suitable range restricted by a threshold that is elucidated by the huge changes in the texture levels and by the maximum of intensity. This method is put into the Mini MIAS database and later on the performance is also measured with some investigated methods. Also, the result achieved is approximately 81% of the overlap measure (AOM).

In [2], the author used a mammogram image segmentation where a new method of region-based active contour is suggested which is established on a bimodal level set formulation. Also, it helps in detecting the regions of high-intensity within mammograms. Further, the procedure deals with region-based SPF function along with the Lee Seo model which is a level set formulation. The phase shift is introduced in the Heaviside function which merges the level set quickly to achieve an optimal solution. It really helps in segmenting into small repetitions with good precision compared to other algorithms.

In [3], the author uses a logical approach in breast mammograms to separate the pectoral muscle and undesired labels are separated by splitting high-intensity regions using convex hulls. To remove the pepper and salt noise, a median filter is used and to separate the breast tissues which appear with the pectoral muscle region, a global thresholding is used. The author used the mini MIAS database with almost 322 mammograms to study the performance of the proposed method.

In [4], the author basically aims at segregating out the ROI (Region of Interest) from the remaining image. This method begins by removing some labels, tags, and annotations from a mammographic image that uses the morphological opening method. The author uses a Sliding Window Algorithm, or SWA, to remove the pectoral muscle from mammograms which is mandatory to be done as it becomes difficult to separate the values of intensity of pectoral muscles which are the same to that of ROI. Further, to disperse the seeds in distinct areas instead of a one bright region, the author has used DRGA (Dispersed Region Growing Algorithm).

In [5], the author has proposed a method which employs a complete FCN (fully convolutional network) to model a potential function which has an end to end network for mammographic mass segmentation. Further, it is followed by a CRF (conditional random field) to perform systematic learning. Later on, the FCN was merged with a position before the mass distribution differed greatly with pixel position. Also, adversarial training is employed to eliminate overfitting due to the small areas of mammogram datasets. Looking at the entire thing, the multi-scale FCN is used to improve the segmentation performance. The results on 2 public datasets, such as DDSMBCRP and INbreast, have shown that the end-to-end network will achieve better performance in comparison to the state-of-the-art approaches.

In [6], the author has introduced an algorithm that is a novel marker-controlled watershed algorithm that is used to highlight the doubtful regions more evidently. It is a morphological function to get watershed lines from a topographic illustration of the input image. The method is applied and observed on various types to diagnose mammograms which are taken from BIRADS and MIAS databases. The results are really commendable for qualitatively and are approved by the radiologists.

In [7], the author tries to cover the effective techniques of segmentation which are used by some researchers to build efficient CADx systems for classifying mammograms. Until now, Active Contour Models and Thresholding were used for the deformation of splines to compare object outline and intensity-based division to split an image into 2 or more regions respectively. This is further followed by clustering and region-based algorithms that help us generate clusters that are based on mathematical standards of inserting pixels into the required areas. This is in progression in regards to designing higher segmentation methods that process foregoing information from the data records so that correct templates can be built to fragment test images. Further, the CADx system is supposed to be sturdy for different sets of mammographic images.

In [8], the author has shown work where the methodology is combined and used to enhance the contrast of the mammogram image where contrast limited histogram equalization (CLACHE), 4th order nonlinear complex diffusion-based unsharpening, and the morphological gradient is included. The mammogram which is enhanced is then segmented using fuzzy c means. The author also analyzes every case with fuzzy c means segmentation: fourth-order nonlinear complex diffusion enhanced, morphological gradient enhanced, combined enhanced, and CLACHE enhanced using the above ways.

In [9], the author has presented an automated segmentation of pectoral muscle and breast tissue in digital mammography which is based on k-means classification and simple histogram operation of pixel intensity. The author has tested his own algorithm on approximately 25 digital MLO (mediolateral oblique) mammograms with settled microcalcifications that are provided by the mini MIAS public database. The algorithm which is proposed can successfully describe the boundary of the pectoral muscle which is near to the breast tissue. With this independence and simplicity to mammogram intensity range, the data may have the capability to be applied in the pipeline of mammographic CAD to assist large scale screening of breast cancer.

In [10], the author has used different types of mass segmentation techniques that are used in mammogram images. The author has used a CAD, i.e., computer-aided diagnosis, system which is also considered as a 2nd reader of the mammographic images so that it can accurately identify lesions. This method is also an intermediate between an input image and radiologist. Also, the author used a segmentation process where it changes the representation of an image so that it makes it easy to analyze. So, this paper compares different mass segmentation methods used in mammogram images.

In [11], the author has proposed the computer-aided design system (CAD) for identifying mammograms. Also, the image is pre-processed by using ROI which is segmented with Otsu's thresholding technique and an adaptive median filter. Further, the classifier took the extracted GLCM features from ROI and classifiers such as KNN and SVM were also used in the computer-aided design system, where it analyzed performance metrics. This helped in demonstrating the automatic identification of cancer with high sensitivity and accuracy in the CAD is more reliable as an aid to radiologists.

In [12], the author has proposed a way where he can detect and classify mass abnormalities using a multi-SVM classifier in digital mammogram images. The author aims to research a way so that it can increase the accuracy of processing images and optimal classification between congenital and malignant abnormalities in mass regions which helps in reducing mismatched breast tissues. The author uses region-based segmentation to detect benign and malignant abnormalities, which also corresponds to the ROI's (regions of interest) or maybe abnormal regions. They also extracted the text-based features from the ROI specimen using GLCMs (Gray Level Co-occurrence Matrices). This paper shows the effectiveness of using classification accuracy which also produced an accuracy of 94%.

In [13], the author presents two enhancement techniques where he used image characteristic based contrast enhancement techniques. Further, he used the modified saturation technique to magnify the mammogram image recommended to its characteristic values and both techniques are validated by monitoring human visual perception.

In [14], the author aims to analyze the computable attributes for distinguishing microcalcification clumps on mammograms for pathological categorization into the malignant and benign category. They included a database of 101 cases where 48 cases are benign and 53 cases are malignant with biopsy being proved. They also used the cranial-caudal (CC) view and mediolateral oblique (MLO) view in mammogram images, which helped in extracting the promising features. In total, they extracted 72 features from the exact view for analysis. Further, they were assessed with an application to classify the mammogram. A DNN, or Deep Neural Network, classifier is being used as supervised learning in the methods of classification. There were three measures used for performance: Specificity, Sensitivity, and Accuracy. The results appeared in such a way where the Mean of Areas of microcalcification spots, CC view, and Mean of Major Axis Lengths of microcalcification spots were carried out better than the other characters which are followed by the Mean Diameter of all microcalcifications and Mean of Minor of Axis Lengths of microcalcification spots. For the Mean of Perimeters of microcalcification spots, MLO view and Mean Diameter of all microcalcifications is recommended over the other characteristics which are again accompanied by Mean of Contrasts of microcalcification spots and diffuseness. It is a good characteristic for both MLO and CC views.

In [15], the author argues a comprehensive assessment of the mass segmentation techniques which require the evaluation and design of the datasets with different effects. To give a more practical analysis, the work has proposed a head to head comparison of improved models with currently suggested techniques based on structured prognosis and deep learning on 4 recommended databases, carrying out a cross sensor evaluation. These obtained outputs help the assertion that the estimation methods from the literature are optimistically distorted when gathered data are evaluated from the same acquisition protocol and sensor.

In [16], the author proposed a method of mask extraction which is done automatically from mammograms which are segmented manually. Generally, medical imaging relies on exact segmentation for CAD applications and it is really important to have a good ground real image to mark a benchmark for the performance in a given segmentation technique. This technique tells the entire way of mask extraction using both digitized and printed images. In MLO (medio lateral oblique), a few important points in the images are to be properly segmented and detected. The extraction of the tissue of the breast and image alignment process and the pectoral muscle from every mammogram in the miniMIAS database has been proposed.

In [17], the author has proposed a FODPSO (fractional-image segmentation). The effectiveness of the suggested technique is compared with other techniques of segmentation which are based on thresholding such as DPSO (Darwinian particle swarm optimization) and PSO (particle swarm optimization). Further, the author compares the individual performances of all considered algorithms and analyses them using a few measures such as SNR, MSE, SSIM, and PSNR.

In [18], the author studies computer-assisted automatic systems for diagnosing breast cancer, which includes the classification and detection of mammary masses. Also, to overcome this issue they proposed a method to detect breast masses in which they assisted the diagnosis for the radiologist where a second potential reader was constructed after the radiologist and to minimize the mistakes done by the physician. The author first showed the mechanism of pre-processing images of mammography so that the quality of an image can be improved by using the method of histogram equalization. This is also based on adaptive limited contrast. In the second stage, they do the segmentation of an image in which prior knowledge is required on the quality and type of the images which will be processed, as well as the composition that has to be segmented. The mammographic images are based on the histogram thresholding technique where it detects the abnormalities. Using this technique, the author got acceptable results, but it is still not perfect as the qualities and structure of the received mammographic images are dissimilar and it makes the stage of segmentation difficult to examine. Here, in the last phase it involves the heap of mammary which are acquired from the specific extraction step and it uses the co-occurrence matrix.

In [19], the author has compared the literature survey techniques and further gave the proposed method. They proposed different scale particular blob identification methods to show the perception of calcification. This scale has been chosen through directed learning. Here, the other component of "Proportion Energy" has been presented by figuring out the vitality for each pixel at different unique scales to present blob discovery. Due to post preparing and forced straightforwardness of the element, the direct picture measure concern is done for calculation.

In [20], the author used a method that is fully automatic and relies on deep learning for mass segmentation in breast images. This also combines heavily connected U Net with AGs (attention gates). It also has a decoder and an encoder where the decoder is of the U NET integrated with attention gates and encoder is a network that is connected convolutionally. The author has proposed ta method which they tested on an authoritative database and the public database. The author also used a few parameters to evaluate the effectiveness, including elements such as sensitivity, F1 score, specificity, overall accuracy, and mean intersection over the union.

In [21], the author has proposed a technique which is a combination of watershed segmentation and multi-thresholding to analyze the DM (digital mammogram) dataset of mini-MIAS. In the first go, CBA+Otsu is applied to increase the unusual section from the DM and later on, the section has been extracted which is improved one from the WS. Also, the texture features of the removed section have been calculated as per the GLCM. In this work, images, like low, medium, dense, and normal images, are inspected using the suggested method. This is also categorized images as malignant or benign based on values of GLCM. It resulted in an efficient way of extracting the abnormal section from the DM.

In [22], the author has studied a new robust level set image segmentation technique which is developed by level set model and wavelet transformation. The proposed method has been verified for the simulated images, as well as for medical image processing under the environment of MATLAB. Through this paper, the author has concluded the integration of the wavelet transform under the process of segmentation which is more useful and accurate in image processing and literature analysis. The author has approached the world of image processing by making a beneficial graphical tool that can also be used as automatic wavelet transform image segmentation.

In [23], the author has implemented a new method so that the border of breast cancer can be highlighted and the filter will be based on the domain of frequency. Further, this will support a decrease in high frequencies and will keep only those that involve the boundary of the breast. The authors found that these techniques helped to reduce the noise, increase the textures, or get moth smooth area. The wavelet transform has been used as a filter and an enhancement stage to: 1) highlight the ROI and 2) reduce the noise and make it clear. Based on the results, the authors found that they still have limitations to get a more clear image for segmentation and increasing texture features.

In [24], the authors proposed a segmentation approach where two complementary techniques are explored individually and the local homogeneity and grey-scale intensities domain are used to address the issue of the precise breast region segmentation. The result coming out from each segmentation method is taken as a knowledge source and is structured using functions formalism where it was carried out using Dempster's combination rule. Further, the two sources are combined using a frequentative process. The output gives the result in quality improvement for exact breast border delimitation and ambiguity removal.

In [25], the authors perform a certain case of enhancement which is basically a mammographic image directly in the DCT compressed domain that uses edge-based enhancement. Using this, the cost of recompression and decompression is circumvented. In the suggested method, the quality of the image is found using a few metrics such as MSE, SSIM, and PSNR and is tested on the MIAS dataset. Further, the computation cost of both the domains is observed and performance metrics are measured with the values in the spatial domain.

In [26], the author focused on a new photoacoustic tomography system which gives a perception of angiographic features in mammogram images and the proposed DSM technique. Further, output images received from this technique can be collated to both MRI and mammogram, as data is obtained and introduced in the CC plane with which radiologists are most familiar with. This proposed method gives comfort to the patient, as it deals with mild compression, lack of ionizing radiation, is non-invasive nature, and has a fast imaging time. Moreover, a portable DSM can be stored and the method is related to a mammogram.

In [27], the author presented an automatic nuclear method of segmentation that used an improvised Hybrid AC model consisting of both region and boundary information. The start of segmentation, which is based on watershed and morphological operations, allows for the production of initial closed curves and reduction in computational load. The segmentation technique was assessed in the context of segmenting the nuclei on high, intermediate, and low-grade breast cancer histopathology.

In [28], the author used 3 techniques which are Gaussian Mixture Model-Expectation Maximization (GMMEM), Fuzzy C-Means (FCM), and K-Means model to segment the IR breast images and compare them. Here, the color space conversion to L*a*b is done to improve the analysis of color so that the malignant and benign cases are classified.

In [29], the author shows the survey and reviews different image segmentation techniques. It helps in segmenting the image according to some similarity with seeded region growing algorithms and this is classical for dynamic segmentation of images.

In [30], the author has suggested methods such as U-Net, SegNet, and FCN. They still need to be enhanced so that better semantic segmentation can be done when diagnosing breast cancer using Ultrasound. The author has also proposed a channel attention module having a multiscale grid and they illustrated Ours-MSGRAP, which outperformed.

In [31], the author has proposed a point of view to efficiently inspect digital mammograms using texture segmentation. It helps in detecting initial stage cancers which will not be susceptible to human error and taking proper steps to reduce the risks linked with Breast Cancer.

In [32], the author used a segmentation technique for identifying breast cancer from thermal images which are initiated based on a CSSA

(Chaotic Salp Swarm Algorithm). It shows ascendancy in single-objective optimization problems that suffer from local optima stagnation and low convergence rate. Here, they used the quick-shift method for extracting superpixels and applied them to the thermal images for the breast area.

In [33], the author compares 5 segmentation methods: fully automatic segmentation (Method 1), distance-based cropping (Method 2), semi-automatic segmentation (Method 3), manual zoom cropping (Method 4), and fully manual segmentation (Method 5). Post-extraction is done through statistical and textural features being found and minimized to only the specific ones.

In [34], the author proposes a CNN-based technique named DL-CNN (Dual Layer CNN) which also uses two layer CNN, where the 1st layer is used for Probable Region Identification and the 2nd is used for segmentation and false-positive reduction. Also, they have used datasets of breast images and other parameters examined are true positive rate at false positive per image.

In [35], the author uses a segmentation technique for identifying the cancer lesions in DCE-MRI images which are majorly based on ACWE (active contour without edges) technique parallel programming with basic purpose, where computation on GPUs (Graphics processing units) is introduced.

In [36], the author studies and aims to make a computerized segmentation system that will use the position of seed as the only priori of an issue. Also, they are approaching a 2 stage segmentation which incorporates shape information of training masses.

For the 1st stage, a new technique of adaptive region growing is used so that they get a rough idea of the mass boundary. For the 2nd stage, a model is introduced to geometric edge-based deformation, which used the output of the 1st stage as the initial contour.

In [37], the author has proposed a novel Docker-based framework that is used to get a comprehensive diagnosis where flexible deep learning methods are taken into consideration. It is drafted by incorporating popular CNN method CDeep3M and it gives an eminent segmentation effect for an ultrasonic image.

In [38], the author presents an architecture which is based on thermography and a DBE processor for a handheld off the shelf intelligent screening and the portable device. Later, an image is pre-processed to get the ROI (Regions of Interest). The texture features are selected very carefully so that efficient hardware can be implemented and they are later fed into a dual classifier which is based on LSVM (Trained Linear Support Vector

Machine) and CNN (convolutional neural network) for deciding the decision boundary.

In [39], the author uses a technique that accurately helps in detecting breast lesions by using a dual-modality system. The author used 3 popular methods which are DPSO (Darwinian Particle swarm optimization), K-means (KM), and Fuzzy-c-Means (FCM), which helped in identifying lesions by using combined mammography and ultrasonography.

In [40], the author aims at researching so that new biomarkers can be validated as breast cancer and this will be done by introducing the electromechanical coupling factor of samples of breast tissue. They have designed a portable tool for diagnosing and a MEMS (microelectromechanical systems) based biochip. This is integrated with a piezoresistive sensing layer so that it can measure the reaction force and a micro-heater for temperature control will be introduced. This helps in showing the statistically significant differences between the 2 groups.

7.3 Proposed Work

7.3.1 Algorithm

To analyze and detect breast cancer, we will use the proposed method which includes the below procedure:

(i) We will start by gathering the mammogram images.
(ii) Images will undergo pre-processing, including:
 (a). Images Flipping
 (b). Removing Image Label
 (c). Noise removal using the median filter
(iii) After this, we will segment the images using the below methods:
 (a). Region of Interest (ROI)
 (b). Pectoral muscle removal using Global Thresholding
 (c). Artificial Neural Network (ANN)
(iv) The morphological operations will be using some compound operations to enhance the tissues and mass region.
(v) We will also analyze abnormalities by applying feature extraction and classification techniques.
(vi) The final result will be obtained, which will help us in identifying if the data taken is Benign or Malignant.

7.3.2 Explanation

The above-proposed method will use the mammogram images and we will apply pre-processing methods so that images will be enhanced and normalized. The segmentation method will help us in getting the Region of Interest (ROI), removing pectoral muscle with the help of global thresholding, and applying the ANN method. The method which helps us in enhancing the tissues and mass region are known as morphological operations. Feature extraction and classification techniques will help us in analyzing the abnormalities in the images.

7.3.3 Flowchart

Over here we are trying to show the entire flow diagram which will give more clarity for the process that is being proposed. This shows end-to-end flow of the same (Figure 7.3).

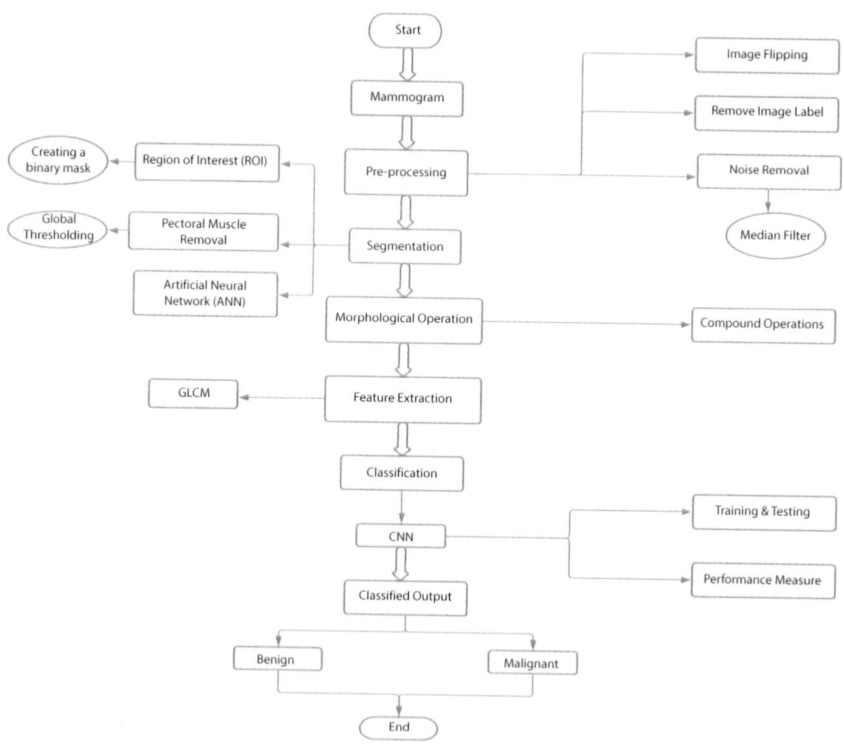

Figure 7.3 Proposed work flowchart.

7.4 Observation Tables and Figures

Table 7.1 helps us in understanding the comparison of the segmentation techniques.

Table 7.2 shows us a good comparison between both compression techniques which helps us in getting better clarity that which is best.

Table 7.3 shows the comparison of base papers which have worked for breast cancer research using segmentation techniques.

Table 7.4 shows the comparison of the research work done using compression techniques.

Table 7.1 Comparison between different segmentation techniques [3, 5, 8, 13, 23, 27, 33, 35, 38].

Technique	Datasets	Pros	Cons
Edge Detection	MIAS, BIRADS	- Low computational complexity - Ease of implementation	- Low effectiveness - Open-bounded or weak-bounded regions - Inability to conform to all supplied images - Leading to improper segmentation
Watershed Transformation	MIAS	Closed edges generally denote the clear-cut object boundaries	- Wrong regions recognized - Over-segmentation - High time complexity
Region Growing	DDSM, FFDM, MIAS	Robustness against noise	- Has difficulty while selecting optimal seed pixels - High time complexity

(*Continued*)

Table 7.1 Comparison between different segmentation techniques [3, 5, 8, 13, 23, 27, 33, 35, 38]. (*Continued*)

Technique	Datasets	Pros	Cons
Thresholding	BIRADS, MIAS, DDSM, INbreast	- Moderate efficacy - Ease of implementation and maximum simplicity	- Has difficulty while deciding for optimal value(s) in division of regions - Unproductive in instances of low contrast between foreground and background
Atlas-based Segmentation	MIAS	Highly efficient for extracting optimal region boundaries based on prior information	Complex images cannot be disfigured to fit into the reference atlases obtained
Active Contour Models	MIAS, DDSM	- Robustness against noise - Effective conforming to object contours	- High complexity of computation and time - Dependent upon initialization parameters
Clustering	MIAS, DDSM	- Easy to implement - k-means produces clear clusters/ regions - Fuzzy c-means allows flexible area membership	- Fixed number of clusters can get by fixing the value of k - Relatively moderate to high computational complexity (k-means is simple)

Table 7.2 Comparison between different compression techniques [24–26, 40].

Technique	Types	Pros	Cons
Lossless Compression	- Run Length Encoding - Area Image Compression - Entropy Encoding - Chain Codes - Predictive Coding - DEFLATE - Adaptive Dictionary Algorithms (LZW)	- Does not add noise to the signal (Noiseless) - Original image can be recovered - Use decomposition/statistics techniques to eliminate/minimize redundancy - Based on finding smart ways to encode the data	- Fewer compression ratios - Used for a few applications such as Medical Imaging, etc.
Lossy Compression	- Chroma Subsampling - Transform Coding - Fractal Compression	- Higher compression ratios - Widely used in many applications	- Does not restore the data in its original form - Decompressed image is close to the original image

Table 7.3 Comparison between breast cancer research work done (segmentation technique) [1, 3, 4, 7, 11, 21].

S.No.	Title	Published year & author	Objective	Techniques/algo/concepts used	Conclusion
1	Hybrid Clustering and Texture Features in Segmentation of Breast Masses in Mammograms	(2018) Moustapha Mohamed Saleck, Abdelmajid EL Moutaouakkil, Mohamed Rmili	The author proposed a method where the mass can be extracted from the ROI based on FCM (Fuzzy C-Means) having setting c=2 and texture features where the user manually elects the area of interest. Further, the procedure of clustering is applied with a proper range limited by a threshold that is interpreted by the huge changes in the texture levels and by the maximum of intensity. This method is put into the Mini MIAS database and later on the show is also measured with some inspected methods.	A. Images Database B. Noise Reduction C. Image Enhancement D. Fuzzy C-Means (FCM) E. Texture Features Extraction F. Morphological Operations	With this paper, a hybrid approach was implemented which was based on the Fuzzy c-means method and texture features which are used for extracting the masses of boundaries from ROI in mammograms. It also uses the fuzzy means FCM method to group the pixel sets. This is limited by the maximum threshold test and grey level into 2 classes where one shows the tumor (the process is replicated by decreasing the threshold the value) and observing the changes in texture features until it suits the threshold. The tumor with high exactness is received when the threshold is suitable and also when there are big changes in texture features.

(*Continued*)

Table 7.3 Comparison between breast cancer research work done (segmentation technique) [1, 3, 4, 7, 11, 21]. (*Continued*)

S.No.	Title	Published year & author	Objective	Techniques/algo/ concepts used	Conclusion
2	Automatic Segmentation of Pectoral Muscle in Mammogram Images Using Global Thresholding and Weak Boundary Approximation	(2017) Syeda Iffat Naz, Monika Shah, Mohammed Imamul Hassan Bhuiyan	The author uses a logical approach in breast mammograms to remove the pectoral muscle and undesired labels are removed by splitting high-intensity regions using convex hulls. To remove the pepper and salt noise the median filter is used and to remove the breast tissues which appear with the pectoral muscle region the global thresholding is used. The author used the mini MIAS database with almost 322 mammograms so that he can study for the performance of the suggested method.	A. Flipping & Removal of Image Label B. Filtering C. Pectoral Muscle Removal Further, other steps are given below: Step 1. Flip an image and remove the labels. Step 2. The left unrelated black region is cropped out. Step 3. After this 1/4th of that image is taken and the median intensity of the nonzero values of the region is set as a global threshold value. Step 4. Then, the thresholding area of unlinked parts are separated by creating a minimal connectivity array.	The author used an efficient and effective method for removing pectoral muscle from mammograms. Also, he used the global threshold which is computed from the max part of the pectoral muscle from mammograms. Later, the image is prepared by using a minimal connectivity array to remove the pieces which are disconnected. Further, the author will study big databases such as DDSM (digital database for screening mammography).

(*Continued*)

Table 7.3 Comparison between breast cancer research work done (segmentation technique) [1, 3, 4, 7, 11, 21]. (*Continued*)

S.No.	Title	Published year & author	Objective	Techniques/algo/ concepts used	Conclusion
				Step 5. The slope of 1 is envisioned on the top middle row of the image, further, all the pieces are removed that lie right to that slope. Step 6. A Window of 5x5 across the image is taken out. Step 7. Finally, the disengaged parts are removed again by the same method described in step 4. Step 8. The image is then recomputed to the original image by padding zeros to it and subtract from the primary image. Step 9. The end image is pectoral muscle removed image.	

(*Continued*)

Table 7.3 Comparison between breast cancer research work done (segmentation technique) [1, 3, 4, 7, 11, 21]. (*Continued*)

S.No.	Title	Published year & author	Objective	Techniques/algo/ concepts used	Conclusion
3	Automated Digital Mammogram Segmentation Using Dispersed Region Growing and Sliding Window Algorithm	(2017) Ayush Shrivastava, Arpit Chaudhary, Devang Kulshreshtha, Vibhav Prakash Singh, Rajeev Srivastava	The author basically aims at segregating the ROI (Region of Interest) from the remaining image. This method begins by removing some labels, tags, and annotations from a mammographic image that uses the morphological opening method. An algorithm, SWA, i.e., Sliding Window Algorithm, to remove the pectoral muscle from mammograms which is important to be done as it becomes difficult to separate the intensity values of pectoral muscles which are the same to that of ROI. Further, to disperse the seeds in different areas instead of a single bright region, the author used DRGA.	A. Artifacts and Label Removal B. Pectoral Muscle Removal Using Sliding Window Algorithm (SWA) C. Dispersed Region Growing Algorithm (DRGA) for Segmentation	The author introduced 2 algorithms, DRGA (dispersed region growing algorithm) and SWA (Sliding window algorithm), for mammogram segmentations to segmentations ROI. These were really useful on the MIAS dataset. The author has given importance to seed selection in the area growing method which is generally neglected and this procedure works well on mammographic images that have microcalcification by dispersing seeds all over.

(*Continued*)

Table 7.3 Comparison between breast cancer research work done (segmentation technique) [1, 3, 4, 7, 11, 21]. (*Continued*)

S.No.	Title	Published year & author	Objective	Techniques/algo/ concepts used	Conclusion
4	Mammogram Segmentation Methods: A Brief Review	(2019) Sarthak Padhi, Suvendu Rup, Sanjay Saxena, Figlu Mohanty	The author tries to cover the effective techniques of segmentation which are used by some researchers to build efficient CADx systems for classifying mammograms. Using this until now, the Active Contour Models and Thresholding are the deformation of splines to compare object outline and intensity- based division to split an image into 2 or more regions respectively. This is further followed by clustering and region- based algorithms that help generate clusters that are established on mathematical standards of inserting pixels into the needed areas.	A. Edge Detection B. Thresholding C. Region Growing D. Watershed Transformation E. Clustering F. Active Contour Models G. Atlas-based Segmentation	The author used some efficient CADx systems for mammogram classification. They used the active contour model which is for deformation of splined to match object outline and thresholding which is an intensity-based division into parts. Further, it is followed by clustering and region-based techniques that help in creating the regions/clusters based on mathematical criteria. Also, it progressed in designing high segmentation techniques and the CADx system proved to be sturdy for different sets of mammograms.

(*Continued*)

Table 7.3 Comparison between breast cancer research work done (segmentation technique) [1, 3, 4, 7, 11, 21]. (*Continued*)

S.No.	Title	Published year & author	Objective	Techniques/algo/ concepts used	Conclusion
5	Performance Analysis of Mammogram CAD System using SVM and KNN Classifier	(2017) D. Saraswathi, E. Srinivasan	The author has proposed the computer-aided-design system (CAD) for identifying mammograms. The images are pre-processed by using ROI which is separated with Otsu's thresholding strategy and an adaptive median filter. Further, the classifier took the removed GLCM features from ROI and classifiers such as KNN and SVM were also used in the computer-aided design system where it analyzed the performance metrics. This helped in demonstrating the automatic identification of cancer with high sensitivity and accuracy in the CAD is more dependable as an aid to radiologists.	1) Pre-processing 2) Segmentation a) Otsu's Thresholding 3) Feature Extraction a) Gray Level Co-occurrence Matrix (GLCM) 4) Classification a) Support Vector Machine b) K-NN (K- Nearest Neighbour)	The author developed a very effective scheme for clustered microcalcifications and masses in mammograms. Also. they have been classifying the developed lesions in this work. Mainly in this work, they have achieved higher classification and false positives are greatly reduced.

(*Continued*)

Table 7.3 Comparison between breast cancer research work done (segmentation technique) [1, 3, 4, 7, 11, 21]. (*Continued*)

S.No.	Title	Published year & author	Objective	Techniques/algo/ concepts used	Conclusion
6	Examination of Digital Mammogram using Otsu's Function and Watershed Segmentation	(2018) S.P. Sachin raj, N. Sri Madhava Raja, M.R. Madhumitha, V. Rajinikanth	In this paper, the author has proposed a technique which is a combination of watershed segmentation and multi-thresholding to analyze the DM (digital mammogram) dataset of mini-MIAS. In the first go, CBA+Otsu is applied to increase the unusual section from the DM and later on, the section has been extracted which is improved one from the WS. Also, the texture features of the extracted section have been computed as per the GLCM. In this study, images, like low, medium, dense, and normal images, are inspected using the suggested method.	A. Image dataset B. Bat algorithm C. Otsu's function D. Segmentation E. Feature extraction	The author has used a combination of WS and multi-thresholding so that they can examine digital mammograms. Earlier, they used CBA+Otsu and later they extracted the section using WS and they used the GLCM for extracting the section. The author has also used images like low, medium, dense, and normal to evaluate using the proposed method which classified the malignant and benign based on values of GLCM. It has been effective in mining the abnormal section from DM.

Table 7.4 Comparison between breast cancer research work done (compression technique) [24–26].

S. no.	Title	Published year & author	Objective	Techniques/algo/ concepts used	Conclusion
1	Two-step evidential fusion approach for accurate breast region segmentation in mammograms	(2018) Rihab Lajili, Karim Kalti, Asma Touil, Basel Solaiman, Najoua Essoukri Ben Amara	The authors proposed a segmentation approach where two techniques are explored individually and the local homogeneity and the grey-scale intensities domain to address the problem of precise breast region segmentation. This is taken as a knowledge origin and is structured using the functions formalism where it was performed using the Dempster's combination rule. Further, the two sources are fused using a frequentative process. There has been a quality enhancement for exact breast border delimitation and ambiguity removal.	1. Foundations of the Dempster–Shafer theory (DST) of evidence 1.1 Basic concepts of DST 1.2 Combination of evidence 2. K-means algorithm 3. 1st info source, grey-scale-based segmentation 3.1 Presentation 3.2 Knowledge modelling and masses estimation 4. 2nd info source local-homogeneity-based segmentation 4.1 Presentation 4.2 Knowledge modelling and masses estimation 5. Information sources fusion	The author addressed the exact issue of accurate breast region segmentation. Due to this, the author proposed a method where segmentation is done on the evidential fusion approach. This resulted in the two complementary info sources. The one method used the image greyscale and the other used the local homogeneity measure. Further, their fusion was executed using the Dempster's combination rule.

(Continued)

Table 7.3 Comparison between breast cancer research work done (segmentation technique) [1, 3, 4, 7, 11, 21]. (*Continued*)

S. no.	Title	Published year & author	Objective	Techniques/algo/ concepts used	Conclusion
2	Enhancement of Mammographic Images in the DCT Compressed Domain	(2018) Marwa Mohiddin, Mohammed Javed	The authors perform a certain case of enhancement which is basically a mammographic image directly in the DCT compressed domain and uses edge-based enhancement. Using this, the cost of recompression and decompression is circumvented. In the suggested method, the quality of the image is found using a few metrics such as MSE, SSIM, & PSNR, and tested on the MIAS dataset. Further, the computation cost of both the domains is observed and performance metrics are measured with the values in the spatial domain.	1. Compressed mammographic images 2. DCT Coefficients in 8X8 block 3. High pass filtering (3X3, 5X5, 7X7 matrix) 4. Modified DCT Coefficients in 8X8 block (Edge enhanced) 5. Edge enhanced compressed image 6. Further medical image analysis by machine	The author introduced an efficient method for enhancing the images using edge segmentation over DCT compressed domain. This helped in improving the contrast and quality of an image. This way it has shown better and comparable results. They concluded by saying the time for computation of enhancement of mammographic images in the DCT domain which is compressed better than the spatial domain. Also, this way the death rate can be reduced.

(*Continued*)

Table 7.3 Comparison between breast cancer research work done (segmentation technique) [1, 3, 4, 7, 11, 21]. (*Continued*)

S. no.	Title	Published year & author	Objective	Techniques/algo/ concepts used	Conclusion
3	Dual Scan Mammoscope (DSM) – A New Portable Photoacoustic Breast Imaging System with Scanning in Craniocaudal Plane	(2019) Nikhila Nyayapathi, Rachel Lim, Huijuan Zhang, Wenhan Zheng, Yuehang Wang, Melinda Tiao, Kwang W. Oh, X. Cynthia Fan, Ermelinda Bonaccio, Kazuaki Takabe, Jun Xia	The author has focused on a new photoacoustic tomography system which gives the perception of angiographic features in mammogram images and the proposed DSM technique. Further, output images received from this technique can be collated to both MRI and mammogram as data is obtained and introduced in the CC plane with which radiologists are most close with. This proposed method gives comfort to the patients as it deals with mild compression, lack of ionizing radiation, non-invasive nature, and fast imaging time. The portable DSM can be stored.	1. System Design 2. Breast Coupling 3. Imaging Procedure 4. Reconstruction and Alignment	The author used the DSM method where both photoacoustic and ultrasonic features of the breast have been acquired. They can be compared directly to both MRI and mammogram. In this lack of ionizing radiation, mild compression, non-invasive, and fast imaging time helps to make comfortable comparisons to other imaging techniques.

7.5 Conclusion

In this paper, I will be using mammogram images to detect breast cancer, which helps us in receiving the best and exact results. Over here. the pre-processing techniques will be using Image flip on all images so that all of them can be aligned in a certain direction. Also, I will be using a technique where the label will be removed by extracting the big area of an image. I will also use the median filter and segmentation methods which will help in removing noise and finding ROI respectively. Further, I will use Global Thresholding for pectoral muscle removal. Once all this is done, then I will use morphological operations and feature extraction using GLCM which will help in getting the spatial relation between pixels. After all this, the CNN will be used to train, test, and measure the performance. Finally, I will get an output where I will be able to identify the benign or malignant tissues.

7.6 Future Work

Based on the above survey, we have thought of a model where we will be using pre-processing techniques, segmentation techniques, morphological operation methods, feature extraction, and classification using CNN. Hence, in the future, I will work on this proposed method so that I can analyze breast cancer before-hand at an early stage.

References

1. Moustapha Mohamed Saleck, Abdelmajid EL Moutaouakkil, Mohamed Rmili; Hybrid Clustering and Texture Features in Segmentation of Breast Masses in Mammograms; 978-1-5386-7266-2/18/$31.00 ©2018 IEEE.
2. Shafiullah Soomro, Kwang Nam Choi; Robust Active Contours For Mammogram Image Segmentation; 978-1-5090-2175-8/17/$31.00 ©2017 IEEE, ICIP 2017.
3. Syeda Iffat Naz, Monika Shah, Mohammed Imamul Hassan Bhuiyan; Automatic Segmentation of Pectoral Muscle in Mammogram Images Using Global Thresholding and Weak Boundary Approximation; 2017 IEEE International WIE Conference on Electrical and Computer Engineering (WIECON-ECE) 18-19 December 2017, WIT, Dehradun, India.
4. Ayush Shrivastava, Arpit Chaudhary, Devang Kulshreshtha, Vibhav Prakash Singh, Rajeev Srivastava; Automated Digital Mammogram Segmentation

Using Dispersed Region Growing and Sliding Window Algorithm; 2017 2nd International Conference on Image, Vision, and Computing.

5. Wentao Zhu, Xiang Xiang, Trac D. Tran, Gregory D. Hager, Xiaohui Xie; ADVERSARIAL DEEP STRUCTURED NETS FOR MASS SEGMENTATION FROM MAMMOGRAMS; 2018 IEEE 15th International Symposium on Biomedical Imaging (ISBI 2018) April 4-7, 2018, Washington, D.C., USA.
6. Arnab Chattaraj, Arpita Das, Mahua Bhattacharya; Mammographic Image Segmentation by Marker Controlled Watershed Algorithm; 2017 IEEE International Conference on Bioinformatics and Biomedicine (BIBM).
7. Sarthak Padhi, Suvendu Rup, Sanjay Saxena, Figlu Mohanty; Mammogram Segmentation Methods: A Brief Review; 2019 2nd International Conference on Intelligent Communication and Computational Techniques (ICCT) Manipal University Jaipur, Sep 28-29, 2019.
8. Monisha Mohan, Lekshmi Priya T, Lekha S Nai; Fuzzy c-means Segmentation on Enhanced Mammograms Using CLAHE and Fourth Order Complex Diffusion; Proceedings of the Fourth International Conference on Computing Methodologies and Communication (ICCMC 2020) IEEE Xplore Part Number:CFP20K25-ART; ISBN:978-1-7281-4889-2.
9. Aulia Rahmatika, Astri Handayani, Agung Wahyu Setiawan; Automated Segmentation of Breast Tissue and Pectoral Muscle in Digital Mammography; 978-1-5386-8448-1/19/$31.00 ©2019 IEEE.
10. Kshema, M. Jayesh George and D. Anto Sahaya Dhas; Efficient Mammographic Mass Segmentation Techniques: A Review; This full-text paper was peer-reviewed and accepted to be presented at the IEEE WiSPNET 2017 conference.
11. D. Saraswathi, E. Srinivasan; Performance Analysis of Mammogram CAD System using SVM and KNN Classifier; International Conference on Inventive Systems and Control (ICISC-2017).
12. G.R. Jothilakshmi, Arun Raaza; Effective Detection of Mass Abnormalities and its Classification Using Multi-SVM Classifier with Digital Mammogram Images; IEEE International Conference on Computer, Communication, and Signal Processing (ICCCSP-2017).
13. P. Shanmugavadivu, S.G. Lakshmi Narayanan; PSYCHOANALYSIS OF CHARACTERISTIC CONTRAST ENHANCEMENT OF DIGITAL MAMMOGRAM IMAGE; 978-1-5090-3239-6/17/$31.00©2017 IEEE.
14. Seng Roty, Cholatip Wiratkapun, Rawesak Tanawongsuwan, Sukanya Phongsuphap; Analysis of Microcalcification Features for Pathological Classification of Mammograms; The 2017 Biomedical Engineering International Conference (BMEiCON-2017).
15. Jaime S. Cardoso, Nuno Marques, Neeraj Dhungel, G. Carneiro, A. P. Bradley; MASS SEGMENTATION IN MAMMOGRAMS: A CROSS-SENSOR COMPARISON OF DEEP AND TAILORED FEATURES; 978-1-5090-2175-8/17/$31.00©2017 IEEE, ICIP 2017.

16. Mario Muštra; Creating Segmentation Masks for Benchmark in Digital Mammography; 978-1-5386-4927-5/18/$31.00 ©2018 IEEE.
17. Santhos Kumar A., A. Kumar, V. Bajaj and G. K. Singh; Fractional-Order Darwinian Swarm Intelligence Inspired Multilevel Thresholding for Mammogram Segmentation; International Conference on Communication and Signal Processing, April 3-5, 2018, India.
18. Adel Dallali, Amel Slimen, Salim El Khediri, Youssra Khemili; Detection of lesion in mammograms; 978-1-5386-4449-2/18/$31.00 ©2018 IEEE.
19. M. Manikandan, P. Surendar; A Survey on Detection of Micro Calcification in Mammogram Images; 2017 International Conference on Electrical, Instrumentation and Communication Engineering (ICEICE2017).
20. SHUYI LI, MIN DONG, GUANGMING DU AND XIAOMIN MU; Attention Dense-U-Net for Automatic Breast Mass Segmentation in Digital Mammogram; Received April 2, 2019, accepted April 23, 2019, date of publication May 7, 2019, date of current version May 17, 2019.
21. S.P. Sachin raj, N. Sri Madhava Raja, M.R. Madhumitha, V. Rajinikanth; Examination of Digital Mammogram using Otsu's Function and Watershed Segmentation; 2018 4th International Conference on Biosignals, Images and Instrumentation (ICBSII), 22-24 March 2018, Chennai.
22. LARBI Messaouda, ROUINI Abdelghani, Zoubeida MESSALI, Samira LARBI; Medical Image Segmentation Based on Wavelet Transformation and Level set method; The 4th International Conference on Power Electronics and their Applications (ICPEA), 25-27 September 2019, Elazig, Turkey.
23. Dilovan Asaad Zebari, Habibollah Haron, Subhi R. M. Zeebaree, Diyar Qader Zeebaree; Enhance the Mammogram Images for Both Segmentation and Feature Extraction Using Wavelet Transform; 2019 International Conference on Advanced Science and Engineering (ICOASE), University of Zakho, Duhok Polytechnic University, Kurdistan Region, Iraq.
24. Rihab Lajili, Karim Kalti, Asma Touil, Basel Solaiman, Najoua Essoukri Ben Amara; Two-step evidential fusion approach for accurate breast region segmentation in mammograms; IET Image Process., 2018, Vol. 12 Iss. 11, pp. 1972-1982 © The Institution of Engineering and Technology 2018.
25. Marwa Mohiddin, Mohammed Javed; Enhancement of Mammographic Images in the DCT Compressed Domain; 2018 International Conference on Control, Power, Communication and Computing Technologies (ICCPCCT).
26. Nikhila Nyayapathi, Rachel Lim, Huijuan Zhang, Wenhan Zheng, Yuehang Wang, Melinda Tiao, Kwang W. Oh, X. Cynthia Fan, Ermelinda Bonaccio, Kazuaki Takabe, Jun Xia; Dual Scan Mammoscope (DSM) – A New Portable Photoacoustic Breast Imaging System with Scanning in Craniocaudal Plane; 0018-9294 (c) 2019 IEEE.
27. Juan Jing, Tao Wan, Jiajia Cao, Zengchang Qin; AN IMPROVED HYBRID ACTIVE CONTOUR MODEL FOR NUCLEAR SEGMENTATION ON BREAST CANCER HISTOPATHOLOGY; 978-1-4799-2349-6/16/$31.00 ©2016 IEEE.

28. R.Meena Prakash, K. Bhuvaneshwari, M. Divya, K. Jamuna Sri, A.Sulaiha Begum; Segmentation of thermal infrared breast images using K-Means, FCM and EM algorithms for breast cancer detection; 2017 International Conference on Innovations in Information, Embedded and Communication Systems (ICIIECS).
29. B.K.GAYATHRI, P.RAAJAN; A Survey of Breast Cancer Detection Based on Image Segmentation Techniques; 978-1-4673-8437-7/16/$31.00 ©2016 IEEE.
30. Haeyun Lee, Jinhyoung Park, Jae Youn Hwang; Channel Attention Module with Multi-scale Grid Average Pooling for Breast Cancer Segmentation in an Ultrasound Image; DOI 10.1109/TUFFC.2020.2972573, IEEE Transactions on Ultrasonics, Ferroelectrics, and Frequency Control.
31. Chaitanya Varma and Omkar Sawant; An Alternative Approach to Detect Breast Cancer using Digital Image Processing Techniques; International Conference on Communication and Signal Processing, April 3-5, 2018, India.
32. ABDELHAMEED IBRAHIM, SHAIMAA MOHAMMED, HESHAM ARAFAT ALI, and SHERIF E. HUSSEIN; Breast Cancer Segmentation from Thermal Images Based on Chaotic Salp Swarm Algorithm; DOI 10.1109/ACCESS.2020.3007336, IEEE Access.
33. Nicholas Lennox, Bertram Haskins; Comparison of segmentation methods for the detection of breast cancer using thermal images; Authorized licensed use limited to: University of Canberra. Downloaded on June 09,2020 at 00:38:07 UTC from IEEE Xplore. Restrictions apply.
34. Nagendra Kumar M, Anand Jatti, C K Narayanappa; Probable Region Identification and segmentation in Breast Cancer using the DLCNN; Second International Conference on Smart Systems and Inventive Technology (ICSSIT 2019) IEEE Xplore Part Number: CFP19P17-ART; ISBN:978-1-7281-2119-2.
35. Olmo Zavala-Romero, Anke Meyer-Baese, Marc B.I. Lobbes; BREAST LESION SEGMENTATION SOFTWARE FOR DCE-MRI: AN OPEN SOURCE GPGPU BASED OPTIMIZATION; 2018 IEEE 15th International Symposium on Biomedical Imaging (ISBI 2018) April 4-7, 2018, Washington, D.C., USA.
36. E. Kozegar, M. Soryani, H. Behnam, M. Salamati and T. Tan; Mass Segmentation in Automated 3-D Breast Ultrasound Using Adaptive Region Growing and Supervised Edge -Based Deformable Model; DOI 10.1109/TMI.2017.2787685, IEEE Transactions on Medical Imaging, 0278-0062 (c) 2017 IEEE.
37. Shida Wang, Jin Huang; Breast Lesion Segmentation in Ultrasound Images by CDeep3M; 2020 International Conference on Computer Engineering and Application (ICCEA).
38. Hafiz Talha Iqbal, Bilal Majeed, Uzair Khan and Muhammad Awais Bin Altaf; An Infrared High classification Accuracy Hand-held Machine Learning based Breast-Cancer Detection System; 978-1-5090-0617-5/19/$31.00 ©2019 IEEE.

39. Kushangi Atrey, Bikesh Kumar Singh, Abhijit Roy, Narendra K. Bodhey; Breast cancer detection and validation using dual modality imaging; 2020 First International Conference on Power, Control and Computing Technologies (ICPC2T).
40. Kihan Park, Wenjin Chen, Marina A. Chekmareva, David J. Foran, and Jaydev P. Desai; Electromechanical Coupling Factor of Breast Tissue as a Biomarker for Breast Cancer; DOI 10.1109/TBME.2017.2695103, IEEE Transactions on Biomedical Engineering.

8

IoT Technologies for Smart Healthcare

Rehab A. Rayan[1*], Imran Zafar[2] and Christos Tsagkaris[3]

[1]Department of Epidemiology, High Institute of Public Health, Alexandria University, Egypt
[2]Department of Bioinformatics and Computational Biology, Virtual University of Pakistan, Punjab Pakistan
[3]Faculty of Medicine, University of Crete, Heraklion, Greece

Abstract

There has been a long-term relationship between health and technology. Yet, lately, there is rapid financing and progress towards the concept of the Internet of Things (IoT) and growth in Big Data research for efficiently dealing with huge interdisciplinary, multi-dimensional, diverse, and scattered data. Such development has shown novel potential in personalized health services. The IoT has revealed a paradigm shift in health, introducing benefits like availability, accessibility, and cost-effective delivery of individualized care. Although Health IoT has provided more options for satisfying health demands, there are many obstacles that should be tackled to make proper, flexible, secure, and effective systems that deal with such demands. Enabling such a shift would need the hardware and software entities to work together to reach wide technical innovations. This chapter covers such crucial elements of modern techniques of IoT for intelligent health such as sophisticated distributive health systems, wearable sensors, and Big Data analytics. It describes novel insights and shows interesting research problems like security, interoperability, scalability, and interfacing between humans, networks, and devices.

***Keywords*:** IoT, e-Health, m-Health, telemedicine, wearable sensors

**Corresponding author*: rehab.a.rayan@gmail.com

M. Niranjanamurthy, Hemant Kumar Gianey and Amir H. Gandomi (eds.) Advances in Data Science and Analytics: Concepts and Paradigms, (181–202) © 2023 Scrivener Publishing LLC

8.1 Introduction

Data analytics have grown into a critical tool because of the evidently existing ambiguous and disparate data worldwide. In healthcare, adapting approaches for data analytics is required for the routinely collected complex big data in many institutions. Examining such data could promote effective healthcare delivery at less cost. The entire world is challenged by critical public health issues regarding controlling highly growing epidemics, the chronically diseased population and elderly people, maternal and infant death, and wretched livelihood factors with increased pollution, poor drinking water quality, and hygiene. Recently, however, the growing demand for more healthcare and the conventional healthcare-unit-oriented approach to mandating patients attend to a healthcare provider remains predominating. For instance, to control chronic diseases, patients must visit the healthcare facility frequently where the healthcare provider monitors the progress of the disease and changes therapy according to medical examinations. Healthcare facilities depend upon a dynamic, disease-provider-oriented approach where the patient is missing as a key player in delivering healthcare [1]. The chief limitations of this approach are mentioned as follows.

Time-constraints: While the quantities of diseased and disabled individuals per population are constantly growing, healthcare providers cannot devote adequate quality time to every case. Rapid examinations yield insufficient history about the patient's lifestyle involving diet, sleeping patterns, physical activity, and societal encounters among other factors. Grasping such elements is vital to accurately diagnosing and managing patients.

Monitoring Compliance: Usually, healthcare providers cannot monitor patients' adherence to prescribed therapies like special diets, medicines, or rehabilitation practices resulting in future hospital admissions, healthcare expenses, and economic load on patients [2].

The Elderly Population: The global number of geriatric people, aged over 60 years, is expected to expand from 841 million individuals in 2013 to almost over 2 billion individuals by 2050 (over 200%,), hence, more healthcare resources would be needed to care for such a growing elderly population [1].

Urbanization: The World Health Organization (WHO) expected that 70% of the world inhabitants would live in urban zones by 2015, showing that densely populated urban cities, potential epidemic centers' promoting the rapid spread of infectious diseases, would demand more infrastructure for the healthcare of this growing population.

Lack of Health Personnel: The demand for healthcare services and, hence, providers, in both urban and rural settings, keeps rising, which requires adopting telemedicine interventions Healthcare Cost: The dramatically growing healthcare expenses are challenging. For instance, in 2017, the United States has spent almost $327 billion on diabetes healthcare, up 26% since 2012 [3].

In recent years, healthcare has been increasingly using IT to deliver smart systems aimed at speeding up health diagnostics and treatment. These systems provide smart health monitoring and medical automation services in various contexts and environments (hospitals, workplaces, houses, while you are on the go...), allowing a major reduction in the cost of doctor visits and a general increase in the quality of patient care [4]. In this sense, the large proliferation of powerful embedded hardware, combined with the production of smart medical sensors and ubiquitous healthcare devices, has significantly altered the way healthcare approaches the globe through the Internet of Medical Things (IoMT) [5].

Smart Health (s-Health) is an area that has developed as a branch of two markets: smart cities and e-Health [6]. Smart cities can be described as cities that are heavily focused on information and communication technologies that invest in human and social resources by fostering economic development, participatory governance, resource management, sustainability, and efficient mobility to enhance the quality of life of their people while ensuring the dignity and safety of citizens [7]. E-health can be defined as "an emerging area at the intersection of medical informatics, public health, and business, with reference to the provision or improvement of health services and information via the Internet and related technologies." In a wider context, the word characterizes not just a technical advancement, but also a state of mind, a way of thinking, an attitude and a contribution to the network, global thinking, using information and communication technology to enhance treatment globally, regionally, and worldwide. There is a cross between s-Health and Mobile Health (m-Health).

8.2 Literature Review

8.2.1 IoT-Based Smart Health

Patient-centered care (PCC) is a growing health framework tailored to the patient's personal healthcare needs that were initially designed by the Picker Institute in 1988 and introduced by the Picker/Commonwealth Program. In 2001, the Institute of Medicine described PCC in the landmark report as healthcare based on recognized collaboration between providers, patients, and families valuing the patient's preference, informing and engaging patients in decision-making regarding their care [8].

PCC was evidently successful on small-scales, however, it is promising for larger scale despite competing with hospital-centered care. PCC will not cancel clinics or hospitals, but it would integrate such organizations in a mutual framework for patients' healthcare via the IoT. IoT offers services through a network of sensors, actuators, telecommunication, cloud computing, and Big Data via the Internet. IoT could be tailored to address the current limitations in health by providing timely and effective services at lower expenses, leading to a sustainable healthcare setting. The Healthcare setting could be classified into big healthcare organizations such as hospitals, small ones such as clinics or pharmacies, and non-clinical settings such as homes or communities [9].

Many patients seek hospitals for healthcare especially operations where hospitals could apply innovative technologies. An IoT-connected intelligent ambulance enables diagnosing cases, hence the hospital and healthcare providers could efficiently get ready prior to the arrival of the patient into the hospital. Intelligent ambulances need clinical diagnostic sensors, a protected connection to the hospital, and techniques to smartly manage processes and devices. For instance, applying the IoT in the operation rooms, intensive or primary care units for efficiently transferring data and harmonizing tasks among the medical personnel and devices [10].

Primary healthcare (PHC) providers are major health caregivers to several patients. IoT can secure PHC physicians a 2-way communication for reserving appointments without phone calls and remotely logging into laboratory findings before patients encounter. IoT would serve as an affordable and time-saving option for screening patients remotely prior to face-to-face interaction with a physician. IoT could facilitate timely confirming insurance coverage and prescribing cost-effective home IoT-self monitoring devices.

Globally, mobile clinics are grappling more attention. In African rural areas, mobile clinics deliver affordable and high-quality care with no need to approach official healthcare providing organizations. For the minimal infrastructure in a mobile clinic, IoT could highly enhance their care-delivering capacity by communicating distantly with hospitals for more specialized diagnosing or therapeutic services [11].

Nowadays, telemedicine is the major IoT representative with an expected global market worth $45.5 billion in 2019 along with estimated expansion in 2026 to reach approximately $175.5 billion [12]. Smartphones are almost in all hands worldwide enabling networking via IoT with other sensors for future tele-screening. Using smartphones, patients could monitor their own health and produce data, which could predict upcoming health-related events. Meanwhile, patients could visit healthcare providers virtually via teleconferencing and growing remote healthcare services would decrease health systems' medical personnel.

Now, more individuals are aware of the significance of early prevention and keeping good health over requiring clinical care later. People are benefiting from IoT networking in self-monitoring medical devices, sports technologies, and fitness-tracking wearables, which allow ongoing monitoring of health. IoT could build an economic structure to minimize expenses on health insurance by using health monitoring to incentivize wellness, creating a more effective, patient-oriented framework, and motivating active patient engagement in healthcare.

Telemedicine services could limit the elderly, disabled, and chronically diseased people's number of visits to healthcare facilities. A technology infrastructure at home could support them effectively and invisibly, facilitating patients living further freely with better quality and well-being. Ambient-assisted life, a European model for an intelligent home, could enhance personal abilities via a sensitive and responsive automated setting. Now, IoT exists in digital home marketplaces such as home controlling systems and gizmos through a smartphone, hence, IoT could serve elderly patients needing healthcare. For instance, intelligent toilets could routinely analyze urine without visiting the physician. Intelligent homes could adjust noise and lights satisfying the sensory needs of autistic patients [13].

Globally, people are moving towards cities, adding to the load over the infrastructure there. Smart cities and connected societies are rising via linking and merging infrastructures to render cities more proficient, affordable, and sustainable. IoT models could supply timely data enabling individuals' rapid and informed decisions. Health is a key system in cities, therefore, it should be integrated into the smart cities' infrastructure. For instance, broad ecological sensors could send data to central sites to be accessed via the health system. Ecological data on contaminants, temperature, humidity, polluted water, or allergens could be disseminated timely to people to avoid health threats. For instance, asthma patients could be alerted to abandon sites high in dust or pollen counts. IoT could merge smart traffic lights to help in routing ambulances, saving lives via collaboration with transportation infrastructure, but IoT needs a smart setting allowing connectivity between stakeholders including healthcare providers, patients, healthcare facilities, cities, and societies.

8.2.2 Advantages of Applying IoT in Health

The Healthcare industry is in a desperate state. Healthcare services are more expensive than ever, the global population has increased, and the incidence of chronic problems is increasing, as healthcare technology promotes consumer engagement and encourages health issues. In such a situation, the possibility of remote care is welcomed more than ever. However, existing health frameworks are not incorporated into technologies that can improve the quality of care by updating them in proper time with patient data and enabling them to take steps in treatment. Novel patient tracking solutions enable physicians to improve the quality of care while focusing on overall cost reduction [14]. What we are approaching is a world where basic health care will be out of reach for most people, a large part of society will be unproductive because of old age, and people will be more prone to chronic illness. Can we assume that this was not the end of the matter, no matter what development of the electronic gateway that people have preserved, although automation will never prevent the population from aging or removing serious diseases it can, in terms of versatility, try to do health benefits in the backpack?

Medical diagnostics consume a large part of hospital costs. Technology can move medical control routines to the patient's home (home-centered) from a hospital (hospital-centered). The right diagnosis also reduces the need to stay in hospital. A modern framework, known as IoT, has a wide application in many areas, including telecommunications [15]. A common expectation is the complete implementation of this model in the healthcare sector, as it enables healthcare facilities to function more efficiently and clinics to provide excellent treatment [16]. There are unmatched benefits of using this technology-based treatment system that can improve the speed and affordability of treatments and improve patients' health [17]. The actual world is connected by IoT to the virtual world of the Internet. Household appliances (such as air purifiers, thermostats, etc.), vehicles, heavy machinery, building, medical devices, and the human body are part of the physical environment [18]. Applying IoT technology to healthcare aims to improve the quality of life of patients, the level of treatment of chronic illnesses, hazard warnings, and life-saving treatments.

There are several uses of IoT for healthcare.

1. Health tracking: The portable devices of today can detect basic human body movements, evaluate human actions, and assess health status. Smart portable devices can reduce patient anxiety and reduce resource waste (such as

smartwatches) [19]. In traditional hospitals, this supplements other responsive health monitoring systems.

2. Patient Help for Health Records: You may remind patients to take medication on time through certain IoT devices in the clinic. Network devices such as electrocardiograms, blood oxygen, and blood pressure will strengthen the continuous structure of the assessment, monitoring, and support for patients and caregivers, enhancing clinical results [20].
3. Service Enhancing: IoT can help link cars with network systems. When a vehicle has an accident, by submitting the location and address of the accident, the device can determine the seriousness of the accident and assist the traffic control department and health center. This will encourage the injured to get treatment quickly [21].
4. Resource Collection for Large-Scale Data Analysis: Large amounts of health data can be produced by health IoT. Health data collection, mining, and usage will further encourage and enhance the production of IoT health [22].

Recently, an increasing interest has arisen in architectures that recognize the partnership between Cloud, Fog, and Edge computing. The key objective is to take full advantage of the capacity for managing not only usable data but also data processing, analysis, correlation, and inference of low-level edge nodes and fog levels. As the intelligent mapping of computational and resource management data across nodes proves to meet the stringent requirements of IoMT systems, such approaches represent a promising response to integrating efficient distributed healthcare applications and services.

8.3 Findings

8.3.1 Significant Features and Applications of IoT in Health

The main applications of IoT in healthcare pertain to mobile health, ambient assisted living (AAL), medications, and implants. The IoT applications in mHealth can be vaguely divided into two categories: apps developed for healthcare professionals and institutions and apps developed for patients, carers, and healthcare workers. Their key features for patients are continuous and real-time remote monitoring, prevention of chronic diseases, early diagnosis of exacerbations (aided by wearables), and proper documentation of health records. Carers, defined here as relatives of patients or third individuals involved in patients' care at home, can enjoy the benefits of IoT smart healthcare through AI-assisted helplines and tracking systems. Employing these modalities can prioritize carers facing an urgent situation. This can also provide carers with educational resources and ad hoc information [23, 24]. Regarding healthcare workers, the advantages of IoT based mHealth comprise flexible staff mobility and performance, speeding up collection and processing of patient data, mitigation of risk of mistakes and decrease of human error risk, and cost-effective treatment, considering the direct and indirect cost of healthcare in the long run [25, 26].

The IoT technologies for ambient assisted living include but are not limited to smart homes and smart environments, ambient assisted living (AAL), agent-based pervasive computing and decision-making methods, and IoT sensing technologies (wireless sensor networks, smart sensors, gateways, etc.). The purpose of these modalities is the creation of smart services and automation features in private and public spaces. The IoT and smart systems' infrastructures comprise intelligent personal assistants, cloud computing, and smart environment paradigms. Easing the lives of older or disabled people can be one of the first goals of the use of this technology in the community [27, 28]. The constant measurement of vitals with patient–friendly devices can help both in detecting emergencies and in properly monitoring the patients. For example, wearable glucose calculators cannot only warn a patient with diabetes about low levels of glucose, they can also detect asymptomatic incidents of hypoglycemia or spikes in blood glucose following a certain food intake. Once the patient or the physician connects the wearable to a smartphone, a full record of this information will be available optimizing the course of treatment [29, 30]. Gradually, wearables may effectively process their input leading to essential decision-making outputs. In ML, widespread collection of patients' data can act as a multiplier of capacity [31, 32].

For medicines, IoT has a great potential both in research and in everyday clinical practice. Drug repurposing has been improved with IoT systems that are capable of compiling and comparing data regarding the chemical structure and clinical features of existing medicines. Regarding research, IoT applications can speed up the collection and processing of data from laboratory experiments to clinical trials. Mokou *et al.* (2020) have described a model of IoT-based drug repurposing for bladder cancer, which can be applied to other neoplastic diseases as well [33]. In terms of clinical practice, IoT can transform the logistics of pharmacies for drug-administration within clinics. Skarmeta *et al.* (2014) have proposed a model of interconnecting patients, physicians, pharmaceutical companies, and regulatory bodies for the timely detection of adverse events. Although confidentiality and anonymization concerns need to be taken into consideration, this is an example of the potential of IoT-based smart healthcare in contemporary medical practice [34]. Tracking or enhancing patients' compliance to pharmaceutical treatments with wearables has also been attempted [35, 36].

The concept of implants is not new in medicine. From pacemakers to neuromodulation and pain management devices, biomedical technology has devised solutions enhancing or replacing a physiological function of the human body. Essentially, what medical implants and IoT have in common is wearables. Implants are the penultimate version of wearable devices. In most cases, they require interventional placement methods and they are expected to remain on the patient for a considerable amount of time. What IoT brings to conventional implants is interconnectivity. So far, patients would visit a healthcare professional to collect and assess the measurements of an implanted device. IoT-based implants provide actual-time monitoring, thorough data collection, and storing in (mostly) online/cloud-based databases [32, 37]. Implants pose greater risks than wearables that can be removed in case of dysfunction. Researchers and manufacturers have issued concerns regarding the interaction between implantable devices, and particularly pacemakers, with IoT signals [38]. A growing body of evidence is focusing on tackling this challenge through electromagnetic filters and standard electromagnetic compatibility tests [39].

8.3.1.1 *Simultaneous Monitoring and Reporting*

Real-time monitoring via mobile networks can save lives in the event of a medical emergency, such as heart failure, diabetes, asthma attacks, etc. [40]. With real-time diagnostic monitoring with a smart healthcare device connected to a mobile app, connected sensors are used to collect necessary medical data and use the mobile network to give a doctor the message received. A study released by the Center for Linked Health Policy showed that there was a 50 percent reduction in 30-day readmission because of remote monitoring of patients with heart failure. The IoT system retrieves and transmits health data: blood pressure, oxygen, blood sugar levels, weight, and ECG [41]. This information is stored in the cloud and can be shared with an accredited doctor, insurance agent, a healthcare provider, or an external consultant to access the information collected regardless of time, place, or unit.

8.3.1.2 End-to-End Connectivity and Affordability

With the help of mobile healthcare technology and other new developments and next-generation treatment facilities, IoT will simplify the emergency management experience. Compatibility, network-to-network connectivity, data availability, and information sharing to determine quality healthcare services are supported by the IoT for socialized care. Link technology including Bluetooth technology, Wi-Fi, Z-Wave, ZigBee, and other creative methods can facilitate the diagnosis of diseases and illnesses in patients and can also be creative in healthcare professionals' treatments [42]. By minimizing unnecessary visits, using high-quality facilities, and optimizing distribution and planning, technology-driven installation reduces costs.

8.3.1.3 Data Analysis

According to its real-time use, the enormous amount of knowledge of a biomedical front surface in a brief time is difficult to store and manage if access to the cloud is not convenient. It is also a tough investment for caregivers to collect and manually review data collected from various devices and sources. IoT devices can capture, report, and analyze information in actual time and reduce the need to store raw data [43]. We can do all this over clouds with only access to final graph reports from vendors. In addition, healthcare practices enable organizations to gain vital health research and data-driven insights that speed up decision-making and are less susceptible to error.

8.3.1.4 Tracking, Alerts, and Remote Medical Care

In life-threatening situations, time is critical. Medical embedded systems collect useful information and send data for real-time monitoring to physicians while sending texts via smartphone devices and other community facilities to individuals on important aspects. Reports and warnings provide a strong insight into the patient's status, regardless of location and time. It also helps to build alternatives that are well known and provide fast treatment. In this way, IoT facilitates real-time warning, reporting, monitoring, and practical treatments, enhances physicians' accuracy and effective interventions, and improves the overall performance of patient care.

Providers of healthcare will call a doctor who is in an immediate situation several kilometers away with smartphone devices. Doctors will review patients easily with healthcare transportation solutions and identify diseases when they are on the move. Via linked systems, machines can transmit drugs based on patient medications and disease-related data and many healthcare supply chains are also available. The IoT will improve hospital patient treatment. This would decrease the comprehensive health treatment of people.

8.3.1.5 *Research*

IoT for health can also be used for research. This is because IoT allows us to get an enormous amount of data about the patient's condition, which may have taken several years if we had collected it individually. Such recorded information would be used for prior results that will assist scientific research. Thus, IoT can not only save time but also our research money. In medical research, therefore, the IoT has an important influence. It facilitates the introduction of major and expanded medical treatments. IoT is used in several techniques that improve the quality of treatment that patients receive. IoT is now also updating existing devices by using intelligent software embedding chips. This chip improves the care and treatment needed for a patient.

8.3.1.6 *Patient-Generated Health Data (PGHD)*

All health-related information created or reported by patients or caregivers is patient-generated health information. PGHD contains information that relates to the patient's health or care history, lifestyle choices, and symptoms that are reported by patients or accessed from smartphones and medical devices that are approved by the Internet. The major difference between PGHD and the data that doctors receive is that patients are primarily educated and can share the previous information.

Remote control of patients is a blessing for people living in daycare or hospitals. Small IoT-based devices can monitor PGHD that can be modified directly by educators and physicians. If an experimental treatment appears to be ineffective, this is an effective way of maintaining the patient's health and proposing changes to the method. Some other benefits of remote monitoring of patients include diagnosis of acute illnesses before they become too severe and detection of drug and alcohol problems with digital drugs in patients seeking care for heart problems.

8.3.1.7 *Management of Chronic Diseases and Preventative Care*

Diseases such as diabetes, heart attack, cancer, obesity, arthritis, and stroke, among others, are becoming more common. It is necessary for individuals affected by these conditions to often take better care of themselves between their medical appointments, meaning they would benefit from IoT-based devices. Besides other devices, such as a glucometer, test equipment, and asthma instruments, flexible instruments can help patients keep track of their health. In addition, Internet-enabled devices store in the cloud their health-related data, which can then be accessed by professionals.

In the medical industry, introducing the IoT will also be beneficial for overweight people who are not recovering from illness and want to avoid problems in the future. Health information can be obtained regularly from anyone and can be shared with caregivers. This will help recognize even a mild issue and stop long-term illness.

8.3.1.8 Home-Based and Short-Term Care

Caregivers can also recognize those who are good enough to stay in their own homes and let them monitor their well-being with IoT-based technology. By tracking their condition in an actual time using data obtained by these devices, they can instantly take care of those who need it. Short-term treatment can be given to patients who have already been discharged from the hospital after an operation or after recovery for an emergency. This treatment method eliminates the need to visit the hospital during the recovery process, enabling patients outside the facility to receive high-quality healthcare.

8.4 Case Study: CyberMed as an IoT-Based Smart Health Model

CyberMed was founded in 2016 and is described as an innovative addition to the telehealth market. CyberMed's products and services merge IoT and telemedicine, enabling people to use medical devices such as digital stethoscopes or pulse oximeters. Patients can use these items during their telemedicine appointments. The collected data gets transmitted to the cloud and becomes instantly available to the doctor, who cannot perform physical examination otherwise. The major challenge that CyberMed addresses is the inability of physicians to thoroughly assess a patient with conventional telecommunication means such as telephone or video calls. The lack of means and experience prolongs the struggle of the patient, increases the risk of mismanagement, and may cause higher expenses if the patient is unnecessarily transported to a hospital [44].

CyberMed offered a comprehensive telehealth approach with actual time modalities and data storing capacity. Healthcare professionals have more means to assess the patient and a detailed record of each consultation. CyberMed's app is known as CDoc. It is compatible with Windows, iOS, and Android, allowing patients to have a doctor visit without leaving their home. Its principal success is the active involvement of the patients in the management of their own health. In a patient-centric communication context, the patient becomes responsible for the accuracy of his vitals and assists the doctor to examine them and make a diagnosis. CyberMed is currently nationwide in the US. It is the first company to bring medical records, telemedicine, and IoT devices together given that it owns and develops all its own components [45].

8.5 Discussions

8.5.1 Limitations of Adopting IoT in Health

Many countries around the world have increasingly tried to integrate new technology into different areas of life. Mobile computer applications have become popular in many areas such as smart homes, e-health, green infrastructure, intelligent network devices, and many more. Some industry watchdogs noted in 2018 that IoT adoption was still in its infancy in Southeast Asia, with just 8 percent adopting the technology. A Gartner Technology Agenda survey conducted in early 2019 by CIOs in Southeast Asia revealed that 11 percent of CIOs rated IoT as their "favorite technology for a game change," while 21 percent said they would increase IoT spending in 2019. Why is IoT adoption not more rapid and widespread with too much hype? Despite the rapid proliferation of actual applications on the Internet, it cannot address many of the security constraints and issues that have recently become a priority for most researchers in this field. IoT, with online patient health monitoring and the use of recently conducted clinical trials, continues to increase in cases of care use [46]. In healthcare, the risks and disadvantages of using smart devices are:

8.5.1.1 Data Security and Privacy

IoT devices can pose a threat to users' security and privacy. Unauthorized access to IoT computers will put people's treatment and their private data at extreme risk [47] to replication, capture, organization, and transmition of health data to the cloud via wireless networks, especially clinical and smartphones. Prefix replication, impersonation attack, wavelength interference, and cloud monitoring are available for the device layer. Traffic is redirected through a man-in-center attack during cloud browsing to allow command injections directly to a device. A direct link attack is proposed using a service discovery protocol such as universal plug-and-play or Bluetooth low energy (BLE) features for locating and targeting IoT devices.

The main problem and danger with IoT technology in general and in the health sector seem to be the security of patient information and confidentiality. Using purpose and configuration, IoT devices collect and transmit cloud information in real-time for data processing. The infrastructure for receiving and processing data will be designed and optimized to be scalable to collect, process, and store data in real-time from millions of research model units to gain insights. However, most IoT devices that receive data suffer from a lack of data standards and protocols. In addition, there is still a significant amount of confusion concealing legislation on data ownership and privacy issues. Cybercriminals who may use stolen data or information for medical identity fraud or extortion are sensitive and useful to patient information collected by various connected devices or portable devices. A hacker or criminal can use patient data to establish a false identity or to purchase drugs or diagnostic supplies that can be resold. Harmful hackers can also claim false compensation claims on behalf of the individual [48].

Telco's infrastructure, equipment suppliers, hospitals, and other participants must take constructive measures to ensure that their communities are safe. When buying "devices or stuff" for healthcare, especially devices that hospitals need to use, hospitals and other healthcare providers must be extremely picky. Hospitals and IT providers need to discuss how best to host large and complex infrastructure given these limitations in IoT technology.

8.5.1.2 Connectivity

To authenticate, authorize, and connect various nodes on a network, today's IoT ecosystems depend on a centralized client/server paradigm. Networks will become bottlenecks as they expand to join billions of users, though adequate now. A potential solution can involve pushing certain tasks to the limit, for example, fog computing is an architecture that uses edge devices to conduct a large amount of local computing, storage, communication, and routing across the backbone of the Internet. Edge devices are usually routers that provide quicker and more powerful backbones and exchanges with authenticated access. The trend is to make the peripheral device smart and the core device "dumb and fast." Here, smart devices such as

IoT, centers take over mission-critical tasks and data processing and analytical roles are taken over by cloud servers. Peer-to-peer communications are other options, where devices directly recognize and authenticate each other and share information without a central server. This model will have its own set of challenges, like security, but with emerging technologies such as blockchain that can be met.

8.5.1.3 *Compatibility and Data Integration*

There is currently no international standard for device identification and tracking efficiency. There is no consensus on IoT standards and requirements, so products made by different vendors do not fit in well with each other. The lack of precision prevents large-scale integration of the IoT, reducing its possible effectiveness. Security and integrity remain important and prohibit users from using artificial intelligence for therapeutic purposes, as there is a risk of violating or hacking remote healthcare strategies. The leakage of confidential information about the health and location of the patient and the manipulation of sensor data can have important implications, which outweigh the benefits of IoT [49]. This limitation is the easiest to address. Manufacturers of this technology, such as Bluetooth, USB, etc., only need to recognize one standard. There is nothing innovative or revolutionary available.

8.5.1.4 *Implementation Cost*

While IoT aims to reduce healthcare costs in the long term, the cost of clinical integration and employee training is very high. Has IoT been the solution to the increase in the cost of medicines? Let us summarize why a currency's value or financial costs are a major opioid crisis for the IoT. The growing prevalence of care is influencing today more than ever. Technical advancements in IoT have never been seen to cover rising medical costs, but on the other hand, they are becoming more expensive [50].

8.5.1.5 *Complexity and Risk of Errors*

The performance of compatible detection devices can be affected by disk failures, anomalies, or even power outages, putting healthcare facilities at risk. Also, skipping a scheduled software update can be much more dangerous than skipping a medical check-up. As in all complex systems, there are many more possibilities for failure. With the IoT, the missteps of a spaceship are going to go wrong. For example, let us say both you and your spouse get a message that they have run out of milk and that you are both going to a store on the way home and that you are both buying milk. As a result, you and your partner have bought twice what you both like. Or maybe even a software bug automatically prevents your printer's new ink cartridge from being imported every hour for a few days, or at worst power failure if you just need a replacement [51].

8.6 Future Insights

IoT will be further established in healthcare in the future. The IoT market in medicine is constantly growing and is expected to reach $158 billion by 2022. This technology can be applied in a wide variety of healthcare settings to remotely monitor patients and guide the right diagnosis. Apart from a standard in the healthcare industry, IoT tends to become a trend among patients. According to recent analyses, wearables alone would attain $222 million in 2021 starting from a volume of $113.2 million in 2017. Within 10 years, the existing 10 billion devices are expected to reach 50 billion [45, 52].

Currently, physicians may assume that IoT devices cannot be suggested or prescribed to older adult patients because of the low level of digital literacy. Accumulating evidence from emergency care suggests that older people are willing and, in most cases, capable of trying telemedicine. As time passes, the digital gap will be filled with patients more and more knowledgeable in smart devices. Accumulating experience with these modalities will make physicians more confident [53]. Moreover, novel IoT research offers the chance of monitoring the patients' residential environment, providing a more comprehensive approach to the disease and the factors creating or sustaining it. In this context, Islam *et al.* (2020) have used a set of sensors collecting information about the heartbeat, body temperature, and at the same time the room temperature and the CO and CO2 levels [54].

The notion of IoT smart healthcare seems to be compatible with new trends in the perception of health. During the last years, the classical definition of health by the WHO as being in a state of complete physical, mental, and social well-being, has been criticized [55]. Modern researchers recognize that this status of welfare is not applicable to most of the population. Consequently, they focus on functionality highlighting the coping mechanisms developed by systems and individuals. This perception suggests a tendency of de-escalating illness to disease. In this context, IoT smart healthcare is expected to transform disease management in a way that increases the functionality and the independence of the patient nearly up to the level of a healthy individual.

8.7 Conclusions

A significant representative of the modern age of information technology is the Internet of Things (IoT). The IoT is growing with more innovative potential. It results from evolution lately in wireless communications and is a network that is expanding across the Internet. To understand the "Internet of Everything," we should link different information sensing devices to the Internet. IoT has been commonly used in different fields at present, such as smart cities, smart houses, smart logistics, smart transport, etc. Among them, one of its significant fields of operation is smart health. Every year, countless individuals lose their lives because of different illnesses or health issues. People are gradually paying interest to health problems. Therefore, a promising research domain in smart health has been applying IoT techniques to address health problems.

Techniques like wearable biosensors, and innovations in Big Data, particularly regarding proficient analysis of huge, multidisciplinary, disseminated, and diverse datasets, enabled personalized e-Health and m-Health services. IoT has the potential for better availability and accessibility, individualized and customized services, and enhanced returns on investments. As IoT-based e-Health expands supporting the current healthcare demands, some key challenges exist prior to coherent, secure, adaptable, and proficient interventions that could be adopted to solve several healthcare issues. This chapter discussed IoT-based e-Health settings along with their applications. It also presented key opportunities and challenges like managing data, scalability, interoperability, legislation, device-network-human interfaces, privacy, and security.

Overall, IoT applications can contribute significantly to the management and monitoring of chronic conditions, in the early detection of exacerbations, and in various levels of disease prevention. The lack of globally standardized IoT processes, the concerns of safety and confidentiality, as well as various implementation costs have set obstacles to the deployment of such solutions.

References

1. Firouzi, F., Rahmani, A.M., Mankodiya, K., Badaroglu, M., Merrett, G.V., Wong, P., Farahani, B.: Internet-of-Things and big data for smarter healthcare: From device to architecture, applications and analytics. Future Gener. Comput. Syst. 78, 583–586 (2018). https://doi.org/10.1016/j.future.2017.09.016.

2. Sokol, M.C., McGuigan, K.A., Verbrugge, R.R., Epstein, R.S.: Impact of medication adherence on hospitalization risk and healthcare cost. Med. Care. 43, 521–530 (2005). https://doi.org/10.1097/01.mlr.0000163641.86870.af.
3. American Diabetes Association: Economic Costs of Diabetes in the U.S. in 2017. Diabetes Care. 41, 917–928 (2018). https://doi.org/10.2337/dci18-0007.
4. Akmandor, A.O., Jha, N.K.: Smart Health Care: An Edge-Side Computing Perspective. IEEE Consum. Electron. Mag. 7, 29–37 (2018). https://doi.org/10.1109/MCE.2017.2746096.
5. Alwan, O.S., Prahald Rao, K.: Dedicated real-time monitoring system for health care using ZigBee. Healthc. Technol. Lett. 4, 142–144 (2017). https://doi.org/10.1049/htl.2017.0030.
6. Solanas, A., Patsakis, C., Conti, M., Vlachos, I.S., Ramos, V., Falcone, F., Postolache, O., Perez-martinez, P.A., Pietro, R.D., Perrea, D.N., Martinez-Balleste, A.: Smart health: A context-aware health paradigm within smart cities. IEEE Commun. Mag. 52, 74–81 (2014). https://doi.org/10.1109/MCOM.2014.6871673.
7. Pérez-Martínez, P., Martínez-Ballesté, A., Solanas, A.: Privacy in Smart Cities - A Case Study of Smart Public Parking. In: PECCS (2013). https://doi.org/10.5220/0004314700550059.
8. Institute of Medicine (US) Committee on the National Quality Report on Health Care Delivery: Envisioning the National Health Care Quality Report. National Academies Press (US), Washington (DC) (2001).
9. Farahani, B., Firouzi, F., Chang, V., Badaroglu, M., Constant, N., Mankodiya, K.: Towards fog-driven IoT eHealth: Promises and challenges of IoT in medicine and healthcare. Future Gener. Comput. Syst. 78, 659–676 (2018). https://doi.org/10.1016/j.future.2017.04.036.
10. Farahani, B., Firouzi, F., Chakrabarty, K.: Healthcare IoT. In: Firouzi, F., Chakrabarty, K., and Nassif, S. (eds.) Intelligent Internet of Things: From Device to Fog and Cloud. pp. 515–545. Springer International Publishing, Cham (2020). https://doi.org/10.1007/978-3-030-30367-9_11.
11. Hill, C.F., Powers, B.W., Jain, S.H., Bennet, J., Vavasis, A., Oriol, N.E.: Mobile health clinics in the era of reform. Am. J. Manag. Care. 20, 261–264 (2014).
12. Mikulic, M.: Telemedicine market size worldwide 2019 vs 2026, https://www.statista.com/statistics/671374/global-telemedicine-market-size/, last accessed 2020/06/19.
13. Rashidi, P., Mihailidis, A.: A Survey on Ambient-Assisted Living Tools for Older Adults. IEEE J. Biomed. Health Inform. 17, 579–590 (2013). https://doi.org/10.1109/JBHI.2012.2234129.
14. Zineldin, M.: The quality of health care and patient satisfaction: an exploratory investigation of the 5Qs model at some Egyptian and Jordanian medical clinics. Int. J. Health Care Qual. Assur. Inc. Leadersh. Health Serv. 19, 60–92 (2006). https://doi.org/10.1108/09526860610642609.
15. Suri, N., Tortonesi, M., Michaelis, J., Budulas, P., Benincasa, G., Russell, S., Stefanelli, C., Winkler, R.: Analyzing the applicability of Internet of Things to

the battlefield environment. In: 2016 International Conference on Military Communications and Information Systems (ICMCIS). pp. 1–8 (2016). https://doi.org/10.1109/ICMCIS.2016.7496574.

16. Hassanalieragh, M., Page, A., Soyata, T., Sharma, G., Aktas, M., Mateos, G., Kantarci, B., Andreescu, S.: Health Monitoring and Management Using Internet-of-Things (IoT) Sensing with Cloud-Based Processing: Opportunities and Challenges. In: 2015 IEEE International Conference on Services Computing. pp. 285–292 (2015). https://doi.org/10.1109/SCC.2015.47.
17. Alansari, Z., Soomro, S., Belgaum, M.R., Shamshirband, S.: The Rise of Internet of Things (IoT) in Big Healthcare Data: Review and Open Research Issues. In: Saeed, K., Chaki, N., Pati, B., Bakshi, S., and Mohapatra, D.P. (eds.) Progress in Advanced Computing and Intelligent Engineering. pp. 675–685. Springer, Singapore (2018). https://doi.org/10.1007/978-981-10-6875-1_66.
18. Greengard, S.: The Internet of Things. The MIT Press, Cambridge, Massachusetts (2015).
19. Abawajy, J.H., Hassan, M.M.: Federated Internet of Things and Cloud Computing Pervasive Patient Health Monitoring System. IEEE Commun. Mag. 55, 48–53 (2017). https://doi.org/10.1109/MCOM.2017.1600374CM.
20. Fernandes, C.O., Lucena, C.J.P.D.: A Software Framework for Remote Patient Monitoring by Using Multi-Agent Systems Support. JMIR Med. Inform. 5, e9 (2017). https://doi.org/10.2196/medinform.6693.
21. Thomas, M.J., Rad, B.: Reliability Evaluation Metrics for Internet of Things, Car Tracking System: A Review. (2017). https://doi.org/10.5815/IJITCS.2017.02.01.
22. Mahdavinejad, M.S., Rezvan, M., Barekatain, M., Adibi, P., Barnaghi, P., Sheth, A.P.: Machine learning for internet of things data analysis: a survey. Digit. Commun. Netw. 4, 161–175 (2018). https://doi.org/10.1016/j.dcan.2017.10.002.
23. Genet, N., Boerma, W.G., Kringos, D.S., Bouman, A., Francke, A.L., Fagerström, C., Melchiorre, M.G., Greco, C., Devillé, W.: Home care in Europe: a systematic literature review. BMC Health Serv. Res. 11, 207 (2011). https://doi.org/10.1186/1472-6963-11-207.
24. Vizer, L.M., Eschler, J., Koo, B.M., Ralston, J., Pratt, W., Munson, S.: "It's Not Just Technology, It's People": Constructing a Conceptual Model of Shared Health Informatics for Tracking in Chronic Illness Management. J. Med. Internet Res. 21, e10830 (2019). https://doi.org/10.2196/10830.
25. Raju, B., Jumah, F., Ashraf, O., Narayan, V., Gupta, G., Sun, H., Hilden, P., Nanda, A.: Big data, machine learning, and artificial intelligence: a field guide for neurosurgeons. J. Neurosurg. 1, 1–11 (2020). https://doi.org/10.3171/2020.5.JNS201288.
26. Zhang, P., Schmidt, D.C., White, J., Mulvaney, S.: Towards Precision Behavioral Medicine with IoT: Iterative Design and Optimization of a Self-Management Tool for Type 1 Diabetes. 2018 IEEE Int. Conf. Healthc. Inform. ICHI. (2018). https://doi.org/10.1109/ICHI.2018.00015.

27. Memon, M., Wagner, S.R., Pedersen, C.F., Beevi, F.H.A., Hansen, F.O.: Ambient Assisted Living Healthcare Frameworks, Platforms, Standards, and Quality Attributes. Sensors. 14, 4312–4341 (2014). https://doi.org/10.3390/s140304312.
28. Sadoughi, F., Behmanesh, A., Sayfouri, N.: Internet of things in medicine: A systematic mapping study. J. Biomed. Inform. 103, 103383 (2020). https://doi.org/10.1016/j.jbi.2020.103383.
29. Rghioui, A., Lloret, J., Parra, L., Sendra, S., Oumnad, A.: Glucose Data Classification for Diabetic Patient Monitoring. Appl. Sci. 9, 4459 (2019). https://doi.org/10.3390/app9204459.
30. Sharma, M., Singh, G., Singh, R.: An Advanced Conceptual Diagnostic Healthcare Framework for Diabetes and Cardiovascular Disorders. ICST Trans. Scalable Inf. Syst. 5, 154828 (2018). https://doi.org/10.4108/eai.19-6-2018.154828.
31. Cox, S.M., Lane, A., Volchenboum, S.L.: Use of Wearable, Mobile, and Sensor Technology in Cancer Clinical Trials. JCO Clin. Cancer Inform. 2, 1–11 (2018). https://doi.org/10.1200/CCI.17.00147.
32. Dimitrov, D.V.: Medical Internet of Things and Big Data in Healthcare. Healthc. Inform. Res. 22, 156–163 (2016). https://doi.org/10.4258/hir.2016.22.3.156.
33. Mokou, M., Lygirou, V., Angelioudaki, I., Paschalidis, N., Stroggilos, R., Frantzi, M., Latosinska, A., Bamias, A., Hoffmann, M.J., Mischak, H., Vlahou, A.: A Novel Pipeline for Drug Repurposing for Bladder Cancer Based on Patients' Omics Signatures. Cancers. 12, (2020). https://doi.org/10.3390/cancers12123519.
34. Jara, A.J., Zamora, M.A., Skarmeta, A.F.: Drug identification and interaction checker based on IoT to minimize adverse drug reactions and improve drug compliance. Pers. Ubiquitous Comput. 18, 5–17 (2014). https://doi.org/10.1007/s00779-012-0622-2.
35. Madanian, S., Parry, D.: IoT, Cloud Computing and Big Data: Integrated Framework for Healthcare in Disasters. Stud. Health Technol. Inform. 264, 998–1002 (2019). https://doi.org/10.3233/SHTI190374.
36. Reinhardt, I.C., Oliveira, D.J.C., Ring, D.D.T.: Current Perspectives on the Development of Industry 4.0 in the Pharmaceutical Sector. J. Ind. Inf. Integr. 18, 100131 (2020). https://doi.org/10.1016/j.jii.2020.100131.
37. Andreu-Perez, J., Leff, D.R., Ip, H.M.D., Yang, G.: From Wearable Sensors to Smart Implants--Toward Pervasive and Personalized Healthcare. IEEE Trans. Biomed. Eng. 62, 2750–2762 (2015). https://doi.org/10.1109/TBME.2015.2422751.
38. Stachel, J.R., Sejdić, E., Ogirala, A., Mickle, M.H.: The impact of the internet of Things on implanted medical devices including pacemakers, and ICDs. In: 2013 IEEE International Instrumentation and Measurement Technology Conference (I2MTC). pp. 839–844 (2013). https://doi.org/10.1109/I2MTC.2013.6555533.

39. Trigano, A., Blandeau, O., Dale, C., Wong, M.-F., Wiart, J.: Reliability of electromagnetic filters of cardiac pacemakers tested by cellular telephone ringing. Heart Rhythm. 2, 837–841 (2005). https://doi.org/10.1016/j.hrthm.2005.03.011.
40. Shaw, R.J., Yang, Q., Barnes, A., Hatch, D., Crowley, M.J., Vorderstrasse, A., Vaughn, J., Diane, A., Lewinski, A.A., Jiang, M., Stevenson, J., Steinberg, D.: Self-monitoring diabetes with multiple mobile health devices. J. Am. Med. Inform. Assoc. JAMIA. 27, 667–676 (2020). https://doi.org/10.1093/jamia/ocaa007.
41. Ali, F., El-Sappagh, S., Islam, S.M.R., Kwak, D., Ali, A., Imran, M., Kwak, K.-S.: A smart healthcare monitoring system for heart disease prediction based on ensemble deep learning and feature fusion. Inf. Fusion. 63, 208–222 (2020). https://doi.org/10.1016/j.inffus.2020.06.008.
42. Ghamari, M., Janko, B., Sherratt, R.S., Harwin, W., Piechockic, R., Soltanpur, C.: A Survey on Wireless Body Area Networks for eHealthcare Systems in Residential Environments. Sensors. 16, (2016). https://doi.org/10.3390/s16060831.
43. Provost, L.P., Murray, S.: The Health Care Data Guide: Learning from Data for Improvement. Jossey-Bass, San Francisco, CA (2011).
44. Makin, C.: Telehealth: CyberMed in East Brunswick aims to carry healthcare evolution to next step, https://www.mycentraljersey.com/story/news/health/2018/07/13/telehealth-next-steps-cybermed-east-brunswick/749334002/, last accessed 2021/02/11.
45. Tian, S., Yang, W., Grange, J.M.L., Wang, P., Huang, W., Ye, Z.: Smart healthcare: making medical care more intelligent. Glob. Health J. 3, 62–65 (2019). https://doi.org/10.1016/j.glohj.2019.07.001.
46. Kang, M., Park, E., Cho, B.H., Lee, K.-S.: Recent Patient Health Monitoring Platforms Incorporating Internet of Things-Enabled Smart Devices. Int. Neurourol. J. 22, S76-82 (2018). https://doi.org/10.5213/inj.1836144.072.
47. Zeadally, S., Bello, O.: Harnessing the power of Internet of Things based connectivity to improve healthcare. Internet Things. 100074 (2019). https://doi.org/10.1016/j.iot.2019.100074.
48. Varadharajan, V., Bansal, S.: Data Security and Privacy in the Internet of Things (IoT) Environment. In: Mahmood, Z. (ed.) Connectivity Frameworks for Smart Devices: The Internet of Things from a Distributed Computing Perspective. pp. 261–281. Springer International Publishing, Cham (2016). https://doi.org/10.1007/978-3-319-33124-9_11.
49. Stergiou, C., Psannis, K.E., Kim, B.-G., Gupta, B.: Secure integration of IoT and Cloud Computing. Future Gener. Comput. Syst. 78, 964–975 (2018). https://doi.org/10.1016/j.future.2016.11.031.
50. Lee, I., Lee, K.: The Internet of Things (IoT): Applications, investments, and challenges for enterprises. Bus. Horiz. 58, 431–440 (2015). https://doi.org/10.1016/j.bushor.2015.03.008.
51. Kai Zhang, Dahai Han, Hongping Feng: Research on the complexity in Internet of Things. In: 2010 International Conference on Advanced

Intelligence and Awarenss Internet (AIAI 2010). pp. 395–398 (2010). https://doi.org/10.1049/cp.2010.0796.
52. Baker, S.E., Xiang, W., Atkinson, I.M.: Internet of Things for Smart Healthcare: Technologies, Challenges, and Opportunities. IEEE Access. (2017). https://doi.org/10.1109/ACCESS.2017.2775180.
53. Gopal, G., Suter-Crazzolara, C., Toldo, L., Eberhardt, W.: Digital transformation in healthcare – architectures of present and future information technologies. Clin. Chem. Lab. Med. CCLM. 57, 328–335 (2019). https://doi.org/10.1515/cclm-2018-0658.
54. Islam, Md.M., Rahaman, A., Islam, Md.R.: Development of Smart Healthcare Monitoring System in IoT Environment. SN Comput. Sci. 1, 185 (2020). https://doi.org/10.1007/s42979-020-00195-y.
55. Bohn Stafleu van Loghum: Towards a new definition of health? Tijdschr. Voor Gezondheidswetenschappen. 91, 138–138 (2013). https://doi.org/10.1007/s12508-013-0050-3.

9

Enhancement of Scalability of SVM Classifiers for Big Data

Vijaykumar Bhajantri[1], Shashikumar G. Totad[1]* and Geeta R. Bharamagoudar[2]

[1]*School of Computer Science & Engineering, KLE Technological University, Hubballi, Karnatak*
[2]*Department of Computer Science & Engineering, KLE Institute of Technology, Hubballi, Karnatak*

Abstract

With todays' modern technology and lifestyle, vast amounts of data are generated exponentially day by day. Storing, processing, and analyzing such huge data is a complex problem and challenging for many applications. Since the data is extremely large, a conventional machine learning algorithm may not perform well with regards to time complexity, data scalability, and accuracy. A good amount of research work is being carried out to solve such problems by different research groups, including distributed and parallel computing, GPU based parallel and distributed computing, etc. A Support Vector Machine is a popular machine learning algorithm for classification problems and a systematic retrospect of SVM algorithms from the perspective of big data are of ample significance, which motivates for development of SVM optimization in parallel distributed computing. In this paper, we describe the state of the art SVM algorithms with their pros, cons, and challenges in parallel and distributed computing methods. Mechanisms for efficient computation of SVM for big data and avenues for the future research are also explored.

Keywords: Support vector machine, challenges, distributed mechanism, shared-memory parallelism, distributed big data architecture, spark

**Corresponding author*: totad@kletech.ac.in

M. Niranjanamurthy, Hemant Kumar Gianey and Amir H. Gandomi (eds.) Advances in Data Science and Analytics: Concepts and Paradigms, (203–232) © 2023 Scrivener Publishing LLC

9.1 Introduction

Big data and machine learning is growing at remarkable rate and fascinating many of researchers. It has become one of prominent research areas and plays a significant role in many fields such as, artificial intelligence, network analysis, image classification and analysis, recommendation system, bioinformatics, fire and safety analysis, face detection, journalism, marketing and logistics, etc. However, the problems belong to different application areas and they share certain important features [2]:

a) Dataset size is enormously large and it contains training examples in hundreds of billions.
b) As the large dataset is stored with detailed information on every training example, the dataset is often high-dimensional in nature.
c) Due to large scale data used by several applications, the data is stored and retrieved generally in a distributed fashion.

Hence, it is essential to develop algorithms that are proficient enough to process large scale data in parallel and distributed manners. According to authors [3–6], simple machine learning models may easily succumb to complex and large datasets while being trained on huge dataset.

Support Vector Machine (SVM) is a supervised machine learning algorithm. It is one of the prevalent classification techniques due to its good generalization performance property for given data [6–8]. Even though it has many advantages, its performance still degrades with respect to extended training process and inadequate memory for solving large scale problems [3, 7, 9–12]. The quadratic programming [14] problem considered by SVM involves computationally expensive tasks [14, 18] such as matrix-to-matrix multiplication [14], inspection of optimality circumstance [19], kernel computation, and gradient update process [33, 34]. With respect to the growing rate of vast amounts of data, size demands adequate memory and effective computation time by using parallel and distributed computing methods to become even more significant [35]. The result of this comprehensive study depicts that parallel and distributed SVM can succeed in substantial speedups compared to a sequential SVM algorithm [12]. The time complexity and memory issues of SVM can be enhanced by using potential parallel techniques, but it is not simple to implement for large scale problems efficiently. The algorithm may not scale well for a large number of data samples or processors and the reason for this is communication overhead, dependency steps in the computation, and inadequate memory [3]. Because of both space and time complexity, it is very important to identify the suitable algorithm for the given problem. Hence, identifying suitable parallel and distributed algorithms and mechanisms has the potential to attain the highest performance of the algorithm for the given large scale dataset.

Shiliang Sun *et al.* [33] givens a comprehensive notion of optimization methods. One of the primary mechanisms of machine learning is optimization. The principle of machine learning algorithms is to build optimization models and learn the parameters in the objective function from the provided dataset. Due to the vast amount of data, it is essential to build efficient and effective optimization methods which will impact applications of the models. In this paper, we will discuss the optimization technique with viewpoints of gradient information. The optimization methods are categorized as [36–38]: i) First order, ii) Higher order, and iii) Derivative-free order. We will discuss and compare the first and higher order methods, wherein first order optimization methods converge at faster speeds but higher order optimization methods face operation and storage challenges.

The rest of the chapter is organized as follows. In section 9.2, we described the outline of the SVM algorithm. The different distributed and parallel mechanisms and corresponding taxonomy are described in section 9.3. Well known parallel distributed implementation binary and multiclass SVM algorithms and their potential advantages and disadvantages are described in section 9.4. In section 9.5, the conclusion and potential scope of work is presented.

9.2 Support Vector Machine

Support Vector Machine (SVM) is one of the performant off-the-shelf supervised machine learning algorithms. SVM [39] is a dominant classification and regression algorithm and it is used for many a number of classification problems magnificently in recent years. In the binary classification problem, the basic notion of SVM is to compute and find a hyperplane that divides the training data point from both sides of hyperplane by using the maximum margin concept [39, 40]. This concept is implemented in two stages: training the machine and testing the model for predicting the new data point. In the training stage of SVM, the machine is trained in search of a hyperplane that is distinct from the specified dataset samples into two classes with identified class labels, that is +1 and -1. Once the trained model is obtained for the given dataset, then testing can be carried out where the model predicts whether the new data points belong to positive or negative class labels [41]. SVM has exceptional features which are used to implement

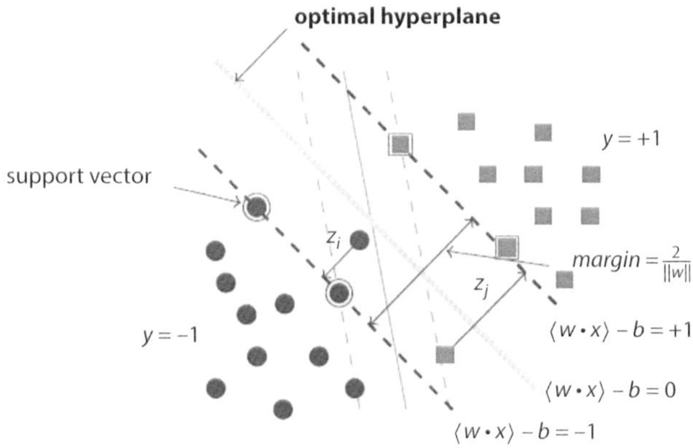

Figure 9.1 Linear separation of data points into two classes.

proficient parallel methods in relation with memory and time. The first features are called support vectors [42] and are found by few data samples and they search and find the separating hyperplane [43]. The second feature is to conduct mapping from non-linear to linear without knowing the mapping function, using predefined methods known as kernels, for calculating the inner product of the mapping function [43]. Another feature of SVM is the solution to the sparsity problem. Figure 9.1 [37] depicts the details of SVM for the binary classification problem, where x is the data point in N-dimensional input space with R^N having correlated labels $y_i \in \{+1, -1\}$. The SVM computes $w.x - b = +1$ for positive class and $w.x - b = -1$ for negative class to maximize the distance between supporting planes for each class (+1 and −1). The distance (margin) between supporting planes is $2/||w||$, where $||w||$ is the 2-norm of the vector w. The hyperplane is defined as $w.x - b = 0$, which separates the two classes and any data point that falls over on the incorrect side of the hyperplane is considered to be an error. Hence, the SVM algorithm has optimized computing the distance between supporting planes (margin) and minimizing the error [37]. Figure 9.1 shows the linear separation of the data points into two classes.

The SVM optimization formulation with inequality constraint given by

$$min\frac{1}{2}\|w\|^2 + C\sum_{i=1}^{l}\zeta_i + \zeta_i^*$$
$$s.t.\begin{cases} y_i - ((w,\varphi(x_i)) - b \leq \varepsilon + \zeta_i) \\ ((w,\varphi(x_i)) + b - y_i \leq \varepsilon + \zeta_i^*) \\ \zeta_i + \zeta_i^* \geq 0 \end{cases} \tag{9.1}$$

with the ε – exhaustive loss function

$$|y - f(x,w)|_{\varepsilon} = \begin{cases} 0, & if, y - f(x,w) \leq \varepsilon \\ |y - f(x,w)| - \varepsilon, & otherwise \end{cases}$$

where ε is the approximation accuracy that can be interrupted by means of slack variables ζ_i, ζ_i^* for the non-feasible solution. In the above equation, w is the weight vector for the hyperplane, x is the vector of observations that is the given dataset, y_i is the class label, $y_i \in \{-1, +1\}$, b is the bias parameter, and $\varphi(x)$ is the map function [1]. In some circumstances, the data point can be classified as liner but in most of the cases it is in non-linear form [7]. For non-linear circumstances, it is essential to map the data point from input space to high dimensional feature space by using the method of non-linear transformation and it maps $\varphi(x)$ input vector x to the feature space [7]. Hence, in the high dimensional space, the data is linearly classified and this is achieved through kernel function. The popular kernel examples are listed in Table 9.1 with the optimization parameters. The kernel function describes the feature space in which training data points are classified, hence it is important to select the suitable kernel function [44].

Table 9.1 Popular kernel functions and optimization parameters.

Kernel function	Kernel type	Inner product	Optimization parameter
Linear Kernel	Linear	$K(x_m, x_n) = x_m^T x_n$	C *and* γ
RBF	Non-Linear	$K(x_m, x_n) = \exp(\gamma\|x_m x_n\|^2 + C)$	C *and* γ
Sigmoid	Non-Linear	$K(x_m, x_n) = \tanh(\gamma(x_m, x_n) + r)$	C, γ *and* r
Polynomial	Non-Linear	$K(x_m, x_n) = (\gamma(x_m, x_n))^d$	C, γ, r *and* d
Laplacian	Non-Linear	$K(x_m, x_n) = \exp(-\gamma\|x_m - x_n\|)$	C *and* γ

9.2.1 Challenges

In machine learning, Quadratic Programming (QP) is a computationally expensive task because it contains computations of the kernel matrix [45, 46] and the training stage of SVM involvesdense quadratic programming, which is expensive. The kernel matrix evaluation involves matrix-matrix and matrix-vector multiplication and optimality [47, 48] and gradient functions updates [33], plus all these tasks are computationally expensive tasks [45, 49]. There are many QP solvers using memory to store the computation results, but it is not feasible due to inadequate size of the memory, therefore such QP solvers are not suitable for solving the QP addressed by SVM [7, 14, 43, 45]. One of the possible proficient solutions to improve the performance of SVM algorithms is the approach of parallelism in the distributed environment, but general purpose QP may not be simply parallelizable [50] and the parallel methods used in QP solvers may not take advantage of special characteristics of SVM [33, 50–52]. Moreover, the large dataset size causes performance problems in SVM algorithms due to the expensive tasks involved. As the dataset size increases the performance of the algorithms starts degrading because of the following reasons:

- Speedup: The kernel operations may take too long to be performed due to high cost computation tasks.
- Memory: Due to limited size of the memory, entire data may not accommodate [5], besides there are also methods of accessing the memory that may affect and reduce the training and testing stage speed [53].
- Accuracy: The accuracy of the algorithms degrades because the size of the original problem is divided into sub-problems, thus it results in poor accuracy of the classification algorithm [54].
- Scalability: Machine leaning algorithms are not made for large data size, hence SVM algorithms may not scale well for a large number of samples or processors [50].

The organization of research about studying parallel and distributed computing of SVMs can be considered in two phases: parallel algorithms, both binary and multiclass, and parallel distributed mechanisms or architectures. In this paper, parallel binary and multiclass SVM are identified and parallel and distributed mechanisms used for the implementation of SVMs are studied. The consequential organization of parallel and distributed SVMs is shown in Figure 9.2.

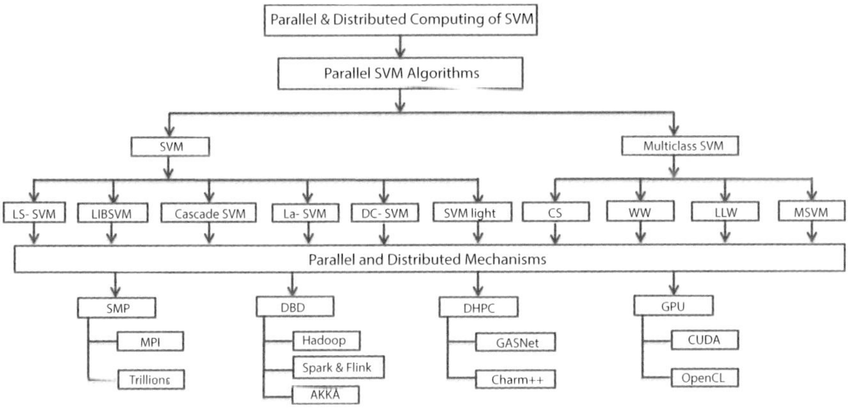

Figure 9.2 Parallel and distributed computing of SVMs containing algorithms and mechanisms. SMP: Shared Memory Parallelism, DBD: Distributed Big Data Architecture, DHPC: Distributed HPC Architecture, GPU: GPU based Parallelism.

9.3 Parallel and Distributed Mechanism

The vast amount of data generated per minute from various fields like internet applications, social media, e-commerce, and scientific research etc., is a trend in rapid growth of the tera bytes of data per day. Wal-Mart has millions of transactions per day worldwide and its warehouse system has touched 4PB and is still growing. In order to discover the knowledge from growing trends in large data, it must depend on large parallel and distributed computing systems [21, 56]. The most commonly used parallel and distributed mechanisms in the field of machine learning are: shared memory parallelism, GPU based parallelism, distributed big data architecture, and distributed High Performance Computing architecture. We will discuss in brief their approaches in machine learning.

9.3.1 Shared-Memory Parallelism

The dataset from a single occurrence in memory is accessed by multi-threads where training tasks are partitioned across multi-threads. This type of shared memory access indicates ignorable communication overhead because all the computing cores can access the data from shared memory, but training data for the problems having large scale data may not be suitable for limited shared memory. One of the most popular mechanisms to overcome such problems is open MPI. The MPI model is the most common messaging-based programming model and it supports shared memory multiprocessing [56]. The advantages of MPI include: good portability that has language independent library functions and nothing to do with hardware and operating system features, good scalability that is extensively successful of parallel machines in distributed environments, and high efficiency communication among computing cores. MPI limitations cannot assure fault tolerance and synchronization between threads. Another emerging framework for share memory parallelism is Trilinos. It is an object-oriented framework for the solution of large-scale, complex multi-physics engineering and scientific problems on new and emerging high-performance computing architecture [57].Most of the Trilinos algorithms are built to solve sparse problems using sparse linear solvers. Trilinos suits for linear and Eigen problem solvers, i.e., for large, distributed systems of equations [57].

9.4 Distributed Big Data Architecture

9.4.1 Hadoop MapReduce

Hadoop MapReduce is one of the well-known distributed big data architectures for processing large scale datasets on parallel and distributed systems. The MapReduce model was developed by Google for big number clusters of machines and this model consists of two basic task mapper and reducer functions, both written by the user [1, 56]. The map function generates key/value pairs by processing the input data. Here, the user basically needs to write logic for processing the input data in the mapper function and the output is used in the reducer function, similar logic is used for reducers to reduce the intermediate results. The user is not required to know how to distribute the input data, how to do cross-cluster scheduling, handling of node failure in the cluster, etc., and the program is concurrently executed automatically on cluster. The illustration of the map-reduce function to count shapes is shown in Figure 9.1. The key issue in map-reduce is the choice of number of map and reduce functions and network bandwidth relatively considered as scarce resource. In recent years, researchers have conducted a lot of research on this model, such as, enhancement of its performance, ease of use and integration with relational databases, and the expansion of application areas.

9.4.2 Spark

AMP Lab, University of Berkeley, designed and implemented the Spark distributed programming model. Spark is designed based on the map-reduce

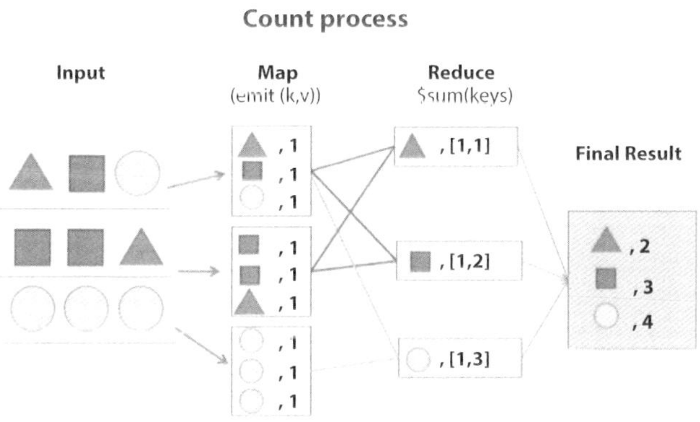

Figure 9.3 Illustration of MapReduce example to count shapes.

model. The program is executed in parallel on multiple working nodes; all the data nodes in the cluster read data from DFS, that is the Distributed File System, and the intermediate results are stored in memory to avoid high-latency disk materialization, therefore it is well-matched for interactive query analysis [56]. Figure 9.3 shows the Illustration of MapReduce examples to count shapes.

Spark computing framework [13, 28] offers various advantages over MapReduce. Explicitly, the caching mechanism and lazy execution model of Spark makes it very fast and fault tolerant, particularly for iterative tasks, compared to MapReduce which needs to write all intermediate data to the disk. The main impression of the Spark model is Resilient Distributed Dataset (RDD), which is a fault-tolerant array of objects distributed across the nodes of the cluster that are executed in parallel [13]. All the intermediate results are cached in the RAM at random, hence data access is faster compared to map-reduce. Developers can ask the Spark model to preserve an RDD in memory, allowing it to be reused efficiently across parallel operations [13, 56]. Eventually, RDDs automatically recover from node failures. MLlib is the machine learning library that supports most machine learning algorithms and it is continuously refined. Figure 9.4 show the Spark model implementation process.

9.4.3 AKKA

Akka is a framework for developing highly distributed, concurrent, and resilient message-driven applications. The framework is built on the actor model, a mathematical model of parallel processing that serves actors as the universal primitives of parallel processing. Actors in the context may

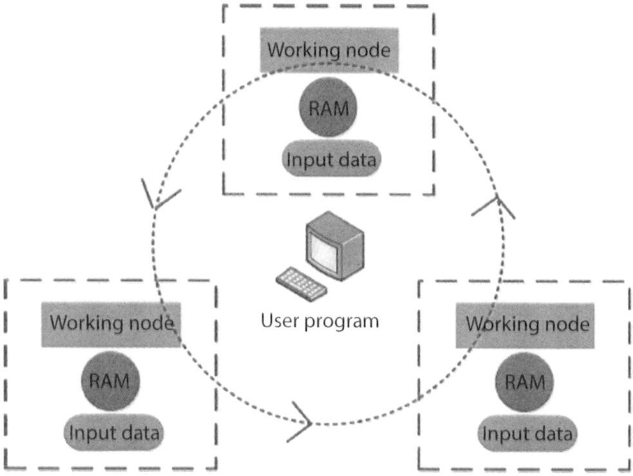

Figure 9.4 Spark model implementation process.

change their individual private state, however messages can affect each other. The Akka cluster is used if you would like to share data among the nodes and we call it Akka distributed data. Here, data is retrieved through an actor providing key-value pair-like API and the values are Conflict Free Replicated Data Types (CRDTs). The CRDT technique has many advantages like replicating data across a network without any synchronization mechanism, avoiding distributed locks, two phase commit, etc., and consistency without consensus. The Akka cluster delivers a fault-tolerant distributed peer-to-peer centered CMS (Cluster Membership Service) with no single point of failure and it achieves this by using gossip protocols and automatic failure detector. The Akka engine works in two modes, that is batch and stream processing. In streaming mode it experiences little delay but also little lower throughput, whereas in batch mode it introduces some delay. Figure 9.5 illustrates the job with different set operators run in parallel at different stages [15].

9.5 Distributed High Performance Computing

9.5.1 GASNet

Global Address Space Network (GASNet) is an open source, portable, high performance, next-generation communication library designed to support efficient communication system for networking necessities of runtime

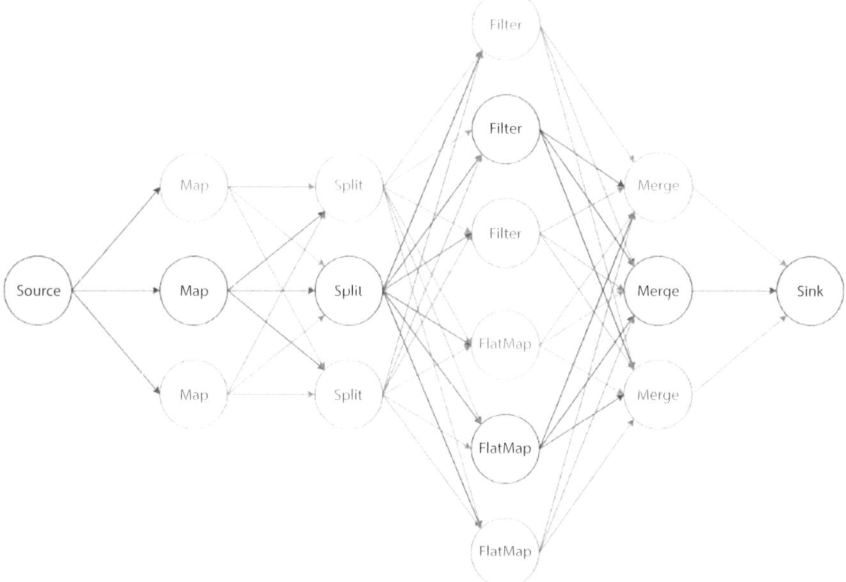

Figure 9.5 Illustration of job operator (map, split, filter, flatmap, merge) example.

systems and other unconventional models in upcoming exascale machines. The primary GASNet API proposes two major modes of communication. 1. RMA (Remote Memory Access) interface for one side that describes the RDMA capabilities of network hardware, facilitates their use to directly execute PGAS (Partitioned Global Address Space) Put/Get operations on user data structures and 2. Streamlined Active Message [16, 58] interface offers extensibility and proficient management of the slaves' parallel runtime systems. The system design objectives for the GASNet communication system consist of network independence, language independence, robust multithreading support, and extensive portability. It is necessary to redesign the GASNet interface and extend in a different way to congregate the requirements of the exascale runtime systems, hence the interface is being redesigned.

9.5.2 Charm++

Charm++ is a grown-up, highly scalable parallel programming framework that facilitates applications to effectively scale in spite of the execution landscape.This parallel programming system has been designed and built with powerful RTS (Run Time System) that can dynamically balance load, component failure tolerance, and control chip temperature to minimize energy. It can optimize communication and expand the array of processors used by a job, which is specifically helpful in cloud environments. The Charm++ programming model is suitable for a wide range of parallel applications and its features were critical in efficiently parallelizing them. The author [17] believes that over decomposition, asynchronous message-driven execution and migratability are essential to empower RTS. According to the author [17], partitioning of the computation in an application into a big number of work and data units, normally much bigger than the number of processing units, is referred as over-decomposition. The essential RTS then maps these work units to PEs as it sees fit. Therefore, this model gives several benefits. Decoupling with an independent number of processors allows the programmer to define his/her module that is in terms of logical entities and which are appropriate for his/her applications. Decoupling is the breakdown of computation from the number of processors and this helps in enhancing the performance of applications by permitting the real time system to intelligently map these units to processing elements. It also supports in synchronous composition of parallel modules and better utilization of cache. For applications which are running on unreliable systems, CHARM++ offers a mechanism called double in memory fault tolerance [17, 59]. In this method, cyclically, two replicas of checkpoints are stored: the first one in the processing elements' local memory and the second in the remote processing elements' memory. When the system starts to malfunction, a new processing element replaces the failed processing element and the latest checkpoints of chares running on the old processing element are copied to it. Subsequently, each processing element rolls back to the last checkpoint and the applications persist to make progress. Hence, systems persist to grow in size and the parallel framework features are important to gain scalable performance.

9.6 GPU Based Parallelism

Today, Graphics Processing Units (GPU) contain an immense number of cores that can be used to harness their computational power for solving computation intensive tasks. GPU is used to accelerate the computationally expensive tasks of SVM, such as kernel evaluation, in decomposition methods [12, 18, 50, 54, 55, 60–68]. The most common approaches that are used to overcome the limitation of GPU besides enhancement of the training process of SVM in GPU based parallelism are: adjusting the data precision [50, 54, 69], selecting suitable working sets [60, 63, 69], and using sparse data format [63, 64, 65]. In the following section we will discuss acceleration of the SVM training process using CUDA and OpenCL.

9.6.1 CUDA

Solving a quadratic optimization task in SVM is complex and in order to evaluate the correspondence of objects, non-linear to linear conversion, i.e., kernel functions, is used. In order to achieve a good model, computation of n^2 kernel execution is essential in worst case, where n is the number of objects. Hence, this operation can be considered as the most time consuming task and generates a model for a collection that consists of a large number of instances that turn out to be a very complex and almost impossible within a reasonable time [28]. This scenario introduces the requirement of techniques which will speed up the computation of kernel functions. One of the popular solutions is CUDA (Compute Unified Device Architecture) technology, which permits us to perform some amount of computation concurrently on GPU (Graphics Processing Unit) and in many applications it accelerates execution speed from 10 to 100 times faster [28]. To enhance the speed in computation of kernel functions, both techniques apply cashing of lately obtained scalar products as well as shrinking [70–72]. At present, LIBSVM [73], DCSVM [30], and SVMLight [74] gpuSVM [69] are the most generally used algorithms on the decomposition technique of the quadratic optimization problem, where in it uses variables which are selected in each step of the algorithms. Both the algorithms work on the principle of decomposition method, LIBSVM [75, 76] uses SMO type decomposition with second order information [77] to select suitable working sets, whereas SVMLight uses the idea of Osuma [80]. Both decomposition methods use caching of acquired scalar products and shrinking to fast-track the computation of kernel functions. In the training phase of SVM, it is required to multiply a matrix by a selected vector in a given iteration step. Hence, it is a time consuming task and needs to bring the scalar product computation on GPU to run parallel which significantly accelerates the training process. Recently developed algorithms, such as CuSVM [78] and GPUSVM [79], apply dense matrix format during kernel matrix calculation which significantly restricts the usage of these methods for big datasets.

9.6.2 OpenCL

OpenCL is a platform for parallel programming that offers a provision for heterogeneous computing on an extensive range of device categories

Table 9.2 Parallel approach and mechanisms for large data samples.

Settings	Parallel approach	Parallel tool	Samples	Speedups	References
LS-SVM column incremental	Parallel incremental	GPU	5 million	190× over LibSVM	Do *et al.* [12]
Random sampling, inexact minimization, normalization, cross-validation, multi-class	ADMM	DMP	~20 million and 30 million features	60× with 8 machines over LibLinear	Zhang *et al.* [84]
Block minimization	Map-Reduce	Hadoop	80 million	Disk throughput is 140 MB/sec	Pechyony *et al.* [85]
Newton SVM	Parallel incremental	GPU	10 million	70 times faster than SVM-Perf	Thanh *et al.* [12]
Data reordering	Parallel kernel computation	DMP	4 million	100× with 48 machines	Durdanovic *et al.* [86]

including FPGA's, GPU's, and multicore CPU's [81, 82]. There is an extensive range of devices, including AMD [CPU, GPU and Hybrid Processors], Intel [CPU and Integrated GPUs], NVIDIA [GPU's that support CUDA], Qualcomm [embedded CPU], Samsung [embedded CPU], Altera [FPGA's], and many others [83]. OpenCL is a promising choice of platform for parallelizing SVM due to design decisions that offer flexible hardware configuration. Ethan Peters and Andreas Savakis [29] experimented with high performance implementation of SVM on heterogeneous systems by using OpenCL and their strategy for accelerating the SVM algorithm is taking individual phases of the SVM algorithm which consumes maximum execution time and adapts them on a parallel accelerator device using OpenCL. The author [29] concluded their experiment with significant speedup for both training and testing for typical image datasets on two GPU's. Still a good scope of research experiment of SVM for large scale datasets using OpenCL. Table 9.2 describes the parallel approaches and mechanisms to enhance the performance of algorithms for large scale dataset. LS-SVM is experimented [12] with parallel incremental approach and GPU over 5 million data samples where the speedup enhances over LibSVM algorithm. similarly Map-Reduce, ADMM, GPU and other approaches have shown better performance of the algorithm.

9.7 Parallel and Distributed SVM Algorithms

Parallelizing Support Vector Machines have a very complex job because of the following reasons: sequential order of instructions of the algorithm, which causes dependency between the steps [17], delaying in memory access [41, 56], and limited size of memory [56] and other resources. Several parallel and distributed versions of SVM have been proposed in the literature [87, 88]. We can categorize them into four groups: parallel [91], distributed [89, 90], heterogeneous (map-reduce based) [92–95], and GPU-based [96].In this section, we have described variants of SVM with advantages and disadvantages. DiP-SVM, or Distribution Preserving Kernel Support Vector Machines, for Big Data help in obtaining local decision boundaries which are in agreement with the global decision boundary, thereby reducing the chance of missing important global support vectors [20]. A parallel SVM training algorithm has more satisfying accuracy and efficiency compared with a standard cascade SVM algorithm in classification precision [24]. As dimensionality increases, so does data sparsity and, consequently, a single binary classifier may separate multiple classes [32].

9.7.1 LS-SVM

The conventional Vapnik's SVM [43] algorithm has a vast computation load due to its inequality constraint and quadratic programming, which is a major disadvantage of the algorithm. As an alternative to conventional SVM, Suykensand Vandewalle [97] developed the least squares version of SVM, very popularly known as an LS-SVM algorithm in the machine learning community. LS-SVM works based on equality constraints instead of Vapniks' [39, 40, 43] inequality constraints and sum squared error (SSE) cost function, as it is often used in training of neural networks. This substantial modification of SVM critically simplifies the problem in a manner that the solution is characterized by a linear system [47].

To assist in the optimization of LS-SVM classifiers [10], the model uses two parallel hyper-planes. Equation 9.1 shows LS-SVM problem and the formulation of LS-SVM problem is the convex quadratic programming with equality constraints.

$$\begin{aligned} \underset{w,b,\eta}{min} \quad & \frac{1}{2}\|w\|^2 + \frac{1}{2}\gamma\sum_{i=1}^{l} e_i^2 \\ s.t. \quad & y_i = ((w.\varphi(x_i)) + b + e_i) i = 1, \ldots\ldots, l \end{aligned} \tag{9.2}$$

where the first term of objective function $\frac{1}{2}\|w\|^2$ denotes the margin between two hyperplanes: $(w.x) + b = 1$ and $(w.x) + b = -1$. The minimization of the second term, $\min\sum_{i=1}^{l} e_i^2$, makes the two hyperplanes locate at the center of the corresponding class of point, $e_i \in R$ are error variables, and $\gamma \geq 0$ is the regularization constant. The Lagrangian is given by

$$L_{LS-SVM} = \frac{1}{2}\|w\|^2 + \frac{1}{2}\gamma\sum_{i=1}^{l} e_i^2 - \sum_{i=1}^{l}\alpha_i\{((w.\varphi(x_i)) + b + e_i - y_i)$$

with Lagrange multipliers $\alpha_i \in R$, after the optimality condition formulation, the resulting least square SVM model for function estimation becomes:

$$f(x) = \sum_{i=1}^{l}\alpha_i K(x, x_i) + b.$$

Compare Equation 9.1 with 9.2 and LS-SVM is a reformulation of the principles of SVM, which contains equality conditions instead of inequality conditions. LS-SVM uses a least square loss function instead of ε-exhaustive loss function. Hence, the solution trails from a linear KKT system rather than computationally expensive quadratic programming problem. Therefore, it is easier to optimize and decrease computation time. The disadvantage of LS-SVM is lack of sparseness. All samples in LS-SVM are support vector, meaning that all training data are used to produce the result. The machine learning research community has contributed to enhance the performance of LS-SVM like solving with incremental models and exact incremental and decrement models [25, 26] and a good research scope aims to improve the algorithm on the sparseness problem. As per our survey, LSSVM is still not explored for large scale problems and distributed computing.

9.7.2 Cascade SVM

The cascade SVM is an SVM training algorithm that uses the filtering technique to enhance the performance at the cost of accuracy. The cascade structure of SVM is developed on the concept of decomposing the problem into independent smaller sub problems and fractional results are combined in subsequent stages in a hierarchical manner. Here, eliminating non-support vectors initially from the optimization proved an effective strategy for accelerating SVM. The advantage of this method is each SVM need not have to deal with the whole training dataset and several SVM classifiers can be trained in a distributed computing network, greatly enhancing speed [21]. This approach offers a speedup since the quadratic programming solvers used in SVM tend to scale with the cube ($O(n^3)$)

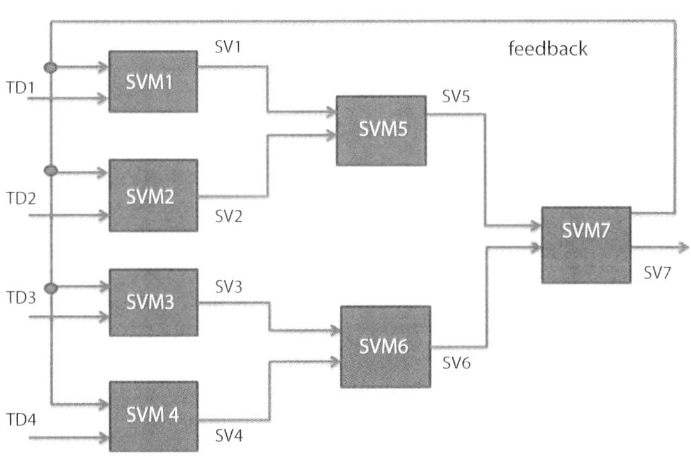

Figure 9.6 Cascade SVM working model.

of the number of training vectors, decomposing the training dataset into smaller parts which can substantially enhance scalability and speedup even on single CPUs [21, 27]. Figure 9.6 describes the cascade SVM working model and here the training dataset is decomposed into subsets TD1, TD2, TD3 and TD4. Support vectors obtained from the first stage of the training dataset are combined in the next stage and then again apply the optimization method at each stage and this continues until only one subset of the support vector is left.

The mathematical formulation of cascade SVM that is the SVM solution for the problem consists in maximizing the quadratic optimization function, given by:

$$\max W(\alpha) = -\frac{1}{2} * \sum_{i}^{l} \sum_{j}^{l} \alpha_i \alpha_j y_i y_j J(x_i, x_j) + \sum_{i}^{l} \alpha_i$$

$$s.t.\ 0 \le \alpha_i \le C, \forall_i\ and \sum_{i}^{l} \alpha_i y_i = 0$$

From the above formulation of cascade SVM, l is the set of training samples (x_i, y_i), where $x_i \in R^k$ denotes a k-dimensional pattern and $y_i = \pm 1$ the class label. $J(x_i, x_j)$ represents the matrix of the kernel values between patterns and α_i the Lagrangian coefficients to be determined by the optimization [27]. The gradient $G_i = \nabla W(\alpha)$ of W, with respect to α then

$$G_i = \frac{\partial w}{\partial \alpha_i} = -y_i \sum_{j}^{l} y_j \alpha_j J(x_i, x_j) + 1.$$

The cascade SVM algorithm is implemented in the parallel and distributed mechanism since it is a working model that is decomposes the training dataset and finds the optimal hyperplane and fewer support vectors.

9.7.3 DC SVM

Cho-Jui Hsieh *et al.*, (2014) [30] proposed, experimented, and analyzed a divide and conquer solver for a kernel support vector machine algorithm to enhance the time complexity of the training phase and accuracy. DC-SVM achieves faster convergence speed compared to an exact solver and better accuracy in less time compared to approximate solvers [30]. DC-SVM divides the problem into sub-problems and each individual sub-problem is solved independently and efficiently in the divide step to partition the problem efficiently. Kernel kmeans is used and in the conquer step, the local solutions of the sub-problem are aggregated to get initial points for the global problem. Given a set of example-label pairs, (x_i, y_i) $i = 1, \ldots\ldots n$, $x_i \in R^d$ *and* $y_i \in \{1, -1\}$. The following is the quadratic optimization problem of kernel SVM to be solved:

$$\min_{\alpha} \quad f(\alpha) = \frac{1}{2}\alpha^T Q\alpha - e^T\alpha, \; s.t. \; 0 \leq \alpha \leq C \tag{9.3}$$

where $\alpha \in R^n$ is the vector of dual variables, e is the vector of all ones, C is the balancing parameter between loss and regularization in the SVM primal problem, and Q is the n x n matrix with $Q_{ij} = y_i y_j K(x_i, x_j)$, where $K(x_i, x_j)$ is the kernel function. The decision value for the test data x can be computed by: $\sum_{i=1}^{n} \alpha_i^* y_i K(x, x_i)$. In a single level DC-SVM algorithm, the data is divided into small subsets and the sub-problem solutions are then used to initialize a coordinate descent solver for the entire problem. For this partition, the dual variables divide into k *subsets* $\{v_{1,} \ldots\ldots\ldots\ldots v_k\}$, then solve the respective sub-problem independently

$$\min_{\alpha_{(e)}} \quad \frac{1}{2}(\alpha_{(c)})^T Q_{(c,c)}\alpha_{(c)} - e^T\alpha_{(c)}, \quad s.t \; 0 \leq \alpha \leq C \tag{9.4}$$

where $c = 1, \ldots\ldots, k$, $\alpha_{(c)}$ denotes the sub-vector $\{\alpha_{(c)} | p \in v_c\}$ and $Q_{(c,c)}$ is the sub-matrix of Q with row and column indices v_c.

The quadratic programming problem (9.3) has n vairables and takes at least $O(n^2)$ time to solve in practice. Dividing into k sub-problems (9.4) can dramatically reduce to $O\left(k\left(\frac{n}{k}\right)^2\right) = O\left(\frac{n^2}{k}\right)$ and memory requirement is also reduced from $O(n^2)$ to $O(\frac{n^2}{k})$. The author [30] has experimented both single and multi-level DC-SVM with RBF and polynomial kernel by varying $C = [2^{-10}, 2^{-6}, 2^1, 2^6, 2^{10}]$ and $\gamma = [2^{-10}, 2^{-6}, 2^1, 2^6, 2^{10}]$ values. Hence, the DC-SVM is a novel algorithm that is much faster than LIBSVM and has a greater accuracy of 96.15%.

In [31], Dinesh Singh and C. Krishna Mohan implemented a distributed kernel support vector machine for big data using subspace partitioning. In the work a dominant eigenvector is used to split the large dataset into smaller subspaces. A decision tree is used to split the dataset recursively at each node in a similar style. Once a partition is accomplished, a kernel SVM is trained independently at each partition in a parallel system. It is required to compute a dominant eigenvector of the whole dataset using an iterative method and the whole dataset is projected on the dominant eigenvector. The extent of the projection is partitioned into B bins, where B is the maximum number of branches at any node in the decision tree. A child node is created for each non-empty bin and the data of the bins are assigned to respective child nodes. It is mentioned in [31] that time complexity for the novel algorithm is $O(nd^2)$, whereas k-means approach time complexity is $O(n^2d)$. Below, Table 9.3 gives a brief overview of the variants of SVM algorithms and their advantages and disadvantages.

9.7.4 Parallel Distributed Multiclass SVM Algorithms

Data analysis requires extensive and powerful computation with a large dimension of classes [22]. However, a good amount of work has been done on multiclass SVM and parallel and distributed binary SVM alone and the research on distributed multiclass SVM demands more investigation by the research community [23]. In 2014, Aruna, G., *et al.* proposed a binary tree based Support Vector Machine and the algorithm implemented in HADOOP framework for parallelism and task distributed among the nodes. The algorithm decreases the number of binary classes when compared with the one versus all and one versus one method. Following are the popular multiclass SVM approaches which contribute to the solution for the multiclass problems and a higher dimension of classes is challenging and a subject of ongoing research. The following Table 9.4 gives brief information about different types of multiclass classification approaches and the advantages and limitations of the algorithms.

9.8 Conclusion and Future Research Directions

Parallelization of Support Vector Machine classifiers is inevitable due to time complexity for large scale data problems, so it is essential to enhance the performance of the SVM algorithm and in this paper we have discussed the methods and mechanisms to improve the performance of SVM. In this survey paper we present state-of-the-art methods and mechanisms used to solve SVM in parallel and distributed methods. Still, there is a good volume for the next level of enhancement with respect to storage, accuracy, scalability, and computational time problems for the growing dimension

Table 9.3 SVM algorithms and their advantages & disadvantages.

Algorithm	Differences	Problem type	Advantages	Disadvantages
SGD-based SVMs	Emphasis on primal optimization	Non-linear and multi-class classifications	It is accelerated for linear SVMs on a single machine, simple to be parallelized	A large number of iterations until convergence, accuracy varies
LS-SVM	Works based on equality constraint, emphasis on sum squared error.	Linear and Non-Linear classification	Reduces numbers of errors and solutions in non-quadratic problem.	Lack of sparseness
DC-SVM	Divide and conquer solver for kernel SVM.	Linear and Non-Linear and multi-class classification	DC-SVM achieves faster convergence speed compared to exact solver and better accuracy in less time compared to approximate solvers.	Balance the computation load between sub-problems.
Cascade –SVM	Data are split into subsets & optimized separately with multiple SVM.	Linear and Non-Linear classification	Advantages over a single SVM are that it can reduce compute, as well as has better storage requirements	Acceleration saturates at relatively small number of layers.
SVM Light	Split the original problem into sequence of smaller sub-problems.	Linear and Non-Linear and multi-class classification	Decomposition of large problem into smaller and accelerated convergence speeds	Objective function of each sub-problem to be solved at each iteration

Table 9.4 Comparison of well-studied multiclass SVM methods.

Multiclass method	One-against-all	One-against-one	Weston-Watkins	DAGSVM	Crammer and Singer
First SVM practice	1995	1996	1999	2000	2001
Methodology	Use several binary classifiers	Use several binary classifiers	Solve single optimization problem	Use several binary classifiers	Solve single optimization problem
Training method	Train single classifier for each class	Train a classifier for each pair of classes	Decomposition method	Same as one-against-one	Decomposition method
Umbers trained classifiers	N	N(N-1) / 2	1	N(N-1) / 2	1
Testing method	Select the class with the biggest decision function value	Max-Wins voting strategy	Use the classifier	Use DAG to make prediction on N-1 classifiers	Use the classifier
Scikit-learn class	LinearSVC	SVC	Not available	Not available	LinearSVC
Disadvantages	Class imbalance	Long training time for large N	Long training time	Not available in popular libraries	Long training time

of real-life data.Combining different methods has been effective in managing large scale datasets since matching methods enhances the potential flaws. The scope and research direction would be attained by considering the development of combination of several techniques which are complementing and matching. A comprehensive study of integrating state-of-the-art methods can expose new boundaries to find a solution for large-scale problems. Considering the special characteristics of SVM is a good scope of future research by taking advantages of parallelism.

References

1. Shirin Tavara. 2019. Parallel Computing of Support Vector Machines: A Survey. *ACM Comput. Surv.* 51, 6, Article 123 (January 2019), 38 pages.
2. Ayan Das, Sourangshu Bhattacharya, 2015. Distributed Weighted Parameter Averaging for SVM Training on Big Data, arXiv:1509.09030v1 [cs.LG] 30 Sep 2015.
3. Guo-Xun Yuan, Chia-Hua Ho, and Chih-Jen Lin. 2012. Recent advances of large-scale linear classification. Proceedings of IEEE 100, 9 (2012), 2584–2603.
4. John C. Platt. 1999. Using analytic QP and sparseness to speed training of support vector machines. In Proceedings of the 1998 Conference on Advances in Neural Information Processing Systems II. MIT Press, 557–563.
5. Valeriu Codreanu, Bob Dröge, David Williams, Burhan Yasar, Po Yang, Baoquan Liu, Feng Dong, Olarik Surinta, Lambert R. B. Schomaker, Jos B. T. M. Roerdink, *et al.* 2016. Evaluating automatically parallelized versions of the support vector machine. In Concurrency and Computation: Practice and Experience 28, 7 (2016), 2274–2294.
6. Tatjana Eitrich and Bruno Lang. 2005. Efficient Implementation of Serial and Parallel Support Vector Machine Training with a Multi-parameter Kernel for Large-scale Data Mining. Citeseer.
7. Hyeran Byun and Seong-Whan Lee. 2002. Applications of support vector machines for pattern recognition: A survey. In Pattern Recognition with Support Vector Machines. Springer, 213–236.
8. Zhao Bin, Liu Yong, and Xia Shao-Wei. 2000. Support vector machine and its application in handwritten numeral recognition. In Proceedings of the 15th International Conference on Pattern Recognition. Vol. 2. 720–723. DOI:http: //dx.doi.org/10.1109/ICPR.2000.906176
9. Janmenjoy Nayak, Bighnaraj Naik, and H. S. Behera. 2015. A comprehensive survey on support vector machine in data mining tasks: Applications & challenges. International Journal of Database Theory and Application 8, 1 (2015), 169–186.

10. R. Ravinder Reddy, B. Kavya, and Y. Ramadevi. 2014. A survey on SVM classifiers for intrusion detection. In International Journal of Computer Applications 98, 19 (2014), 34–44.
11. G. Wang. 2008.Asurvey on training algorithms for support vector machine classifiers. In 4th International Conference on Networked Computing and Advanced Information Management (NCM'08). Vol. 1. 123–128. DOI:http://dx.doi.org/10.1109/NCM.2008.103
12. Thanh-Nghi Do, Van-Hoa Nguyen, and Francois Poulet. 2008. Speed up SVM algorithm for massive classification tasks. In Advanced Data Mining and Applications. Springer, 147–157.
13. Sauptik Dhar, Congrui Yi, Naveen Ramakrishnan, Mohak Shah, 2015. ADMM based Scalable Machine Learning on Spark, 2015 IEEE International Conference on Big Data (Big Data).
14. Kristian Woodsend and Jacek Gondzio. 2009. High-performance parallel support vector machine training. In Parallel Scientific Computing and Optimization. Springer, 83–92.
15. Ivan Kholod, Ilya Petukhov, and Andrey Shorov, 2016, Cloud for Distributed Data Analysis Based on the Actor Model, Hindawi Publishing Corporation, Scientific Programming, Volume 2016, Article ID 1050293, 11 pages, http://dx.doi.org/10.1155/2016/1050293.
16. Dan Bonachea, Paul H. Hargrove, 2019, GASNet-EX: A High-Performance, Portable Communication Library for Exascale, Lawrence Berkeley National Laboratory Technical Report (LBNL-2001174) doi:10.1007/978-3-030-34627-0_11
17. Bilge Acun, Abhishek Gupta, Nikhil Jain, 2014. Parallel Programming with Migratable Objects: Charm++ in Practice, SC14: International Conference for High Performance Computing, Networking, Storage and Analysis, IEEE Computer Society, DOI 10.1109/SC.2014.58
18. AUSTIN Peng, Yanxia Zhang, and Yongheng Zhao. 2011. CUDA-accelerated SVM for celestial object classification. In Astronomical Data Analysis Software and Systems Xx, Vol. 442. 119–122. Astronomical Society of the Pacific.
19. H. X. Zhao and Frederic Magoules. 2011. Parallel support vector machines on multi-core and multiprocessor systems. In 11th International Conference on Artificial Intelligence and Applications (AIA'11), R. Fox (Ed.). IASTED, 75–81.
20. Dinesh Singh, Debaditya Roy, C. Krishna Mohan, 2017. DiP-SVM: Distribution Preserving Kernel Support Vector Machine for Big Data, IEEE Transactions on Big Data (Volume: 3, Issue: 1, March 1 2017), Pages: 79 – 90, DOI: 10.1109/TBDATA.2016.2646700
21. ANG, Hock Hee; Gopalkrishnan, Vivekanand; HOI, Steven C. H.; and NG, Wee-Keong, 2013. Classification in P2P Networks with Cascade Support Vendor Machines. (2013). ACM Transactions on Knowledge Discovery from Data. 7, (4), 20-1-29. Research Collection School Of Information Systems. https://ink.library.smu.edu.sg/sis_research/2267

22. Alber M, Zimmert J, Dogan U, KloftM, (2017) Distributed optimization of multi-class SVMs. PloS ONE 12(6): e0178161. https://doi.org/ 10.1371/journal.ponc.0178161.
23. Arun Govada, Shree Rajani, Aditi Viswanathan, S.K. Sahay, 2015, A Novel Approach to Distributed Multi-Class SVM, Transactions on Machine Learning and Artificial Intelligence, Vol. 2, No. 5, p. 72,
24. Jian-Pei Zhang, Zhong-Wei Li, Jing Yang, 2005.A Parallel Svm Training Algorithm On Large-Scale Classification Problems, IEEE Proceedings of the Fourth International Conference on Machine Learning and Cybernetics, Guangzhou.
25. Fuqiang Sun, Xiaoyang Li, Haitao Liao and Xiankun Zhang,2017. A Bayesian least-squares support vector machine method for predicting the remaining useful life of a microwave component, Advances in Mechanical Engineering, 2017, Vol. 9(1) 1–9, DOI: 10.1177/1687814016685963.
26. Hyunsoo Kim, Haesun Park, 2004. Incremental and Decremental Least Squares Support Vector Machine and Its Application to Drug Design, Proceedings of the IEEE Computational Systems Bioinformatics Conference.
27. Hans Peter Graf, EricCosatto, Léon Bottou, Igor B Durdanovic, Vladimir N Vapnik, 2004, Parallel support vector machines: the cascade SVM, NIPS'04: Proceedings of the 17th International Conference on Neural Information Processing Systems Pages 521–528.
28. Krzysztof Sopy_la, Pawe_l Drozda, and Przemys_law Górecki, 2012. SVM with CUDA Accelerated Kernels for Big Sparse Problems, ICAISC 2012, Part I, LNCS 7267, pp. 439–447, 2012. Springer-Verlag Berlin Heidelberg 2012.
29. Ethan Peters and Andreas Savakis, 2015. SVM with OpenCL: High performance implementation of support vector machines on heterogeneous systems, 2015 IEEE International Conference on Image Processing (ICIP), DOI: 10.1109/ICIP.2015.7351622
30. Cho-Jui Hsieh, Si Si, Inderjit S. Dhillon, 2014. A Divide-and-Conquer Solver for Kernel Support Vector Machines, Proceedings of the 31st International Conference on Machine Learning, Beijing, China. JMLR: W&CP volume 32.
31. Dinesh Singh; C. Krishna Mohan, 2019. Projection-SVM: Distributed Kernel Support Vector Machine for Big Data using Subspace Partitioning, 2018 IEEE International Conference on Big Data (Big Data), DOI: 10.1109/BigData.2018.8622478
32. Duleep Rathgamage Don, Ionut E. Iacob, 2019. DCSVM: fast multi-class classification using support vector machines, Springer-Verlag GmbH Germany, part of Springer Nature 2019, International Journal of Machine Learning and Cybernetics. https://doi.org/10.1007/s13042-019-00984-9
33. Dominik Brugger. 2006. Parallel Support Vector Machines. Arbeitsbereich Technische Informatik, Universitat Tubingen. 27 pages.
34. Emmanuel Didiot and Fabien Lauer. 2015. Efficient optimization of multi-class support vector machines with MSVM-pack. In Modeling Computation

and Optimization in Information Systems and Management Sciences. Springer, 23–34.

35. Ana Gainaru, Emil Slusanschi, and Stefan Trausan-Matu. 2011. Mapping data mining algorithms on a GPU architecture: A study. In Foundations of Intelligent Systems. Springer, 102–112.
36. D. F. Shanno, 1970. Conditioning of quasi-Newton methods for function minimization, Mathematics of Computation, vol. 24, pp. 647–656.
37. J. Hu, B. Jiang, L. Lin, Z. Wen, and Y.-x. Yuan, 2019. Structured quasi newton methods for optimization with orthogonality constraints, SIAM Journal on Scientific Computing, vol. 41, pp. 2239–2269.
38. J. Pajarinen, H. L. Thai, R. Akrour, J. Peters, and G. Neumann, 2019. Compatible natural gradient policy search, Machine Learning, pp. 1–24.
39. Corinna Cortes and Vladimir Vapnik. 1995. Support-vector networks. Machine Learning 20, 3 (1995), 273–297.
40. Bernhard E. Boser, Isabelle M. Guyon, and Vladimir N. Vapnik. 1992. A training algorithm for optimal margin classifiers. In Proceedings of the 5th Annual Workshop on Computational Learning Theory. ACM, 144–152.
41. John Platt. 1998. Sequential Minimal Optimization: A Fast Algorithm for Training Support Vector Machines. Technical Report MSR-TR-98-14. Microsoft Research. 21 pages. Retrieved December 12, 2018 from http://research.microsoft.com/apps/pubs/default.aspx?id=69644
42. Vladimir Vapnik. 2013. The Nature of Statistical Learning Theory. Springer Science & Business Media. 314 pages.
43. John iu Ivanciuc. 2007. Applications of support vector machines in chemistry. Reviews in Computational Chemistry 23 (2007), 291–400.
44. Tao Li, Hua Li, Xuechen Liu, Shuai Zhang, KaiWang, and Yulu Yang. 2013. GPU acceleration of interior point methods in large scale SVM training. In 12th IEEE International Conference on Trust, Security and Privacy in Computing and Communications (TrustCom'13). IEEE, 863–870.
45. John C. Platt. 1999. Using analytic QP and sparseness to speed training of support vector machines. In Proceedings of the 1998 Conference on Advances in Neural Information Processing Systems II. MIT Press, 557–563.
46. Valeriu Codreanu, Bob Dröge, David Williams, Burhan Yasar, Po Yang, Baoquan Liu, Feng Dong, Olarik Surinta, Lambert R. B. Schomaker, Jos B. T. M. Roerdink, *et al.* 2016. Evaluating automatically parallelized versions of the support vector machine. In Concurrency and Computation: Practice and Experience 28, 7 (2016), 2274–2294.
47. Kristian Woodsend and Jacek Gondzio. 2009. Hybrid MPI/OpenMP parallel linear support vector machine training. Journal of Machine Learning Research 10 (Dec. 2009), 1937–1953.
48. Fernando Pérez-Cruz, Anıbal R. Figueiras-Vidal, and Antonio Artés-Rodríguez. 2004. Double chunking for solving SVMs for very large datasets. In Proceedings of Learning (2004).

49. Tatjana Eitrich and Bruno Lang. 2005. Efficient Implementation of Serial and Parallel Support Vector Machine Training with a Multi-parameter Kernel for Large-scale Data Mining. Citeseer.
50. AUSTIN Carpenter. 2009. CuSVM: A CUDA implementation of support vector classification and regression. Retrieved December 12, 2018 from http://www.patternsonascreen.net/cuSVMDesc.pdf.
51. Thomas Serafini, Gaetano Zanghirati, and Luca Zanni. 2005. Gradient projection methods for quadratic programs and applications in training support vector machines. Optimization Methods and Software 20, 2-3 (2005), 353–378.
52. Andrew Cotter, Nathan Srebro, and Joseph Keshet. 2011. A GPU-tailored approach for training kernelized SVMs. In Proceedings of the 17th ACM SIGKDD International Conference on Knowledge Discovery and Data Mining. ACM, 805–813.
53. Edward Y. Chang. 2011. PSVM: Parallelizing Support Vector Machines on Distributed Computers. Springer, Berlin, 213–230. DOI:http://dx.doi.org/10.1007/978-3-642-20429-6_10
54. Andreas Athanasopoulos, Anastasios Dimou, Vasileios Mezaris, and Ioannis Kompatsiaris. 2011. GPU acceleration for support vector machines. In 12th International Workshop on Image Analysis for Multimedia Interactive Services (WIAMIS'11), Delft, the Netherlands, April 13-15, 2011. TU Delft; EWI; MM; PRB.
55. Yunmei Lu, Yun Zhu, Meng Han, Jing (Selena) He, and Yanqing Zhang. 2014. A survey of GPU accelerated SVM. In Proceedings of the ACM Southeast Regional Conference (ACM SE'14). ACM, Article 15, 7 pages. DOI:http://dx.doi.org/10.1145/2638404.2638474
56. Yunlu Gong and Lianguo Jia, 2019. Research on SVM environment performance of parallel computing based on large data set of machine learning, Springer Science + Business Media, LLC, part of Springer Nature 2019, The Journal of Supercomputing, https://doi.org/10.1007/s11227-019-02894-7
57. MICHAEL A. HEROUX, ANDREW G. SALINGER, 2005. An overview of the Trilinos Project, ACM Transactions on Mathematical Software, Vol. 31, No. 3, September 2005, Pages 397–423.
58. Von Eicken, T., Culler, D.E., Goldstein, S.C., Schauser, K.E.: Active Messages: a Mechanism for Integrated Communication and Computation. In: Proceedings of the 19th International Symposium on Computer Architecture. Pp. 256{266. Gold Coast, Australia (May 1992). Doi:10.1145/139669.140382
59. G. Zheng, L. Shi, and L. V. Kale, 2004. FTC-Charm++: An In-Memory´ Checkpoint-Based Fault Tolerant Runtime for Charm++ and MPI, IEEE Cluster, San Diego, CA, September 2004, pp. 93–103.
60. Xueqin Zhang, Yifeng Zhang, and Chunhua Gu. 2014. GPU implementation of parallel support vector machine algorithm with applications to detection intruder. Journal of Computers 9, 5 (2014), 1117–1124.

61. Qi Li, Raied Salman, Erik Test, Robert Strack, and Vojislav Kecman. 2011. GPUSVM: A comprehensive CUDA based support vector machine package. Open Computer Science 1, 4 (2011), 387–405.
62. Sergio Herrero-Lopez, John R. Williams, and Abel Sanchez. 2010. Parallel multiclass classification using SVMs on GPUs. In Proceedings of the 3rd Workshop on General-Purpose Computation on Graphics Processing Units (GPGPU-3). ACM, New York, NY, 2–11. DOI:http://dx.doi.org/10.1145/1735688.1735692
63. Quan Liao, Jibo Wang, Yue Webster, and Ian A. Watson. 2009. GPU accelerated support vector machines for mining high-throughput screening data. Journal of Chemical Information and Modeling 49, 12 (2009), 2718–2725.
64. Krzysztof Sopyła, Paweł Drozda, and Przemysław Gorecki. 2012. SVM with CUDA accelerated kernels for big sparse problems. In Artificial Intelligence and Soft Computing. Springer, 439–447.
65. Qi Li. 2011. Fast Parallel Machine Learning Algorithms for Large Datasets Using Graphic Processing Unit. Ph.D. thesis. AAI3489482.
66. Tsung-Kai Lin and Shao-Yi Chien. 2010. Support vector machines on GPU with sparse matrix format. In 9th International Conference on Machine Learning and Applications. IEEE, 313–318.
67. J. Vaněk, J. Michalek, and J. Psutka. 2017. A GPU-architecture optimized hierarchical decomposition algorithm for support vector machine training. IEEE Transactions on Parallel and Distributed Systems 28, 12 (Dec 2017), 3330–3343. DOI:http://dx.doi.org/10.1109/TPDS.2017.2731764
68. Yang You and James Demmel. 2017. Runtime data layout scheduling for machine learning dataset. In 46th International. Conference on Parallel Processing (ICPP'17). IEEE, 452–461.
69. Bryan Catanzaro, Narayanan Sundaram, and Kurt Keutzer. 2008. Fast support vector machine training and classification on graphics processors. In Proceedings of the 25th International Conference on Machine Learning. ACM, 104–111.
70. Nanbo Peng, Yanxia Zhang, and Yongheng Zhao. 2011. CUDA-accelerated SVM for celestial object classification. In Astronomical Data Analysis Software and Systems Xx, Vol. 442. 119–122. Astronomical Society of the Pacific.
71. Fan, R.-E., Chen, P.-H., Lin, C.-J. 2005. Working set selection using the second order information for training svm. Journal of Machine Learning Research 6, 1889–1918.
72. Osuna, E., Freund, R., Girosi, F, 1997. Training support vector machines: an application to face detection. In: Proceedings of IEEE Computer Society Conference on Computer Vision and Pattern Recognition, vol. 6, pp. 130–136.
73. Chang, C.C., Lin, C.J.: LIBSVM, 2011. A library for support vector machines. ACM Transactions on Intelligent Systems and Technology 2, 27:1–27:27.

74. L. PALAGI and M. SCIANDRONE, 2014. On the convergence of a modified version of SVMlight algorithm, Optimization Methods and Software ISSN 1055-6788 print/ISSN 1029-4937 online © 2005 Taylor & Francis Group Ltd http://www.tandf.co.uk/journals DOI: 10.1080/10556780512331318209
75. Keerthi, S., Shevade, S., Bhattacharyya, C., Murthy, K., 2001. Improvements to platt's smo algorithm for svm classifier design. Neural Computation 13(3), 637–649.
76. Platt, J, 1988. Fast training of support vector machines using sequential minimal optimization. In: Schoelkopf, B., Burges, C., Smola, A. (eds.) Advances in Kernel Methods – Support Vector Learning. MIT Press.
77. Fan, R.-E., Chen, P.-H., Lin, C.-J, 2005. Working set selection using the second order information for training svm. Journal of Machine Learning Research 6, 1889–1918 .
78. Carpenter, A., 2005. Cusvm: A cuda implementation of support vector classification and regression. Tech. rep.
79. Catanzaro, B., Sundaram, N., Keutzer, K, 2008. Fast support vector machine training and classification on graphics processors. In: Proceedings of the 25th International Conference on Machine Learning, ICML 2008, pp. 104–111. ACM, New York .
80. Osuna, E., Freund, R., Girosi, F, 1997. Training support vector machines: an application to face detection. In: Proceedings of IEEE Computer Society Conference on Computer Vision and Pattern Recognition, vol. 6, pp. 130–136.
81. The OpenCL Specification, Khronos OpenCL Working Group, URL www.khronos.org/opencl/
82. H. Gasparakis, 2014. "Heterogeneous Compute in Computer Vision: OpenCL in OpenCV," IS&T/SPIE Electronic Imaging, Visual Information Processing and Communication V, San Francisco, CA.
83. Khronos OpenCL Conformant Products, URL: http://www.khronos.org/conformance/adopters/conformant-products.
84. Caoxie Zhang, Honglak Lee, and Kang G Shin. 2012. Efficient distributed linear classification algorithms via the alternating direction method of multipliers. In Proceedings of the Fifteenth International Conference on Artificial Intelligence and Statistics, Neil D. Lawrence and Mark Girolami (Eds.), and In Proceedings of Machine Learning Research (PMLR'12), Vol. 22. 1398–1406.
85. Dmitry Pechyony, Libin Shen, and Rosie Jones. 2011. Solving large scale linear SVM with distributed block minimization. In NIPS 2011 Workshop on Big Learning: Algorithms, Systems and Tools for Learning at Scale. Citeseer.
86. Igor Durdanovic, Eric Cosatto, and Hans-Peter Graf. 2007. Large Scale Parallel SVM Implementation. MIT Press,105–138.

87. X. Ke, R. Jin, X. Xie, and J. Cao, "A Distributed SVM Method based on the Iterative MapReduce," in Proc. Of the IEEE Int. Conf. on Semantic Computing (ICSC), Anaheim, CA, USA, 7–9 Feb 2015, pp. 7–10.
88. X. Wang and S. Matwin, "A Distributed Instance-weighted SVM Algorithm on Large-scale Imbalanced Datasets," in Proc. Of the IEEE Int. Conf. on Big Data (ICBD), 2014, pp. 45–51.
89. A. Bordes, L. Bottou, and P. Gallinari, 2009. "SGD-QN: Careful Quasi-Newton Stochastic Gradient Descent," J. of Mach. Learning Res. (JMLR), vol. 10, pp. 1737–1754.
90. Y. Lu, V. Roychowdhury, and L. Vandenberghe, 2008. "Distributed Parallel Support Vector Machine in Strongly Connected Networks," IEEE Trans. On Neural Networks, vol. 19, no. 7, pp. 1167–1178.
91. L. Zanni, T. Serafini, and G. Zanghirati, 2006."Parallel software for training large scale support vector machines on multiprocessor systems," J. of Mach. Learning Res. (JMLR), vol. 7, pp. 1467–1492.
92. Z. Sun and G. Fox, 2012. "Study on Parallel SVM Based on MapReduce,"in Proc. Of the Int. Conf. on Parallel and Distributed Processing Techniques and Applications, pp. 16–19.
93. N. K. Alham, M. Li, S. Hammoud, Y. Liu, and M. Ponraj, 2010. "A distributed SVM for image annotation," in Int. Conf. on Fuzzy Systems and Knowledge Discovery (FSKD), Yantai, Shandong, China, pp. 2983–2987.
94. N. K. Alham, M. Li, Y. Liu, S. Hammoud, and M. Ponraj, 2011."A distributed SVM for scalable image annotation," in Proc. Of the Int. Conf. on Fuzzy Systems and Knowledge Discovery (FSKD), Shanghai, China,, pp. 2655–2658.
95. N. K. Alham, M. Li, Y. Liu, and S. Hammoud, "A MapReduce based distributed SVM algorithm for automatic image annotation," Computers and Mathematics with Applications, vol. 62, no. 7, pp. 2801–2811, 2011.
96. S. Herrero-Lopez, J. R. Williams, and A. Sanchez, 2010. "Parallel multi-class classification using SVMs on GPUs," in Proc. Of the 3rd Workshop on General-Purpose Computation on Graphics Processing Units – GPGPU '10, Pittsburgh, PA, USA, pp. 2–11.
97. J.A.K. Suykens and J. Vandewalle, 1999, Least Squares Support Vector Machine Classifiers, Kluwer Academic Publishers. Printed in the Netherlands.vap

10

Electrical Network-Related Incident Prediction Based on Weather Factors

Hongda Tian[1*], Jessie Nghiem[2] and Fang Chen[1]

[1]*Data Science Institute, University of Technology Sydney, Sydney, Australia*
[2]*Data and Analytics, Energy Safe Victoria, Melbourne, Australia*

Abstract
Accurate prediction of electrical network-related incidents has great implications for improving network safety. This paper focuses on the correlation between such incidents and weather factors and aims to develop incident prediction models using weather variables. The key weather factors leading to the incidents will be identified quantitatively. Specifically, the problem will be divided into three sub-problems: classification of incident and normality, natural language processing-based incident categorization, and classification of multiple types of incidents. A variety of machine learning techniques will be investigated to solve these problems. The proposed methods will be tested using the data relating to incidents occurring at the electrical network within the state of Victoria in Australia.

Keywords: Predictive analytics, supervised classification, factor analysis, natural language processing

10.1 Introduction

Electrical network-related incidents (e.g., fire) often cause substantial economic and ecological damage, as well as endanger the lives of people. As a result, it is crucial to develop effective methods and equipment that can reduce the risk/loss of future incidents. To improve network safety, one important aspect is to predict such incidents accurately so that related decision makers could take proactive measures to prevent them

**Corresponding author*: hongda.tian@uts.edu.au

M. Niranjanamurthy, Hemant Kumar Gianey and Amir H. Gandomi (eds.) Advances in Data Science and Analytics: Concepts and Paradigms, (233–246) © 2023 Scrivener Publishing LLC

effectively. However, a variety of factors (e.g., aging infrastructure and human behaviour) could cause these incidents, which makes it a challenging task.

In this work, we aim to investigate the relationship between electrical network-related incidents and daily weather factors (e.g., daily maximum temperature). Specifically, machine learning models will be developed for incident prediction using weather variables. The key weather factors leading to the incidents will be identified quantitatively. By the leverage of the data regarding ten years of incidents occurring at the electrical network throughout the state of Victoria in Australia, three specific sub-problems are investigated in this paper.

Firstly, the problem of whether weather variables could be used for differentiating incidents from normal status will be investigated. Except for weather factors, spatial information for weather observations is also incorporated into feature vectors. Various popular modelling techniques are considered in this study. Cross validation will be performed to evaluate and rank the implemented models.

The second task is focused on automatic categorization of incidents. The existing practice on incident categorization is usually a semi-manual process. It defines each reported incident into one of fifteen categories based on information such as incident cause and event description, which are generally free text input by humans. The objective of this task is to classify incidents into correct categories, automatically using the aforementioned information. Thus, classification models using natural language processing will be developed to deal with this task. A bag-of-words model will be used in order to turn the incident descriptions into a bag of standardized tokens that could be read by machine learning models in a supervised learning setting.

Finally, based on the classified incident categories and related weather data, we could further study their correlations. For such a multi-class classification problem, different machine learning models will be built for multiple types of incident differentiation. The widely used metrics and cross validation will be adopted for model evaluation. In addition, for both binary and multi-class classification, the driving weather factors leading to the incidents will be identified through an analysis of feature importance.

Following this introduction, we review the related literature in Section 10.2. The proposed methods are presented in Section 10.3. The experimental results are provided in Section 10.4. Finally, we conclude the paper in Section 10.5.

10.2 Related Work

A Poisson regression model and a Bayesian network model were used for modelling failure rates of overhead distribution lines in [1]. Power outages caused by extreme weather conditions (e.g., hurricanes) were studied in [2–4]. A boosting-based ensemble learning method was presented to estimate outages caused by wind and lightning in overhead distribution systems in [5]. A prediction for the number of damages in electrical distribution systems resulting from a weather event was performed in [6]. Damages were divided into six types including single-customer outage, low-voltage, tree-trim, other, multi-customer outage, and wire-down-no-outage. Weather variables such as temperature, wind speed, rain rate, precipitation, pressure, and humidity were considered in the work. A Bayesian prediction model estimating the number of outages caused by storms was developed in [7]. A method for predicting power outages due to convective storms was proposed in [8], which is a combination of storm cell identification and tracking and state-of-the-art machine learning techniques.

Generally, there are two key differences between the existing work and ours. As can be noticed, most existing work only focuses on the impact of single weather factor on network incidents. In this paper, we will study the effects of multiple weather factors. Additionally, all the incidents are considered as a whole in most previous research. However, incidents will also be disaggregated into different types in our work.

10.3 Methodology

10.3.1 Binary Classification of Incident and Normality

We first attempt to answer the question of whether weather variables could be used for differentiating incidents from normal status. For this purpose, weather observations at both normal and incident situations are used to build a binary classification model. Except for weather factors, spatial information for weather observations is also incorporated into feature vectors. Instead of including the raw values of longitude and latitude as features, they are converted into three dimensional features (x, y, z) according to trigonometry based on Equation 10.1. Such converted location features can be properly scaled with the weather data. A variety of widely used modelling techniques are considered in this study including Naive Bayes,

Logistic Regression, Random Forest, Decision Tree, K-Nearest Neighbors, Bernoulli, and Support Vector Machine.

$$\begin{aligned} x &= cos(latitude) \times cos(longitude) \\ y &= cos(latitude) \times sin(longitude) \\ z &= sin(latitude) \end{aligned} \tag{10.1}$$

10.3.2 Incident Categorization Using Natural Language Processing

Some incidents may be strongly related to weather factors, while others could have a weak correlation with weather. Additionally, incidents could be disaggregated into certain categories according to different weather patterns. In order to investigate the relationship between different types of incidents and weather variables, we need to divide all the incidents into a few categories first, which will be studied in this section.

For the incident data used in this study, each incident is described by "incident cause" and "event description", which are unstructured free texts input manually. A straightforward idea is to test whether it is possible to perform incident categorization by means of natural language processing techniques based on these descriptions. Currently, incident categorization is conducted manually. There is a potential to automate this process if promising results could be achieved.

A bag-of-words model is considered here, which involves reducing sentences to collections of words where punctuation, word order, and grammar are ignored. Specifically, tokenization is first performed to turn free texts into a collection of smaller parts called tokens. Two types of tokenization methods are tested, namely stemming and lemmatization. Then, a histogram is constructed using the appearance frequency of all the tokens for feature extraction. Furthermore, term-frequency and inverse-document-frequency (TF-IDF) transformation is adopted for feature normalization, which assigns higher weight to terms that appear more frequently within an incident's description but appear less frequently elsewhere. Finally, the extracted features input multiple classifiers as presented before for incident categorization.

10.3.3 Classification of Multiple Types of Incidents

Compared with the differentiation between incidents and normal situations based on weather factors conducted in Section 10.3.1, we study the

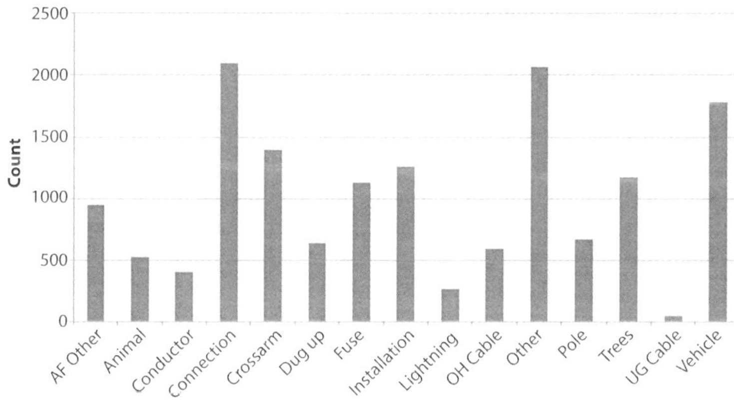

Figure 10.1 Number of samples for fifteen categories of incidents.

relationship between different types of incidents and weather variables in this section. Specifically, the objective is to build classification models using weather variables for differentiating fifteen types of incidents that are predefined. All the well-known models mentioned before will be tested here as well. A distribution chart based on the number of samples for fifteen categories is shown in Figure 10.1. As can be observed, the sample number across different incident categories is heavily imbalanced. SMOTE [9] is adopted to address this issue, which is a data augmentation method generating synthetic samples for minority classes based on K-Nearest Neighbors.

10.4 Experiments

10.4.1 Data Sets

The incident data used in this study involves incidents occurring at the electrical network within the state of Victoria in Australia from 2010 to 2019. For each standard incident record, the corresponding date and location information are available. Each incident has been assigned one of fifteen category labels. In addition, each record is accompanied by "incident cause" and "event description" describing the incident using free texts.

To obtain the weather condition when the incidents occurred, we first downloaded the historical weather data for the whole of Victoria between 2010 and 2019 from SILO [10]. The data has a gridded format in terms of geographic coverage and the grid has a resolution of 0.1° latitude by 0.1° longitude (approximately 10 km × 10 km). Thus, the whole of Victoria is divided into 4316 locations. For each location with specific latitude and longitude, numerical values for fifteen weather variables are available on a daily basis. The meanings of these weather variables are summarized in Table 10.1. For each incident, the weather data recorded on the same date at the nearest location to the incident site are considered as its corresponding weather condition.

Table 10.1 Weather variables and their meanings.

Abbreviation	Meaning
T_Max_oC	Maximum Temperature
T_Min_oC	Minimum Temperature
Rain_mm	Daily Rainfall
Evap_mm	Evaporation
Radn_MJm2	Solar Exposure, consisting of both direct and diffuse components
VP_hPa	Vapour Pressure
RHmaxT_	Relative Humidity at the time of maximum temperature
RHminT_	Relative Humidity at the time of minimum temperature
FAO56_mm	Potential Evapotranspiration calculated using the FAO Penman-Monteith Formula
Mlake_mm	Morton Evaporation over shallow lakes
Mpot_mm	Morton Potential Evapotranspiration over land
Mact_mm	Morton Actual Evapotranspiration over land
Mwet_mm	Morton Wet Environment Areal Evapotranspiration over land
Span_mm	A calibrated estimate of class A pan evaporation based on vapor pressure deficit and solar radiation
MSLPres_hpa	Mean Sea Level Pressure

10.4.2 Evaluation Metrics

To evaluate the performance of a series of classification models, accuracy, precision, recall, and F1-scores are adopted, which are defined in Equations 10.2 to 10.5. All these metrics are derived from true positives (TP), true negatives (TN), false positives (FP), and false negatives (FN).

$$Accuracy = \frac{TP + TN}{TP + TN + FP + FN} \tag{10.2}$$

$$Precision - \frac{TP}{TP + FP} \tag{10.3}$$

$$Recall = \frac{TP}{TP + FN} \tag{10.4}$$

$$F1 - Score = \frac{2 \times Precision \times Recall}{Precision + Recall} \tag{10.5}$$

Additionally, the area under the receiver operating characteristic (ROC) curve (AUC) is also adopted to evaluate the performance for binary classification of incident and normality.

10.4.3 Binary Classification

We conduct the experiments related to binary classification of incident and normality in this section. The weather data collected at the nearest locations to incident sites when no incidents were reported are selected to represent normal situations. There are 4,741,082 records representing normality in total. We first randomly select 70% from the weather data for incidents and the same amount for normal status to construct a training set. All the rest of the weather data are used for testing. Among different models, as presented in Section 10.3.1, Random Forest leads to the best performance with an accuracy of 99.91%. Thus, we only report the results based on Random Forest in this section. The confusion matrix is shown in Table 10.2. As noticed, 4,485 samples are correctly classified among 4,503 incident records with a recall rate of 99.6%. As for a large amount of 4,730,575 normal records, the false alarm rate is less than 0.1%. We further calculate the AUC in this case, which has a very high value of 0.999988.

Table 10.2 Confusion matrix for binary classification of incident and normal data.

		Predicted label	
		Incident	**Normal**
True label	**Incident**	4,485	18
	Normal	4,269	4,726,306

These results indicate that the fifteen weather factors are very useful for differentiating incidents from normality.

In order to understand which weather variables are more critical for the binary classification, an analysis about recursive feature elimination is performed. The importance for the fifteen weather factors is illustrated in Figure 10.2. As can be seen, daily rainfall and relative humidity at the time of minimum temperature are the top two significant factors, while evaporation has the least contribution to the classification performance.

Furthermore, we conduct a 10-fold cross validation for comprehensive evaluation, which results in a high average accuracy of 99.93%. The confusion matrices for the best and worst fold are shown in Table 10.3 and Table 10.4, respectively. As can be observed, both cases lead to a similar recall rate (above 99.5%) for incident class. This demonstrates that the chance of misdetecting incidents is rather low. In the worst fold, more normal samples are misclassified as incidents. However, even at the worst case, a low false alarm rate of 0.09% could be achieved. The AUC for the best and worst fold are calculated as 0.999995 and 0.999983, respectively.

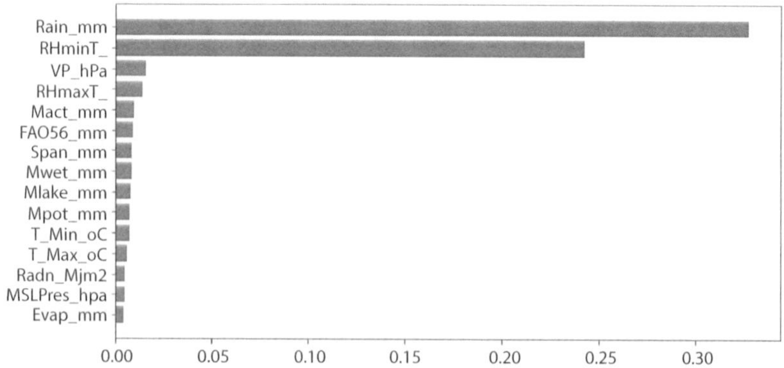

Figure 10.2 Feature importance for binary classification of incident and normal data.

Table 10.3 Confusion matrix for best fold of 10-fold cross validation of binary classification.

		Predicted label	
		Incident	**Normal**
True label	**Incident**	1,494	7
	Normal	1,451	4,721,619

Table 10.4 Confusion matrix for worst fold of 10-fold cross validation of binary classification.

		Predicted label	
		Incident	**Normal**
True label	**Incident**	1,496	5
	Normal	4,353	4,718,717

10.4.4 Incident Categorization

In this section, we present the experimental results about incident categorization based on the techniques described in Section 10.3.2. For each incident category, 70% of samples are selected at random for model training and the rest are used for testing. The classification results obtained using different models are shown in Table 10.5. In

Table 10.5 Classification results for incident categorization using different models.

Method	**Accuracy**	**Precision**	**Recall**	**F1-score**
Support Vector Machine	0.789	0.789	0.789	0.788
Logistic Regression	0.781	0.780	0.781	0.779
Random Forest	0.755	0.753	0.755	0.737
K-Nearest Neighbours	0.689	0.702	0.689	0.684
Naive Bayes	0.685	0.672	0.685	0.671
Decision Tree	0.659	0.661	0.659	0.659
Bernoulli	0.658	0.678	0.658	0.656

Table 10.6 Category-wise classification performance for incident categorization based on support vector machine.

Category	Precision	Recall	F1-score
Vehicle	0.90	0.92	0.91
Trees	0.90	0.92	0.91
Animal	0.92	0.85	0.88
Lighting	0.91	0.76	0.83
Dug Up	0.88	0.88	0.88
Fuse	0.84	0.87	0.85
Other	0.86	0.82	0.84
Crossarm	0.82	0.84	0.83
Installation	0.77	0.80	0.78
Connection	0.72	0.76	0.74
Pole	0.61	0.67	0.64
UG Cable	0.67	0.20	0.31
AF Other	0.59	0.59	0.59
Conductor	0.55	0.49	0.52
OH Cable	0.56	0.46	0.50

terms of all the evaluation metrics, Support Vector Machine achieves the best performance. We then perform a 10-fold cross validation using the Support Vector Machine. The average classification performance for each category is provided in Table 10.6. In consideration of all the evaluation metrics, the best performance is noticed for 'Trees' and 'Vehicle' categories. 'Conductor' and 'OH Cable' have the worst classification performance.

10.4.5 Multi-Class Classification

The experimental results for multiple types of incident classification are provided in this section. Among all the models tested, Random Forest yields the best average accuracy of 27% for 10-fold cross validation. It seems the fifteen weather factors are not very effective for multiple types of incident differentiation. The best performance is observed for the 'Crossarm' category. Due to the very limited data for 'UG Cable' category, it shows the worst performance. The average classification performance for the top four performing categories is shown in Table 10.7.

We further conduct an experiment using the top four performing categories only, namely 'Crossarm', 'Other', 'Fuse', and 'Trees'. The classification performance is shown in Table 10.8. Compared with the case where all the fifteen categories are considered, the performance for each of the four categories is improved significantly. One explanation for this could be these categories are more related to the fifteen weather factors and each category is associated with unique weather condition. Furthermore, we investigate the importance of the fifteen weather factors in this case, which are plotted in Figure 10.3. Compared with the case of binary classification, there are no significant dominant features. However, mean sea level pressure is identified as the most important weather variable while daily rainfall is the least important.

Table 10.7 Multi-class classification performance for top four performing categories based on random forest by considering all fifteen categories.

Category	Precision	Recall	F1-score
Crossarm	0.433	0.416	0.422
Other	0.390	0.428	0.406
Fuse	0.294	0.378	0.331
Trees	0.277	0.264	0.268

Table 10.8 Performance for the classification of top four performing categories.

Category	Precision	Recall	F1-score
Other	0.683	0.776	0.725
Crossarm	0.621	0.595	0.607
Fuse	0.569	0.584	0.576
Trees	0.538	0.415	0.469

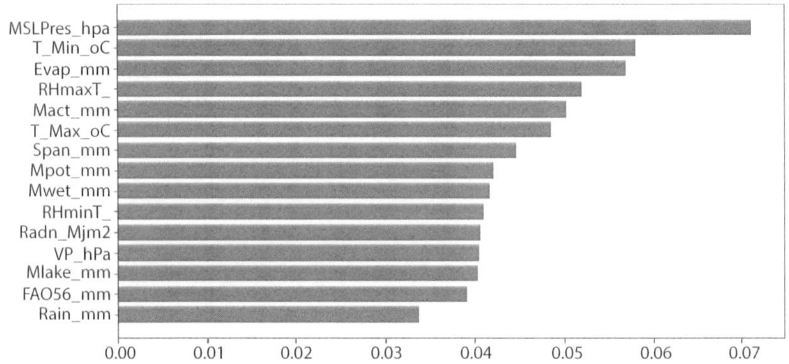

Figure 10.3 Feature importance for classification of top four performing categories.

10.5 Conclusion and Future Work

In this paper, we have studied the problem of electrical network-related incidents prediction using daily weather factors. More specifically, three sub-topics, namely classification of incident and normality, natural language processing-based incident categorization, and classification of multiple types of incidents, have been investigated by means of various machine learning techniques. The experimental results have indicated a very good performance for binary classification. In consideration of practical applications, weather forecast data could be fed into the developed classification models to predict the occurrence probability of potential incidents. Decision makers may take this information into consideration and adopt proactive measures to further improve network safety. Reasonably good performance has been achieved for incident categorization. Although the differentiation of multiple types of incidents is not very successful at the current stage, it is very promising to improve the performance by considering the following items in the future: 1) include more weather factors (e.g., wind speed) at a finer temporal granularity (e.g., hourly measurement) into analysis; 2) incorporate data related to network infrastructure, human behaviour, terrain, vegetation, etc. into modelling; 3) design incident categories through other methods such as unsupervised learning.

Acknowledgements

We would like to thank Energy Safe Victoria for providing the electrical network-related incident data for this research work.

References

1. Zhou, Y., Pahwa, A., Yang, S. S.: Modeling weather-related failures of overhead distribution lines. *IEEE Transactions on Power Systems* 21(4), 1683–1690 (Nov 2006)
2. Nateghi, R., Guikema, S., Quiring, S. M.: Power outage estimation for tropical cyclones: Improved accuracy with simpler models. *Risk Analysis* 34(6), 1069–1078 (Jun 2014)
3. Chen, P. C., Kezunovic, M.: Fuzzy logic approach to predictive risk analysis in distribution outage management. *IEEE Transactions on Smart Grid* 7(6), 2827–2836 (Nov 2016)
4. He, J., Wanik, D. W., Hartman, B. M., Anagnostou, E. N., Astitha, M., Frediani, M. E. B.: Nonparametric tree-based predictive modeling of storm outages on an electric distribution network. *Risk Analysis* 37(3), 441–458 (Mar 2017)
5. Kankanala, P., Das, S., Pahwa, A.: Adaboost+: An ensemble learning approach for estimating weather-related outages in distribution systems. *IEEE Transactions on Power Systems* 29(1), 359–367 (Jan 2014)
6. Li, Z., Singhee, A., Wang, H., Raman, A., Siegel, S., Heng, F. L., Mueller, R., Labut, G.: Spatio-temporal forecasting of weather-driven damage in a distribution system. *In: Proceedings of the IEEE Power and Energy Society General Meeting*. pp. 1–5 (Jul 2015)
7. Yue, M., Toto, T., Jensen, M. P., Giangrande, S. E., Lofaro, R.: A Bayesian approach-based outage prediction in electric utility systems using radar measurement data. *IEEE Transactions on Smart Grid* 9(6), 6149–6159 (Nov 2018)
8. Tervo, R., Karjalainen, J., Jung, A.: Short-term prediction of electricity outages caused by convective storms. *IEEE Transactions on Geoscience and Remote Sensing* 57(11), 8618–8626 (Nov 2019)
9. Chawla, N. V., Bowyer, K. W., Hall, L. O., Kegelmeyer, W. P.: SMOTE: Synthetic minority over-sampling technique. *Journal of Artificial Intelligence Research* 16, 321–357 (Jun 2002)
10. Jeffrey, S. J., Carter, J. O., Moodie, K. B., Beswick, A. R.: Using spatial interpolation to construct a comprehensive archive of Australian climate data. *Environmental Modelling & Software* 16(4), 309–330 (Jun 2001)

11

Green IoT: Environment-Friendly Approach to IoT

Abhishek Goel[1] and Siddharth Gautam[2*]

[1]*Department of Information Technology, Guru Gobind Singh Indraprastha University, Delhi, India*
[2]*Department of Information Technology, Research Fellow, NSUT, Delhi, India*

Abstract
The Internet of Things, better known as IoT, has been a great area for research and has also gained fame in recent years. Nowadays, we all have advanced and sophisticated devices around us. Some instruments are often related to an IoT system. Such a high number of instruments being connected to the IoT system has led to a high consumption of energy. This high consumption of energy by devices connected to IoT has been turned into a major research area. Hence, G-IoT, i.e., the main focus of G-IoT, is on lowering the consumption of electrical power by the IoT instruments to attain a continual environment for the IoT system.

Keywords: G-IoT, energy efficiency, RFID, sensors, green techniques, green environment

11.1 Introduction

In this era of technology, the internet has changed our living standards. It has turned the whole world into a small piece of land where everything is connected to everyone. These things not only include our smart devices, i.e., mobile phones, watches, etc., but also include things like our house items including the lights, fans, electrical appliances, etc. We, humans, have advanced ourselves so much that we can even control our car parked in a parking lot just with a click. Figure 11.1 represents the different components

**Corresponding author*: siddharthinfo92@gmail.com

M. Niranjanamurthy, Hemant Kumar Gianey and Amir H. Gandomi (eds.) Advances in Data Science and Analytics: Concepts and Paradigms, (247–274) © 2023 Scrivener Publishing LLC

Figure 11.1 Components of an IoT system.

that are there in an IoT system. This is the beauty of the Internet of Things, wherein anything can be communicated with, anytime and anywhere [1, 2].

Though this beauty allows machines to interact with each other automatically, intelligently process data, and achieve a common solution, it generates a huge amount of data that needs to be processed regularly and, hence, possesses high energy consumption which in turn puts an extra burden on society [1, 3].

The community is continuing towards a viridescent scope to limit the pessimistic effects of innovation implementations on human and condition by creating strategies and strategies without hurting impacts on the earth and anthropoid well-being, preserving characteristic assets, and producing techniques for the maintainable turn of events—to represent individuals, the planet, and benefits for both. Innovation usage without harming, over-misusing, or draining regular assets, decrease of vitality utilization, the obtainment of totally reused or recovered items, diminishing the measure of garbage and discharges during creation and use and options to innovations which do not cause a pessimistic effect on wellbeing and the characteristic condition, are the main objectives of viridescent, ecological, or neat innovation. At the end of the day, green innovation includes ecologically reasonable structuring, assembling, utilizing, and discarding, with no or fundamentally diminished away on the earth [3, 4].

Due to all this, there is a need for better solutions to make our living environment sustainable by reducing carbon dioxide emissions and reducing power consumption. To solve this problem, G-IoT comes into play [2, 4].

Figure 11.2 represents the areas where Green - IoT can be put to use. Due to the emerging crisis of the environment, G-IoT techniques must be taken into consideration. Nowadays, we have an estimate of 31 billion devices connected to the internet. Have you ever thought that the cellular network you are using now leads to CO2 emissions? According to a projection, there are around 345 million tons of CO2 emissions due to cellular networks. Hence, the G-Iot in an attractive area of research.

Our main aim is to describe what green-IoT is, techniques currently available, and future prospects. Section 11.2 discusses the Green-IoT and

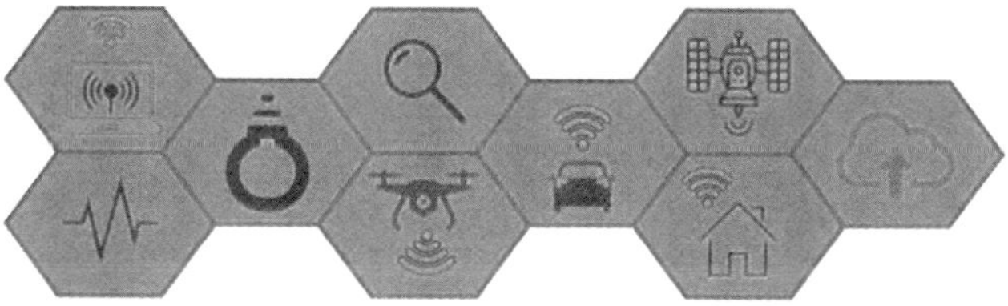

Figure 11.2 Green-Internet of Things (G-IoT).

different components of IoT. In Section 11.3, we will discuss the techniques available and also summarize them in a tabular form. Section 4 consists of a case study to understand the working schema of G-IoT [5, 6].

11.2 G-IoT (Green Internet of Things)

Green-IoT can be referred to as the system of saving or reducing energy consumption by devices in an IoT system. This, in turn, further reduces CO2 emissions and helps in the development of a sustainable environment. There are various techniques available for the implementation of G-IoT and they are discussed in further sections. Using these techniques we are trying to reduce the greenhouse effects caused due to the ever-increasing connected devices in an IoT system. Gradually, we will move forward advancing our technology in such a way that it stops creating the greenhouse effect [6–8].

To achieve this, first we segregated the components of the IoT devices in power-hungry and non-power-hungry components as described in Figure 11.3 [3].

There are four major pillars on which the whole concept of Green IoT stands. These four pillars are mentioned in Figure 11.4.

- Green Design is a practice in which, while building, we opt for an eco-friendly alternative to neutralize the harmful repercussions on individual lives as well as the abode. Its major focus is on safeguarding air, water, and earth [4].
- Green Production is the resumption of manufacturing tactics and the established order of nature-pleasant functions inside the production field. Fundamentally, it is the "greening" of production, in which people use less natural resources, lessen contamination and garbage, reuse and recycle materials, and average discharge in the strategies [4].

  Viridescent producers investigate, grow, or employ automation and applications to reduce their effect on nature.

Figure 11.3 IoT components classification.

- Green Utilization includes the utilization of eco-friendly goods while constructing a device that is going to be used in an IoT system. It also includes the application of upgraded algorithms, gateways, nodes, etc. to minimize the effect on the environment [4].
- Green Recycling includes the recycling and reuse of electronic devices that are partially non-working. It will reduce the generation of a brand new device. Hence, it reduces the cost of manufacturing, the material used, etc. It also helps in the development of a green environment. According to a survey, we get to know that there is no possible way in which waste can be disposed of safely. It contaminates the environment in one way or another [4].

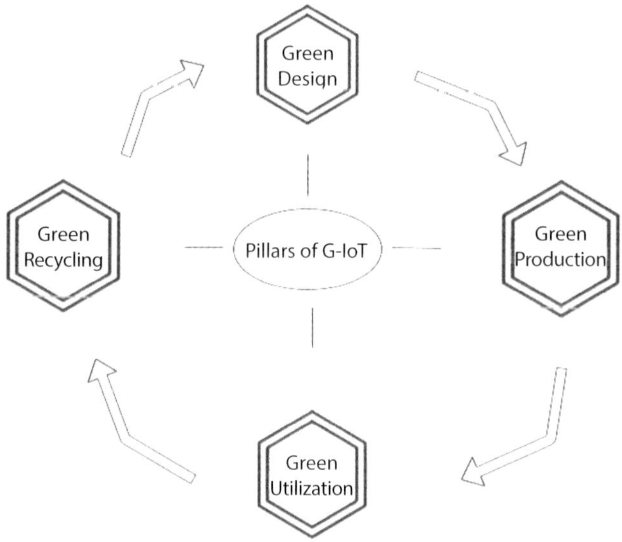

Figure 11.4 Pillars of G-IoT.

To overcome this problem, we need a proper strategy for waste management. It can only be ensured when each material that is used in production can either be reused or recycled so that we can use it again or recycle it in such a way that it gives back to the environment [6].

11.3 Layered Architecture of G-IoT

Since we understand the Green IoT, it is now time to understand the architecture of the G-IoT. The architecture of Green IoT can be divided into 6 major layers, as shown in Figure 11.5 [9].

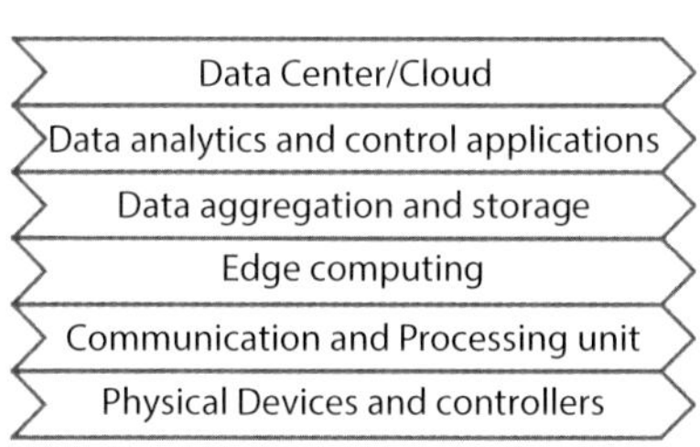

Figure 11.5 Architecture of G-IoT.

Here you are going to learn the purpose of each layer and components that are present in each layer.

11.3.1 Data Center/Cloud

It is the network of computers and storage devices that are used by various organizations for the purpose of transmission, storage, and processing. Due to the direct dependencies of these organizations on data centers, they play a vital role in the daily activities of the organization.

Data centers include components like routers, networking switches, power supply, backup generators, cooling systems, etc. Due to the hype of greener technologies, green data centers include low emission materials used for construction, catalytic converters, and renewable power sources [9, 10].

11.3.2 Data Analytics and Control Applications It

These are used for analyzing data and help in optimizing security in high-risk regions. The application control includes processes like code sway, filtering control, output sway, and probity control.

Controlling a program is a safety norm that squares unauthorised apps from compiling in manners that controls data in danger. The power storage swap depends on the privacy reason for a specific application and the principal objective is to guarantee the privacy and security of data used by and transferred between softwares [5, 9, 10].

Software support assimilates fulfilment and checks authenticity, ID, approval, input source, and criminal records.

- Fulfilment Examines: commands guarantee data handling from inception to finish
- Legitimacy Examines: commands guarantee substantial data is input or handled
- ID: commands guarantee extraordinary, verifiable recognizable documents, all things considered
- Verification: commands give an application frame validation component
- Approval: commands guarantee permission to the software framework by affirmed company clients as it is
- Information Control: commands guarantee data series takes care of the software framework from other sources

- Legal Control: commands guarantee experimentally and the scientifically true collection of data, in view of abstract data and information

Specifically, implementation controls guarantee legitimate indulgent and the classification, respectability, and accessibility of the application and its related information. With the correct application controls, organizations and associations significantly diminish the dangers and dangers related to application utilization since applications are kept from executing in the event that they put the system or touchy information in danger [10].

11.3.3 Data Aggregation and Storage

Data aggregation is any procedure whereby information is accumulated and communicated in a synopsis structure. At the point when information is accumulated, nuclear information lines, ordinarily assembled from various sources, are supplanted with sums or rundown insights. Gatherings of watched totals are supplanted with outline measurements dependent on those perceptions. Total information is ordinarily found in an information distribution center, as it can give answers to systematic inquiries and furthermore significantly diminish an opportunity to question enormous arrangements of information [5, 9, 10].

Storing the data generated in an IoT system is a huge challenge. Because of the voluminous amount of data, there is a need of around 507.5 ZB of storage. This huge amount of data is generated by around 5 million devices connected to an IoT network across the globe. Cloud storage used in this framework is the best option provided and needs to be taken forward. We cannot rely on the physical servers setup by big players like Google, Amazon, Facebook, etc. for data storage [5, 9, 10].

11.3.4 Edge Computing

Edge Computing is the part of the computer network in the IoT framework where the information that is either consumed or produced by the users is stored at the edges. At its fundamental extent, edge computing brings estimative and informative volume closer to the appliances or gadgets where they are being congregated, instead of being controlled by a chief area that can be thousands of miles apart. This is usually done so that information, particularly real-time information, does not endure inactivity issues that can influence an application's execution. In expansion, companies can spare cash by having the handling done locally, decreasing the sum of information that ought to be prepared in a centralized or cloud-based area. These edge gadgets can incorporate numerous distinctive things, such as an IoT sensor, an employee's scratchpad computer, their most recent smartphone, the security camera, or even the internet-connected microwave stove within the office break room. Edge portals themselves are considered edge gadgets inside an edge-computing foundation [5, 9, 10].

11.3.5 Communication and Processing Unit

This layer consists of components that provide communication over other layers as well as the devices connected in a similar framework. It consists of different protocols that manage communication among two or more devices. Various physical components in this veneer are WSN nodes, cloud servers, big data gateway nodes, base stations, etc.

The processing unit is required to process the information that is being delivered over various devices in the IoT network [5, 9, 10].

Physical Devices and Controllers

These include components like sensors, gateways, routers, etc. Here, we are going to discuss various physical components present in the G-IoT frameworks in detail.

The components are majorly divided into 4 broad categories as shown in Figure 11.6 below [5, 9, 10].

a. Sensors can be defined as the module, machine, or instrument that are used to dig out the changes in the surrounding environment. After sensing the event, the information

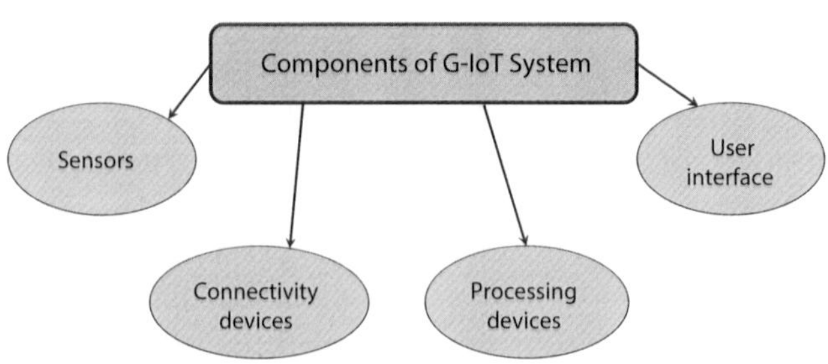

Figure 11.6 Components of G-IoT System.

is then sent to an electric device or a computer processor. Various types of sensors are listed below [11–15]:

- Temperature Detector
- Proximity Detector
- Acceleration Sensor (Accelerometer)
- IR Sensor (Infrared Sensor)
- Pressure Detector
- Light Detector
- Ultrasonic Detector
- Smoke, Gas, and Alcohol Sensor
- Touch Detector
- Color Detector
- Humidity Sensor
- Tilt Sensor
- Flow and Level Sensor

b. RFID stands for Radio Frequency Identification. If broken down into pieces, RF stands for wireless communication and ID stands for tag identification. Therefore, RFID tags are used to store the information about the object in a unique coded form. When a radio wave falls over the RFID tag, the information on the tag is retrieved by a receiver and performs the required task. It works very similarly to the barcode system that is available in many malls and shops nowadays. The only difference between barcode and RFID is that RFID does not need the LOS, i.e., line of sight, whereas the barcode system scanner needs to be aligned with the barcode. Due to this reason, RFIDs are used in identifying real-world objects. A recent example of an RFID tag is "fastag", launched by Paytm to pay tolls automatically from a bank account without any human intervention [11–15].

Other applications of RFID include personnel tracking, inventory management, ID badging, etc.

RFID mainly consists of 4 components: a tag (that carries data for identification), a reader (used for reading data over the tag and in the system database), an antenna (for transmission and receiving the radio signals), and the base station (for data processing) [11–15].

Since we are discussing the green environment, there are some ways we can do efficient use of RFID. First of all, the size of the RFID tags needs to be reduced as they are hard to recycle. Secondly, energy-efficient techniques should be applied and overheating of the RFID system should be reduced and maintained [11–15].

c. Sink Nodes can be understood as the data collector of the network as all data after being sensed by various sensors is sent to sink nodes. It can either be a base station or an access point. It is the middleware between the sensor and the human. All data transferred in the networking system needs to go through the sinks. Sink nodes are also known as the gateway between the sensor nodes and the data processing center. In repent, IOT sink nodes need to be dynamic as they not only upgrade the lifetime of the G-IoT system, but also help in overcoming the power constraint that is a major challenge with the G-IoT components [11–15].
d. Data Centers are the physical places of an organization where all the data being used is stored. The major constituent of the chief figures are routers, switches, firewalls, storage systems, servers, and application delivery controllers. Nowadays, we have the data stored over the cloud instead of the physical devices. Due to this, in this era, our whole data is connected over various data centers, public or private clouds, and edges. Besides the technical components, data centers also have facilities like cooling systems, ventilation systems, UPS, power generators, etc. [11–15].
e. Gateway Nodes are the coordinating unit of the system. They basically provide the interface for the modules of the sensors present in the system. They are used to manage and configure the sensors and the devices present in a G-IoT network. Gateways also help to keep track of activities being performed inside the network. All this data is stored inside the gateway memory and is also available if the system or network gets restarted. Since it is the controller unit, security plays a vital role in it. Therefore, G-IoT gateways are designed in such a way that they provide data security at each and every level of transaction. To detect the unauthorized devices, gateways are provided with Crypto Authentication Chips. To ensure further safety, gateways are also provided with the Secure Boot so that the system does not get rebooted by any malicious or unauthorized devices [11–15].
f. Resource Allocators: In the G-IoT network there are many devices connected to each other and each node is described

as the nodes. There are two types of nodes present in the G-IoT network. First, includes the nodes where services are used by various resources. The second one is the gateways that are connected to various resources. All the communication is controlled by the gateways, therefore it is necessary to design a network in which resource allocation is done in such a way that there exists the minimum cost of the communication and does not overburden the system. The resource allocators make sure that the network is distributed in such a way that each gateway gets connected to the minimum number of possible resources, which in turn reduces the total cost of the network [11–15].

g. Wireless sensor nodes include the group of sensors that allow sensing of the surrounding activities using various phenomena. The sensors communicate among themselves using radio signals. WSNs are equipped with sensing and computing devices, power components, transmitters, etc. Some of the drawbacks of WSN include the limited processing speed, low bandwidth for communication, and low storage capacity. Nowadays, people have focused on making the sensors ss that they have a long life and use a minimum amount of power when under usage [11–15].
h. Base Station is a place where all signal transmissions take place. It requires a huge amount of electricity to run such stations. Hence, they contribute a high proportion to the greenhouse effect. To reduce this, there is a need to use advanced equipment to reduce the power consumption [11–15].
i. Processor/Cloud
j. Actuators

11.4 Techniques for Implementation of G-IoT

Green Internet of Things is totally based on the notion of IoT. It does the same work as IoT, which includes connecting devices, protocols for communication between devices, and networking architecture. The only difference is that G-IoT tries to accomplish all this in an ecological manner by applying energy efficiency techniques and aids. All this is enabled using the new forms of ICTs in addition to RFID (Radio-Frequency Identification), Wireless Sensors Network (WSN), and M2M, which means communication via machines or in other words machine to machine communication, power-saving tools/instruments and transmission, cognitive radio, Edge/Fog/Cloud computing, and Big Data analysis.

To satisfy the needs of Green IoT there are certain principles that need to be followed. These principles are known as ICT (Information and Communication Technology) principles. It may include the working of the sensor nodes only when required, also high storage units must be scaled down to narrow energy and space utilization and apportion of the memory resources can be done by sharing data over multiple devices connected to the G-IoT framework. To please various essence of G-IoT, the tasks mentioned below need to be performed [11–17].

- Eco-accommodating structures and the dissipation of bio-items in congregate G-IoT segments (the hereafter is underway and biodegradable gadgets operations and nano-powder handling units);
- Reducing energy dissipation through various gadgets and tools can be achieved by following a sleep scheduling algorithm in which the device only works when it is required in the system, otherwise it remains in the sleep mode.
- Usage of renewable forms of energy that include solar, wind, geothermal, hydro, etc.
- Installing all kinds of powerful and decentralized storage at the perimeter where data generation takes place. This, in turn helps in overcoming cost, privacy, bandwidth, and latency challenges.
- Application of smart communication techniques, which includes MIMO, i.e., Multiple Input Multiple Output
- Reduction of data transfer path lengths
- Using biodegradable materials for designing of the mechanisms used in a G-IoT system

Since ICT uses various tags and techniques to ensure the application of Green IoT, in this section we are going to discuss various green tags that are present in ICT and are explained below.

- Green M2M

  It is considered to be one of the fundamental units of G-IoT. Green M2M refers to the interaction between two machines or objects with merely no intervention of human communication. The futuristic market of such types of communication has better scopes than the traditional human to human interaction. This helps a company reduce its revenue generated due to communication facilities.

There are certain techniques through which M2M is applied. It includes techniques like information redundancy, spatial redundancy, and temporal redundancy. Since M2M communication is done using the communication nodes, they are the major source for power consumption. So, by applying better communication protocols, power consumption can be reduced. This is also possible by turning several nodes to low power consumption (i.e. sleep mode) when not in use. While applying the sleeping algorithm, we can have a check over the area where the communication nodes are present [11–17].

- Green RFID

  One of the best wireless technologies of all time is Green Radio Frequency Identification, specifically due to its present advantages in pliability, lifetime, and low cost. RFID allows vast prospective profit in recognition and trailing of tools. RFID is chiefly the extract and communication automation. Therefore, it is perceived as having a poor influence on nature. Therefore, RFID tags are non-corroding and recoverable. RFID is also without wire and without power technology. RFID grants new opportunities in many industries. RFID supply chains reduce CO2 emissions to improve goods sales, command room temperatures for depletion in wastage and improving quality, elevate pickups and delivery effectiveness, maintain the reusing citation of reclaiming plastic automobiles parts, improve waste administration efficiency, enhance strength manufacturing and management, provide a surrogate to battery energy for protection alert gadgets, place inclined prerequisites created by using strength plants, etc. In consequence, a proper RFID device affords options to be extra environmentally accountable and friendly. Otherwise, considerable investments and studies are centered on the investigation of new tag fabrication (e.g., textile, adhesive, plastics), the enhancement power harvesting, the discount of RFID chip, the abilities for localizing or positioning objects or individuals, the improvement of passive wi-fi RFID, etc. Some illustration examples committed to a variety of functions can be cited [11–17].

- Nestle makes use of temperature management to decrease spoilage, enhance quality, and decrease energy-related costs.
- Argonne National Laboratory has developed an RFID onboard sensor suite to tune and reveal programs containing nuclear and radioactive products.
- Since 2010, Walmart Stores has been working with marketers of men's denims and fundamentals to be capable to tune these gadgets to use RFID tags to optimize the administration of stock and decrease CO2 emissions.
- In Paris, timber has an RFID tag underneath their lower back permitting less difficult monitoring with the aid of the municipal officials.
- Airfield Architects place RFID at the carrier of the grant chain. They declare that RFID purposes permit tightly closed work-flows, decrease waste, and store time, dealing with transportation and, consequently, eat much less energy.
- RFID technological know-how additionally helps producers set up an inexperienced grant chain to attain the aim of an environmentally pleasant automobile and healing fee of life. RFIDs are turning into units integrating sensing and sign capacity capable to supply monitoring and vicinity of individuals. Though now it has no issues, RFID is a dependable technological know-how predicted to end up formidable in the coming years, fixing troubles in supply, private ID, asset tracking, etc. and additionally enjoying fundamental functions in order to advise options for a greener industry. Green RFID purposes will require advances on more than one new tag designs inclusive of sensor integration and integration in future wi-fi cognitive networks.
- Green CC

  The main supply of CO2 emissions consists of electricity and industries such as concrete. One of the designs to seize CO2 from some sources is the oxyfuel emission. The power demand for this kind of technique comes from O2 generation, which is carried out as air liquefaction. This strength demand can specially decrease the use of thermal built-in separation as ceramic oxygen transport membranes. It is least if the oxygen transport membrane is divided in a 4-end mode, which includes oxygen and is swept and immediately dilutes the usage of recirculated flue gas. 55-60% depletion in seize electricity demand in contrast to cryogenic air separation and up to 45% depletion in contrast to post-combustion seize strategies can be achieved [11–17].

GREEN-CC offers a high-efficiency seize method based totally on oxyfuel combustion. The focal point in particular is on the improvement of integration strategies for oxygen transport membrane-modules in energy plant life and concrete enterprise thinking about minimum strength associated with CO2 collection with minimum investment. It will be determined by using fee calculations. GREEN-CC will additionally discover the use of oxygen transport membrane-based gas combustion in exclusive energy-demanding industrial processes, e.g. refining and petrochemical enterprises and permeable membrane substances exhibit a chemical CO2 and different flue gasoline components. The main project confronted by way of GREEN-CC is consequently to become aware of and enhance membrane materials and factors for 4-end mode oxygen transport membrane integration. The required membrane line will consist of membrane strains supported on oxygen discount catalysts with excessive and steady outcomes in flue gas. A planar membrane module will be constructed, which includes hurdles like becoming a member of technology [11–17].

- Green WSN

A WSN is a diverse database where the data is stored continuously by tracking sensors to serve different applications for which the WSN has been developed. This database is to be controlled judiciously so that required information can be originated from it by resources such as energy, time, etc. All efforts done are towards achieving this goal.

Green wireless sensor networks (WSNs) faced vital importance due to the growing significance of sensor enabled smart environments. Energy optimization and communication optimization are two modes of investigation for Green CC. Due to the growing sensor mass in smart environments, honestly finding the shortest way for green communication has been proven to be an NP problem. Literature in Green CC mainly focuses on finding the main optimal path. The optimal path finding solutions are suitable for application specific traditional WSN. The cutting-edge sensor enabled smart environments supporting heterogender applications require scattered optimal path finding solutions to green communication.

Specifically, finding the optimal path solution in the worldwide network, the signed algorithm identifies paths in a short search space called divisional forward zone. The idea of forward zone improves the searching speed and reduces the computation centric communication cost [11–17].

One of the vital challenges WSNs face today is low power consumption. Important WSN frameworks are a main issue in green communications due to many protocols, strategies, and optimization algorithms. The green wireless sensor network is an uprising concept in which the lifetime and performance of the network is maximized while minimizing the carbon prints. This energy network serves in a vast range of green applications. Applications include healthcare, environmental engineering, industry, military, smart home, etc. It is also used in intrusion detection and energy harvesting, storage, and usage of data [11–17].

- Green DC

  A green data center is a deposit for the storage, management, and assembly of data in which mechanical, electronic, electrical and computer systems are shaped for maximum energy efficiency and minimum environmental impact. The construction and operation of a green data center involves advancement in technologies and strategies. Some examples are:
  - Waste recycling
  - Sustainable landscaping
  - Use of low-emission building material
  - Installation of catalytic converters on backup generators
  - Use of alternative energy technologies such as heat pumps and evaporative coolers
  - Use of hybrid vehicles

Demand for new data centers is ample in India, driven by the high scale facilities that Internet giants such as Amazon Web Services, Microsoft, and Google Cloud demand to power their clouds, etc.

The green tech services market is expected to reach Rs. 539681400000 by the end of 2020, reflecting an annual growth rate of nearly 6 percent over this time. This growth is majorly attributable to green data center initiatives introduced by enterprises looking to not only reduce their carbon print, but also manage increasing costs [11–17].

Data center solutions accelerate the speed of work by delivering new packages for data center facilities. The pre-engineer targets specific parameters, including deployment cost, reliability, performance, and speed [11–17].

Building data centers in cold environments contributes significantly to effective and efficient data center cooling and data center facilities can double this effect by installing air economizers that extract from the natural environment instead of artificial power sources. Extensive air conditioning using surrogate cooling sources while adjusting the speed of exact requirements can make a difference in impact on power consumption [11–17].

The techniques used in ICT have been summarized in Table 11.1.

Power saving techniques in various components have been described in Table 11.2.

Table 11.1 Techniques used in ICT [1–5].

Schema for ICT	Techniques used
Green M2M	• Implementing vitality reaping • Efficient correspondence convention plans • Adjusting and calibrating the relaying power • Utilizing components of energy saving
Green RFID	• Manufacturing tags using eco-friendly materials • Adjusting and calibrating the relaying power • Using advanced protocols for optimizing the sensing of data
Green CC	• Use of varying hardware and software to optimize energy consumption • Using cloud-based services
Green DC	• Use of renewable sources of energy • Designing an energy-efficient architecture for data centers
Green WSN	• Contraction and compression of data • Optimization of the radio spectrum
Common Green ICT	• Minimization of data transfer path lengths • Use of renewable sources of energy

Table 11.2 Power saving techniques in various components [1–5].

Physical components	Reasons behind energy consumption	Methods for saving energy	Parameters improved
Sensors	Regular sensing of data all round the clock	Applying the sleep scheduling algorithm; compressive sensing; self-powered sensors	Mobility, placement in the circuit, QoS
RFID	Identification of the sensed data	Passive sensors can be used where data is detected using light, vibration, radiation or any other physical phenomenon.	Improved performance and delays in communication.
Sink nodes	All data is stored and analysed using the sink nodes.	Optimization in processing the data; core mapping	Complexity of network, scheduling the on-off timer, cost optimization
Data centers	Data processing over cloud and heavy computation tasks	Load distribution; minimizing the path for data transfer	Positional accuracies, reduced complexities, enhanced QoS
Gateway nodes	Links various sensing nodes, controls communication of the network	Storage control; scheduling of events	Power control, intervals of sleep, optimized battery levels

(Continued)

Table 11.2 Power saving techniques in various components [1–5]. *(Continued)*

Physical components	Reasons behind energy consumption	Methods for saving energy	Parameters improved
Resource allocator	Allocation of resources with the gateway for their operation	Service migration; service shutdown	Proper allocation, scheduling the access time
WSN	Communication and networking among the devices	Various algorithms like multiple constraint routing and cluster head communication can be used	Range of network, latency, improved power levels
Base station	Used for storing and fetching information for the resources so that it can be used later	Optimization of communication pathway; load balancing algorithm	Interoperability, deployment of various topologies, load allocation
Processor/cloud	Complex computations, assigning tasks to different nodes	Reducing the path length of the data; edge computing	Use of less number of resources
Actuators	Triggers the task upon certain stimulus	Analysing the energy consumption by various devices	Privacy, security

11.5 Power Saving Methods Based on Components

In Section 11.3, we discussed various physical components present in the G-IoT framework. Here we are going to discuss various power-saving techniques with regards to each component.

11.6 Applications of G-IoT

There are various applications of G-IoT. It is all because of the constant changes occurring in our environment. Though there is IoT available to all of us, it has also contributed to degrading our environment. Development of IoT leads to high production of e-waste, hazardous emissions, and also very high power usage. All these factors have led to the development of G-IoT where we can overcome the drawbacks of IoT and make it sustainable with our natural environment.

Various applications of G-IoT include smart cities, smart agriculture, smart healthcare, etc. [34].

- Water
  This method of water supply and sanitation is considered one of the essential ultimatums of sustainable development. The growing scarcity of useful water resources in the world requires better management of these precious plant resources. ICT based technologies can be used to improve the sustainable management of water resources because even water flowing through an ICT region can be important. This can be achieved by moving towards inexperienced ICT and G-IoT concepts [30]. Technologies such as satellite television for PC image transmission, geographic mapping, and Internet-based applied sensor science are targets for use in the water sector. The logs accumulated and analyzed in real-time on modern premises allow individuals, companies, and water agencies to predict and manage preventive movements and make various conscious choices in sustainable water management [29]. G-IoT speculation will play a huge role in translating current IoT activities into hydroponics where aquaculture is more sustainable. The move to an inexperienced water finance system requires insurance policies for sustainable water management and increased funding to improve water subsidies and productivity. Proper management of water resources is

essential for the conservation of freshwater ecosystems and represents social and financial development. Creative and forward-thinking G-IoT has the potential to contribute to water conservation, particularly in agriculture, energy, construction and business, and in the ICT sector.

- Forestry
  Forestry associated with agriculture brings about great changes and technological changes. At the same time, forests and agricultural lands have a significant impact on local climate trade due to the importance of their carbon inventory and the transformation of greenhouse gases between the environment, soil, and land, and vegetation, which can move in both directions [18, 19]. Therefore, it is very important to reduce deforestation and increase afforestation. The IoT based forest Wi-Fi monitor is able to detect the growth facts and the forest environment at any time and is only as good as smart behavior and special treatment. In other words, the sensors and lockout structures are used to detect and transmit information from high definition forest monitoring wirelessly or via the mobile community to an online database for updates in real-time [28]. Information published in the cloud is accessible to employees from any computer, anywhere [18, 19]. Analyzing the data allows you to better understand the growth of the bush, the effects of local weather conditions, pests, and diseases and helps you make correct forecasts, early warnings, and preventative manoeuvres. For example, if a wood stove is detected, firefighters will benefit from the speed and development paths of the oven and suddenly, it will be possible to respond to an emergency. Besides forest resources and their management, applied sciences using information and communication technologies play an important role in different sectors of the forest chain, such as harvesting, transport, processing, production, and processing transformation [18].

  Compared to ICT and IoT, inexperienced ICT and G-IoT conserve what is achievable, dramatically reduce carbon dioxide emissions, protect weeds and predictive sources, and make smart choices to maintain a durable forest chain. The Forest Initiative, therefore, plays a key role in the transition to a greener financial system and a more sustainable society. The forestry investment themes will accelerate the transition to a greener economy [18].

- Waste Management
  Electronic waste electrical and digital equipment is the fastest waste transfer of 3 to 5 per year and enjoys global interest. At the same time, it is one of the most regulated components of the waste stream [20]. Greening this area allows equipment used in science or practice to reduce or inhibit emissions and pollution generated during operation and occurring nearby, as well as collect and reuse or recycle waste, transforming it into a valuable resource. The most pressing waste needs are to decouple waste from financial development and respond to the growing e-waste challenges and increase recycling rates. For this reason, e-waste recycling leads to shifting health and environmental risks to the protection of useful resources, lower energy consumption, and financial development. In addition, many of the benefits of waste management in the 21st century are also the result of advanced ICT options in the industry [17, 18].

  Companies all over the world are building IIoT facilities for better waste management, for example, Energy, Compology, Bigbelly, Sutera, etc. Cloud options receive data from Wi-Fi sensors that measure container capacity as well as from several different sensors and data sources, e.g., Global Positioning System, smart devices, or RFID tags that track garbage trucks and crowding of visitors and disseminate all collected statistics so that recycling companies can obtain information that they want to analyze, predict, and optimize for the most important offers. They offer, for example, optimization routes and time spent by garbage trucks between containers [17, 18]. Upgrading the IoT option to G-IoT will lead to many improved, sustainable, and cost-effective waste management practices and will provide additional benefits to many parties directly or indirectly involved in waste disposal. Some of the current and projected financial benefits of recycling e-waste include:

  - Energy saving and protection of valuable, important, and rare plant substances, e.g. gold, silver, platinum, as well as copper, aluminium, and precious iron, including plastic and glass. Recycling e-waste allows you to sell up to 70 of electricity, which is the end result of saving valuable energy and resource costs. These energy savings have many indirect benefits, such as less reliance on finished oil reserves, reducing pollution and greenhouse gas emissions [17, 18, 22–34].

- Replaced and refurbished electronic products are cheaper and more practical than brand new products [30–34].
- Companies that recycle e-waste create additional jobs and strengthen the economy. E-waste recycling revenues are approximately 2 billion and are expected to rise to nearly 3.5 billion by 2020 [17–20].

11.7 Challenges and Future Scope

Besides all the advances and research toward G-IoT, there are still some areas left and are still many challenges to overcome. Until now, we have described various studies and processes to have a socially viable environment with IoT, but the technical challenges which still remain unresolved have been listed below:

- Models for implementation of Green IoT should be reliable with the energy consumption models
- Complexity of the network should be reduced
- Recyclable material used for making sensors needs to be studied thoroughly
- Awareness among the common users of G-IoT needs to be triggered. There is a need for the common man to be aware of the techniques used for the implementation of G-IoT.
- Security of the G-IoT system needs to be optimized as well
- All the physical devices should operate on the minimum possible power to reduce the overall power consumption [30–34]

As G-IoT will grow, it will contribute in making our environment much greener and healthier. Besides this, our living standards will not only socially but economically rise in the near future. There are some fields that still need to be researched, which will help us in greening the IoT [15–20].

11.8 Case Study

To have a better understanding of the Green IoT concept, let us dive into a practical example where the above discussed techniques have been implemented to maintain the balance between the Internet of Things and the environment. Since we have been talking about electric power consumption, either reduce it or make electricity through the conventional sources. Here, we will talk about the Cochin International Airport, the first ever airport that is totally working on solar power [21].

We all know airports require huge amounts of electricity as there are a number of sensors, cameras, and other electrical devices working simultaneously. This leads to high energy consumption. To deal with this problem, the authorities decided to have electricity from solar power. They started off with a 100 KW project that helped them generate power around 400 KW. Marking and analyzing the success of the project they scaled it up. In 2015, they were able to have a setup of 29.5 MW that produced around 120000 units of electricity every day. This much energy was not only enough for their daily needs, but enough for banking as well. The banked power can be used later on non-sunny days [29–35]. Before the deployment of the solar panels, the daily consumption of electricity by the airport was 48000 units per day which cost around Rs. 6.8 for each unit. This consumption led the airport to generate a daily electric bill of around Rs. 3.26 lakhs. The area consumed by these panels is also used for car parking and the growth of organic vegetables. If we account for the total power generated till date it is around 4 crore units that estimates to around Rs. 30 crore. It has been a great initiative by Cochin International Airport. Now, seeing this example many others are heading towards the same path.

11.9 Conclusion

It is the need of an hour to have a sustainable environment for living and development of human beings. All this can be achieved by preserving the natural resources of our planet. Our society has been highly influenced by the new ICT principles and the introduction of Green IoT. Despite this fact, there has been increasing consumption of energy and other natural resources. All of these have led to deterioration of the environment due the increase in carbon-dioxide release and high production of e-waste, i.e., material used in making sensors, devices, etc. According to the well stated quote, "Modern problems require modern solutions", our society has also decided to switch to green technologies. Switching to greener technology will lead to less consumption of energy as well as the other resources. It will also ensure that the negative effect of the technology currently in use leads to less negative effects on all associated things. This in turn will help in the development of a sustainable environment for all living species.

Here, we demonstrated the concept of Green Internet Of Things and its ability to bring transformation in various sectors, which intend to have a crucial role towards the green economy. When put to practical application, Giot has shown a great response in sectors like agriculture, forestry, fisheries, aquaculture, etc. Many realize the G-IoT includes smart buildings, smart industries, and a smart grid because these are the sectors where there are high consumption of energy and natural resources and they are the largest producers of greenhouse gases. Not only in the above sectors, but G-IoT also finds its application in transport, tourism as well as the waste management sectors. Involvement of G-IoT in these sectors will lead to a significant growth in socioeconomic and environmental benefits.

References

1. Alsamhi, S. H., Ma, O., Ansari, M. S., & Meng, Q. (2019). Greening internet of things for greener and smarter cities: A survey and future prospects. *Telecommunication Systems, 72*(4), 609–632. doi:10.1007/s11235-019-00597-1
2. Sadiku, M. N. (2020). Green Internet of Things. *Emerging Green Technologies,* 77–84. doi:10.1201/9780429344213-8
3. Shah, K., & Narmavala, Z. (2018). A Survey on Green Internet of Things. *2018 Fourteenth International Conference on Information Processing (ICINPRO).* doi:10.1109/icinpro43533.2018.9096789
4. Maksimovic, M. (2017). Greening the Future: Green Internet of Things (G-IoT) as a Key Technological Enabler of Sustainable Development. *Studies in Big Data Internet of Things and Big Data Analytics Toward Next-Generation Intelligence,* 283–313. doi:10.1007/978-3-319-60435-0_12
5. Shah, K., & Narmavala, Z. (2018). A Survey on Green Internet of Things. *2018 Fourteenth International Conference on Information Processing (ICINPRO).* doi:10.1109/icinpro43533.2018.9096789
6. Nazir, T., & Banday, M. T. (2018). Green Internet of Things: A Survey of Enabling Techniques. *2018 International Conference on Automation and Computational Engineering (ICACE).* doi:10.1109/icace.2018.8686974
7. Sadiku, M. N. (2020). Green Internet of Things. *Emerging Green Technologies,* 77–84. doi:10.1201/9780429344213-8
8. Huang, J., Meng, Y., Gong, X., Liu, Y., & Duan, Q. (2014). A Novel Deployment Scheme for Green Internet of Things. *IEEE Internet of Things Journal, 1*(2), 196–205. doi:10.1109/jiot.2014.2301819
9. Vidas-Bubanja, M. (2014). Implementation of green ICT for sustainable economic development. *2014 37th International Convention on Information and Communication Technology, Electronics and Microelectronics (MIPRO).* doi:10.1109/mipro.2014.6859819

10. Diófási-Kovács, O., & Valkó, L. (2016). Transition to Green Economy: Green Procurement Implementation Strategies Experiences from Hungarian Public and Private Organizations. *World Sustainability Series Sustainable Economic Development,* 243–257. doi:10.1007/978-3-319-45081-0_14
11. Bansal, A. K., Das, G., Pandey, S., Ghosh, A., Kapoor, S., Qadeer, M. S., . . . Gani, K. M. (2020). Implementation of Sustainable Green Technologies in Waste Management. *Green Innovation, Sustainable Development, and Circular Economy,* 115–128. doi:10.1201/9781003011255-10
12. Sarkar, N. I., & Gul, S. (2020). Green Computing and Internet of Things for Smart Cities: Technologies, Challenges, and Implementation. *Green Computing in Smart Cities: Simulation and Techniques Green Energy and Technology,* 35–50. doi:10.1007/978-3-030-48141-4_3
13. Vikram, S. (2015). Green computing. *2015 International Conference on Green Computing and Internet of Things (ICGCIoT).* doi:10.1109/icgciot.2015.7380566
14. Taneja, M. (2015). A mobility analytics framework for Internet of Things. *2015 International Conference on Green Computing and Internet of Things (ICGCIoT).* doi:10.1109/icgciot.2015.7380440
15. Zungeru, A. M., Ketshabetswe, L. K., Mtengi, B., Lebekwe, C. K., & Chuma, J. M. (2020). Introduction to Green Internet of Things Sensor Networks. *Green Internet of Things Sensor Networks,* 1–8. doi:10.1007/978-3-030-54983-1_1
16. Singh, S., & Mittal, K. (2015). Internet of everything smart environment. *2015 International Conference on Green Computing and Internet of Things (ICGCIoT).* doi:10.1109/icgciot.2015.7380668
17. Goel, A., Gautam, S., Tyagi, N., Sharma, N. and Sagayam, M. (2021). Securing Biometric Framework with Cryptanalysis. In Intelligent Data Analytics for Terror Threat Prediction (eds S.K. Pani, S.K. Singh, L. Garg, R.B. Pachori and X. Zhang). https://doi.org/10.1002/9781119711629.ch9
18. IoT Based Smart Farming: Applications, Technologies and Future Vision. (2019). *International Journal of Recent Technology and Engineering Regular Issue, 8*(4), 6129–6134. doi:10.35940/ijrte.d8826.118419
19. Smart Farming: IoT Based Water Managing System. (2020). *International Journal of Innovative Technology and Exploring Engineering Regular Issue,* 9(4), 2383–2385. doi:10.35940/ijitee.d1796.029420
20. Comparative Analysis of 3-D Password Using Various Techniques ', International Journal of Emerging Technologies and Innovative Research (www.jetir.org), ISSN:2349-5162, Vol.6, Issue 6, page no. 711–718, June 2019, Available :https://www.jetir.org/papers/JETIR1907Q08.pdf
21. Wawryk, A. S. (2005). Green Pricing and Green Power Marketing: Demand-Side Mechanisms for Promoting "Green Power" in Deregulated Energy Markets. *The Law of Energy for Sustainable Development,* 138–155. doi:10.1017/cbo9780511511387.012
22. Wakasa, K., & Konomi, S. (2016). Weaving Urban Spaces through Visible Green to Increase the Awareness of Green Networks. *Proceedings of the*

Second International Conference on IoT in Urban Space - Urb-IoT '16. doi:10.1145/2962735.2962758

23. Praba, T. S., Laxmi, S. P., Sethukarasi, T., Harshitha, R. D., & Venkatesh, V. (2020). Green IoT (G-IoT): An Insight on Green Computing for Greening the Future. *Advances in Greener Energy Technologies Green Energy and Technology,* 579–600. doi:10.1007/978-981-15-4246-6_33
24. Green House Monitoring And Control System Using Iot. (2020). *Journal of Xidian University, 14*(9). doi:10.37896/jxu14.9/098
25. Zeb, S., Habib, A., Amin, Y., Tenhunen, H., & Loo, J. (2018). Green Electronic Based Chipless Humidity Sensor for IoT Applications. *2018 IEEE Green Technologies Conference (GreenTech).* doi:10.1109/greentech.2018.00039
26. Hijawi, U., Gastli, A., Hamila, R., Ellabban, O., & Unal, D. (2020). Qatar Green Schools Initiative: Energy Management System with Cost-Efficient and Lightweight Networked IoT. *2020 IEEE International Conference on Informatics, IoT, and Enabling Technologies (ICIoT).* doi:10.1109/iciot48696.2020.9089443
27. Lenka, R. K., Rath, A. K., & Sharma, S. (2019). Building Reliable Routing Infrastructure for Green IoT Network. *IEEE Access, 7,* 129892–129909. doi:10.1109/access.2019.2939883
28. Gautam, S., Malik, A., Singh, N., & Kumar, S. (2019). Recent Advances and Countermeasures Against Various Attacks in IoT Environment. *2019 2nd International Conference on Signal Processing and Communication (ICSPC).* https://doi.org/10.1109/icspc46172.2019.8976527
29. Mann, P., Tyagi, N., Gautam, S., & Rana, A. (2020). Classification of Various Types of Attacks in IoT Environment. *2020 12th International Conference on Computational Intelligence and Communication Networks (CICN).* https://doi.org/10.1109/cicn49253.2020.9242592
30. Malik, A., Gautam, S., Abidin, S., & Bhushan, B. (2019). Blockchain Technology-Future Of IoT: Including Structure, Limitations And Various Possible Attacks. *2019 2nd International Conference on Intelligent Computing, Instrumentation and Control Technologies (ICICICT).* https://doi.org/10.1109/icicict46008.2019.8993144
31. Md. Mamunur Rashid, Joarder Kamruzzaman, Mohammad Mehedi Hassan, Sakib Shahriar Shafin, Md. Zakirul Alam Bhuiyan, "A Survey on Behavioral Pattern Mining From Sensor Data in Internet of Things", Access IEEE, vol. 8, pp. 33318–33341, 2020.
32. Ankita Sindhu, Nihar Ranjan Roy, "A Comparative Analysis of Important Energy Conservation Approaches in IoT", Cloud Computing Data Science & Engineering (Confluence) 2021 11th International Conference on, pp. 546–551, 2021.
33. V. Tahiliani and M. Dizalwar, "Green IoT Systems: An Energy Efficient Perspective," 2018 Eleventh International Conference on Contemporary Computing (IC3), 2018, pp. 1–6, doi: 10.1109/IC3.2018.8530550.

34. Tyagi, N., Gautam, S., Bharadwaj, J., Goel, A. (2020). B-IoT (Blockchain Internet of Things): A Way to Enhance IoT Applications via Blockchain. SSRN Electronic Journal. https://doi.org/10.2139/ssrn.3747476
35. K. R. Swetha, N. M, A. M. P and M. Y. M, "Prediction of Pneumonia Using Big Data, Deep Learning and Machine Learning Techniques," 2021 6th International Conference on Communication and Electronics Systems (ICCES), 2021, pp. 1697–1700, doi: 10.1109/ICCES51350.2021.9489188.

12

Big-Data Analytics: A New Paradigm Shift in Micro Finance Industry

Vinay Pal Singh[1], Rohit Bansal[2] and Ram Singh[1]*

[1]School of Business, Quantum University Roorkee, Uttarakhand, India
[2]Department of Management, Vaish Engineering College Rohtak, Haryana, India

Abstract

In the 21st Century, Big Data Analytics assume a critical part in the improvement of MFIs through effective utilization of Dashboards and Score checking, and offering profound bits of knowledge into the information, builds up organizations to accomplish more noteworthy perceivability, adaptability, veracity, and speed. Big Data Analytics is the use of advanced analytic techniques against very large, diverse data sets that include structured, semi-structured, and unstructured data from different sources and in different sizes, from terabytes to zettabytes. The use of Predictive Analytics and profitability based investigation in the space of microfinance resembles a hint of something larger. These would permit the MFIs a more conscious methodology to oversee hazard in a superior way. This part features the large difficulties of the microfinance business, how enormous information will be helpful for the microfinance business, what kinds of difficulties will be for huge information in the business, and furthermore, the helpfulness of huge information in the business. Through Mobile and Cloud-Based investigation, the executives exploit to rethink and overhaul the association's arrangements for the advancement of the foundations and for their forthcoming customers. This chapter discusses Big Data Analytics, a new paradigm shift in the micro-finance industry.

Keywords: MFI, Big Data, Microfinance, RBI, NBFC

**Corresponding author*: ramsinghcommerce@gmail.com

M. Niranjanamurthy, Hemant Kumar Gianey and Amir H. Gandomi (eds.) Advances in Data Science and Analytics: Concepts and Paradigms, (275–292)

12.1 Introduction

Microfinance is a development where low pay families and independent venture have lasting admittance to a scope of great monetary administrations to fund their pay delivering exercises, construct resources, balance out utilization, and ensure against hazard. These administrations are not restricted to credit, but incorporate saving, protection, and cash moves. Miniature accounts and micro-credit assume a significant part in fostering country regions by giving advances to individuals at lower or financed paces of interest. It has been perceived as another standard for reducing neediness from the world through friendly and monetary strengthening of the poor, especially ladies. The respectable idea of microfinance is certainly not a new idea; it was presented by Professor Muhammad Yunus with the formation of the Grameen Bank in 1976 in Bangladesh. The fundamental test for MFIs is a topographical one. Past the metropolitan urban communities, its populace is spread all over inside rustic regions. "According to the Bharat Microfinance Report, microfinance "through MFIs" is upgrading 43 million records; around 85 percent of the records updated with 83 percent gross credit portfolio are being changed through NBFC MFIs". "NBFCs and NBFC MFIs are clearly coordinated by RBI for microfinance undertakings where the quantum in everyday advancing to the borrower, the quantity of providers for each borrower, the speed of interest, and additional charges is determined by RBI, in less troublesome terms, a borrower can be a person from one Self Help Group or Joint Liability Group; the borrower can get up to Rs 1,25,000 from 2 NBFC and MFIs as a person from Self Help Group or Joint Liability Group or in his individual cutoff". The speed of interest is similarly decided by quarterly calculations of RBI. Dealing with costs and credit security insurance charges can be charged from the borrowers. Particulars are through the "Qualifying Asset" standard of "RBI for the microfinance region. In the microfinance region, NBFC/NBFC MFIs and u/s 8 associations are qualified", by the exemplary nature of the importance of "credit establishments" of the "Credit Information Company (Regulation) Act" to move the borrower level data to the "Credit Information Bureau".

12.2 Reality of Area and Transcendent Difficulties

The overlooked details are the main problem. Indian microfinance is incredibly mind boggling. There are distinctive authoritative documents dynamic in the business sectors, for example Banks, NBFCs, NBFC MFIs,

U/S 8 organizations, social orders, trusts, cooperatives, and so on are the revenue driven portion and U/S 8 organizations, social orders, and cooperatives are the "Not-For-Profit" section. There are assorted models, including Self Help Groups, Joint Liability Groups, people, Limited Liability JLGs, and so forth. There is no uniform guideline for microfinance, NBFC, and NBFC MFIs, as they are straightforwardly controlled for microfinance activities. U/S 8 organizations are money organizations that work with the exceptional agreement not to enroll with RBI. Societies, Trusts, and Cooperatives Societies are according to their enlistment and follow every one of the standards implied for NBFC MFIs. To get a bank account, particularly Priority Sector Lending, banks are managed but do not go under the immediate guideline for microfinance activity, so they do not need to follow the rules for NBFC and NBFC MFIs. In spite of organizations with various authoritative documents having monetary activities, just like NBFCs NBFC MFIs, banks are qualified to transfer borrower-level information on CIBs. Here, every one of these establishments is working in similar regions and the needy individuals can be an individual from these gatherings. Microfinance incorporates every one of the drives taken by various organizations regardless of authoritative documents and models. MFIs and SHGs were there anyway and, as of late, banks are showing revenue and, for the most part, due to work by the Business Correspondence Model joining forces with MFIs. Different contestants are the P2P NBFCs. Lamentably, because of the non-comprehensive nature of the CICR Act and in spite of notice from RBI, around 15 percent of the SHG part level information is being transferred on CIBs and developing of thorough informational index is an overwhelming errand. All things considered, to comprehend the market, an exertion is being made by arranging the information from various sources on pieces of the pie. The accessible information is on various time spans, but have nearness. The information for "Not for Profit MFIs" is as of March 2019 and the SHG information is as of October 2019 and the rest August 2019.

There is a test to comprehend the effort. CIBs have the information on dynamic records and to eliminate this test, the advance has been taken for a superior thought. Thinking about the general portfolio of NBFC, NBFC MFIs, BC of Banks, and NFP MFIs, the microfinance area has 43.5 percent of the area and it would be more on the off chance that we add on the information of helpful social orders. In any case, there is information stirred up, as information of around 15 percent of the SHG's portfolio is in the bank section and it may not be that huge a sum. Limiting that reality, the business might self-assertively seem as though the pie diagram. In this intricacy of the microfinance area of India and the inaccessibility of comprehensive information and administrative system, four circumstances have arisen.

12.2.1 Probable Overlending

To begin with, it is conceivable for over-loaning by the banks to occur, however taking into account a similar helpless populace, they do not need to follow the rules of RBI for NBFC and NBFC MFIs. The Not for Profit revenue driven MFIs are likewise not under direct guidelines and the government is actually thinking about limiting them, as they do not have assets for a greater sum and cross the cut-off. The inquiry here is if the borrowers in RBI specified pay classification and by considering their reimbursement limit, the loan to them has been confined, which is why the banks are saved open for interest in a similar class of the populace with a bigger sum, which is crushing the RBI's push to shield helpless borrowers from overconsumption.

12.2.2 Information Imbalance

Second, due to the limitations radiating from the Credit Information Company (Regulation) Act, banks, NBFCs, and NBFC MFIs are transferring information on CIBs, keeping social orders, trusts, and agreeable social orders out. At last, there is no solid information on agreeable social orders, which can in the end can be gigantic in number. Individual conversation with CIBs uncovered that just 15 percent of the SHG's part level information is transferred by the banks on CIBs, regardless of clear guidelines from RBI. So, until now, the data given by CIBs on obligation is not full confirmation. The inquiry here is indeed, why RBI is not advising every one of the establishments giving credits to the specified pay bunch for transferring information on CIBs. RBI may raise the issue of the realness of the information as the other NFP MFIs are not managed by them. In the present circumstance, they can generally work with the SROs for NBFC MFIs for guaranteeing the credibility of the information.

12.2.3 Retreating Not-for-Profit Sector

Third, the beginning of the microfinance area through NFP MFIs is not difficult to set up and they have a significant presence in the more profound regions. In spite of their positive side, they are not getting support from the banks since they are not controlled by RBI. NFP MFIs take into account the need of the customers and are sourcing costly assets from NBFCs, resounding to the provisioning of expensive credit to the borrowers. Also, the pay over consumption of these establishments returns to the framework and by one way or another the non-revenue driven target of the microfinance business is retreating. Setting up of NBFC MFI also needs a lot of money and the prevalent steady condition is not favorable for activities of NFP MFIs. Numerous social disapproved of business people are being disallowed, so this condition is denying new participants and working with restraining infrastructure. The inquiry emerges as to why the public authority is not fostering an administrative system for these foundations which are still out of direct guideline of RBI. MUDRA, RMK, and so forth can be worked with as the controller of this fragment. For instance, Uganda has set up an administrative structure for other monetary establishments and brought all the monetary incorporations under guidelines.

12.2.4 Neighbourhood Pressure

Aside from these, the nearby political pioneers are exploiting the non-comprehensive nature of the strategy structure. They are tweaking the data, misleading the borrowers, and affecting reimbursement in a generously adverse way and as of late, a portion of the spaces of Assam, Tamil Nadu, Maharashtra, Uttar Pradesh, and others show this pattern is progressing and it is malicious for the area. In light of the fact that there is no solid general strategy design for the microfinance business, the instructions to different partners and invested individuals, on the business, are not solid and deficient. From the above examination, unmistakably the Indian microfinance area is perplexing and it needs the quick consideration of RBI to proclaim a comprehensive arrangement system to ensure help for poor and monetarily minimized individuals. In RBI, FIDD is proclaiming Priority Sector Lending which is the principle wellspring of assets for the microfinance area, DNBR is controlling the NBFCs and NBFC MFIs, which are the biggest fragment in the microfinance area, and DBR is managing the banks that are coming as a significant disturbance in the market, most likely in a negative way [18]. RBI needs to fix this jigsaw puzzle by setting up and organizing a council, quickly, to chip away at a significant goal to make an adept and comprehensive strategy system for the entire microfinance section.

Nowadays, MFIs have deployed a mobile banking application to reach out to remote areas and islands. Even though these initiatives are enjoyed by MFIs, they are not guaranteed to tap the market. Various issues faced by MFIs such as lack of applicant data and the risk of default loan undertaken by the banks in dispensing loans has not been sufficiently addressed. Financial institutions cannot possibly disburse loans to every applicant as it has to mitigate the risk of default and cater to their own interests as well. To assess the risks, banks would require the applicant's data, such as his credit history, which is usually not readily available for this group of consumers. Currently, institutions have personnel who conduct manual background verification of applicants such as by speaking with the applicants' neighbors and village leaders. Even then, this does not sufficiently address the risk of default. The expansion of MFIs indirectly supports economic development and, importantly, more power to women. To sustain growth of MFIs, Big Data Analytics have to be optimally leveraged.

12.3 Data Analytics in Microfinance

The application of analytics in the area of microfinance is just the tip of the iceberg. Insights derived from analytics can help these institutions achieve greater visibility, versatility, veracity, and velocity. This would allow them to take a more deliberate approach, manage risks better, and design their services for prospective microfinance clients. Big Data plays an innovative role in the Microfinance ecosystem. It helps to fulfill evolving customer demands and expectations. Better penetration of mobile devices worldwide increases the opportunity to understand consumer behavior, comprising how they spend their income to know the pattern of savings and creditworthiness. They can now target a distinct group of people using such knowledge.

12.3.1 Types of Data Analytics Used in Microfinance

Analytics can offer probable solutions for the challenges that these institutions face in microfinance. One possible approach is to introduce the concept of credit scoring to microloans. The lack of credit information is a challenge, as microfinance borrowers typically fall into the category of little or no credit history. However, using advanced analytics approaches, it is possible to derive credit worthiness scores for such clients. Microfinance institutions can also look to Big Data as another possible result. Given the lack of conventional credit data, institutions may believe in supplementing with the use of unconventional data sources to enhance the credit view of their potential customers by using geospatial analytics. Geospatial analysis includes individual population forecasting by filtering out appropriate data and applying it to provide accurate trend analysis, modeling, and predictions. By utilizing this insightful procedure, the customer sourcing executives can extend their customer base by focusing on the individuals who have not been tapped at this point. Understanding personal conduct standards utilizing prescient investigations can likewise assist with resolving the issue of default hazard. A miniature money foundation needs to present the KYC (Know Your Customer) information to an outer office which accumulate the information from all micro account institutions working in the country. They likewise amass information of all acquiring defaulters. Investigation performed on this information base can think of examples concerning customer conduct with the goal that the MFIs can stamp just those who have a perfect history. This will diminish wrongdoings generally. As more information becomes open after some time, the insightful models can be additionally refined, empowering more prominent honesty in client knowledge. Most of the MFIs are climbing to little back banks to convey pretty much to their current customer base. In the event that the MFIs utilized profitability based analytics to classify the productive client base, Client Lifetime Value, or CLTV, is an action utilized for deriving the worth of a client relationship in view of the net present value of the assessed future earnings from the customer relationship. Clients with a superior net present worth are the beneficial ones. With the assistance of analytics, the MFI can outline such customers to take them to a more significant level and the negative net present worth should be overlooked in this regard, while exertion ought to be made to improve recovery from such customers".

12.3.2 Use of Big Data in Microfinance Industry

With the fast upgrade in innovations and new players and colossal speculations coming up in monetary innovation, cell phone infiltrations are renovating the monetary administrations vista. With improved infiltration of cell phones universally, the chance to acquire understanding about buyer conduct, containing how they invest their cash and energy, has additionally upgraded. They would now be able to focus on an unmistakable gathering of individuals utilizing such information. The large information examination market likewise depends on a few versatile applications as their mode of data is put away in an information stockroom. Not simply for the portable business, Big Data impacts different business sectors like MFIs. By consolidating digitisation, Big Data assumes an imaginative part in the one of a kind biological system. It assists with satisfying the developing client requests and assumptions. The microfinance business has seen fast development. This development has become a reality because of financial backers' preceded with help of MFIs with a value implantation of around Rs. 9,443 crores, which is an expansion of 55 percent from Q1 FY19-20. With last-mile availability set up to arrive at an enormous number of customers, it is quickly advancing into a powerful channel to achieve one of the public inclinations: monetary consideration. Taking into account that numerous customer accounts are served under the umbrella of the microfinance area, it is the center point of considerable granular information. This informational index is improved with client data containing age, pay gauges, occupation, participation at meeting focuses, and others, prompts four key viewpoints. In India, speedy advances in development, phone entrance, new players, and immense interests in money-related development are changing the financial organization scene. The unavoidable issue is the manner in which colossal data can enable MFIs to accept an inventive part in the new climate, while meeting propelling customer suspicions and prerequisites by melding digitization and uniting with various accomplices in the natural framework. The microfinance region is evaluated to serve almost 200 million end clients with a credit portfolio noteworthy of over Rs. 2.5 lakh crore across the Joint Liability Group (JLG) and Self Help Group (SHG) model of advancing as of the completion of March 2019. With last-mile accessibility set up to arrive at in excess of 200 million clients at any rate once each month, it is rapidly progressing into a stunning channel to achieve one of the public requirements of financial thought. Something valuable about microfinance is the openness of a gigantic proportion of granular data, considering 200 million customer accounts spread the country over [17]. This instructive list is rich, covering age, sex, occupation, pay checks, repayment plans, interest at meeting centers, and others, with most credit foundations chipping away at IT-enabled crediting stages and four dynamically recognized divisions being invigorated for all the data.

12.3.3 Risk and Data Based Credit Decisions

This can be used to satisfactorily cultivate application scorecards for a convincing and impartial selection of customers for financing, key information, and customer individual lead norms got from industry data can similarly be set up into such scorecards. At the front end, such credit decisions are available through cutting edge channels of the handheld contraption of the customer care official, shockingly quickly and they would, along these lines, have the option to execute the piece of a fulfilment chief, which puts convincing energy in affirmation, endorsement, and reference checks. Modified Big Data disturbed computation based customer advance requesting dealing with support and administering by crediting the customer's record very soon, is likely what the valuable stone ball is expecting.

12.3.4 Product Development and Selection

Large information stirring at the back-end, utilizing state of the art factual models and examination, man-made brainpower, and AI can be successfully bridled to support clients in the nick of time for their monetary necessities, with the perfect advance ticket size and reimbursement frequencies. It additionally permits one to investigate the future in anticipating the portfolio practices at different geologies and fragments and thus, foresees likely defaults or credit misfortunes all the more precisely. This will empower right danger estimating of the advances being offered, consequently charging upgraded financing costs to clients in accordance with the worldwide administrative norms being ordered by national banks and controllers all throughout the planet.

12.3.5 Product or Service Positioning

Soon, through huge information, the business will be in a situation to offer items that the client needs as opposed to items that are planned inside. This would help in strategic pitching of monetary incorporation items, administrations like ledgers, annuities, protection, speculations, and settlements and so on, by showing the necessities of the clients produced through examination information displaying client division and value demonstrating.

12.3.6 M-Commerce and E-Payments

With the assistance of huge information, m-trade will permit clients to pick administrations on layaway by empowering a credit endorsement component through examination. Huge information will likewise help unite installment alternatives. A gauge puts over a billion exchanges happening each year in the area, which can be e-empowered to profit clients and cut working costs down. Different information, organized and unstructured, accessible in the universe is taken care of into the organization to break down and react viably and rapidly to issue proclamations. Large information combined with different aspects of man-made brainpower (AI) has effectively begun to change the manner in which choices are made. Be that as it may, it is similarly critical to comprehend the pertinence of dissecting the correct information and dispensing with the trash. Envision how it could deal with an area where the current degree of incorporation across FI items and administrations is just around 20 percent in a country with a populace of 1.3 billion and developing.

12.3.7 Making Reliable Credit Decisions

It can help in the advancement of utilization scorecards for making an unprejudiced determination of clients for financing. Client personal conduct standards and basic data from industry information incorporation into such scorecards help to determine fast credit choices. In a couple of minutes, at the front end, such credit choices are achievable through advanced channels of the client care official's handheld gadgets. Accordingly, this assists with saving the time spent in confirmation, reference checks, and approval by the satisfaction chiefs. Amounting to this, huge information drives client credit endorsement, demand handling, and payment of the advance sum.

12.3.8 Big Data-Driven Model Promises Psychometric Evaluations

The huge information driven models can likewise be useful for psychometric assessments. A few psychometric apparatuses help assess the candidate's answers, which help to catch data that can assist with anticipating credit reimbursement conduct containing candidates' convictions, execution, perspectives, and honesty [21, 22].

12.3.9 Product Build-Up, Service Positioning, and Offering

With the assistance of Big Data, the Microfinance Industry will arrive at a position where they will give items that clients precisely need. In light of the client needs apparent through investigation, for example, value displaying, client division, and information demonstrating, MFIs will actually want to support clients with in-the-nick-of-time monetary necessities, with the correct credit ticket size and protection plans. Microfinance organizations will actually want to anticipate portfolio practices at different geologies and consequently, properly investigate defaults or credit misfortunes all the more exactly. As needs be, organizations can choose the correct portfolio for their monetary items.

12.4 Opportunities and Risks in Using Data Analytics

Generally, MFI utilizes individual relations of customers with officials at a specific branch. Notwithstanding, this mode has a few limits, for example, when clients are new or when field officials are moved to another branch.

A great many clients think that it is hard to maintain customized relations with the officials. These days, Microfinance organizations can use enormous information to recommend customized administrations to a huge number of customers. For instance, Banorte, a Mexican management account with an excess of 13 million clients, is considering client banking conduct to distinguish which monetary items best suit the client, make customized offers when customers utilize Banorte's application, and increment clients' immediate associations with branch work force. Barclays has utilized customer feeling in online media to recognize and address inadequacies in its application [16].

MFIs are likewise utilizing enormous information to target clients and advance strategic pitching of their monetary items. Rather than starting "one-size-fits-all" showcasing efforts, huge information permits MFIs to utilize a wide assortment of individual attributes to section clients into surprising gatherings and give altered proposals as per their decision. A few foundations are, in any event, utilizing enormous information to foresee customer's future prerequisites [1]. These financial organizations can utilize huge information to foster their client base. One of the fundamental explanations behind denying advances is absence of or deficient advance history, which keeps micro-finance organizations from surveying imminent clients' financial soundness. Large information can alleviate this worry by empowering monetary foundations to profile potential borrowers dependent on the reimbursement of administrations other than advances, for example, previous history installments of lease, utilities, or cell phone plans. This crucial data is not new and monetary organizations previously assembled installment information through online installments of bills. Be that as it may, new versatile advances are making it simpler to put together this important information and report them to credit offices. Monetary establishments are taking advantage of large information to fabricate elective FICO assessments for low-pay families. Models incorporate Fintech organizations like Lenddo and Tala with a presence in Africa, Asia, and Latin America and these Fintech organizations commonly offer an application that an individual can download onto their telephone and use to apply for borrowings. At the point when they present a credit application, the application checks the advanced impression of a cell phone and follows the contacts, interpersonal organization profile, topographical examples, and promptly concludes whether to expand the advance. A considerable lot of these elective credit suppliers are situated in East Asia, like Ayannah (the Philippines), CredoLab (Indonesia, Malaysia, and Singapore, among different nations), and Kakao Bank (Korea) [2] and automated credit scoring can help in increment credit while additionally saving additional time and may diminish a portion of the human ambiguity that can arise in the assessment cycle [19, 20].

Big Data can likewise elevate admittance to back for SMEs. MFIs experience issues evaluating the danger of SMEs in light of the fact that they might not have been doing business long and public data about them is restricted. Huge online retailers, like Alibaba, Amazon, eBay, and Mercado Libre, are utilizing large information to accumulate and break down data on firms taking part in their foundation and afterward giving loans [3]. Micro-finance and mobile innovation assume a huge part in Big Data and help carry out advancing monetary consideration. A wide scope of information is produced by Smartphone applications. These aid in creating different arrangements of information focuses that can be utilized by monetary establishments to assess expected clients for loaning, particularly in far off regions where no record is accessible. It is a fantastic mix of innovation, information examination, and microfinance to tap the immaculate market of monetary services [4]. Big information is a help for MFIs for monetary comprehensiveness. Important information is produced through versatile devices and microfinance exchanges which help in the following ways:

1. Better procedures are utilized to distinguish the market
2. Design suitable monetary plans
3. Identify and serve the likely customers
4. Evaluate forthcoming clients all the more proficiently and successfully

Enormous information creates monetary administrations and advance monetary incorporation as monetary specialist organizations acquire comprehensive bits of knowledge helpful in making important business choices.

In this plan of action, huge information is used to overview a customer's dependability. It is portrayed as gigantic volumes of coordinated and unstructured information that can be aggregated from a customer's entire profile for online action, be it via web-based media stages, item buys, or electronic registration. Regularly, such information is gathered from different information focuses, which shift as per the sort of online movement performed. An illustration of this is telephone propensity information of customers incorporates call length, as well as the recurrence of calls. It is the sort of information that will be utilized to assess a client's ability to repay a credit by means of a miniature financing plan. What is utilized is not the immediate substance of the information, but rather the personal conduct

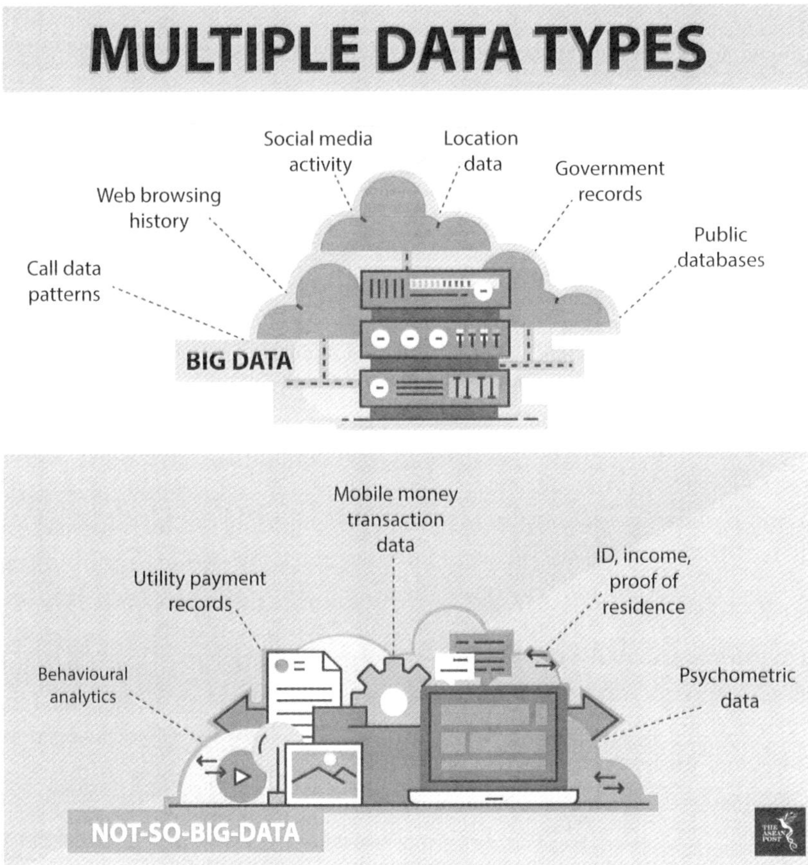

Figure 12.1 Multiple data types used in big data.

standards associated with the information gathered. Enormous information examination is an undeniably fundamental piece of the Fintech environment. The ability to change crude data into critical encounters is the establishment of cross industry headway. Figure 12.1 shows the multiple data types used in Big Data.

12.5 Risk in Utilizing Big Data

With big data comes the biggest risk of data privacy. Enterprises worldwide make use of sensitive data, personal customer information, and strategic documents. When there is so much confidential data lying around, the last thing you want is a data breach at your enterprise. Data scientists break Big Data into four dimensions:

1. Volume
2. Variety
3. Velocity
4. Veracity

This infographic explains and gives examples of each. Broadly speaking, the risks of Big Data can be divided into four main categories: security issues, ethical issues, the deliberate abuse of Big Data by malevolent players (e.g., organized crime), and unintentional misuse. Big Data has the potential to change the manner in which monetary administrations give. Effectively utilizing huge information presents some significant difficulties that, if not tended to, could affect customers and society. These worries are not select to the monetary sector [4]. Using enormous information in micro-finance establishments includes building huge informational indexes that incorporate private data presented by people, uninhibitedly or true. Miniature money foundations can improve their own information by employing outsiders to assemble customer information for their sake. Monetary establishments could be charmed to offer their restrictive information to intrigued outsiders, for example, showcasing and retail organizations that are worried about realizing the ways various segments and social groups manage money [5]. In this point of view, information protection is a significant concern. Miniature financial foundations should be straightforward and immediately uncover what data they have on shoppers and how are they doing it. In certain conditions, purchasers could concede the ability to restrict monetary establishments from selling specific data. Whenever data is assembled, monetary organizations need to safeguard the data. In some unacceptable hands, it very well may be utilized to submit wholesale fraud, tricks, and coercions. Presently, monetary organizations have expanded spending on IT wellbeing measures and the quantity of information penetrates has risen. Around one-fourth of monetary establishments detailed an information break in 2018 and half of them said that it was not the first time [6]. Monetary establishments need to find essential ways to improve information security.

Another test is an overabundance in reliance on enormous information that occasionally leads to predispositions whenever utilized without the most extreme consideration [7]. During the time spent examining huge information through calculations, human assumption can be presented in various stages, from picking the factors in the model and their general ramifications to how the example is gathered and results deciphered. Besides, models cannot intentionally present predispositions when they are not modified to do such. For instance, compulsory inclination can hap pen when models are estimated utilizing authentic information that was produced under states of disparity [8].

Monetary establishments may not just utilize enormous information to offer items that shoppers may show interest in, but could likewise tailor costs to extricate the most extreme benefit from every customer. For instance, calculation based loaning can bring about higher loan costs being charged to minorities in the wake of confirming that these gatherings once in a while do cost examinations and live in regions where the stock of monetary administrations, and in this way rivalry, is limited [9]. Some monetary organizations even utilize large information to recognize vulnerable gatherings needing quick money and recommend monetarily dangerous plans and items, for example, payday credits. Extra information does not really mean better investigations. Informational indexes can be huge to such an extent that is difficult to recognize where to begin and what to show up for. The important data may be covered up under a heap of pointless data [10]. Analytical instruments utilized in huge information can be acceptable at discovering relationships between factors but not great at recognizing connections from real causation. Customary methods to surmise causation, for example, randomized control preliminaries and characteristic trials, may likewise be needed [11]. Furthermore, large information is not in every case totally precise. For instance, an overview in the United States tracked down that more than 66 percent of respondents guaranteed that their buyer data was just 0–50 percent correct [12]. Different elements can clarify these blunders, including the expense of keeping up forward-thinking data and people intentionally giving incorrect data to secure their protection [13–15].

As close to home information is gathered without information on customers, the utilization of such information gets exploitative and may lead purchasers to feel uncertain about it. Information should be gathered and investigated with straightforwardness. Enormous information investigates how shoppers act, without considering the conditions clarifying why they acted that way. Genuine circumstances ought to be investigated notwithstanding Big Data examination to stay away from segregation dependent on socioeconomics. Enormous information gives extraordinary knowledge into the requirements of purchasers with the goal that monetary specialist organizations can more readily meet them. In any case, such experiences are normally maintained as a mystery so organizations can utilize them for business purposes, subsequently expanding their control over buyers.

Nations need to guarantee that the customers additionally approach the information and can question errors depending on the situation.

12.6 Conclusion

Big Data Analytics can drive beneficial development for micro-finance establishments through powerful use of score checking and dashboards, which offer profound bits of knowledge into the information which assists the association with making essential choices. With the assistance of Predictive Analytics and profitability based examination, MFIs can recuperate the nature of advances and accomplish higher benefit. Zeroing in on five key spaces of information science including Artificial Intelligence, markets, engineering, streamlining, and reproduction has given a superb chance to make the potential business sectors all the more successful. Further mechanical headways in micro-financing may in any case be drawing nearer and finally, the future lies in the point of view of large information.

References

1. Armendàriz, Beatriz and Jonathan Morduch (2010). The Economics of Microfinance, Second edition. Cambridge, MA: MIT Press.
2. Asrow, Kaitlin, and Joanne Xu. 2018. The 2018 California Consumer Privacy Act: Understanding Its Implications and Ambiguities. Fintech Edge Special Report. Federal Reserve Board of San Francisco
3. Athey, S. 2017. "Beyond Prediction: Using Big Data for Policy Problems." Science 355 (6324): 483–85.
4. Banerjee, Abhijit, Dean Karlan, and Jonathan Zinman (2015). "Six Randomized Evaluations of Microcredit: Introduction and Further Steps." American Economic Journal: Applied Economics 7(1): 1–21.
5. Banerjee, Abhijit, Timothy Besley, and Timothy Guinnane (1994). "Thy neighbor's keeper: The design of a credit cooperative with theory and a test." Quarterly Journal of Economics 109(2): May: 491–515.
6. Barocas, S., and A. D. Selbst. 2016. "Big Data's Disparate Impact." California Law Review 104 (3): 671–732.
7. Bartlett, R., A. Morse, R. Stanton, and N. Wallace. 2019. "Consumer-lending Discrimination in the FinTech Era." NBER Working Paper 25943, National Bureau of Economic Research

8. Bauchet, Jonathan and Jonathan Morduch (2010). "Selective Knowledge: Reporting Bias in Microfinance Data." Perspectives on Global Development and Technology 9 (3–4): 240–269.
9. Collins, Daryl, Jonathan Morduch, Stuart Rutherford, and Orlanda Ruthven (2009). Portfolios of the Poor: How the World's Poor Live on $2 a Day. Princeton, NJ: Princeton University Press.
10. Conning, Jonathan and Jonathan Morduch (2011). "Microfinance and Social Investment." Annual Review of Financial Economics, vol. 3, ed. Robert Merton and Andrew Lo. 2011: 407–434.
11. Cull, Robert, Asli Demirgüç-Kunt, and Jonathan Morduch (2009). "Microfinance Meets the Market." Journal of Economic Perspectives 23(1), Winter: 167–192.
12. Cull, Robert, Aslı Demirguç-Kunt, and Jonathan Morduch (2016). "The Microfinance Business Model: Enduring Subsidy and Modest Profit." World Bank Policy Research Working Paper 7786.
13. Deaton, Angus. 1992. Understanding Consumption. Oxford: Oxford University Press/Clarendon. Helms, Brigit. 2006. Access for All: Building Inclusive Financial Systems (An Excerpt).
14. Economist, The. 2019. "South Korea is Trying to Make Banking Fun." May 2
15. Fintech News. 2017. "Alternative Credit Scoring Providers in Southeast Asia You Have to Know." June 9
16. FTC (U.S. Federal Trade Commission). 2016. Big Data: A Tool for Inclusion or Exclusion? Understanding the Issues.
17. Korea Joongang Daily. 2019. "Big Data Means Big Money." May 20
18. Lucker, J., S. K. Hogan, and T. Bischoff. 2017. "Predictably Inaccurate: The Prevalence and Perils of Bad Big Data." Deloitte Review 21 (July): 8–25.
19. Thales. 2018. Thales Data Threat Report
20. Washington DC: CGAP. Morduch, Jonathan. 2000. "The microfinance schism." World Development 28(4) (April): 617–629.
21. B. Pavithra, J. K. Shaker and F. M. S. Mani,et.al. "The study of big data analytics in E-commerce", International Journal of Advanced Research in Computer and Communication Engineering , vol. 5, no. 2, pp. 126–131, Oct. 2016.
22. K. R. Swetha, N. M, A. M. P and M. Y. M, "Prediction of Pneumonia Using Big Data, Deep Learning and Machine Learning Techniques," 2021 6th International Conference on Communication and Electronics Systems (ICCES), 2021, pp. 1697-1700, doi: 10.1109/ICCES51350.2021.9489188.

13
Big Data Storage and Analysis

Namrata Dhanda

Amity University Uttar Pradesh, Lucknow, India

Abstract
With the recent advancements in information technology and the growing number of electronic devices, data is evolving at a very rapid rate. This humongous data needs to be efficiently managed and utilized. Hence, the primary concern is the storage, management, and exhaustive analysis of this enormous amount of data. Due to the increased volume of data, the term data is replaced by Big Data. Certain properties are possessed by Big Data like Volume, Variety, Velocity, Veracity, Value, and Variability. These six properties are also referred to as 6V's of Big Data. Now, unlike the simple relational database system, Big Data is in various formats as it is being generated and collected from different sources. It need not necessarily be structured in a tabular format. Most of the data that is generated these days is either semi-structured or unstructured. Hence, the traditional database systems are no longer sufficient to handle this Big Data. We need to adopt new methods to handle such varied forms of data. This chapter will give a brief introduction to the concepts of Big Data, its components, and the various forms of data that are generated by different devices. It also provides an introduction to the data processing of Big Data in a distributed fashion, which is done using Hadoop and MapReduce.

Keywords: Big Data, Hadoop, MapReduce, HDFS, Structured Data, Unstructured Data, Semi-Structured Data, NoSQL

13.1 Introduction

The word Big Data seems to be getting bigger every day with the increasing volumes of data gathered from different sources. Due to the size and complexity of this data, conventional methods are not capable enough

Email: ndhanda510@gmail.com

M. Niranjanamurthy, Hemant Kumar Gianey and Amir H. Gandomi (eds.) Advances in Data Science and Analytics: Concepts and Paradigms, (293–312) © 2023 Scrivener Publishing LLC

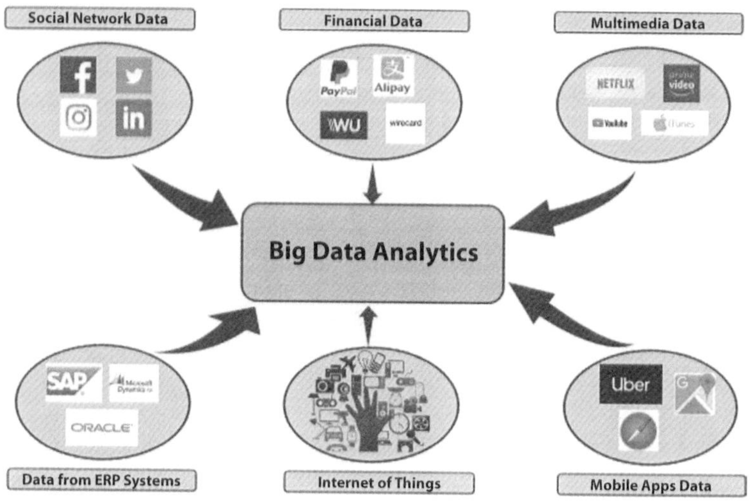

Figure 13.1 Common sources of big data generation.

of storing, processing, and analyzing this data. According to Gartner [1], data is the new oil. IDC quotes that the rate of growth of the Big Data market is seven times the rest of the IT market. IBM views Big Data as a business strategy for enhancing profits and visualizing future trends. It is estimated that by 2025 there will be 175 Zettabytes of data in the datasphere. The most prominent sources of Big Data include social media sites, IoT devices, mobiles, cameras, transactional data, weblogs, search engines, health records, archives, military surveillance, research data, e-Commerce, and so on (Figure 13.1). With Big Data arises the requirement for Data Analytics to find solutions to the existing problems to discover new opportunities and predict future possibilities. Big Data companies are in the continuous process of devising methods to extract meaningful information from the accumulated data and gain insights for making accurate decisions.

13.1.1 6 V's of Big Data

The following are the common properties of Big Data. The 5Vs in [12] have been extended to 6 V's:

a. Volume refers to the tremendous amount of data generated from multiple sources.
b. Velocity is the rate of generation of data. Big Data statistics for the year 2020 demonstrate that there are around 40000

searches that are performed per second on Google, which accounts for approximately 1.2 trillion searches every year. About 65 billion messages are exchanged every day by a WhatsApp base of 2 billion users. Twitter, a commonly used social networking site, generates more than half a million tweets every single minute. According to IDC, there could be a substantial increase in the quantity of IoT devices by the year 2025. It could rise to 41.6 billion. So, from some of these statistics, we can visualize the speed at which data is being generated and the need for methods to store, process, and analyze it using intelligent learning techniques [2].

c. Variety refers to the various forms of data that are being generated. We are no longer restricted to the relational form of data. Data exists in various forms like images, videos, weblogs, E-mails, tweets, PDFs, documents, etc. The different forms of data could be structured, unstructured, semi-structured, or quasi-structured, each of which is discussed in detail in the next section.
d. Veracity means the trustworthiness of the data. Is the data actual and complete in itself? The existence of missing values or inconsistencies in data may lead to uncertainty.
e. Value refers to how important or relevant the data is. It means that the data being dumped is useful for making any kind of analysis that may prove fruitful for the organization or society, otherwise the data is said to be redundant.
f. Variability refers to variance concerning several factors. Variability could be because data is being generated from different sources and will be in different formats and maybe following a slightly different nomenclature, which might lead to inconsistency. Also, variability may refer to the speed at which the data is transferred to the database.

13.1.2 Types of Data

Data may be broadly classified into the following four types:

a. Structured Data: Data having a fixed format is known as structured data. Usually, such data is in a tabular format consisting of columns representing the fields or attributes and rows holding the values of those fields, as depicted in Figure 13.2. Structured data is easy to handle and can be

Student Name	Roll No	Branch	Grade
Ram	1001	EE	A
Aryan	1006	EC	A
Abhi	1007	CSE	B

Figure 13.2 Structured data in form of relational table.

manipulated using traditional methods of database handling. SQL is generally used to handle relational databases.

b. Unstructured Data: Almost 80% of data that is generated these days is unstructured. Data that is not structured falls under the category of unstructured data. It could be in the form of text documents, images, video, tweets, etc., which are all examples of unstructured data. It is typical to store and process unstructured data as compared to relational data. Also, the storage requirement is more in the case of unstructured data [3].
c. Semi-Structured Data: This kind of data lies in between the above two types. It possesses a certain format but is still not relational. For instance, E-mail is an example of semi-structured data because it is structured in the sense that it contains certain mandatory fields like the address of the sender, the address of the receiver, and the date and time at which the mail was sent. However, it is unstructured because the content it holds in the mail body is in textual format. Another example of semi-structured data could be an XML file, Server logs, JSON files, and sensor outputs.
d. Quasi-Structured Data: Textual data with irregular formats is known as quasi-structured data. Formatting such data requires efficient tools and efforts. Examples include clickstream data, Google search results, web scrapping data, etc. The point of difference between semi-structured and quasi-structured data is that the first one has some metadata associated with it, with the help of which formatting of that data can be easily done with the available information. However, in the case of quasi-structured data no metadata is available, hence intelligent tools are required to extract useful information from the data.

13.1.3 Issues in Handling Big Data

There are several challenges linked with Big Data [4, 5] that must be dealt with to make data useful:

- The exponential growth of data and its storage management: As data is being continuously generated at a rapid rate, it is quite necessary to extract useful information from it that can be used for analysis. Also, the storage of large volumes of data in itself is a big task. Distributed storage is adapted to store this complex data across various systems.
- Processing data having a complex structure: As data is being gathered from multiple sources and is in different formats, we need to do some kind of data preprocessing before performing any kind of analysis on it. There are many issues that must be dealt with like inconsistency, different naming conventions being followed in different sources, redundancy, missing values, outlier detection, etc.
- Processing speed of data: As data is evolving at a rate much higher than it is capable of being processed, there is a requirement for specialized systems or a large number of computers connected to perform distributed computing [6, 8].

13.2 Hadoop as a Solution to Challenges of Big Data

Hadoop is the solution to all the issues related to Big Data. Hadoop is an open-source, Java-based framework that is capable enough of storing and processing large data files by using the concept of distributed computation. Hadoop originated from the Apache project that was run by the Apache Software Foundation. Hadoop was created by Doug Cutting of Yahoo along with Mike Cafarella for the distribution of the Nutch search engine. Hadoop was named after the name of toy elephant of Doug Cutting's kid. They were inspired by Google's MapReduce concept which proposed splitting a large file into several small subfiles and running them on several nodes in the network. The initial version of Hadoop, Hadoop 1.0, was launched in the year 2006. In 2007 Yahoo started using Hadoop on a 1000 node cluster. Thereby, Apache released the first stable version of Hadoop in the year 2011. The public announcement of the second Hadoop which included YARN was made in November 2012. The second updated version of Hadoop, that is Hadoop 2.3.0, was out in February 2014 with some updation in the previous version. In 2017, the third version of Hadoop, that is Hadoop 3.0, was launched and in the year 2020, Hadoop 3.1.3 was released. Many giant companies like Facebook, Yahoo, Twitter, Google, LinkedIn, etc. are using Hadoop for analytical processing. Scalability is the main feature of Hadoop. Instead of relying on a single large server to store and process data, the system can be scaled up by adding commodity hardware as per the needs of the application without causing much change to the existing setup [7].

13.2.1 The Hadoop Ecosystem

The Hadoop Ecosystem contains a bundle of services for efficiently storing and processing data using various Hadoop components which are dedicated to performing a particular task, as shown in Figure 13.3. The main components include HDFS, MapReduce, YARN, and other common Hadoop utilities [9]. A detailed description of these components is given below.

The Hadoop framework consists of three main components:

a. Hadoop Distributed File System: Abbreviated as HDFS, the world's most efficient and trustworthy storage system is HDFS. Google published a paper on Google File System (GFS) [10, 11]. Inspired by that paper, HDFS was developed.

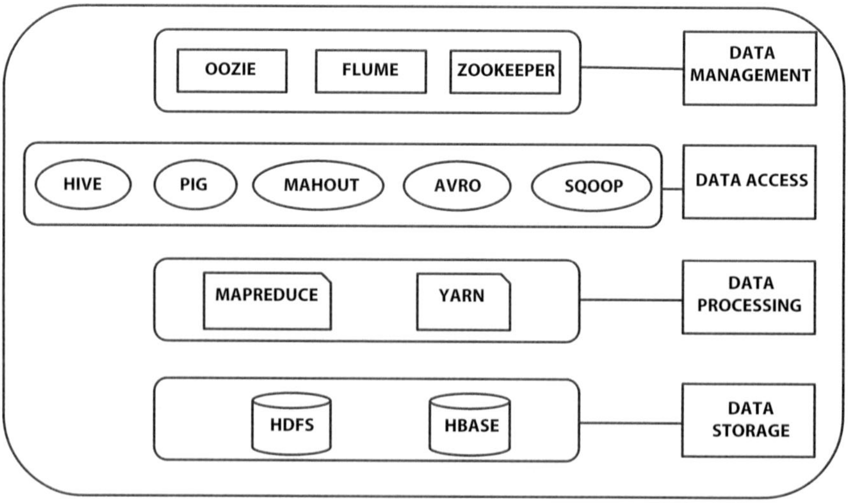

Figure 13.3 The Hadoop Ecosystem.

Instead of using high-end systems to build a cluster, HDFS is designed to run on commodity hardware. Instead of storing some small-sized files in the cluster, HDFS prefers to store a smaller number of large files. HDFS offers a fault-tolerant system by defining a strong replication policy for its data. The data is recoverable even after any kind of failure occurs. The throughput of the system is increased as parallel accessing of data is possible. Hadoop has two core components:

NameNode: It is also referred to as the Master Node. As the size of the files is quite large, we break the files into many small-sized segments referred to as blocks. The blocks are stored in the cluster on different nodes known as Data Nodes. The NameNode stores the location of these blocks in the HDFS cluster or we can say that NameNode is responsible for holding the metadata about each of these fixed-size blocks. It contains the file permissions, block size, location of each block, etc.

Data Node: Data Nodes are the slave or worker nodes. They contain the actual data or the block or file segment. The usual size of the block in HDFS is 128MB, however, it can be set per the requirements and system configuration. It keeps notifying the NameNode at frequent intervals about the updation in the block to keep the metadata updated in the NameNode.

b. MapReduce: HDFS solves the problem of storage of a massive amount of data by providing a distributed environment. In addition, it also helps in achieving scalability and fault tolerance. However, it is needed to process and analyze this data to gain useful insights from it. For that, we have the second main component of Hadoop which is known as MapReduce. MapReduce is the processing layer of Hadoop. It is a sub-project of the Apache Hadoop Project. Hadoop MapReduce is a software framework for distributed processing of large data sets on computing clusters. MapReduce is a parallel programming model for writing distributed applications devised at Google for efficient processing of large amounts of data (multi-terabyte data-sets), on large clusters (thousands of nodes) of commodity hardware in a reliable, fault-tolerant manner. In MapReduce, we divide a bigger task into several small tasks, each of which runs parallel on a different node across the cluster ([13–15]). The outputs obtained by each node are merged to achieve the resultant output. The execution of the Mapper and Reducer program on the dataset results in the full execution of the job or task requested by the client. The MapReduce job consists of the data file, the logic of the task to be performed in the form of a program, also referred to as a MapReduce program, and the configuration files. The configuration files are run either using the default setup values or can be initialized as per the application needs. There are specifically two tasks that are being performed while processing:

Mapper: Mapping is the first phase of the MapReduce program. The input is first split into fixed-size chunks and then fed to the Mapper in the form of key/value pairs. A reference to the input value is referred to as the key. The actual data on which operation is to be performed is called the value. The Mapper is a user-defined logical program depending on the problem at hand. The first step is splitting all inputs in the form of key and value pairs. The output of the Mapper is another set of key/value pairs obtained after processing. It is not the final output but the intermediate output that is generated from the Mapper. This is the intermediate output and is stored on the local disk.

Reducer: The results produced by the Mapper act as input to the Reducer program. Here, the input to the Reducer is in the form of a key/value pair. Usually, in the reducer, we do aggregation or summation computation. The output produced by the Reducer is the final output and is stored on the HDFS. In between the Map and the Reduce phase, we have two other intermediate phases known as Shuffle and Sort. As the output of the mapper traverses to the Reducer, this transfer is referred to as Shuffle. The values are sorted based on their key values before being given as input to the Reducer. This operation is known as Sorting.

Figure 13.4 illustrates the functioning of a MapReduce program. The objective is to count the frequency of each word occurring in the input file.

Two entities control and manage the execution of a MapReduce job:

- Job Tracker: There is only one Job Tracker for a particular job. The client request is first submitted to the Job

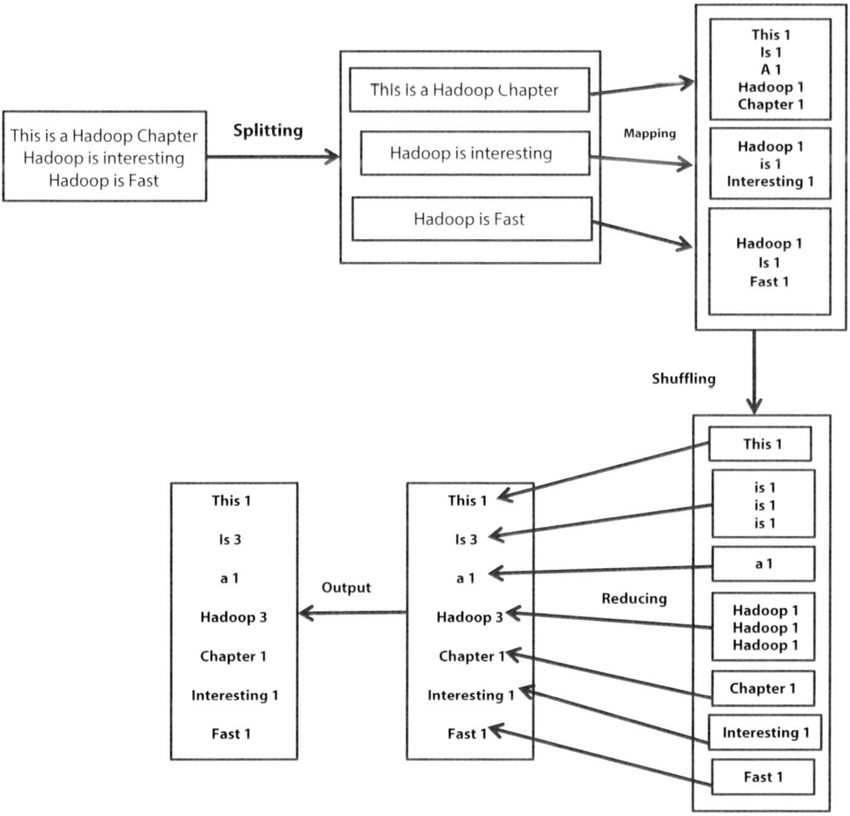

Figure 13.4 Working of a MapReduce program for word count example.

Tracker, which acts as the master node, and is responsible for the overall execution of the job.

- Multiple Task Trackers: Task Trackers are the slaves and there can be any number of Task Trackers. Each of them is responsible for executing the job assigned to them by the Job Tracker.
- Job Trackers reside on the NameNode and Task Trackers reside on the Data Node.

c. Yet Another Resource Negotiator (YARN): It is responsible for proper job scheduling among the different Data Nodes and allocation of resources for the proper execution of the program. The key components that assist in the functioning of YARN are the Resource Manager (RM), the Node Manager (NM), and the Application Master (AM).

Resource Manager is the top authority without whose consent the resource allocation is impossible. It manages the resource allocation to all the nodes in the cluster as per the requirement of the application. The Node Managers perform like agents and manage an individual node like CPU, Memory, network, etc. They are in direct communication with the Resource Manager. The third and the last are the Application Masters which act as an intermediary between the above two. It negotiates resources with Resource Manager and works with one or more Node Managers to execute tasks for which the resources were allocated.

d. Hadoop Utilities: It is a set of common files, libraries, and configuration files needed to execute the above three components.
e. Apache Hive: Hive was developed by Facebook and is currently being used by a lot of big companies like Amazon, IBM, Yahoo, Netflix, etc. As it is cumbersome to write programs in MapReduce, professionals at Facebook devised a language similar to SQL to handle, query, and analyze large databases. It came to be known as Hive Query Language (HiveQL). HiveQL automatically translates the SQL-like queries into MapReduce programs and produces the results, saving time and effort.
f. Apache Pig: Pig was brought in by Yahoo. It is a high-level data flow platform for executing Map-Reduce programs of Hadoop. Pig Latin is the language of Pig. Scripts written in Pig are quite simple compared to those written in MapReduce. It facilitates the user with a lot of built-in functions like union, sorting, and ordering. Also, it makes use of a lot of nested data types like bags, tuple, and maps. The Pig scripts are automatically converted to MapReduce programs after fetching data from HDFS. Apache Tez or Apache Spark can also be used to execute Pig scripts. Pig can handle almost any type of data. After executing, it stores the results in HDFS. Apache Pig operates into two modes:
    - Local Mode: Local Mode executes on a single JVM and is used for prototyping purposes usually. The files are first installed and then run using localhost.
    - MapReduce mode: It is the default mode and is also known as the Hadoop mode.

Pig scripts are written and executed on the Grunt Shell, which is invoked using the "Pig" command. The architecture of Pig is depicted in Figure 13.5. Pig scripts are internally converted into MapReduce jobs using the Script Parser, Pig Optimizer, Pig Compiler, and the Pig Execution Engine.

g. Sqoop: Sqoop is an acronym for SQL Hadoop. It is used for importing and exporting data between Hadoop and relational database systems. It is an ETL (Extract-Transform-Load) component of the Hadoop ecosystem. Figure 13.6 shows the ETL operation in Sqoop.
h. Apache HBase: It is a NoSQL database used for storing huge volumes of data in the form of a database table. It is capable of storing semi-structured as well as unstructured data with real-time read/write access to the data. It is built on

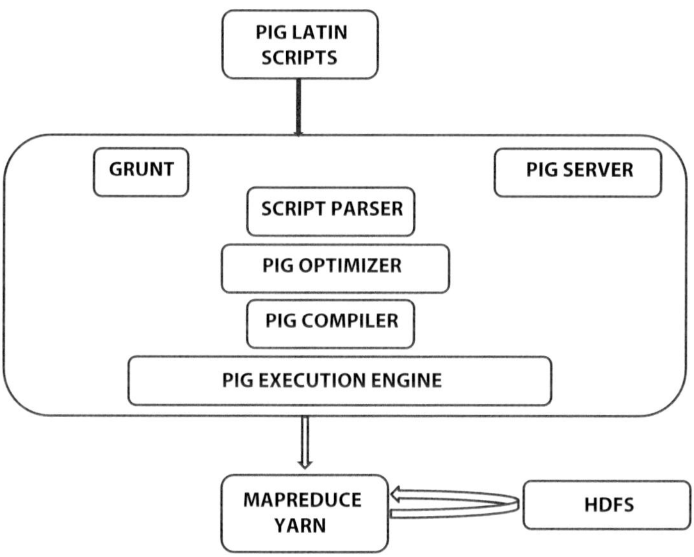

Figure 13.5 Pig architecture.

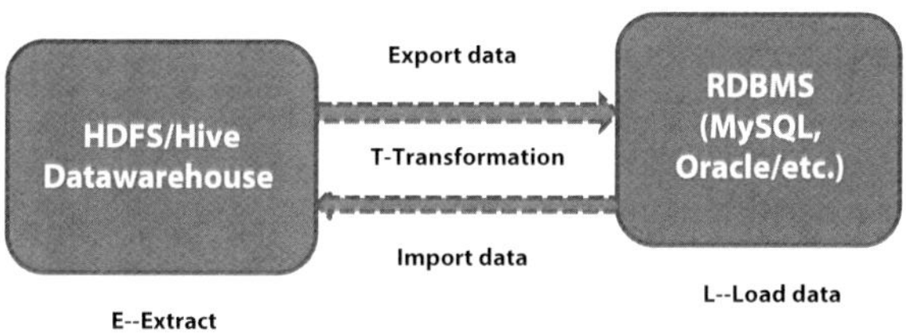

Figure 13.6 ETL operation in Sqoop.

top of HDFS. It has two main components called the HBase Master and the Region Server. The HBase Master is mainly the administrative node that does load balancing across the Region Servers. It acts as an interface between the client and the Region Server. On the other hand, Region Servers are the nodes where the actual data is stored, updated, or deleted as per the client's request. Region Servers are slave nodes.

i. Apache Mahout: For the creation of scalable machine learning algorithms, we have a component of Hadoop which is named Mahout. Like all other components of Hadoop, it is also an open-source framework. To analyze the data stored in HDFS, Mahout provides a set of tools to perform various operations like classification, clustering, prediction, etc.

j. Apache Flume: Real-time data can be ingested into HDFS using Apache Flume. Mainly the data is in the form of weblogs. Moving data from the application server generating weblog into HDFS or HBase can be easily done using Flume at a high speed. Most of the time, the rate of data generation is greater than the rate at which the data is written to the destination and in such cases Flume acts as a mediator and stabilizes the flow of data between the source and destination. Flume also provides contextual routing that allocates two channels for each message: one for the sender and the other for the receiver. This guarantees a reliable and fault-tolerant system.

k. Zookeeper: To manage a large number of nodes in the cluster, a distributed coordination service called the Zookeeper is available. Through its simple API and distributed computing environment, Zookeeper manages the distribution of resources across different nodes. This helps the developers concentrate on the application logic instead of being worried about the availability of resources necessary to execute the application. This framework was designed by Yahoo. It helped them access their applications robustly. Slowly and gradually, Apache Zookeeper became a standard for organized service used by multiple frameworks. This includes Hadoop, HBase, etc. Apache HBase uses this coordination service for tracking the status of distributed data. The prominent services that are offered by Zookeeper include:

- Naming Service: It is responsible for naming all the nodes in the cluster.
- Configuration Management: If any new node is added to the system, it makes sure that it is updated with the latest configuration or is in sync with the existing system.
- Cluster Management: The status of the node in real-time is monitored by the Zookeeper. Also, the information about any node joining or leaving the cluster is kept track of by the Zookeeper.
- Leader Election: Zookeeper selects one of the nodes as the Leader node for the synchronization of various services.
- Locking and Synchronization Service: Another service provided by the Zookeeper to maintain the consistency of the system is that it locks the data when it is being modified so that incorrect reads are not performed by any node in the network. Atomicity property is taken care of by Zookeeper.
- Reliable Data Registry: Even if one or more nodes in the system fail due to any reason, it is the responsibility of the Zookeeper to ensure that the information or data stored in them is still accessible so that the operations do not come to a halt. It also helps in resolving deadlocks if they occur.

l. Oozie: Apache Oozie is a scheduler for how the job workflow is to be executed. It is a tool by which we can pipeline a set of tasks to be performed either sequentially or in parallel to run in a Hadoop distributed environment. One of the main advantages of Oozie is that it is tightly integrated with the Hadoop stack, supporting various Hadoop jobs like Hive, Pig, and Sqoop, as well as system-specific jobs like Java and Shell. Oozie is an open-source Java Web-Application that is available under Apache license 2.0. It is responsible for triggering the workflow actions, which in turn uses the Hadoop execution engine to execute the task. Hence, Oozie can leverage the existing Hadoop machinery for load balancing, fail-over, etc. Oozie detects the completion of tasks through callback and polling. When Oozie starts work, it delivers a distinguished callback HTTP URL to the word and informs that URL as soon as it is completed. If the invoking operation fails, then Oozie can poll the task for successful completion. A few jobs in Oozie are mentioned below:

- Work-Flow Jobs: These jobs are illustrated in the form of a directed Acyclic Graph to demonstrate the sequence in which the tasks are to be executed.
- Coordinator Jobs: These are workflow jobs are initiated at times and according to their availability.
- Oozie Bundle: It is a collection of workflow jobs and coordinator jobs.

m. Apache Ambari: Ambari is a popular constituent of the Hadoop ecosystem. It is a platform that performs management operations such as managing, monitoring, provisioning, and securing the Apache Hadoop cluster. Ambari gives a consistent and secured platform for operational control. The following are the main characteristics of Ambari:

- Simplified Operational Management: It can easily manage the clusters.
- Security Setup: It reduces the complexity to administer and gives flexibility to configure the cluster security.
- Customization: It provides customizable services under management.
- Visibility: It verifies that the cluster is good and healthy. It also ensures availability with an overall aspect to monitoring.

n. Avro: Data Serialization is a service provided by the component of Hadoop known as Avro. One can exchange data or serialize data using this open-source project. Big Data can exchange programs written in distinct languages using this component of Hadoop. The data can be serialized into files or messages with the help of Avro. The metadata and data are together stored in one single file or message so that it is easy to comprehend the data stored in two different files.

- Avro Schema: Avro requires schema for performing read and write operation and for serialization and deserialization of data/files or messages. It depends on schemas for the concept of serialization as well as deserialization. In order to ensure that the files may be accessed by any program at any time, Avro files are stored with their schema.
- Dynamic Typing: It can perform serializing and deserialization without much writing of code. It provides the

facility to optimize the code with the help of statistically typed language.

o. Solr and Lucene: These two utilities are responsible for searching and indexing purposes. Java libraries, basically Lucene, are well-built on Java that permits the mechanism of spell-check.

13.2.2 Rack Awareness Policy in HDFS

To make the system fault-tolerant, HDFS uses the Rack Awareness Policy so that there is no loss of data even if any kind of failure occurs. In this, several copies of the file are stored on the Data Nodes so that in case one copy is destroyed, we can recover the data from the other copies. To understand this concept, first we must understand what is meant by a Rack. A Rack is a group of nodes; as an example consider 40-50 Nodes that are connected to one identical network switch. We can construct many Racks in the cluster as there will be thousands of nodes in the cluster. If in any case the network degrades, then all the nodes in that Rack will go downwards. So, we have to devise a policy in such a way that in case of shutdown of a switch, the data available on the nodes connected to that switch is retrievable. The communication between Data Nodes lying on the same Rack is much faster and easy as compared to the communication between nodes lying on different Racks. It is the responsibility of the NameNode to assign blocks of data-to-Data Nodes lying in the cluster by following the Rack Awareness Policy.

Working: The NameNode maintains a list of Rack IDs along with the Data Node that each Rack contains. The NameNode selects the Data Node on the closest Rack for performing the read/write operation requested by the client. This concept of selecting the nearest Data Node based on Rack location is referred to as the Rack Awareness Policy. Now, the next point of concern is how to place the replicas on different Data Nodes using this Policy. To recover from failure, HDFS maintains replicas of the data blocks. As the network bandwidth and retrieval speed are more if we access blocks on the same Rack rather than accessing them on different Racks, we do Rack Allocation accordingly. The default number of replicas is three, though the same can be set per the user requirements. Now, if we place all three replicas on the Data Nodes on the same rack, the rack might likely fail and we will not be able to recover the block stored on that Rack as all three copies have been stored in it. On the other hand, if we store all three replicas on different Racks, then the cost of writes will increase as we need to write the same data block on three different Data Nodes existing on three different Racks. So, we must devise an alternative policy that lies as

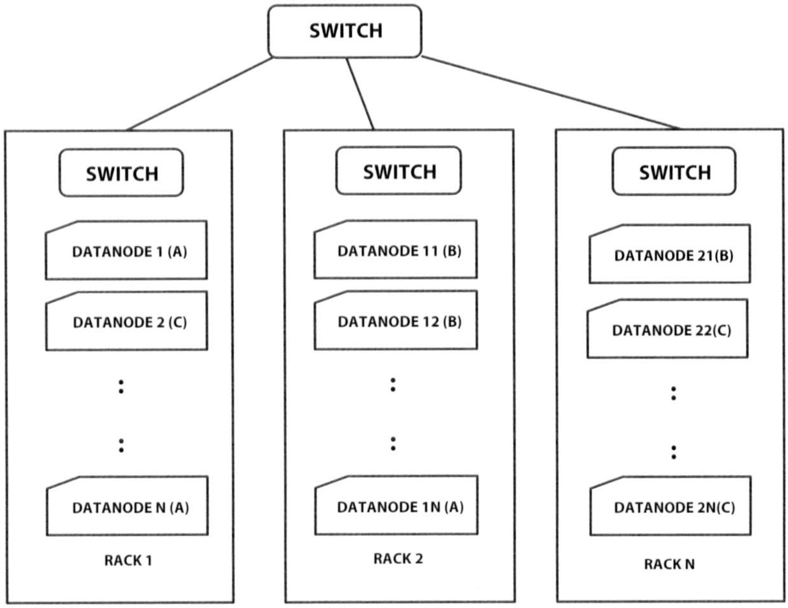

Figure 13.7 Diagrammatic representation of rack awareness policy.

an intermediary between the above two cases and this is known as Rack Awareness Policy. It works according to the following rules:

- No more than one replica should be placed on the same Data Node.
- A maximum of two replicas can be placed in one Rack on different Data Nodes.
- The number of Racks used for storing the replicas should not be greater than the number of replicas to be stored. The number of replicas to be created for a particular data block is predefined.

In the Figure 13.7, A, B, and C represent the data block stored on Data Nodes according to the Rack Awareness Policy. This kind of policy helps in making the system fault-tolerant and highly available.

13.3 In-Memory Storage and NoSQL

In-memory NoSQL databases are databases that store data in the main memory and the results of updation persist on the disk. The main purpose of in-memory databases is to reduce the time required for reading and write operations as the number of disk accesses is reduced because of the data being stored in memory. As the data is stored in memory, there are chances that it might be lost if the system fails due to hardware failure, software failure, power failure, or any other type of failure. To overcome this loss of data, the data is stored on the disks and each operation is recorded on the log which is stored on the disk. Such databases are useful in applications where we require minimal response time like real-time bidding, gaming, etc. RDBMS is capable of handling structured data, but when we talk about unstructured, semi-structured, or quasi-structured data which consists of many formats like audio, video, log file, text, or PDF documents, sensor data, time-series data, etc., SQL takes a back-foot. NoSQL comes to the rescue in such cases [16]. It can handle almost any type of unstructured data. NoSQL is an abbreviation for "No SQL or Not only SQL". The four main categories of NoSQL databases are as follows.

13.3.1 Key-Value Data Stores

For non-transactional data, the key-value NoSQL databases are capable of performing fast read and write operations. Any type of values, be it text, video, etc., are stored in the form of binary objects and each value can be accessed using a key. The application has full control over what is stored in the value field, thus making it the most frequently used database. For ensuring the availability and scalability of data, such key-value pairs are replicated across different nodes in the cluster [17]. That is why it is generally not used for transactional data, as it might lead to inconsistency. Redis, Riak, and Berkeley DB are some diverse examples of Key-Value Databases.

13.3.2 Document Stores

Document databases generally are used to store files that have metadata associated with them like XML files, JSON files, or BSON files. They are quite similar to key-value databases except for the fact that in this case, the value is the entire document that holds all data related to a specific key. Indexing techniques can be applied to the most frequently used fields in the document for faster access. The documents in this store can have the same or different structures. MongoDB, OrientDB, CouchDB, and Terrastore are some diverse examples of document stores.

13.3.3 Wide Column Stores

They are similar to the row-column database used in SQL, except for the difference that in wide column stores each row can have a separate name and format for its columns. Each row is defined by a Row Key. Columns may be added and deleted from any row at any instant without worrying about the other rows. Similar columns may be grouped. Then, such a container of columns is referred to as a super column. A single query can retrieve the required data as similar columns may be grouped. Cassandra, HBase, Hypertable, and Amazon DynamoDB are the common column databases that are in the market.

13.3.4 Graph Stores

It is a graph database that uses graph data structures for the storage and linking of values. Just like a graph consists of nodes and a set of edges connecting the nodes, similarly, in graph databases, each entity is defined by a node. The entity has certain properties. The entities are connected using edges representing the relationship between the two entities. Since the adjacent nodes or values are linked together, there is no need for any kind of indexing technique in it. Some of the graph databases are OrientDB, Neo4J, Infinite Graph, and FlockDB.

13.3.5 Multi-Modal Databases

They are a combination of the above four databases and are the most prominently used ones.

13.4 Advantages of NoSQL Database

The following are the advantages of NoSQL databases over the traditional RDBMS [18]:

- Scalability: Horizontal scalability is supported by NoSQL databases so that the number of commodity hardware can be added or reduced as per the requirements. This is more cost-effective than RDBMS, which incurs a lot of expenditure when the system scales up or down.
- Performance: The addition of low-cost commodity hardware can speed up the system, increasing its performance and delivering better user experiences.
- High Availability: NoSQL databases are highly available and are not as complex as relational databases. In a distributed

masterless architecture, the data is equally distributed among all the nodes so that there is no breakdown in case a failure occurs.

- Flexible Data Modeling: Since NoSQL is schemaless, the developers can perform the modifications at any time without worrying much about the backend details, thereby making the system more flexible and agile.
- Global Availability: By creating redundant data on diverse servers, data centers, and other cloud resources, the data is easily accessible at all times. Also, the burden of configuration management as required in RDBMS is eliminated, hence the developer can focus more on the application logic.

13.5 Conclusion

The chapter gives a brief outline of the emergence of Big Data and how technology revolutionized the market trends. With the increasing growth in data, there is an urgent need to analyze it from different perspectives to gain insights that would help make futuristic decisions. The failure of traditional database management systems to handle Big Data and evolvement of Hadoop for the storage and processing of Big Data, as well as the components of Hadoop that would assist in resource management, data accessing and processing have been explained in detail. The use of NoSQL over SQL to handle unstructured data is a benefit. Big Data can be analyzed using Machine Learning techniques [19].

References

1. Chaudhari, P., & Patel, B. (2017). Future of Big Data. International Research Journal of Engineering and Technology, 4(1), 595–597.
2. Ziaie Tabari, A., & Ou, X. (2020, October). A Multi-phased Multi-faceted IoT Honeypot Ecosystem. In Proceedings of the 2020 ACM SIGSAC Conference on Computer and Communications Security (pp. 2121–2123).
3. Davenport, T. H., Barth, P., & Bean, R. (2012). How'big data'is different.
4. Labrinidis, A., & Jagadish, H. V. (2012). Challenges and opportunities with big data. Proceedings of the VLDB Endowment, 5(12), 2032–2033.
5. Sagiroglu, S., & Sinanc, D. (2013, May). Big data: A review. In 2013 international conference on collaboration technologies and systems (CTS) (pp. 42–47). IEEE.
6. Madden, S. (2012). From databases to big data. IEEE Internet Computing, 16(3), 4–6.
7. George, G., Haas, M. R., & Pentland, A. (2014). Big data and management.
8. Marx, V. (2013). The big challenges of big data. Nature, 498(7453), 255–260.

9. Bhosale, H. S., & Gadekar, D. P. (2014). A review paper on big data and hadoop. International Journal of Scientific and Research Publications, 4(10), 1–7.
10. Saraladevi, B., Pazhaniraja, N., Paul, P. V., Basha, M. S., & Dhavachelvan, P. (2015). Big Data and Hadoop-A study in security perspective. Procedia computer science, 50, 596–601.
11. Patel, A. B., Birla, M., & Nair, U. (2012, December). Addressing big data problem using Hadoop and Map Reduce. In 2012 Nirma University International Conference on Engineering (NUiCONE) (pp. 1–5). IEEE.
12. Anuradha, J. (2015). A brief introduction on Big Data 5Vs characteristics and Hadoop technology. Procedia computer science, 48, 319–324.
13. Condie, T., Conway, N., Alvaro, P., Hellerstein, J. M., Elmeleegy, K., & Sears, R. (2010, April). MapReduce online. In Nsdi (Vol. 10, No. 4, p. 20).
14. Dean, J., & Ghemawat, S. (2008). MapReduce: simplified data processing on large clusters. Communications of the ACM, 51(1), 107–113.
15. Dean, J., & Ghemawat, S. (2010). MapReduce: a flexible data processing tool. Communications of the ACM, 53(1), 72–77.
16. Han, J., Haihong, E., Le, G., & Du, J. (2011, October). Survey on NoSQL database. In 2011 6th international conference on pervasive computing and applications (pp. 363–366). IEEE.
17. Strauch, C., Sites, U. L. S., & Kriha, W. (2011). NoSQL databases. Lecture Notes, Stuttgart Media University, 20, 24.
18. Stonebraker, M. (2010). SQL databases v. NoSQL databases. Communications of the ACM, 53(4), 10–11.
19. Dhanda, N., Datta, S. S., & Dhanda, M. (2019). Machine Learning Algorithms. In Computational Intelligence in the Internet of Things (pp. 210–233). IGI Global.

14

A Framework for Analysing Social Media and Digital Data by Applying Machine Learning Techniques for Pandemic Management

Mutyala Sridevi

VTU Research Centre - Department of MCA, BMS Institute of Technology and Management, Bengaluru, Karnataka, India

Abstract

The volumes of data available in the form of social media posts and content, along with digital data serves as a rich source of information that can be processed and analysed to draw valuable insights from it. The use of social media in the healthcare domain by its stakeholders has seen a steep rise in the context of the COVID-19 pandemic for healthcare provision, vaccination trials, and faster information dissemination. Harnessing the data from social media with digital data would become a treasure trove to dig knowledgeable insights. Rather than applying machine learning techniques at an abstract level of pandemic management, viewing the pandemic as a disaster would help to divide the cycle of events into phases to better tackle the situation. The current work focuses on identifying problem statements at each phase of pandemic management and suggest suitable machine learning techniques that can be applied to address them. A generalized framework for the application of machine learning techniques for pandemic management is proposed.

Keywords: Machine learning, social media, pandemic, disaster, healthcare

Email: sridevim@bmsit.in

M. Niranjanamurthy, Hemant Kumar Gianey and Amir H. Gandomi (eds.) Advances in Data Science and Analytics: Concepts and Paradigms, (313–326) © 2023 Scrivener Publishing LLC

14.1 Introduction

Social media use has become prevalent in present days to stay connected with the world virtually. It is undeniable that people have stronger social networks online than offline. Though lots of deliberations are happening on the digitalized emotions and relations between people, it is an interesting fact that social media interactions serve as a rich source of data that can be analysed to draw valuable conclusions. Hordes of people share humongous volumes of data in the form of posts, blogs, news articles, etc. on social media and this is multiplied during remarkable happenings in the world. The avenues that usage of social media in healthcare provides has started realising no bounds and is flattered by its stakeholders to alleviate many of the healthcare provision issues that generally arise in an offline environment. Especially during the spread of a pandemic, social media acts as a source of information, though sometimes unreliable, a means of marketing, influencer of emotions, and a powerful weapon to bring positive waves of thinking in the disturbed mobs. While this is one phase of social media, on the other side, it serves as a rich source of data for healthcare research to make appropriate decisions to predict and contain spread along with formation of government policies and plans to foresee any adverse contingencies and act accordingly to mitigate the consequences. In this context, it is required to view the pandemic as a disaster to better enable the concrete level approach to identify the problem statements, data sources, and machine learning techniques that can be applied to address them. Section 14.2 presents the work done so far, followed by understanding pandemic as a disaster, application of machine learning techniques at various phases of pandemic management, generalized framework to apply machine learning techniques for pandemic management, and the conclusion.

14.2 Literature Review

The onset of a pandemic in current days with most of the countries in the world densely populated, created newer challenges than the pandemic that swept the world almost a century back. The way that information is generated, utilized, and propagated on platforms of social media, public attitude, prediction of spread of the disease, mental health status of the people, and how government responds to the contagion during the pandemic are the points that attracted huge amounts of research and the non-exhaustive list continues as new variants of the virus come into existence. Data accessibility, sample sizes that are non-representative, study design in terms of prospective or retrospective terms, and selection bias are the limitations that are posed by social media platforms to be open for research [1].

Health measures suggested during the pandemic like social distancing, wearing of masks, and personal hygiene resulted in new issues with the mental health of people and the status of their social relationship, giving more importance to digital bonding. The term "Infodemic" was coined in 2003 to represent information that spreads with far reaching effects that may be either accurate or inaccurate and it gained a newer usage during the COVID-19 pandemic.

The findings in [2] highlighted the prevalence of issues with mental health positively correlated with high exposure to social media during the current outbreak. It further sought the attention of the government towards problems like anxiety and depression in people to combat with the infodemic during widespread health emergencies. The research in [3] presented the results of sentiment analysis performed on a group of people who are active users of Weibo, a Chinese social media platform, before and after the announcement of COVID-19 in the month of January, 2020. They unveiled an increase in negative polarity of emotions compared to positive ones and deterioration in life satisfaction and was able to throw light on people's mental health post the outbreak.

The studies in [4, 5], and [6] analysed the usage of Twitter by people in decisive roles during the COVID-19 outbreak, how social media was used to retransmit official communication during the pandemic, and examination of the crisis communication by the government and its stakeholders on Twitter in the early stages of the outbreak.

The study of responses to an online questionnaire prepared to determine the effects of social media in self-reporting of mental health and COVID-19 panic spread in Iraq [7] revealed that the nature of its impact differs from individual to individual based on their level of literacy, age, and gender. The longitudinal analysis performed on United States' tweets during COVID-19 in [8] noticed an increase in social media interactions with a steep increase during the self-quarantine mandates. It also added that extensive use of social media would exacerbate negative emotions in the long run for most of its participants given the manipulative power of social media.

The work in [9] collected the data using an online survey with cross-sectional design to understand the correlation between the role of various aspects in coping with COVID-19 and the usage of social media. The authors performed an analysis of structural relationship, cluster analysis of text corpus, and sentiment and entropy analysis which identified the functional role of usage of social media in multiplying a positive viewpoint towards factors that act as pressure points during the outbreak.

A review article [10] tabulated the positive and adverse impact of social media in the current COVID-19 crisis. The positive aspects help healthcare providers to quickly share key data irrespective of the geographical location, decrease time for knowledge transfer, and allow the public to rapidly obtain announcements from the government to follow their instructions that help in crisis management. At the same time, overwhelming volumes of information, cognitive overload faced by the healthcare providers, transmission of panic and low quality information, sharing of invalidated data by the influencers in social networks, etc. were the negative aspects that were presented in the article.

The work reviewed in the studies referred so far focused more on the mental issues and adverse effects of using social media during the pandemic. There is more research that is directed towards the application of data analytics and machine learning in the control/prediction of COVID-19. Machine learning will help the research community to deal with huge amounts of data, train the machine on historical data to learn from experience, and predict essential elements into the future. Social media data combined with mobile and sensor data, patient health parameters, hospital records about the resources available, and travel data of patients [11] would be an invaluable resource to contain/predict various aspects of the contagion.

An article [12] related to application of machine learning to study effects of COVID-19 beliefs highlighted that scientific publications along with non-scientific content like political speeches and content posted by them equally affect trends in health beliefs on social media. It also presented a few applications of machine learning that identified drugs to treat the disease, uncovered links between risk of acquiring chronic disease and diet, and the importance of social media platforms like Reddit in understanding people's thoughts and designing strategies to address their concerns.

The survey conducted by [13] explores the research avenues related to COVID-19 through the application of deep learning. Despite the limitations posed by deep learning techniques like lack of generalization metrics, limited labelled data, issues with data privacy and interpretability, the opportunities are very vast in areas of Natural Language Processing, Computer Vision, Life Sciences, and Spread Forecasting in Epidemiology.

The authors in [14] proposed a machine learning model to forecast COVID-19 in India using methods like Linear Regression, Multilayer Perceptron, and Vector Autoregression to understand the spread of COVID-19 cases in the country. The dynamic SEIR (Susceptible – Exposed – Infectious – Removed) model proposed in [15] and an artificial intelligence approach were successful in predicting the peaks of the pandemic in China and the size of its spread.

Combining the areas of healthcare and social media research with applications of machine learning in the study of a pandemic as a disaster is a new perception of study which is attempted in this chapter. This chapter will provide an idea of perceiving the pandemic as a disaster and discusses various machine learning techniques that can be applied at each stage to efficiently and effectively deal with the pandemic. This will further provide a clear approach for beginners with respect to applications of various machine learning algorithms at various stages of the pandemic. The author discussed the prediction of Pneumonia using Big Data, deep learning, and machine learning techniques and studied Big Data analytics in E-commerce [18, 19].

14.3 Understanding Pandemic Analogous to a Disaster

Disaster was defined as "a serious disruption of the functioning of a community causing widespread human, economic, or environmental losses that exceed the ability of the affected community to cope using its own resources" by the World Health Organization in 1998. The key terms in this definition very well apply to the COVID-19 pandemic, also characterizing it as the largest disaster faced by mankind in recent years. Mitigation, preparedness, response, and recovery are the main phases that constitute the disaster management life cycle that are applicable to COVID-19 management as well. The pandemic management cycle analogous to a disaster management cycle can be depicted as in Figure 14.1.

The four phases in the above cycle are considered to be recurrent owing to the first, second, and third waves that are commonly noticed during a pandemic according to historical evidences provided by the Centres for Disease Control and Prevention (CDC) [16] and the characteristic of COVID-19 being an SIRS (Susceptible – Infectious – Recovered – Susceptible) model rather than SIR (Susceptible – Infectious – Recovered) model [17] due to the new variants of COVID-19 emerging from time to time. Table 14.1 provides various aspects to be considered during the four phases of Pandemic Management Cycle to effectively manage and further contain the spread of the pandemic.

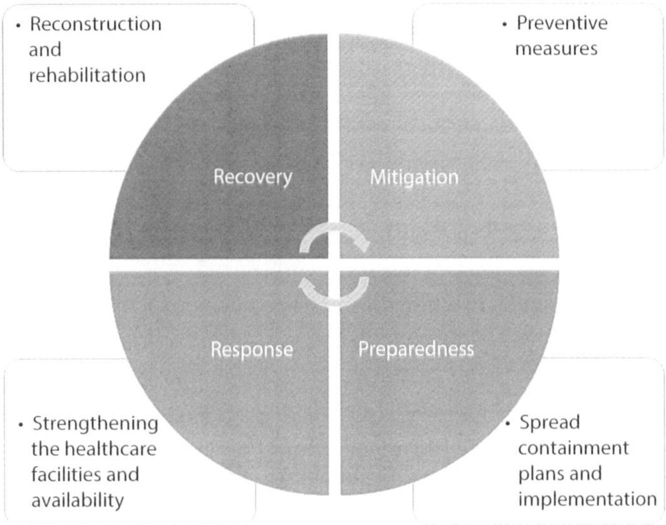

Figure 14.1 Pandemic management cycle.

Table 14.1 Measures to be considered under the four phases of pandemic.

Name of the phase	Measures
Mitigation	Preventive measures like early diagnosis, contact tracing, personal hygiene, social distancing, and vaccination
Preparedness	Forecast and predict the disease trends to strategize spread containment plans and implementation measures
Response	Harnessing hospitals/health resource availability
Recovery	Reconstruction of economy and health rehabilitation for the affected people

14.4 Application of Machine Learning Techniques at Various Phases of Pandemic Management

Machine learning (ML) helps with smart solutions to analyse humongous volumes of data. Machines generally learn from experience and data to be precise without having to program directly. When these ML applications encounter unseen data, they iteratively evolve to work more accurately. So, application of ML in pandemic management could efficiently serve the purpose to obtain better outcomes. This section provides an elaboration on various ML techniques that can be applied at each phase of the pandemic management cycle.

14.4.1 Mitigation Phase

This phase involves preventive measure like early diagnosis, contact tracing, maintaining social distancing, wearing masks, personal hygiene, and vaccination. The following Table 14.2 provides machine learning techniques that can be applied at this phase.

Table 14.2 Machine learning techniques suitable for mitigation phase.

Problem statement	Data source	Machine learning techniques
Diagnosis of correct symptoms to prescribe medical care	Health parameter data gathered by mobile medical apps/social media posts on health conditions	Classification techniques with respect to binary/ multi-class to diagnose correct variant of the SARS associated coronavirus
Monitor adherence to health behaviour guidelines issued to contain the spread like social distancing, wearing mask, etc.	Images captured from public places	Convolutional neural network models that perform real-time image analysis to detect crowds or people in close proximity and mask down moments in public places to raise an alert in case of non-compliance
Contact tracing to break the chain of virus transmission and contain the spread	GPS location data of individual and his/her contacts	Density-based clustering techniques to predict the spread through contact and quarantine them as a precaution
Effectiveness of vaccination and maximizing its availability	Online surveys and social media posts by vaccinated crowds	Use of tools like Spearman and Pearson rank correlations for preliminary investigation and in depth data analysis to study the effects of vaccination with respect to various demographic factors through longitudinal studies that may be prospective or retrospective

14.4.2 Preparedness Phase

This phase includes developing models to forecast/predict spread of the disease, effectiveness of containment measures, requirement of healthcare facilities, provisioning of medicine/critical care, and location based vaccination requirement. Table 14.3 shows appropriate ML applications corresponding to the above problem statements.

Table 14.3 Machine learning techniques suitable for the preparedness phase.

Problem statement	Data source	Machine learning techniques
Forecast the rate of spread of the disease and predict the probable time of wave occurrences in the pattern of a pandemic	Online data of reported coronavirus cases from authentic sites	Time series forecasting that predicts the future based on the data supplied
Prediction of healthcare facility requirement and emergency needs	Data from apps that provide single point information	Regression techniques to predict the demand versus availability of hospital beds and oxygen concentrators
Provision of lifesaving drugs and critical care on time	Online alerts by chatbots and mobile apps on remote requirements	Multilinear regression techniques to learn the correlation between demographic factors and healthcare requirements
Prediction of location specific vaccination requirement to avoid large crowds and optimize the waiting time	Location specific population census data from government websites	Feature engineering and methods like random forest for demand forecasting
Alleviate the task of booking vaccination slots by raising alerts about vaccine availability based on GPS location	Online vaccination booking versus slot availability information	Chat bots based on Natural Language Processing and prediction models

Table 14.4 Machine learning techniques suitable for the response phase.

Problem statement	Data source	Machine learning techniques
Single window information availability about medical facilities	Hospital resource data available online/reported on social media platforms	Multi-linear regression models to map various parameters of resources to size of spread
Demographic analysis based on GPS location to meet the emergency requirements	Electronic Health Records of patients	Location specific requirement forecasting using ensemble models that combine regression and time series forecasting techniques
Maximizing the reach of genuine information that alleviates pandemic panic	Social media posts, tweets, data about influencers on social network communities	Social network analysis techniques focused on bridges, local bridges, structural holes, etc. to understand the pace of information dissemination

14.4.3 Response Phase

This phase involves bringing the information of medical resource availability in terms of healthcare providers, beds and oxygen supply, critical care facilities, and supply of life saving drugs. The ML applications corresponding to the given problem statements are presented in Table 14.4.

14.4.4 Recovery Phase

The recovery phase involves reconstruction of the economy, as well as health, through rehabilitation that can reduce the aftermath of a pandemic. This includes boosting various sectors that strengthen the economy and rejuvenating the health of the affected people by incorporating various measures to combat the post-recovery effects from the disease that vary from person to person. Table 14.5 shows ML techniques that can be used in this phase.

Table 14.5 Machine learning techniques suitable for recovery phase.

Problem statement	Data source	Machine learning techniques
Study of effects of lockdown and other related measures to curb the spread of the disease	Demographic factors and economic performance indicators reported by government sites	Correlation between pandemic related safety measures and economic growth related to various sectors by regression techniques and Principal Component Analysis
Cohort studies about herd immunity and mob mentality during and after the pandemic	Social media interactions, Electronic Health Records of patients	Clustering techniques to unveil the characteristics of a cluster that share common features
Effectiveness of vaccination over long periods of time	Social media data, Online survey data	Social network analysis to study the SIR and SIRS compartmental models of epidemiology to study the sustained effect of vaccination in combating the new variants of the virus.

14.5 Generalized Framework to Apply Machine Learning Techniques for Pandemic Management

This section presents a generalized framework that acts as a reference to develop various machine learning applications that use social media and digital data to manage the pandemic at its different phases as depicted by Figure 14.2.

The data from Electronic Health Records (EHRs), population census, social media, and mobile and sensor data captured through various apps and hospital resource data provides the content to perform processing and further analysis. Based on the problem statement and phase of the pandemic for which the machine learning application is being developed, an appropriate data source has to be selected and a problem needs to be conceptualized. In the later steps, a list of assumptions should be made to conceptualize the solution and select appropriate tools and techniques to

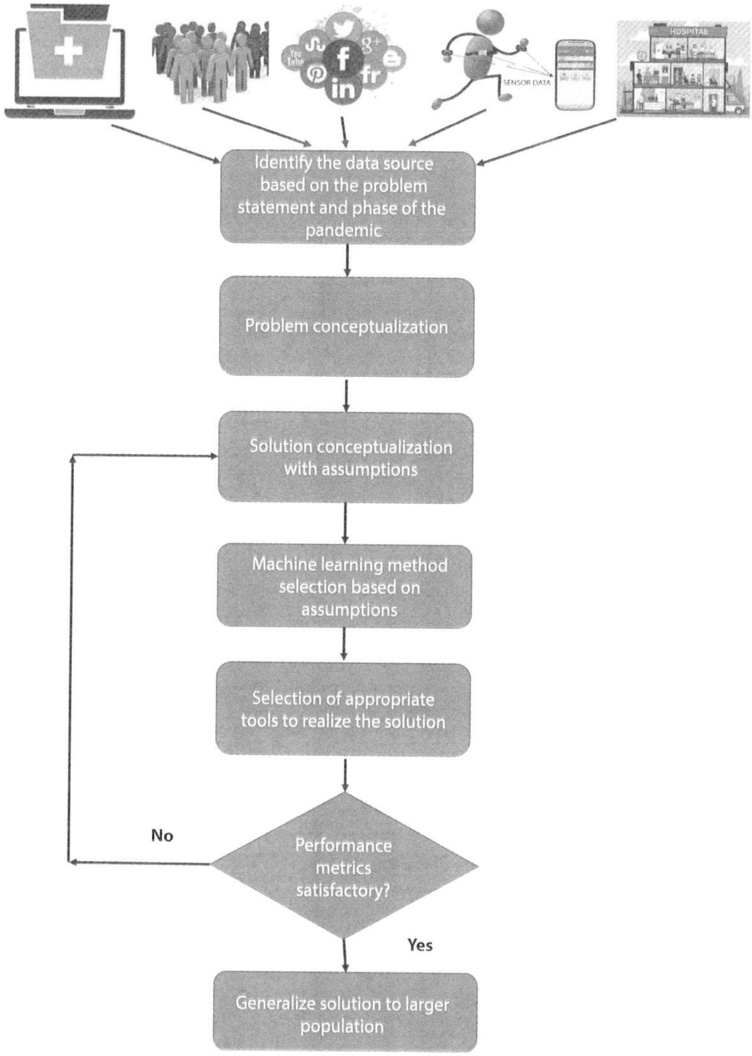

Figure 14.2 Framework to apply machine learning techniques for pandemic management.

realize it. At this stage, the selected technique needs to be evaluated using performance metrics and if the numbers are not satisfactory, the list of assumptions made has to be checked, which becomes an iterative process until the best performing model is built that can generalize well with the new data.

As one single machine learning technique does not prove to be an exact match for a given dataset and a list of assumptions made to select an algorithm to fit the data at hand cannot be tested appropriately, the evaluation of the techniques has to happen iteratively until the best performing machine learning technique for the selected data is identified. The finalized machine learning technique should best explain the behaviour of the data with performance metrics that give satisfying numbers.

Performance metrics include training and test set accuracies, coefficients of determination (R-squared measure) and F-statistics for regression problems, and AUC (Area Under Curve) for Precision-Recall curves if the classes in the dataset are imbalanced and AUC for ROC (Receiver Operating Characteristic) curve for classification problems. The solution that is conceptualized should be generalizable so that the machine learning application works with the same efficiency on unseen data as it does on the training data. The nature of data, type of data, and diversity and scale of data play a significant role in deciding the machine learning techniques that have subtle differences among them though they fall under a larger umbrella of regression and classification models.

14.6 Conclusion

This present study focuses on reviewing the existing work on using machine learning to understand various pre and post effects of a pandemic by using widely available social media and digital data. The work presented a new perception of comparing the pandemic to a disaster and discussed different problem statements that can be formulated at each phase of the pandemic management cycle, data sources that provide data for analysis, and suitable machine learning techniques that can be applied for a given problem statement. Further, the importance of performance metrics and the nature of data in the evaluation of a machine learning model were presented to provide a complete understanding of the framework proposed for pandemic management by applying machine learning techniques.

References

1. S. Tsao, H. Chen, Y. Yang, Z.A. Butt, S.-F. Tsao, H. Chen, T. Tisseverasinghe, Y. Yang, L. Li, Z.A. Butt, What social media told us in the time of COVID-19: a scoping review, Lancet Digit. Heal. 3 (2021) e175–e194. https://doi.org/10.1016/S2589-7500(20)30315-0.
2. J. Gao, P. Zheng, Y. Jia, H. Chen, Y. Mao, S. Chen, Y. Wang, H. Fu, J. Dai, Mental health problems and social media exposure during COVID-19

outbreak, PLoS One. 15 (2020) e0231924. https://doi.org/10.1371/journal.pone.0231924.
3. S. Li, Y. Wang, J. Xue, N. Zhao, T. Zhu, The impact of covid-19 epidemic declaration on psychological consequences: A study on active weibo users, Int. J. Environ. Res. Public Health. 17 (2020). https://doi.org/10.3390/ijerph17062032.
4. S.R. Rufai, C. Bunce, World leaders' usage of twitter in response to the COVID-19 pandemic: A content analysis, J. Public Heal. (United Kingdom). 42 (2020) 510–516. https://doi.org/10.1093/pubmed/fdaa049.
5. J. Sutton, S.L. Renshaw, C.T. Butts, COVID-19: Retransmission of official communications in an emerging pandemic, PLoS One. 15 (2020) e0238491. https://doi.org/10.1371/journal.pone.0238491.
6. Y. Wang, H. Hao, L.S. Platt, Examining risk and crisis communications of government agencies and stakeholders during early-stages of COVID-19 on Twitter, Comput. Human Behav. 114 (2021) 106568. https://doi.org/10.1016/j.chb.2020.106568.
7. A.R. Ahmad, H.R. Murad, The impact of social media on panic during the COVID-19 pandemic in iraqi kurdistan: Online questionnaire study, J. Med. Internet Res. 22 (2020) e19556. https://doi.org/10.2196/19556.
8. D. Valdez, M. ten Thij, K. Bathina, L.A. Rutter, J. Bollen, Social media insights into US mental health during the COVID-19 pandemic: Longitudinal analysis of twitter data, J. Med. Internet Res. 22 (2020) e21418. https://doi.org/10.2196/21418.
9. Y. Marzouki, F.S. Aldossari, G.A. Veltri, Understanding the buffering effect of social media use on anxiety during the COVID-19 pandemic lockdown, Humanit. Soc. Sci. Commun. 8 (2021) 47. https://doi.org/10.1057/s41599-021-00724-x.
10. A. Verner Venegas-Vera, Gates B Colbert, Edgar V. Lerma, Positive and negative impact of social media in the COVID-19 era, Rev. Cardiovasc. Med. (2020) 561–564. https://rcm.imrpress.com/article/2020/2153-8174/RCM2020195.shtml (accessed June 7, 2021).
11. S.J. Alsunaidi, A.M. Almuhaideb, N.M. Ibrahim, F.S. Shaikh, K.S. Alqudaihi, F.A. Alhaidari, I.U. Khan, N. Aslam, M.S. Alshahrani, Applications of big data analytics to control covid-19 pandemic, Sensors. 21 (2021) 2282. https://doi.org/10.3390/s21072282.
12. Jessica Kent, Machine Learning Shows Social Media Greatly Affects COVID-19 Beliefs, Heal. IT Anal. (2021). https://healthitanalytics.com/news/machine-learning-shows-social-media-greatly-affects-covid-19-beliefs (accessed June 7, 2021).
13. C. Shorten, T.M. Khoshgoftaar, B. Furht, Deep Learning applications for COVID-19, J. Big Data. 8 (2021) 1–54. https://doi.org/10.1186/s40537-020-00392-9.
14. R. Sujath, J.M. Chatterjee, A.E. Hassanien, A machine learning forecasting model for COVID-19 pandemic in India, Stoch. Environ. Res. Risk Assess. 34 (2020) 959–972. https://doi.org/10.1007/s00477-020-01827-8.

15. Z. Yang, Z. Zeng, K. Wang, S.S. Wong, W. Liang, M. Zanin, P. Liu, X. Cao, Z. Gao, Z. Mai, J. Liang, X. Liu, S. Li, Y. Li, F. Ye, W. Guan, Y. Yang, F. Li, S. Luo, Y. Xie, B. Liu, Z. Wang, S. Zhang, Y. Wang, N. Zhong, J. He, Modified SEIR and AI prediction of the epidemics trend of COVID-19 in China under public health interventions, J. Thorac. Dis. 12 (2020) 165–174. https://doi.org/10.21037/jtd.2020.02.64.
16. 1918 Pandemic Influenza: Three Waves | Pandemic Influenza (Flu) | CDC, (n.d.). https://www.cdc.gov/flu/pandemic-resources/1918-commemoration/three-waves.htm (accessed June 7, 2021).
17. P. Adda, D. Bichara, Global stability for SIR and SIRS models with differential mortality, Int. J. Pure and Applied Mathematics. 80 (2012) 425–433. https://ijpam.eu/contents/2012-80-3/14/14.pdf.
18. B. Pavithra, J. K. Shaker and F. M. S. Mani,et.al. "The study of big data analytics in E-commerce", International Journal of Advanced Research in Computer and Communication Engineering , vol. 5, no. 2, pp. 126–131, Oct. 2016.
19. K. R. Swetha, N. M, A. M. P and M. Y. M, "Prediction of Pneumonia Using Big Data, Deep Learning and Machine Learning Techniques," 2021 6th International Conference on Communication and Electronics Systems (ICCES), 2021, pp. 1697–1700, doi: 10.1109/ICCES51350.2021.9489188.

About the Editors

M. Niranjanamurthy, PhD, is an assistant professor in the Department of Computer Applications, M S Ramaiah Institute of Technology, Bangalore, Karnataka. He earned his PhD in computer science at JJTU. He has over 10 years of teaching experience and two years of industry experience as a software engineer. He has published four books and 56 papers in technical journals and conferences. He has two patents to his credit and has won numerous awards.

Hemant Kumar Gianey, PhD, is an assistant professor in the Computer Science and Engineering Department at Thapar Institute of Engineering and Technology, Patiala, Punjab, India. He obtained his PhD from Rajasthan and was a post-doc in Computer Science and Engineering at the National Cheng Kung University, Taiwan. He has over 15 years of teaching and industry experience and has also published papers in and acted as a reviewer and guest editor for several technical and scientific journals.

Amir H. Gandomi, PhD, is a professor of data science in the Department of Engineering and Information Technology, University of Technology Sydney. Prior to joining UTS, he was an assistant professor at the School of Business, Stevens Institute of Technology, NJ, and a distinguished research fellow in BEACON center, Michigan State University. He has published over 150 journal papers and four books and collectively have been cited more than 14,000 times. He has been named as one of the world's most influential scientific minds and a Highly Cited Researcher (top 1%) for three consecutive years, from 2017 to 2019. He has also served as associate editor, editor and guest editor in several prestigious journals and has delivered several keynote talks. He is also part of a NASA technology cluster on Big Data, Artificial Intelligence, and Machine Learning.

Index

Also of Interest

Check out these other related titles from Scrivener Publishing

Also in the series, "Advances in Data Engineering and Machine Learning"

ARTIFICIAL INTELLIGENCE AND DATA MINING IN SECURITY FRAMEWORKS, Edited by Neeraj Bhargava, Ritu Bhargava, Pramod Singh Rathore, and Rashmi Agrawal, ISBN 9781119760405. Written and edited by a team of experts in the field, this outstanding new volume offers solutions to the problems of security, outlining the concepts behind allowing computers to learn from experience and understand the world in terms of a hierarchy of concepts. *NOW AVAILABLE!*

MACHINE LEARNING AND DATA SCIENCE: Fundamentals and Applications, Edited by Prateek Agrawal, Charu Gupta, Anand Sharma, Vishu Madaan, and Nisheeth Joshi, ISBN: 9781119775614. Written and edited by a team of experts in the field, this collection of papers reflects the most up-to-date and comprehensive current state of machine learning and data science for industry, government, and academia. *NOW AVAILABLE!*

MEDICAL IMAGING, Edited by H. S. Sanjay, and M. Niranjanamurthy, ISBN: 9781119785392. Written and edited by a team of experts in the field, this is the most comprehensive and up-to-date study of and reference for the practical applications of medical imaging for engineers, scientists, students, and medical professionals. *EXPECTED IN EARLY 2023*

SECURITY ISSUES AND PRIVACY CONCERNS IN INDUSTRY 4.0 APPLICATIONS, Edited by Shibin David, R. S. Anand, V. Jeyakrishnan, and M. Niranjanamurthy, ISBN: 9781119775621. Written and edited by a team of international experts, this is the most comprehensive and up-to-date coverage of the security and privacy issues surrounding Industry 4.0 applications, a must-have for any library. *NOW AVAILABLE!*

Other related titles

CYBER SECURITY AND DIGITAL FORENSICS: Challenges and Future Trends, Edited by Mangesh M. Ghonge, Sabyasachi Pramanik, Ramchandra Mangrulkar, and Dac-Nhuong Le, ISBN: 9781119795636. Written and edited by a team of world renowned experts in the field, this groundbreaking new volume covers key technical topics and gives readers a comprehensive understanding of the latest research findings in cyber security and digital forensics. *NOW AVAILABLE!*

DEEP LEARNING APPROACHES TO CLOUD SECURITY, edited by Pramod Singh Rathore, Vishal Dutt, Rashmi Agrawal, Satya Murthy Sasubilli, and Srinivasa Rao Swarna, ISBN 9781119760528. Covering one of the most important subjects to our society today, this editorial team delves into solutions taken from evolving deep learning approaches, solutions allow computers to learn from experience and understand the world in terms of a hierarchy of concepts. *NOW AVAILABLE!*

MACHINE LEARNING TECHNIQUES AND ANALYTICS FOR CLOUD SECURITY, Edited by Rajdeep Chakraborty, Anupam Ghosh and Jyotsna Kumar Mandal, ISBN: 9781119762256. This book covers new methods, surveys, case studies, and policy with almost all machine learning techniques and analytics for cloud security solutions. *NOW AVAILABLE!*

SECURITY DESIGNS FOR THE CLOUD, IOT AND SOCIAL NETWORKING, Edited by Dac-Nhuong Le, Chintin Bhatt and Mani Madhukar, ISBN: 9781119592266. The book provides cutting-edge research that delivers insights into the tools, opportunities, novel strategies, techniques, and challenges for handling security issues in cloud computing, Internet of Things and social networking. *NOW AVAILABLE!*

DESIGN AND ANALYSIS OF SECURITY PROTOCOLS FOR COMMUNICATION, Edited by Dinesh Goyal, S. Balamurugan, Sheng-Lung Peng and O.P. Verma, ISBN: 9781119555643. The book combines analysis and comparison of various security protocols such as HTTP, SMTP, RTP, RTCP, FTP, UDP for mobile or multimedia streaming security protocol. *NOW AVAILABLE!*

Printed in the USA/Agawam, MA
January 24, 2023

804855.002